THE RISE AND FALL OF FLEET STREET

By the same author

Pressures on the Press

THE RISE AND FALL OF FLEET STREET

Charles Wintour

Hutchinson
London Sydney Auckland Johannesburg

This edition first published in Great Britain by Hutchinson, an imprint of Century Hutchinson Ltd, Brookmount House, 62–65 Chandos Place, London WC2N 4NW

Century Hutchinson Australia Pty Ltd, 20 Alfred Street, Milsons Point, Sydney NSW 2061, Australia

Century Hutchinson New Zealand Ltd, PO Box 40–086, Glenfield, Auckland 10, New Zealand

Century Hutchinson South Africa (Pty) Ltd, PO Box 337, Berglvei, 2012 South Africa

Phototypeset by Input Typesetting Ltd, London

Printed and bound in Great Britain by
Butler and Tanner Ltd, Frome, Somerset

British Library Cataloguing in Publication Data
Wintour, Charles
    The rise and fall of Fleet Street.
    1. London (City). Fleet Street. National newspaper
    publishing industries
    I. Title
    338.4′707212

ISBN 0–09–170920–2

Contents

Acknowledgements   vii

Illustration credits   ix

Preface   xi

1 Northcliffe   1

2 The Berry Connection   30

3 Lord Snow White and the Daily Herald   49

4 The Cocoa Press is Swallowed   64

5 Beaverbrook   82

6 The Prudent Prince of Publishers   106

7 The Man Who Would Be King   128

8 Victor Matthews   151

9 Rothermere – The Heir Who Flourished   172

10 Robert Maxwell   190

11 Rupert Murdoch, the Invader from Adelaide   215

12 The Abuse of Power   238

13 New Beginnings   248

Appendix   264

Index   265

To Audrey with love

Acknowledgements

I have drawn on all those sources which I acknowledge in the endnotes to each chapter. In addition I have studied the Northcliffe Papers in the Manuscript Room of the British Library and John Cruesemann undertook the labour of reading, on my behalf, the Beaverbrook Papers in the House of Lords Library. I am grateful to the Trustees of the Beaverbrook Foundation for allowing me to quote from those papers.

I have consulted many individuals on various aspects of the book and some of them spoke to me at length. I wish to thank the following most warmly for their help:

Tom Baistow; Frank Barlow; Sir Gordon Brunton; Sir Eric Cheadle, CBE; Lord Cudlipp; Jeremy Deedes; Stuart Dempster; Chief Librarian, Press Association, and his staff; Sir David English; Harry Fieldhouse; John Gold; Sir Denis Hamilton, DSO; Paul Hamlyn; Louis Heren; Cyril Kersh; Francis King; Andrew Knight; Brian MacArthur; Bruce Matthews; Lord Matthews of Southgate; Robert Maxwell, MC; Bill Miles; Rupert Murdoch; Bill O'Neill; Huw Richards; Sir Frank Rogers; Lord Rothermere; Anne Sharpley; Jocelyn Stevens; Lord Thomson of Fleet; Colin Webb, Editor-in-Chief, Press Association.

And a particular word of thanks to my sons, James and Patrick Wintour. James calculated the value of the £ over the decades with the help of the indices provided by the Central Statistical Office. Patrick regards my views on the print unions as 'outrageous', but nonetheless read several chapters and corrected a number of errors and misconceptions on my part.

Of course none of the authorities I have mentioned are responsible in the slightest for my views, or for any mistakes of fact which I may, inadvertently, have made.

Finally, many thanks to Harold Harris, one-time literary editor of the *Evening Standard* and later editorial director of Hutchinson, who suggested that I write another book about Fleet Street. I am also most grateful to Richard Cohen, publishing director of Hutchinson, and to my agent Hilary Rubinstein, both to whom made a number of constructive comments.

Illustrations

PLATES

Between pages

Plate 1　Northcliffe in 1896; towards the end of his
　　　　　life; with Wickham Steed in 1921　　　　　80 and 81

Plate 2　Laurence Cadbury; Viscount Southwood;
　　　　　Viscount Camrose　　　　　　　　　　　　80 and 81

Plate 3　Beaverbrook in 1924; with Churchill aboard
　　　　　HMS *Prince of Wales*; Lord Thomson in 1962;
　　　　　with Beaverbrook and Max Aitken in 1964　112 and 113

Plate 4　Hugh Cudlip and Cecil King; Lord Matthews;
　　　　　Jocelyn Stevens　　　　　　　　　　　　112 and 113

Plate 5　Lord Northcliffe, Hon. Esmond Harmsworth
　　　　　and Lord (Harold) Rothermere; the second
　　　　　Lord Rothermere in 1955; Sir David English　176 and 177

Plate 6　Robert Maxwell in 1988; Maxwell with the
　　　　　third Lord Rothermere and Rupert Murdoch
　　　　　in 1987　　　　　　　　　　　　　　　176 and 177

Plate 7　Murdoch in 1960; with Harry Evans and
　　　　　William Rees-Mogg in 1981　　　　　　　208 and 209

Plate 8　Wapping demonstrators in 1986; Eddie Shah;
　　　　　Andreas Whittam-Smith　　　　　　　　208 and 209

ILLUSTRATIONS WITHIN TEXT

Page

1　*News Chronicle* in 1960 and *Daily Telegraph* in 1937　42

2　*Sunday Express* in 1931　　　　　　　　　　　　90

3　*Daily Mirror* in 1926　　　　　　　　　　　　　93

4　*The Times* celebrating its 60,000th edition
　　in 1977; and announcing its suspension, 1978　124–5

5　*Daily Mirror* in 1936　　　　　　　　　　　　138

6　*Daily Mirror* in 1968　　　　　　　　　　　　147

7   The first *Mail on Sunday*, 1982, and the
     last *Evening News*, 1980   184
8   *Daily Mirror* in 1984   210
9   Murdoch buys *The Times*, 1981; the *Sun* in 1984   229

ILLUSTRATION CREDITS

p. 1   Popperfoto; Popperfoto; Keystone Collection
p. 2   Camera Press; Popperfoto; Press Association
p. 3   Hulton Picture Library; Keystone Collection; Popperfoto;
       Popperfoto
p. 4   Popperfoto; Popperfoto; Central Press
p. 5   Popperfoto; Popperfoto; *Daily Mail*
p. 6   Popperfoto; Popperfoto
p. 7   Keystone Collection; Popperfoto
p. 8   Popperfoto; Popperfoto; Popperfoto

Preface

Although I edited the *Evening Standard* for nearly twenty years and held several other enjoyable jobs in the Express group I felt for most of my career that I was an amateur journalist and extremely lucky to be employed among the real pros. Perhaps this helped me to keep a slight sense of perspective about some of Fleet Street's larger lunacies, but it was basically true. I got a job there through sheer fluke.

In the winter of 1944 I was among a group of junior officers sitting in a garret of the Trianon Palace Hotel at Versailles, then the focus of Supreme Headquarters, Allied Expeditionary Force (better known as SHAEF). We were discussing what we wanted to do after the war. I confessed I wanted to be a journalist. Then Arthur Granard, an acute and very amiable aide to deputy supremo Air Chief Marshal Tedder, said out of the blue, 'If you ever want an introduction to Lord Beaverbrook, let me know.' As Lord Forbes (he was the son of the eighth Earl of Granard) he had written the gossip column in the *Sunday Express* after the death of Beaverbrook's court jester, Lord Castlerosse, another Irish peer. There were many months to go before the war ended, and even longer before I would be demobilised. But it was not an offer I would forget.

My parents were both fairly appalled when I said I wanted to be a journalist but were pleased and slightly startled when my first article, about the interesting seventh hole on the local golf course, was accepted by the *Western Gazette*, and paid for. While still at Oundle School I had had a couple of articles published by the *Radio Times* and I had won £5 from the *Daily Mail* for selecting the week's most interesting postal bargain. Later at Cambridge I became part of *The Granta*'s editorial team and eventually shared the editorship with Eric Hobsbawn, now the leading Marxist historian. I was meant to be the humourist and he was the brains. But war clouds were gathering.

When I went down from Peterhouse in the summer of 1939, I was convinced that war was imminent and regarded the job I obtained at J. Walter Thompson, the leading advertising agency, as purely temporary. So it turned out. The job ended immediately war was declared. I applied for a commission and soon found myself in a bleak Officer Cadet Training Unit outside Colchester along with Woodrow Wyatt, later as rebellious a Labour MP as he had been an officer. Eventually I went to the junior staff college and in 1943, when I was helping to run one of those endless exercises requiring plenty of imagination and a very few troops, had the luck to bump into an army Colonel with whom I had shared an office at a Corps headquarters after the retreat from France. He was now working on the second front invasion plan. He invited me to join his team at Norfolk House in St James's Square. There I worked very hard under the glamorous title of GS02 (Strat Plans). Strat stood for 'strategy' about which I knew nothing but I helped to draft the ideas of others, only for the whole lot to be overturned when Monty, as commander of the Army Group, arrived on the scene demanding more of everything. With the invasion imminent I was transferred to the operations side of SHAEF and was expected to help coordinate the activities of resistance groups with the main strategic thrust. That was why I had become friendly with such a glamorous figure as Tedder's PA for he could organise airborne supplies for the resistance.

With the war over I fetched up in an army headquarters at Preston - a sobering change from the Trianon Palace at Versailles, the Champagne Club at Rheims and the IG Farben building at Frankfurt. I wrote nervously to Arthur Granard reminding him of his offer, half expecting to hear no more. A fortnight later I was amazed to receive an invitation to visit Lord Beaverbrook at his flat in Park Lane. With apprehension I presented myself the following week and was greeted with the utmost courtesy and apparently deep interest in what I was doing. Arthur must have written in very friendly terms. Beaverbrook suggested that I should write an article on the difference between British and American methods of work – one of the subjects we had been discussing – and personally escorted me to the lift; it was all so unlike an interview with an army chief.

Shortly after I sent off the article I received an offer of a three months' trial as assistant leader-writer on the *Evening Standard* at a salary of £14 a week. After five months, unable to bear the suspense any longer, I approached the editor, Herbert Gunn, as he passed my desk and enquired whether the trial had been satisfactory. 'Oh, don't bother about that,' he said ambiguously and marched on to more important business. So far as I knew the trial continued. But I did notice that Lord Beaverbrook seemed to be taking an interest in me and that Gunn, whose judgment could be appalling but who was a marvellous guide to young journalists, sometimes included me in the group that went across Shoe Lane to have a mid-morning drink at the Two Brewers.

Eventually promotion came my way – first as political editor of the *Evening Standard*, then as assistant editor of the *Sunday Express*. I went back to the *Evening Standard* as deputy editor and then to the *Daily Express* as managing editor. Eventually I got the job I had wanted all along: the editorship of the *Evening Standard*, surely the best job in Fleet Street. And most days when Beaverbook was in the country he would ring me up and make that familiar nasal-voiced enquiry, 'Now tell me what's noo, Mr Win*tour?*' The *Evening Standard* was not important financially; it did not lose much money and it didn't make much money. So it had a charmed existence as Beaverbrook's pet. I was allowed to recruit an exceptionally able group of journalists who enjoyed the paper and each other's company. Beaverbrook also agreed that I could start the *Evening Standard* Drama Awards which have now been a feature of the London theatre scene for thirty years. Both Sir Max Aitken and Victor Matthews also allowed the *Evening Standard* considerable freedom; it was a considerable help to be in another building, away from the office intercom, but their main worry was always the *Daily Express*. Under the super-charged management of Jocelyn Stevens the *Standard* actually began to make quite a lot of money. Eventually I became a director of Beaverbrook Newspapers, chairman of Beaverbrook Western and a member of the Press Council. I was also on the Standing Committee of the London School of Economics for a time. So for one reason or another I met most of the leading personalities in the industry.

When I retired in 1982 at the age of sixty-five, I picked up a number of odd jobs, notably the editorship of the *UK Press Gazette* which I held for a year until it was clear that the owner, Timothy Benn, did not quite share my view of the editor's position. But it was a marvellous time to edit the trade paper as the year included Rupert Murdoch's earth-shattering move to Wapping, Eddy Shah's launch of *Today*, the take-over of Express Newspapers by United Newspapers and Conrad Black's gradual assumption of control at Telegraph Newspapers.

For some time I had been thinking of writing a book about Fleet Street but I wished neither to write an autobiography – my life was not of sufficient general interest – nor to compile another collection of well-honed tales. Others can tell the stories much better than I ever could.

So I responded with enthusiasm to an idea from Harold Harris that I should write a book about the rise and fall of Fleet Street as a publishing centre. Harris had been literary editor of the *Evening Standard* during my time there and had left to become editorial director of Hutchinsons, where he had launched Freddie Forsyth on to his best-selling career. Now he was a consultant to Century Hutchinson. My first thought was to write a seamless narrative starting with the rise of the mass circulation papers and winding up with the desertion of the Street by all the principal publishing houses. 'Fleet Street's association with printing and publishing is of long standing,' said the *London Encyclopaedia* in 1983.[1] Indeed the first printers moved into Fleet Street around 1500 although newspapers did not start there for another 200 years. A survey of the Fleet Street story from say the launch of the *Daily Telegraph* in 1855 would have been worthy, interesting and, hopefully, worthwhile. But it could have missed all the fizz and surprise and excitement caused by the succession of truly amazing characters who built up the industry to extraordinary heights of power, influence and prosperity. Northcliffe was the most brilliant genius of them all, with his instinctive understanding for what interested the ordinary man and woman. William Berry, later Lord Camrose, was a true professional, trained in his teens, who made the *Telegraph* into a fine newspaper with strong traditions of reliability in reporting and paternalism in staff relations. Julius Elias, later Lord Southwood, poured millions into circulation stunts for the *Daily Herald* and in so doing permanently enlarged the newspaper reading public in this country. Beaverbrook was the greatest journalist of the lot and probably got more sheer fun from his papers than any other publisher. Roy Thomson allowed his editors a free hand; he cared more about the bottom line than exercising personal influence on political affairs. Cecil King, whose partnership with Hugh Cudlipp brought the *Mirror* to mass market supremacy for a few years, eventually became so intoxicated by a sense of his own superiority that he precipitated the board-room revolt which sacked him. Victor Matthews, a builder, rescued the *Express* from near-bankruptcy and began the long and difficult task of bringing some discipline into the industry. Vere Rothermere skilfully rescued his inheritance from collapse. Robert Maxwell, despite spending five years in the wilderness following the Leasco fiasco, showed superhuman drive, energy and resource in building up a media empire of world stature. Rupert Murdoch, the most complete newspaperman of them all, raised his hand whenever opportunity offered and never stopped expanding. The rivalry between the two R.M.'s makes fiction pallid by comparison. Only Laurence Cadbury failed the test; he completely lacked the spirit of adventure and enterprise.

I therefore determined to write a series of biographical portraits which, taken together, tell the story of the rise and fall of Fleet Street as a newspaper publishing centre. It is not intended to be completely comprehensive. There is no mention of the valiant efforts of the two branches of William Waldorf Astor's family to raise the tone of the British press. John Jacob Astor of Hever Castle – he was the younger son – and his family maintained the quality of *The Times* from Northcliffe's death until a combination of taxes and organisational viscosity dragged them down, so that they sold control to Thomson. Waldorf Astor of Cliveden, the second Viscount and husband of Nancy, inherited *The Observer* and J. L. Garvin with it. His younger son David Astor took over the editorship in 1948 and assembled an idiosyncratic, well written and intelligent Sunday newspaper with a fine foreign service. One month before the British attack on Suez *The Observer* had actually passed the circulation of Kemsley's *Sunday Times*. In bravely opposing that adventure David Astor took an unpopular course and lost some 30,000 readers. *The Observer* never regained its lead. Eventually he too found the drain on the family's finances was too heavy and sold out to an American oil company, Atlantic Richfield. So the Astors' involvement in the industry, regarded as so important at the time, was relatively tangental. Nor have I examined the fortunes of the *Financial Times*, that outstanding financial newspaper which has been the British pioneer in global production, for its specialist nature removes it from the scope of this book. Equally, *The Guardian*'s arrival in the environs of Fleet Street did not take place until 1959 and, while its political posture had been of compelling interest to the Left, its economic fortunes, closely associated with the prosperity of the *Manchester Evening News*, have been less central to the state of the national newspaper industry.

So my book may seem less well organised than a broad historical survey but I believe it gives a more accurate picture, and one which is perhaps more faithful to the spirit of Fleet Street. For the history of the newspaper industry can be told only through the personalities who made it. In each chapter I have attempted to begin with a particularly significant or character-revealing event and then move into a more chronological vein. The ebb and flow of editorial policies are relevant in this book only in so far as they bear on the characters and the fortunes of the participants.

Finally the general reader should never forget that Fleet Street was a collection of print factories with vast and costly presses in the basements, roaring and shaking every night as they spewed out newspapers by the million. The compositors, process workers, readers, foundry men, engineers, electricians, machine minders and circulation staff together with all their various grades of colleagues and assistants frequently showed tremendous loyalty to their paper and could, when roused by the excitement of a big story, perform miracles of production and distribution. Unfortunately the gradual accumulation of power by the print unions provided an ominous rumbling Wagnerian *Leitmotiv* to the more visible pyrotechnics of publishers and editors. As I recount in the closing chapters, the unions were finally defeated after the most bitter struggle in the history of the industry. They may regroup, but they will never exercise the same grip that once they held, for the final chapter in the rise and fall of Fleet Street was also the story of the eclipse of print union power.

Note:
[1] *The London Encyclopaedia* edited by Ben Weinreb and Christopher Hibbert, Macmillan, 1983.

1
Northcliffe

I am but mad north-north-west; when the wind is southerly, I know a hawk from a handsaw.

Hamlet to Rosencrantz and Guildenstern

On Sunday, 4th June 1922, Lord Northcliffe,[1] the most powerful and inventive newspaper genius of the century, was in Boulogne where he had checked into the Hotel Christol under the name of Leonard Brown. He was behaving increasingly strangely. The day before he had sacked the golf professional who had been with him for more than a decade. He had despatched no less than seven telegrams to London complaining about the number of directors' relations employed in his organisation. He was exasperated with his 'overpaid directors'. He felt surrounded by treachery and was fearful of being attacked. From under his pillow he pulled out a little black silk bag which had been left at the hotel for 'Mr Leonard Brown'. 'Do you see the colour?' he asked his secretary. 'It is the colour of death.'

Back in London his staff were getting more and more worried. Yet their 'Chief', as he liked to be called, had often behaved pretty curiously before and he was, without doubt, the sole creator and inspiration of the largest publishing empire in the world. They all owed everything – their money and in some cases their titles - to him. More than 20 million copies of his publications were sold every week, and most of these publications he had actually launched rather than bought. Lord Beaverbrook was to call him 'a man of brilliant creative talents, touched by the hand of genius'.[2] The author H. G. Wells talked of Northcliffe's 'big and undoubtedly unco-ordinated brain', but no one ever questioned the drive and dynamism with which he had built up his amazing realm of print. He was the one and only begetter of the modern newspaper industry.

But now, in Boulogne, this meant very little. Northcliffe wrote a six-page letter to his friend, Sir Robert Hudson, who was also his

1

wife's lover and was staying with her at the Swiss resort of Evian-les-Bains. A well known doctor, Sir Frederick Treves, was with them. The letter contained the following pathetic passage:

> You have with you the most distinguished medical man in the world. Will you kindly ask his opinion as to my sanity? I have begun to have doubts whether it is too little work and too much money, or whether it is simply decay of my faculties; I do not know, but I think I am going mad. Please wire me at once to relieve my suspicions.

To assist in the diagnosis Northcliffe added that he had dreamt he had run off with Princess Mary and started a boarding house in Blackpool.[3]

Sir Robert Hudson's reply is not recorded, but the letter cannot have come as a complete surprise. There had been earlier signs that Northcliffe was becoming unhinged and rumours about his mental state were multiplying. More than three years earlier the Prime Minister, Lloyd George, speaking in the Commons debate on the Paris Peace Conference, had launched a devastating, and far from unprovoked, attack on Northcliffe. (The press magnate had demanded a preview of Cabinet appointments as the price of his support as well as an important role in the peace negotiations.) Lloyd George never mentioned the name, although his target was easily identified when he referred to Broadstairs where Northcliffe had his favourite home close to the North Foreland, and added that 'even great newspapers will forgive me for saying so' as he swept into the most ferocious passage of his speech:

> 'When a man has deluded himself, and all the people whom he ever permits to go near him help him into the belief that he is the only man who can win the war, and he is waiting for the clamour of the multitude that is going to demand his presence there to direct the destinies of the world, and there is not a whisper, not a sound, it is rather disappointing; it is unnerving; it is upsetting. Then the war is won without him. There must be something wrong. Of course, it must be the Government!'

Far crueller than any words he used was a gesture: as he launched into this passage the Prime Minister tapped his forehead, hinting at mental imbalance or worse.[4]

Northcliffe had been a hypochondriac for years. His letters were always complaining of bronchitis, neuritis, neuralgia, chills, headaches, trouble with his eyes (not surprising considering the acres of small print he read every week), fatigue, influenza, liver trouble, sore throat, ptomaine poisoning, and so forth. A rather sad page of his 'weight diary', headed 'A Fat Man's Gallant Fight Against Fate', showed that from 10th January, 1920 to 30th May, 1921 he was able, with difficulty, to reduce his weight from fourteen stone ('horrible') to thirteen stone ten lbs eight oz – a reduction of three and a half lbs. Northcliffe was 5 foot 8 inches tall so he was more than two stone over-weight.

In fact there is some evidence that Northcliffe's health had been gradually deteriorating from as early as 1909, when he was in his mid-forties. Paul Ferris, who studied the subject with the help of private papers in possession of the Harmsworth family, concluded there was a possibility that Northcliffe went to Germany that year to obtain treatment for syphilis from the famous Dr Ehrlich of 'magic bullet' fame; that the treatment did not work and that Northcliffe eventually suffered from tertiary syphilis which affected his brain.[5] (Both Wickham Steed, Northcliffe's appointee as editor of *The Times*, and J. L. Garvin of *The Observer* seem to have believed this disease was the problem.) His wife, Lady Northcliffe, writing to his secretary in 1910, said 'everyone in London says that Lord Northcliffe has an incurable disease'[6] but reported that 'the Chief' looked better than he had for ten years. There is in fact no firm evidence on the subject; the doctors announced the cause of death as ulcerative endocarditis, an insidious form of blood poisoning; there was no post-mortem and the matter remains an open question.*

What is not in doubt is the paranoid megalomania of Northcliffe's last weeks when his abuse of senior employees, transmitted by telegram or telephone, became so immoderate that two of the directors, Sir Andrew Caird, general manager of Associated Newspapers, and Walter Fish, assistant editor of the *Daily Mail*, issued writs for libel against him after being accused of an outrageous attempt to cut down wages and of lying. In March 1922 Wickham Steed, whom Northcliffe was attempting to remove from the editorship of *The Times*, to which he had been appointed with the warmest expressions

* Ferris. The author's verdict: 'not proven'. Cecil Harmsworth King, according to Hugh Cudlipp, 'always asserted in private and in public that General Paralysis of the Insane was the cause'. See *The Prerogative of the Harlot* by Hugh Cudlipp, Bodley Head 1980.

of goodwill only two years earlier, consulted the distinguished solicitor, Sir Charles Russell, who had recently seen Northcliffe. Russell told him that, in his view, Northcliffe's condition had deteriorated to such an extent that he was no longer capable of doing business and that he was unlikely to live long. The following month Steed travelled with Northcliffe to Geneva and formed the impression that Northcliffe was going mad.

Yet on most occasions during the last few years Northcliffe was in complete command of his faculties, and he was certainly plotting with a high degree of success to bring *The Times* (of which he had been the principal owner since 1908) as completely under his control as the *Daily Mail*. The co-proprietor, John Walter, sold shares to Northcliffe in June 1922 and lost his option to buy Northcliffe's shares in the event of the latter's death without realising the true state of his colleague's health.

In 1919 Northcliffe had undergone an operation for the removal of a benign tumour in his throat but his physical health had become increasingly uncertain. Stories about his condition had been multiplying: J. L. Garvin wrote to Northcliffe that there had been 'rumours, some mild, some wild'.

Northcliffe himself chased after any hope of a cure for the unknown affliction. At one moment he was off to see a Dr Mackay, who was thirty-two, in Birmingham for a vaccine treatment, and shortly afterwards he was wondering whether he should not be seeing some younger medical man. The doctor whom he respected most, a Scot called Sir James Mackenzie, advised him to slow down but he couldn't do it. The publisher Newman Flower, summoned to see Northcliffe, recorded in his autobiography, *Just as it Happened*,[7] that Northcliffe, pacing up and down his office, said he had seen his thirty-second specialist that day and repeated again and again, 'I am going to die'.

Curiously those who saw Northcliffe most frequently, his secretaries and his servants, saw nothing much wrong with their boss. He had always been autocratic and peremptory and he showed little change to them. But in the final months he was often clearly demented.

He dictated sometimes for hours at a time; he thought people were out to assassinate him; he flourished a loaded pistol at his own dressing gown under the impression it was a lurking figure; he despatched abusive telegrams to his most loyal servants until they were intercepted; he was appallingly rude to many of those who tried to serve him; he insulted his wife; his behaviour and threats became so outrageous that the general manager of *The Times*, hearing of the sick man's return to England, gave orders for a guard to be placed on the door to prevent Northcliffe from entering Printing House Square.

His last days at his house in Carlton Gardens were completely macabre. He was guarded by a team of male nurses supplied by Sir Thomas (later Lord) Horder, the leading doctor of the day, but he could, for a time, still use the telephone and was thus able to 'sack' many of the staff at his newspapers, ignorant of the fact that his orders were now being disregarded. When Horder came to visit him, Northcliffe shouted, 'Another of George's bloody knights!' and grabbed a pistol from under his pillow. It was soon removed and found to be unloaded. Apparently cut off from all telephones, he found one in his wife's bedroom and used it to telephone the *Daily Mail* news desk with instructions on how he should be rescued from incarceration. His final days were spent, on Horder's advice, in a hut built on the roof of the Duke of Devonshire's house in Carlton Gardens. (Northcliffe's own roof was found unsuitable for the structure.) Meanwhile his brothers, well aware of the vast fortune that was about to be divided, were appalled to discover that Northcliffe had made two new wills in which he left everything to his wife to use exactly as she liked under Sir Robert Hudson's guidance, and that he urged her to marry again. While subsequently protesting that Northcliffe had never been certified insane, they were quick to prove, with the help of Lord Horder, that the great man was nonetheless in no fit state to make a new will. To avoid scandal a settlement was reached on the basis of the original will but Lady Northcliffe received an extra £250,000, though slightly less income; she soon married Sir Robert Hudson.

Shortly before his death Northcliffe dictated final instructions to his doctor: they were absolutely clear. He wished to be buried near his mother and he wanted nothing on the burial stone but his name, together with the year of his birth and the year of his death. 'In *The Times* I should like a page reviewing my life-work by someone who really knows and a leading article by the best man available on the night.' It was a graceful gesture by the sorely tried editor, Wickham Steed, that he wrote the leader himself, and in generous terms. The family history records a final change in his appearance: 'Death had given him back his youth'.

*

There was little in his early youth to suggest that Alfred Harmsworth would become one of the most famous and influential men in England. His father, also called Alfred, was a school teacher with the gift of the gab who later became a bibulous and fairly briefless barrister; his mother was the daughter of a reasonably prosperous Irish land agent. He was their 'first born' as he never ceased reminding his mother who eventually had thirteen other pregnancies to cope with, the last in her forty-seventh year.

The family left Ireland, where young Alfred, known in the family as 'Sunny', had been born in July 1865, so that the father could pursue his legal career in London. They moved from one house to another in the Hampstead and St John's Wood areas. Cash was often very short, for the land agent died shortly after the marriage, and so the father's hoped-for job in the land agent's office never materialised, nor did much of the legacy.

Perhaps the most significant event of those early years was Sunny's eighth birthday when a friend of his father, Mr George Jealous, gave him a printing set. Mr Jealous was the editor of the *Ham and High*,[8] still one of the best local papers in the country, and on press days he had allowed Sunny into the composing room. In spotting and encouraging the boy's early passion for print Mr Jealous gave him an experience he was still talking about fifty years later.

Possibly for financial reasons Sunny (later named Dodger by some of his school chums) did not go to school until he was eight, and apart from being noted for dazzlingly good looks seems to have had an unremarkable career until, at the age of thirteen, he arrived at Henley House School, St John's Wood, presided over by one J. V. Milne, father of A. A. Milne and grandfather to Christopher Robin. There, despite his total inability to master arithmetic, he soon emerged as a leading figure among the boys, becoming captain of both the football and the cricket teams.

Two other interests began to dominate his life. First, he persuaded Mr Milne to allow him to start a school magazine, and the first issue duly appeared in March 1881 with a little item under the heading 'Entre Nous': 'I have it on the best authority that the H.H.S. Magazine is to be a marked success.' (Northcliffe was always good at 'booming' his own products.) The magazine had been printed locally and, again, the young editor hung around the works until the job was done. Moreover Mr Jealous gave him some reporting jobs to do on the *Ham and High* and the boy used to frequent the editor's home, reading papers and magazines with quiet concentration.

Secondly he took up bicycling with immense enthusiasm, owning a half-share in a smart bicycle and riding it over vast distances in all weathers.

Then calamity struck. When only sixteen, out of school and out of work, he got the Harmsworths' maid pregnant and was shipped off to the Continent as secretary-companion to a young man on a tour of France. The maid, who was called Smith, went back to her family and eventually gave birth to a boy who was called Alfred. Although the boy's father later watched over the boy through the medium of solicitors, paid for his education and tried to help him start a career, he was a miserable disappointment, bringing tears to his father's eyes according to a confidential secretary, and eventually emigrated to Australia where he is said to have died of drink.

Back from the Continent young Harmsworth had to earn his own living, and began freelancing around Fleet Street. Money was still short and to eat Sunday dinner with his family he sometimes had to walk from his lodgings in Clapham to St John's Wood. The poverty of the family in his early days was never forgotten and may explain the closeness of the Harmsworths in later years. But at the time he kept up with his bicycling, falling ill after riding from Bristol to London on a penny-farthing in the rain. He also persisted with his journalism and eventually called on George Newnes, founder of *Tit-Bits*, because he was said to pay as much as a guinea a column. Soon he was a regular contributor. He quickly realised that Newnes was tapping a vast market, telling his friend Max Pemberton, 'This man has got hold of something bigger than he imagines.' He tried and failed to raise capital to start a rival magazine, but eventually accepted a job with William Iliffe's publishing firm in Coventry as editor of *Bicycling News* at a salary of £2 10s a week. He was nearly twenty-one.

He soon introduced a number of touches which foreshadowed his newspaper technique. He cut stories ruthlessly. He introduced a gossip column. He promoted the idea of women's cycling, and appointed a woman correspondent. Soon the circulation was rising and his pay was increased but he was dissatisfied, confiding in a friend, 'This Coventry life is too middling – you are not quite down, but you are by no means up. I must be up!' He suggested to Iliffe, head of the firm, that they should start a rival to *Tit-Bits* in the form of 'Answers to Correspondents' but Iliffe felt it would not fit in with his successful specialist magazines. He did however offer to print such a magazine on credit if young Harmsworth could find other backers.

It took about eighteen months for Alfred to raise the money, largely from a retired army captain called Beaumont who had married a rich widow, but might have been physically attracted by the handsome, debonair young man with the golden hair. The ex-soldier was tapped first for £1,000 which was invested in a small publishing company Alfred had set up with the help of a couple of friends, and then for another £1,000 specifically for the new publication, *Answers to Correspondents*. With typical self-confidence young Alfred got married during this period, to a pretty girl called Mary Milner whom he had been courting for some time, and meanwhile in his office he worked on a large file called 'SCHEMO MAGNIFICO', outlining other publications he hoped to launch in the future.

The opening issue, the foundation of his whole publishing empire, appeared in June 1888. At first it was very tough going indeed. The print bills could not be paid right away and the formula, of appearing to answer queries from correspondents on such subjects as 'How to Cure Freckles', 'Strange Things that Happen in Tunnels' and 'Why Jews don't ride Bicycles', was attracting less than 20,000 readers a week. (His sister, Geraldine, later the mother of Cecil King, spent much of her time in the British Museum finding suitable answers to mythical letters.) Gradually, by shortening the title to *Answers*, by ingenious mail order offers, by simple competitions, and by developing the editorial formula to include short stories and interviews with famous people, the sale increased to 33,000 and the paper neared solvency. By the time of the first annual meeting in June 1889 his brother Harold, who had been persuaded to give up a safe civil service career to look after the financial side of the enterprise,[9] was able to report a sale of 48,000 and a gross profit of £1,097.

But the big breakthrough came when Alfred launched a competition for '£1 A WEEK FOR LIFE'. It was said that he had got into conversation with a tramp on the Embankment (how many press barons of a later age would find the time for that?) and the tramp said he would be happy if only he had that amount. The competitors had to guess the amount of bullion in the Bank of England on a certain day. (Again it was Alfred who had spotted a little paragraph in *The Times* giving a figure for the previous day.) But the key to success was that each entry had to be signed by five witnesses, none from the same address as the entrant. As the fame of *Answers* was thus being spread, extra staff had to be hired to vet the postcards;

Harmsworth brothers and sisters were roped in; and on the last day alone 295,000 entries were received, bringing the total up to 718,218. The sale of the Christmas issue which contained the name of the winner, one Sapper Austin of the Ordnance Survey in Southampton, exceeded 200,000 copies.

The profits of *Answers* were now rising to £150 a week and with typical audacity Alfred and Harold decided to launch another publication, but this time they formed the company themselves, leaving their original partners (who soon dropped out, or were pushed out) with a share of the *Answers* company. The new publication, which first appeared in May 1890, was *Comic Cuts*. It certainly lived up to its name, cutting many jokes from American publications and containing snippets of the most juvenile punning 'Jokes' and 'Tiny Chips.' Alfred coined the slogan, 'Amusing without being vulgar'. It was soon making even more money than *Answers*, despite a cover price of only ½d, and sold 300,000 copies a week. Ten weeks later the brothers launched a third publication, *Illustrated Chips*, soon shortened to *Chips* and also selling at ½d; it was the beginning of comic strip journalism. Alfred was in his element, supplying wheezes of every kind, such as *Answers* pens and *Answers* cigarettes and *Answers* toothache cures, while a new character called 'Mr Answers' was despatched on various adventures such as sleeping in a haunted house and being hypnotised. Meanwhile Harold was slashing printing and paper costs to the absolute minimum and piling up the profits; some time in the summer of 1890 he was able to tell Alfred that he could look forward in the next twelve months to receiving not less than £10,000 (worth as much as £450,000 a century later). On the proceeds Alfred bought himself Elmwood, the house near Broadstairs which he was always to regard as his favourite home, but the brothers also looked after their immediate family, buying a house in Maida Vale, paying for the education of younger brothers and sisters, and setting them up in other ways. Nor were contributors neglected; they were paid 'on acceptance' - an admirable system which is far from universal nearly a century later.

The publications factory was now in full spate: *Forget-Me-Not* was launched in November 1891 and after a hesitant start was soon contributing to profits. Harold was able to report in July 1892 that *Answers* was selling 375,000, *Comic* 420,000, *Chips* 212,000 and *Forget-Me-Not* 83,000, a total of 1,090,000. Short story magazines soon followed: *Home, Sweet Home* in 1892, *Half-penny Marvel* and

Union Jack a year later as well as a group of magazines for boys, including *The Wonder* and *The Marvel* which published the Sexton Blake detective stories.

In July 1894 the fertile brain of Alfred produced another sort of publication: the *Sunday Companion*, a non-denominational religious weekly. Again there was a slow start and Harold was quick to urge, 'Knife it', but Alfred persisted and in ten years it was making £20,000 a year. As usual a batch of similar titles was launched to protect the big money-maker from attack; one of them, *Golden Stories*, used the work of a little-known writer called Ethel M. Dell.

As owners of such a successful and profitable magazine business it was only a question of time before the Harmsworth brothers were asked if they were interested in buying a newspaper. The moment came in the summer of 1894 when two journalists, Louis Tracy and Kennedy Jones, then employed by the loss-making evening paper, *The Sun*, obtained an option to buy the *Evening News* which was also in debt, incurring losses at the rate of £100 a week,* and up for sale by the executors of a former Conservative MP who had supported it and another who had helped keep it going. Harold reckoned it was worth having 'if we could pick up the paper for a song', and Alfred must have liked the idea. After all, the paper was already selling 100,000 copies a day. They brought it for £25,000 including plant and building. Then they set to work in their separate ways, Harold to cut the costs, Alfred to steam up the circulation with the help of Kennedy Jones, a brusque but able Scot who was soon made editor.

Alfred went into what is now a familiar routine but was then a pioneering path: larger headlines, shorter stories, a women's page, shorter leading articles, less racing (but only down from twelve columns to nine), more features including a daily short story. He plundered *Answers* for material, causing Kennedy Jones to exclaim, 'God, man, you're not going to turn the paper into an evening *Answers*, are you?' Aided by heavy coverage of a murder trial (Alfred had visited the accused , James Canham Read, in his cell at Chelmsford jail and described the prisoner, his clothes and the execution chamber in an unsigned article in the *News* – Alfred always had a taste for the macabre), the paper made big gains in circulation, selling 390,000 on the last day of the trial. In the first year of Harmsworth ownership the *Evening News* switched from substantial

* It was said that when Harold saw the 'books' for the first time he was so appalled that he burst into tears. Later the same story was told about him when he first examined the accounts of *The Times*.

loss to profit, making £14,000, nearly doubling that figure in the second year.

Alfred's horizons were now expanding fast. Writing to two of his brothers in October 1894 he reported, 'Our next scheme is a daily paper which we talk of starting in February.' The paper was the *Daily Mail*, but like many other newspapers it did not meet its original launch date, eventually hitting the streets on Monday, 4th May 1896, priced only ½d while other papers were 1d. The first issue does not look so revolutionary today, with its front page full of small advertisements and its conservative type, but the paper did call for an end to the requirement that motorists should be preceded by men with red flags.

Alfred was thirty; his career as a newspaper proprietor was nearing full flood. He told Kennedy Jones the venture meant 'bankruptcy or Berkeley Square'. Hoping for a sale of 150,000 he was ecstatic when the first day's figure nearly touched 400,000; his remark to Kennedy Jones, 'We've struck a gold mine', has gone down in Fleet Street history. It was perfectly true.

At one time or another, apart from the *Daily Mail*, the *Evening News* and his string of magazines, he owned *The Observer*, the *Weekly Despatch*, the principal shareholding in *The Times*, a string of regional newspapers, and he launched the *Daily Mirror*. In a famous television broadcast Beaverbrook said, 'I hold one-fifth of the newspaper market, but Northcliffe had *one-half!*' He was not far out.

Yet what was Alfred Harmsworth's secret? Many highly intelligent men worked for him or knew him well and most of them tried to sum up just why he was so successful. Perhaps Norman Angell, the general manager of the *Continental Daily Mail* who later won a Nobel prize for his book *The Great Illusion*, got the key element right when he said, that 'Northcliffe possessed the common mind to an uncommon degree'. Northcliffe himself said, 'Most of the ordinary man's prejudices are my prejudices and are therefore the prejudices of my newspapers.' On another occasion he said, 'We don't direct the ordinary man's opinion. We reflect it.' To this extent his lack of a university education which he often professed to regret proved an advantage. Nonetheless he was well read, being particularly fond of Dickens and Hardy, writing to the latter author that he could tell the story of *A Pair of Blue Eyes* backwards. Another close observer saw Northcliffe as 'for all time a boy . . . He had the audacity, the impatience, the impetuosity, the follies and tricks, the mischief, even the thoughtless cruelties of a boy. He had a boy's passion for having things explained . . .' He certainly impressed his young nephew Cecil King by telling him that he was always learning.

Northcliffe was much more than self-educated. He had phenomenal energy, often working in the early days until four in the morning. He had a dominating, autocratic personality with an absolutely appalling temper which at times became quite ungovernable: he was known even to make a man kneel before him, and on another occasion literally kicked a man out of his office. He had a good memory, being able to recall a sermon he had heard at the church of St Augustine in Kilburn forty years earlier. He was thoroughly versed in every branch of newspaper production, often corresponding directly with Charles Hart, mechanical superintendent at Carmelite House where his beloved *Daily Mail* was printed, on such subjects as typefaces, quality of paper, linotypes, stereotyping and autoplate.

He wrote powerful prose, punchy slogans and selling headlines. It was Northcliffe who, in 1915, after writing the *Daily Mail* leader attacking Kitchener for failing to give the army enough ammunition, ordered the famous bill, 'KITCHENER'S TRAGIC BLUNDER'; the paper was burnt at the Stock Exchange; service clubs banished it from their premises; and sales slumped by 238,000 copies a day. ('I don't care,' said Northcliffe, but the attacks on Kitchener were softened while the general campaign on the shell shortage continued.) Before the war he commissioned the Berlin correspondent of the *Daily Mail* to write a book about Germany. When published the book was virtually ignored, so he had stories written about it under the heading, 'THE BOOK THAT WILL NOT SELL'. Eventually it sold 200,000 copies. It was said that he had learnt much from American journalism; certainly he cribbed many stories from American papers in the early days. Yet he had something to teach the Americans; when he took over Pulitzer's *New York World* for a day he cut the page size and would not allow any story to run for more than 250 words. Hearst said later, 'We all thought it a clever stunt, but few of us realised the vital importance of the principle, "peptonised journalism".'

He was remarkable in the backing he gave to technical progress of many kinds. He was one of the first to have a telephone installed at his country home (at a time when William Mudford, the editor of the *Evening Standard*, was refusing to have it either in his office or at home). He was an early motorist, setting out at short notice in

1899 to drive from London to Oldham in his 6 hp Panhard so that he could help Winston Churchill in an election campaign. After five punctures he had to abandon the car. (Churchill failed to get in, but wrote a charming note suggesting that neither 'my career or your car will be seriously damaged'.) Later he was to take a keen interest in the Rolls-Royce motor car, suggesting it should have a self-starter. ('We have not yet found one good enough for Rolls-Royce,' replied the managing director.)

He was among the first to give powerful encouragement to the aviation industry, having confidential reports sent from the US on the progress of the Wright brothers whom he subsequently met at Pau in France; they became friends. Soon he was offering a succession of *Daily Mail* prizes for pioneer flights – £1,000 for the first flight across the Channel, £10,000 for the first flight from London to Manchester, £10,000 for the winner of the first round-Britain race (all these prizes were won by Frenchmen), £10,000 for the first transatlantic flight. One biographer of Northcliffe says that despite his enthusiasm for aviation he never flew.[9] In fact he had a short flight in a French military aircraft in 1911, but his mother then made him promise, in writing, that he would never do that again without her written consent.

Broadcasting was less appealing to him. He foresaw the competition. All the same, he persuaded Dame Nellie Melba, the world famous Australian soprano, to give the first broadcast concert. (She had to go to the Marconi works at Chelmsford where she was fed chicken and champagne.) It gave a tremendous fillip to the development of the new medium. He was also well ahead of his time in demanding a twice-weekly column of film criticism, and he was supporting decimal coinage as early as 1916.

Clearly he could exercise immense charm when he was ready to make the effort. R. D. Blumenfeld, editor of the *Daily Express* and a leading figure in Fleet Street between the wars, wrote of meeting Northcliffe early in his career: he was 'a fascinating young man – buoyant, enthusiastic, clear-eyed, exceedingly good-looking . . . He was endowed with a smile that lasted in the memory.' Tom Clarke, later to be appointed news editor of the *Daily Mail*, wrote of 'grasping a large friendly hand and looking into magic eyes . . . feeling I had met a human dynamo.' To his favourites, like Clarke, he could be exceptionally generous, suddenly ordering him to take his wife on a holiday in France, all expenses paid. On another occasion Clarke made a mistake on a story and expected a tremendous dressing down; instead Northcliffe increased his salary saying, 'I have increased your salary because I want men in my business who can make decisions even if they are wrong.'

There was a black reverse side to this kind of treatment. On one occasion he rang up the editor of one of his newspapers. 'Who am I speaking to?' he asked. 'The editor,' came the reply. 'You *were* the editor,' said Northcliffe and rang off. The editor left within a week. One journalist who had been employed at *The Times* wrote, 'The regime resembled a petty German court with its heel-clickings, grovellings, slander, espionage and jealousies of those who desired to bask in the sunshine of patronage.'[10] Yet Northcliffe, who was a mass of inconsistencies, claimed to dislike flattery and told his secretary of one man, 'He is impossible . . . He agrees with everything I say.'

Again and again he talked of his 'spies' and his 'ferrets' in the organisation. Certainly he was well informed of what was going on. Some thought that reports went to him from the telephone operators. *The History of The Times*, written by Stanley Morison, named the people responsible for defending the historic quality of the paper and went on:

> Their actions were reported by spies in the office chosen by the Chief for their capacity to render a slavish obedience to their ennobled employer. Northcliffe had plumbed the depths of the English petty bourgeois appetite for titles . . . Leading members of his staff must have titles . . . It amused him to employ knights and baronets . . .[11]

Apart from members of his own family this could refer only to *Sir* Campbell Stuart, knighted for services on Northcliffe's British War Mission to the United States, and later managing director of *The Times; Sir* Andrew Caird, vice-chairman of Associated Newspapers; and *Sir* George Sutton, chairman of the Amalgamated Press and Northcliffe's former confidential secretary. (Pomeroy Burton, a very pushy character whom Northcliffe had hired from the *World* because he was the only member of the staff who refused to wear a dinner jacket when Northcliffe edited the paper for a night, was general manager of Associated Newspapers and persistently pressed for an honour but did not get it until after Northcliffe's death.)

If some of Northcliffe's methods were obnoxious he could also behave with extraordinary sympathy and understanding in a personal crisis. A young humorous writer on the *Daily Mail*, called Twells Brex, who was mortally ill with cancer, wrote to say that he wanted to go on working as he felt he could not continue to draw his money unless he did so, Northcliffe wrote back at once to say that if Brex wanted to work, 'Why not?' He added, 'Please do not worry about salary. I have not put in eighteen hours a day since I was fifteen in order that those who help me should be deprived in the hour of need.' Brex suffered greatly before the end, but wrote a moving reflection on death which was published in the *Mail*. Northcliffe was frequently at his bedside, sitting silently until Brex wanted to talk. After his death, apart from generous financial provision, he arranged for the young widow and her son to stay at Elmwood for several weeks. Mrs Brex's letter of thanks, to be found in the British Library's collection of Northcliffe MSS, is still quite heart-rending even at this distance of time.

Northcliffe must also count as a pioneer of women's emancipation. In December 1916, in correspondence with Mrs Fawcett and Lady Betty Balfour, two leaders of the women's suffrage movement, he suggested that a major united deputation should await on the Prime Minister. He talked with the Prime Minister, whom he found sympathetic, and also with the editor of *The Times*, who was also ready to give support. Eventually the deputation called on Lloyd George and, aided by a report from the Speaker's Conference on Electoral Reform, the women won their case.

From the beginning Northcliffe was concerned that his newspapers should contain material especially interesting to women and of course it was his idea that the *Daily Mirror*, founded in 1903, should be a paper for women, edited and written by women. The idea was a flop; the women were insufficiently skilled and had to be sacked. 'It was a horrid experience – like drowning kittens,' wrote the new editor, Hamilton Fyfe. But Northcliffe never lost his concern that women should have an important role in his organisation, employing them as reporters, war correspondents and diplomatic correspondents as well as feature writers. And he wanted women staff to be properly looked after. In 1919 he was writing to the general manager of *The Times* that all women workers should have a half day off, morning or afternoon, once a fortnight, in addition to Saturday afternoons, when they could see something of the world and of the shops. (On the other hand he did not like women pictured in breeches, saying, 'I don't like masculinity in women. Many people [probably meaning his mother] think it is interfering with the birthrate.')

Reading the notes he dictated to his staff and colleagues on every aspect of the newspaper business more than fifty years later, it is impossible not to admire his drive, his knowledge, his understanding of the human element and his instinctive touch on most editorial matters. He prided himself on the political independence of his papers and on his own isolation from politicians. 'He often told me that he was better off as a journalist,' wrote Lord Beaverbrook, 'because he did not consort with Ministers or ex-Ministers.'[12] Two notes to Marlowe, editor of the *Daily Mail*, on political independence are worth quoting today: first, 'I do not believe in headlines that contain political bias or comment'; second, 'The *Daily Mail* was not made by licking Ministers' boots'. And how many reporters over the years would not agree with the comment: 'Sub-editors at night destroy the individuality of the writer.' Another note to Keith Murdoch, the Australian newspaper publisher who admired him immensely, would be echoed by any publisher of a monopoly evening paper:

'Remember that it is very difficult to run one [afternoon] paper in a town. You have only the morning papers to compare with it, and they are dead by the afternoon. If you had got another paper to compete with, you would be on the strain every hour of the day, as you probably are now, but racing against yourself is different to racing against a pack of other people.'

(Later he was to lend Keith Murdoch £5,000 so that Murdoch could gain control of the *Evening News* of Sydney, the start of his newspaper group. When Murdoch told him he would have to wait for the return of the money, Northcliffe told him to forget it. Indirectly, therefore, Keith's son, Rupert, was given some help in the launch of his own meteoric career by the founder of Associated Newspapers.)

He was an absolutely superb propagandist. Part of the success of the *Daily Mail* launch was due to the cross-publicity it received in all the Harmsworth titles, a technique he was always ready to use again. He reminded a manager, 'Wisdom dictates that *Daily Mail* topics get the fullest possible attention'. These topics, really *Daily Mail* publicity stunts, included the Titanic fund, the *Daily Mail* aeroplane, a thousand-pound holiday ('one of my own inventions'), a campaign for the Small Ads, the *Daily Mail* yearbook and constant attention to the Paris edition and the Paris Travel Bureau. Some of his stunts were so good they were copied in the United States. The New York *Journal* had run the circulation schemes which had appeared in *Answers* and the *Daily Mirror*, including a journalist given the name of 'Mr Raffles' who daily mingled with the crowd without disguise and if challenged successfully handed over a prize.* 'One day last week it had the unheard of effect of completely blocking Wall Street' wrote a Northcliffe employee, 'causing the suspension of business, the closing of the Treasury doors, and of Pierpont Morgan's office, against possible attacks of theft.'

Perhaps the most curious aspect of his character was his obsessive love for his mother. There cannot be many young men of twenty-three who write to their mother 'In Bed, My Wedding Day' and then write again on the first day of their honeymoon to assure her 'how happy we are' and sign 'Your loving Boy'. (Usually he signed 'your First Born', perhaps because he felt that she gave too much attention to some of the later progeny.) On his birthday he would write, telephone or cable to remind her 'This is our day'. During the war, visiting British General Headquarters in France he asked for facilities to send an immediate telegram. The staff agreed. The telegram was a message of love for his mother. On a trip to the United States his watch was kept to 'Totteridge time' so that he would know what his mother was doing at the home he had bought her, and he arranged to read a devotional book she had given him, *Daily Light on the Daily Path*, at the same time as she did. 'I think of you every second daily,' he wrote, 'and thank God I have had so good and brave a Mother.' On another occasion he wrote, 'Just a tiny little love letter, darling Mum . . .'

Cecil King, her grandson, wrote that she gave an exceptional expression of 'unchanging strength, deep affection and earthy wisdom'. He adds that Northcliffe's love for her was 'deeply embarrassing' to her. But she knew how to take advantage of it. Once, when Northcliffe's nephews and nieces were present, he said something that displeased her. 'Alfred,' she said, 'I will not have such talk in my drawing room. Please leave the room.' He meekly departed. On another occasion when she was seventy and Northcliffe was over forty he contradicted her. She said she knew he must be ill. It was the first time in his life that he had gone against her wishes.

---

* The idea was later copied by the *News Chronicle* with 'Lobby Lud'.

She had considerable influence on the conduct of his papers. While they were sensational by the standards of the time, they were not prurient; indeed they were quite prudish in some respects. Further, Northcliffe deferred to her views on policy matters as well. After writing his famous leader on Kitchener he drove out to Totteridge for his mother to vet it. She made some amendments which he incorporated in the final text. And in his final days one of the few intelligible remarks to have been recorded were the words, 'Tell Mother she is the only one.'

Mother was of course not quite the only one. Northcliffe had a succession of mistresses of whom a lady called Mrs Wrohan, of mysterious origins, seems to have been the principal, bearing him three children. Lady Northcliffe, who was childless, developed a long-standing affair with Sir Robert Hudson who raised vast sums of money for the Red Cross during the First World War with Northcliffe's assistance. Northcliffe seemed fully aware of what was going on and gave it his blessing. Indeed on one occasion he used Hudson to transmit a veiled warning to his wife about her conduct, writing to him in January 1920:

> I am very glad that you are staying on to look after the ladies. Attractive women of means have been having a hard time of it lately, as you may have seen from the published accounts, and there are reports known to the press which have not been printed. An interesting French book called 'L'Age Dangereux' throws an interesting light on this engaging topic. I thought I would say this to you as I know it would not be read to you if I had written it in another quarter.'

The last decades of the nineteenth century saw a number of developments which eased the transition from small circulation quality papers, mostly subsidised, to the publication of mass circulation papers in Fleet Street. The transport system had been revolutionised by the coming of the railway age. The first special newspaper train was run in 1845 by agreement between *The Times* and Hudson, 'the Railway King'. 'By 1852,' writes Christopher Hibbert, 'all the main railway lines had either been finished or authorised.'[13] The means of carrying papers printed in London to the furthest corners of the kingdom for people to read on the very same day were now available.

Meanwhile taxation on newspapers was rapidly being removed. Taxes on advertisements were abolished in 1853; the stamp duty on newspapers went two years later. And Gladstone got rid of the paper duties, 'a tax on knowledge', in 1861.

The appetite for newspapers was growing too. The Education Act of 1870 made attendance at school compulsory bringing virtually universal literacy by the end of the century. As W. T. Stead, then editor of the *Westminster Gazette*, wrote in 1892, 'The Education Act has practically created a new reading public, for which the morning daily, as we have it, makes next to no provision.' Northcliffe's papers, with their emphasis on shorter stories, 'talking points' and entertainment, were to fill the gap.

There was also a big breakthrough in printing techniques. The old sheet-fed presses were on the way out. By 1870 rotary presses fed by great rolls of paper had largely replaced them, with the result that output of copies per hour increased ten fold or more. By 1904 *Lloyds Weekly*, using seven Hoe presses, was able to print 55,000 copies an hour. At the same time paper was becoming much cheaper. *The Times* was paying 55s a ream in 1845 and only 38s a ream in 1861, a reduction of nearly thirty-five per cent. At that time the use of esparto grass imported from North Africa had overtaken the supply of rags as the principal component of newsprint. Shortly afterwards the chemical treatment of woodpulp as a means of producing the raw material of newsprint was perfected, and that is still the basis of the modern newsprint industry. Northcliffe himself, writing in the eleventh edition of the *Encyclopaedia Britannica*, noted that woodpulp was at the root of the expansion of the modern newspaper industry.[14]

Finally the actual setting of type was speeded up immensely by the invention of keyboard machines which could cope with the job previously done by hand. One of the first to appear was the Hattersley which emerged in the 1860s. Unsurprisingly, its introduction was bitterly opposed by the London craftsmen; after use the type had to be redistributed by hand and the London craftsmen refused to work with unskilled women recruited for the purpose. It was first used by the *Eastern Morning News* of Hull in 1866. But the Hattersley suffered from repair and maintenance problems and it was soon overtaken by the arrival of Mergenthaler's Linotype machine, which redistributed the type automatically. Once again provincial newspapers led the way with the *Leeds Mercury* installing it first; *The Times*, a non-union shop, was the first London newspaper to use it. Perhaps influenced by the attitude of the printers who gave a foretaste of the future by being generally bloody-minded and obstructive about the introduction of new technology, and deliberately misusing it, Northcliffe did not even see one until 1893, seven years after it had been installed in the United States at the *New York Tribune*. Then, of course, he was quick to realise its potential for his new paper. All the same, where type was concerned he was a traditionalist; leading articles in the *Daily Mail* and *Evening News* continued to be set by hand for years.

The new plants with their rotary presses and linotypes were extremely expensive and in consequence the need of lucrative advertising contracts to help pay the bills became more pressing. Fortunately for the new magnates of Fleet Street, there was plenty of advertising looking for a home. The manufacturers of branded goods were seeking to make their mark; drapers like D. H. Evans announced 'white sales'; multiple retailers like Gordon Selfridge were crying their wares; breakfast cereals like Quaker Oats were beginning their assault on the breakfast tables of Britain; the makers of patent medicines wished to make known the beneficent effects of their dubious potions; and the growth of classified advertising was just beginning.

Northcliffe knew what had to be done, and was ready to promote readers' interest in the advertisements. As late as 1921, just before setting off for the Continent, he sent some 'peppers' to Caird, the vice-chairman of Associated Newspapers, with instructions that they should be used regularly in the *Daily Mail*. The 'peppers' included such teasing advice as 'You will find some novel announcements among the *Daily Mail* advertisements this morning' and 'Cast your eyes over the advertisements today. There may be something for you there.' Yet all his adult life he was complaining about obtrusive advertisements. *Answers*, his first publication, had no advertisements at all at the outset. He sent countless memoranda to his managers on the need to control advertising, particularly obtrusive typography. In 1908 he was writing to *The Times* advertising manager, 'I would rather see no advertisements at all in the paper and pay the dividends out of my own pocket than have the whole of the good work of the editorial staff ruined in this way.' In 1914 he sent a telegram to the advertisement manager of the *Daily Mail*: 'MOST STRONGLY PROTEST AGAINST YOUR INJURING MY NEWSPAPER BY SUCH TYPE AS IN OXO ADVERTISEMENT PLEASE SEND ME WRITTEN EXPLANATION WHY YOU DISOBEY MY ORDERS.' In March 1915 a note to Lints Smith, associate manager of *The Times*: 'I must say I was thunderstruck to find after my repeated protest that you have destroyed the appearance of two whole pages by that abominable tyre advertisement.' In 1919, complaining about the *Daily Mail*, he wrote to the directors: 'Foolish things are being done such as cutting out football to make way for an advertisement.' His final insult to the advertising departments was to appoint Mr Glover, a burly hall porter at Carmelite House, 'head critic of advertisements', charged to keep out offensive advertising. After a good lunch with 'the Chief' at Carlton Gardens Mr Glover addressed the advertising staffs of Carmelite House; he got a rise of £100 a year for his extra responsibilities and appears to have played no further part in deciding advertising policy.

These then were the factors which led to the foundation of an immensely profitable mass circulation newspaper business based in Fleet Street, hub of the London printing trade since the early sixteenth century and home of most London newspapers from the eighteenth century. The railways had been built which could carry the papers swiftly from the metropolis to the major centres of population in the crowded island. The rotary presses had increased the speed of production. The new linotype machines had the capacity to set fat newspapers overnight. A growing audience existed for easily digestible news and entertaining, untaxing feature stories. A large and increasingly prosperous group of commercial enterprises was looking for opportunities to display its wares to a mass readership. And in Northcliffe there was a newspaper genius, the first who really understood and sympathised with the man on the Clapham omnibus – perhaps as only a man who had sometimes been too poor to find the fare could possible do – and who delighted in providing him and his wife with a newspaper they could read, understand and enjoy.

Yet even as the conditions for the successful foundation of the Fleet Street industry all came together, so were the seeds of its eventual destruction being sown by the very same man who had launched the whole massive enterprise – Lord Northcliffe. It was all done with the best of intentions. He believed that the people who wrote and printed the newspapers were underpaid. (And of course he was right at that time.) 'When I was a working journalist,' he wrote in 1919, 'I always felt that the proprietor had too much of the swag. I am still of that opinion.' Another example of his attitude can be seen in an exchange of notes with Caird, the vice-chairman of Associated Newspapers, in September 1919. Caird wrote:

Men are not working as they used to. An extra page in the foundry brings a deputation downstairs for an interview. In one department last week was displayed a card bearing the words:-
Don't hurry
Don't worry

Northcliffe replied at once:

You will find that Don't hurry, don't worry, is not confined to our work people, but is general throughout the middle and upper classes who are swarming to Scotland. Why should you expect the 'workers' to hurry and worry when the capitalists such as myself and you are lying back in the heather listening to the humming of the bees, or waiting at each tee on an overcrowded links for a game that takes four hours to play?

It was a constant theme in his ceaseless flow of notes to his management team. In January 1922 he wrote to Howard Corbett, an assistant manager of *The Times:*

I do not wonder that our Messengers are joining a union if they are only paid three pounds a week. Girl Messengers get a guinea and I understand that 77s a week is the smallest sum on which a married man can live in the humblest circumstances in London. How would you or I like to do it? Personally I would organise a strike.

Again he wrote to Caird in March 1922:

Our responsibilities are chiefly to those who have invested money in our companies ... Our other responsibilities are to the newspaper workers who since 1888* I have paid well. There is hardly a wealthier group of men in Great Britain than newspaper owners, big and little. So long as I am engaged in this kind of work I shall join in no combination for reducing salaries and wages.

Northcliffe's interest in the wages of his work force was much more than talk. His notes to managers like Caird and Lints Smith

---

* The first issue of *Answers* was printed in June 1888.

of *The Times* repeatedly enquire about low payments. For instance in 1917 his secretary wrote to Caird: 'The Chief asks how are the boys and girls paid at Carmelite House? What wages do boys of 16 get? There are quite a number of children employed there.' The answer was that boys got between twenty and thirty shillings a week, and girls about the same. In June 1918 there was a dispute in the Manchester office. Caird wearily reported that the comps who had received four advances of wages since the war began were asking for a further fifteen shillings a week. The lino operators who were getting 53s 3d in 1914 were now receiving 76s 9d. The case hands had been raised from 45s 6d to 67s. 'The question for us,' wrote Caird, 'is shall we, as we did last year, give way and pay the demand. If we do so others will be compelled to do the same and the other unions will be encouraged to go ahead. We shall all suffer.' Northcliffe replied. 'It is quite impossible for a man with children to live on £3 7s a week ... I have no intention of going into any fight to keep working men's wages down to £3 7s a week and I should like you to tell these people so in Manchester.' In 1918 he wrote to Lints Smith: 'I am hearing of cases (not in our business) of wounded soldiers coming back to their old jobs and being taken on at *lower wages* because of the pensions they are getting. I am sure you will see to it that none of your subordinates re-engage old employees on these terms.' In March 1919 he was writing to Caird: 'I hope the utmost care is being taken that no section of our employees – clerks or otherwise – have any sort of grievance as to hours of work, payment or accommodation.'

He was equally alert to pay and conditions of his journalists. Right at the start of his publishing career he was paying two guineas a column, more than twice the usual going rate. After the war he saw three young reporters from the *Daily Mail* and encouraged them to talk. Later he told Tom Clarke they had said that when reporters were working late at the office they should have a meal paid for. 'I agree.' And that when out working on a job all day long, reporters should have lunch paid for. 'I agree.' Then in Edinburgh he found that the local correspondent received the same retainer and lineage as in 1914 though prices had more than doubled. He presumed the same applied to provincial correspondents. 'No wonder they lack the enthusiasm displayed by highly paid directors, departmental heads and lino operators at Carmelite House.' And writing to a director of Associated Newspapers in 1917, after deputations of journalists had called on the Newspaper Proprietors' Association, he said:

> I am very glad to see that the journalists have at last had the courage to tackle the proprietors. We are rolling in money and it is time to disgorge to the staff. I have been a constant advocate of increased remuneration since I was a reporter. I do not know of any occupation which is more ill-paid.

In fact Northcliffe gave immense encouragement to the National Union of Journalists during its early years. The union was actually founded in 1906 but progress in recruitment was slow until the National Insurance Act of 1911 under which anyone earning less than £160 a year had to join the State Insurance scheme. A large number of journalists turned out to be in that category and membership of the NUJ climbed to more than 3,000. To celebrate, a banquet was held at the Hotel Cecil with Lloyd George, Chancellor of the Exchequer, as guest of honour. Northcliffe could not attend but sent a letter, reproduced facsimile in the union's official history,[15] which says it 'holds a permanent place of honour in our annals'. Northcliffe pointed out that during the past twenty years 'our craft has risen from a humble, haphazard, and badly paid occupation to a regular profession'. It was therefore all the more necessary that newspaper workers should combine for mutual protection and encouragement. The key paragraph followed: 'The introduction of all manner of time saving machinery within the last few years has made the work less arduous, but more nerve exhausting, and it is incumbent that journalists should unite for the obtaining of longer annual holidays and better pay.' Not surprisingly the reading of this letter was interrupted by bursts of applause, and the union's historian reports that it had a tonic effect on the membership. The letter was framed. Five years later Lord Northcliffe showed that he was as good as his word by supporting the NUJ when they wanted recognition from the Newspaper Proprietors' Association. In a confidential note to his own secretary Northcliffe wrote that in his opinion any worker who did not join a union was a fool, but he hoped (perhaps foreseeing the horrors of closed-shop journalism) that no one would be forced to join who did not want to join.

Consistency was never Northcliffe's strong point and he was appalled when in 1920 the NUJ was discussing a claim that included a demand for some kind of grading for journalists. In a leading article the *Daily Mail* said that these demands, if pressed, would result in a 'reluctant but complete shut-down'. A later report referred, in Northcliffe's phrase, to 'Jam Factory Journalism', but he did allow a lengthy reply by the union's general secretary to be printed in the *Mail*. The claim was dropped.

On several other occasions Northcliffe showed exasperation with union demands, being particularly sensitive to any hint of union interference with editorial freedom, and towards the end of his life kicking a union official out of his Paris office after calling him a 'damned ungrateful swine'.

Yet on balance he was a fair employer. Left to themselves it looks as if several other newspaper proprietors would have paid out as little as possible to their staffs. But Northcliffe frequently acted as their goad. He was genuinely cherished by the printers and idolised by almost all his journalists. When paper sizes had to be cut during the First World War and staff dismissed, Northcliffe wrote to each dismissed printer saying that he could take the letter to the cashier and claim £5 for each year of service. The head printer at Carmelite House wrote to say, 'For a couple of hours the room had more the appearance of a general holiday than a working department...' then, perhaps more ominously, 'A gift of this nature is a precedent in the newspaper section of the trade'. There was equal goodwill at Printing House Square; the Imperial Father of the Composing Room Chapel wrote, accepting an increase of 8s a week saying, 'If the same spirit existed in government departments as prevails between the management of *The Times* and the composing room staff we would not have to deplore the lamentable squabbles we have today.' And the night editor of the *Daily Mail*, after the whole staff had received a Christmas bonus, wrote, 'The air of delight radiated through the office this evening would have rejoiced your heart'.

Cecil King has said that his uncle started the Newspaper Proprietors' Association as a breakaway body from the Master Printers' Association.[16] Details are sketchy because the NPA records were destroyed during the war, but Northcliffe had very little time for his co-proprietors. As his family biographers put it, 'his resentment was transferred in latter years to the "amateur proprietors" (his term), who acquired newspapers as they acquired oil wells, factories or chain stores, and who had no experience of or special regard for newspaper working conditions'.

The full extent of his resentment can be seen in one of the most extraordinary pamphlets ever published about Fleet Street –

'Newspapers and their Millionaires' by Lord Northcliffe – which was first serialised in the *Daily Mail*. The copy in the British Library is said to be the 18th edition, price 3d; it may well have been the first edition because Northcliffe always liked to give the impression that anything he produced was selling like hot cakes. The cause of this outburst was an attempt by the Newspaper Proprietors' Association to cut wages. Northcliffe resigned rather than be a party to any such move. It was the first of many such resignations by publishers who didn't like uniting with their business rivals even on industrial relations. As he said in the pamphlet, written in his own fascinating staccato style: 'I object to being a member of a Combination in which capitalists ignorant of Fleet Street dictate terms to those who have spent their lives trying to understand the complex questions of newspapers.'

Northcliffe explained that 'a member of the Combine' had visited him to remonstrate over the high wages paid in Fleet Street and his refusal to cut them. 'The wages are preposterous,' this man had said. 'Some of these men have motor cycles and side cars; more than one of them drives a motor car.' Northcliffe had seen nothing wrong with that. British newspapers were just as prosperous as they had ever been. For the first time, he wrote, he had realised that behind every single London daily newspaper there was a multi-millionaire, a millionaire, or a very wealthy colleague, a Shipping King (Sir John Ellerman who had substantial interests in *The Times* and was chief shareholder in the *Tatler*), a Cotton-waste King (Sir John Leigh of the *Pall Mall Gazette*), Coal Kings (he meant the Berry brothers, who came from South Wales and owned the *Daily Graphic*), an Oil King (Lord Cowdray, then of the *Westminster Gazette*) and the rest of them.

These were not actually named, though their pictures were displayed in the centre of the pamphlet. But he did name a few, being particularly scathing about the 'chocolate millionaires behind the *Daily News*', the Cadbury family. He added a curious story that the head of the family, which was of course based at Bourneville, had once invited him to launch a paper there with Cadbury money to 'purify the press of Birmingham'. But he was complimentary about three people – 'the beautiful and accomplished director of the *Morning Post*, Lady Bathhurst', who had inherited control from her father, Lord Glenesk; Lord Burnham (the rather ineffectual chairman of the *Daily Telegraph*) 'fine work for the NPA ... secured a well-deserved step in the peerage'; and Lord Beaverbrook, now sole owner of the *Daily Express* and the newly launched *Sunday Express* 'whose career is a credit to Canada'. It may be noted that these three all owned newspapers in close rivalry either with *The Times* or the *Daily Mail*.

The key passage appeared at the foot of page 12 of the 24-page squib: 'There is no case for a reduction in the wages of our daily printers, and as regards what are called the Northcliffe journals there will be none.'

By the time he wrote this highly enjoyable, idiosyncratic brochure (the summer of 1922), his brain was beginning to disintegrate; nonetheless he could still make clear exactly what he really thought. After all it was only a variation of what he had been saying to Caird towards the end of the war following a dispute at their Manchester printers:

> The printers are realising that the invention of the rotary press and woodpulp paper have enormously increased the power and profit of the newspaper owners. As soon as newspaper owners were hit by the war they doubled and in some cases trebled the price of their product. I have not yet heard that they have doubled or trebled the wages of their workers.
>
> On the other hand the cost of living of these workers has, in many cases, doubled or trebled, and most of them are living cheek by jowl with munitioners and munitionettes who are earning more than highly skilled workers in the printing house.
>
> *Many newspaper owners and printers are not so favourably placed as we are, and I therefore feel that we must act by ourselves alone, pointing out to our workers that it will be unfair of them to expect the same terms from small printers and newspaper owners.*

So the founder of the modern British newspaper industry, who was also the founder of the Newspaper Proprietors' Association, destroyed any hope that the newspaper owners might stick together long before they had any idea of what might hit them in future years. His trust that the printers would not act unfairly in demanding the highest rate throughout Fleet Street might have been well founded as long as he was alive, for he had a very close relationship with George Isaacs, leader of the principal printing union. But there was no hope that his brother Harold, Lord Rothermere, the financial scourge of the organisation, would maintain the same patriarchal benevolence towards the staff. On his deathbed Northcliffe started up and told young Cecil King, 'Harold will ruin my paper. He thinks too much of money.'

He was a great, if flawed, genius. He liked to model himself on Napoleon whose hat, he was delighted to find on a visit to Versailles, fitted him exactly; but unlike his hero he had no capacity for organisation and relied entirely on instinct. H. G. Wells wrote of the 'extraordinary mental and moral conflicts' created by the great challenges he met compared with the total inadequacy of his education. Yet if he had been better educated he might neither have realised the vastness of the opportunities before him, nor had the mental energy to seize them so successfully. His ability to produce publications people actually wanted to read transformed the newspaper trade into a vast and prosperous industry. To his credit he strove to see that employees benefited from the money that was flowing so abundantly to the publishers. It was too much to expect that a man with such a fertile imagination for 'talking points', stunts and human interest stories should also have realised the long-term industrial implications of what he was doing. Northcliffe may well have been the greatest newspaper man in history; he was not the greatest industrialist.

Notes:
1. There is vast documentation on Northcliffe's life. Almost a dozen biographies have been produced as well as innumerable reminiscences by people who worked for him. The value of all this work is very uneven. The greatest store of material can be found in the massive 933 page family biography *Northcliffe* by Reginald Pound and Geoffrey Harmsworth, Cassell 1959. They had full access to all the papers, but omitted any details of Northcliffe's sex life and illegitimate children. This omission was amply rectified by Paul Ferris in *The House of Northcliffe*, Weidenfeld, 1971. Ferris was helped by Sir Geoffrey Harmsworth as well as by other members of the family. The Northcliffe papers in the British Library have clearly been carefully filleted, but they are still worth reading. Perhaps the best short life is *Lord Northcliffe* by A. P. Ryan, Collins, 1953. An admiring direct account of Northcliffe at work can be found in *My Northcliffe Diary* by Tom Clarke, Gollancz, 1931. Clarke was news editor of the *Daily Mail* in Northcliffe's last years and much favoured by 'the Chief'. Clarke later went to Australia and then came back to edit the *News Chronicle* for a time.
2. *Men and Power, 1917–1918*, by Lord Beaverbrook, Collins, 1956, p. xxi.
3. Pound and Harmsworth, op cit.

4. *History of The Times*, Volume IV, Part 1, Times Publishing, 1952, p. 500.
5. Ferris, op cit, particularly Chapter 14, 'Signs and Symptoms'.
6. Pound and Harmsworth, op cit, p. 399.
7. *Just as it Happened*, by Sir Newman Flower, Cassell 1950.
8. The *Hampstead and Highate Express*.
9. *Northcliffe* by Harry J Greenwell, Allan Wingate, 1957.
10. Sisley Huddlestone (of *The Times*) in *In My Times*, 1938, quoted in Brendon, *Life and Death of the Press Barons*, Secker and Warburg, 1982.
11. *History of The Times*, op cit, Volume IV, Part 2.
12. *Politicians and the War, 1914–1916*, by Lord Beaverbrook, Collins, 1960, p. 91.
13. *The English, A Social History, 1066–1945*, by Christopher Hibbert, Grafton Books, 1987.
14. Pound and Harmsworth, op cit p. 101.
15. *Gentlemen, the Press! Chronicles of a Crusade* by F. J. Mansfield, NUJ President, 1918–1919, W. H. Allen 1944.
16. *Strictly Personal*, by Cecil King, Weidenfeld, 1969.

2
The Berry Connection

I believe that more unhappiness comes from this source than from any other – I mean from the attempt to prolong family connection unduly ...

From Samuel Butler's *Note Books*

Three months after one Colonel Arthur Burroughes Sleigh founded the *Daily Telegraph* in 1855 with the object of carrying on a vendetta against the royal Duke of Cambridge (in a vain attempt to blight the Duke's prospects of becoming Commander-in-Chief of the British army) he had to sell ownership of the paper to his printer, Joseph Moses Levy,[1] for the vendetta was a dreadful failure in every way and the Colonel could not pay his bills. Mr Levy was already the chief proprietor of the *Sunday Times* (perhaps for similar reasons) but he must have decided that the *Daily Telegraph* was a better proposition for he sold his interest in the Sunday and set up a separate company for the daily. He divided the company's shares into sixty-fourths, with a quarter for himself and a eighth for his son Edward, a half for his successful businessman brother, Lionel Lawson Levy, and the final eighth for the manager of his printing works which were located at Peterborough Court in Shoe Lane. Meanwhile his son was learning the rudiments of journalism at the *Sunday Times*.

Joseph Levy had very clear ideas about journalism. 'What we want is the human note,' he said. In practice that meant sensational stories, law reports of murder and libel cases and a considerable reliance on the techniques of James Gordon Bennett's salacious *New York World*. So such headlines as 'Horrible Atrocity. A child devoured by pigs' and 'Felonious Assault on a Young Female' were to be found in early issues. Combined with outspoken support for Gladstone, this caused absolute fury in some intellectual circles. The *Saturday Review* wrote a particularly scathing attack on the *Telegraph* under the heading 'Newspaper Sewage': 'When Mr Gladstone is out of town and the daily service of praise and worship in honour of the most pious of Ministers is for the moment suspended, it turns with equal relish to the no less congenial occupation of mastering the "inner life" of a Chelsea brothel.' The paper was certainly far more radical than in later years, denouncing prostitution and urging the reform of the House of Lords as well as publishing attacks on the Prince Consort and criticising state pensions for the Queen's relations.

Yet Joseph Levy's real innovations lay in the area of management and particularly pricing policy. When he bought the paper it was selling four pages at 2d; within a few weeks he reduced the price to 1d and set about capturing a million readers. The effect on circulation was dramatic. By October he announced. 'We have every reason to be satisfied with the support we have received: our circulation, which already exceeds that of all our daily contemporaries put together (*The Times* excepted), is every day increasing.' In fact sale was less than 30,000 (against 56,000 for a 4d *Times*) but it was certainly climbing. Spurred by competition from the morning *Standard* which also cut its price to 1d but managed to produce eight pages for the money, the *Telegraph* also expanded to eight pages for 1d and kept its advertising rates very low. Six years after Joseph Moses Levy took over the paper it was selling 141,000 copies and had outstripped *The Times*. He was a real pioneer: other novelties he introduced to Fleet Street were the box number for classified advertisements and uniformed newspaper sellers.

His son Edward emerged as a brilliant journalist in his own right. He took his uncle's name and became Edward Lawson-Levy (he was created a baronet in 1892 and a peer, the first Lord Burnham, in 1903 – probably the first press baron proper). He also abandoned the Jewish faith and entered the Church of England. Together with Thornton Leigh Hunt, son of the essayist, he considerably broadened the scope of newspaper journalism. Book and theatre reviews, together with musical essays, were quickly added, while news reporting was expanded to cover science, fashion, provincial news and special reports from the American Civil War. An embryonic foreign service was added; the *Telegraph's* staff correspondent in Paris was actually furnished with the first newspaper telephone to London. The London staff was tiny; in the 1860s there were only three sub-editors, each of whom could turn his hand to anything. The same was expected of their bibulous but versatile star writer George Augustus Sala who once received a note saying, 'Please write a leader on Billingsgate and start for St Petersburg this evening'. (Sala could even get away with insulting the owner, lurching into his room and saying 'You bladdy Jew, give me some money!', after which he would disappear for days.)

The formula worked. The sale reached 196,000 by 1870 and 242,000 by 1877. With success came respectability. Lawson-Levy, who at one time saw Gladstone or his secretary nearly every day, switched to the cause of Disraeli and Conservatism. With intense loyalty to his friends and his staff it seemed that no one ever got sacked.* John le Sage was appointed editor in 1885 and did not retire until 1923 when he was eighty-three; the paper which once had been among the revolutionaries of Fleet Street was now in the hands of an editor who would not use the telephone and who gave reporters their daily assignments written in his own hand. As for recruitment, the chroniclers of the *Sunday Times* wrote: 'If there was a vacancy in a department which required someone presentable, such as the circulation department, it was automatically filled by an officer of the Royal Bucks Hussars, of which Lord Burnham, who lived in great state at Hall Barn, Beaconsfield, was honorary colonel.'[2]

This was not a paper likely to respond very energetically when a real competitor, in the shape of Northcliffe's *Daily Mail*, emerged in 1896. Nor was Burnham immune to disarming flattery from Northcliffe who, on his eightieth birthday, presented him with an illuminated address from newspaper publishers. A picture exists of the two press barons seated together, with Northcliffe, cigar in hand, leaning attentively forward, while plump little Lord Burnham, wearing tweed cap, plus-fours and spats, with an orchid in the buttonhole, gazes at his rival as if transfixed by a hypnotist.

When Northcliffe also gained control of *The Times* in 1908, Lord Burnham's troops found that they were being attacked on two fronts. Lacking energetic leadership, they did not distinguish themselves. Not even the war could help. Sale declined from 280,000 at the start of the war in 1914 to 180,000 by 1918. By 1927 it was only 84,000 of which 10,000 copies were sold at reduced rates.

The second Lord Burnham, who had succeeded to the title in 1916, was really more interested in politics than newspapers. He

---

* The tradition was maintained by the Berrys. Many years later I suggested to a member of the family that one of the *Telegraph* critics was really past his best and might honourably be pensioned off. 'Oh no! We couldn't possibly do that. He's been with us for nearly forty years,' was the scandalised reply.

was also conscious that a number of beneficiaries of the various family trusts created by the original owners depended on their annual dividends and he looked after their interests rather more carefully than was wise. The *Telegraph* badly needed re-equipping but the money went to the family instead. When, finally, he was appointed a member of the Simon Commission on India which would entail a lengthy absence from the country, he decided the time had come to sell. In 1927 he approached two brothers from Wales, William and Gomer Berry.

It was a very sensible choice. William Berry had been the driving force in setting up a growing publishing enterprise in London and his brother was an admirable support in getting the revenue and watching the books. Such was their trust in each other that they shared a joint bank account on which either could draw without reference to the other; and that arrangement lasted until 1936 when the older brother was nearly sixty. Their relationship was remarkably similar to the partnership between Northcliffe and his brother, the first Lord Rothermere, but rather more genteel.

Their father, John Matthias Berry, was a reasonably prosperous estate agent and auctioneer in Merthyr Tydfil. He was a Methodist, an alderman, a justice of the peace and a devoted Liberal. There was something remarkable about the family, for each of the three sons became a peer. The eldest brother, Seymour, captured the early patronage of Lord Rhondda and emerged as Lord Buckland, a major Welsh industrialist. He was chairman of Guest, Keen and Nettlefolds with large interests in collieries, iron and steel, but died in 1928 following a hunting accident.

William Ewert (*sic*), presumably named after William Ewart Gladstone, took to journalism at an early age. When he was only fourteen, the editor of the local newspaper, W. W. Hadley, commended an essay the boy had written and said, 'This boy must become a journalist'; he meant what he said for he gave the boy a job and enlisted him as an articled reporter for four years. But although William remained loyal to Merthyr for the rest of his life, he decided to seek his fortune in London as soon as he was free to move. He found employment on the *Investors' Guardian* at a salary of 35s a week but suddenly he was sacked. He managed to conceal from his family for three months that he was out of work. It is quite conceivable that the stress of that period influenced his later determination not to fire anyone from the *Telegraph* if he could possibly avoid it.

Eventually he found another post: this time he was a reporter for the Commercial Press Association. In that role he made an intelligent suggestion at the annual meeting of Harmsworth Brothers and promptly was offered a job by Lord Northcliffe – an offer he did not take up. Instead he decided it was time to start a publication of his own. He formed a company called Ewart*, Seymour & Co, backed by £100 from his successful elder brother and launched a magazine called *Advertising World*, the forerunner of such media milch cows as *Campaign* and *Marketing Week*. It is said that he wrote all of the first number himself, subbed it, laid it out and canvassed for the advertisements as well. He lived frugally and walked to work every day from Forest Gate to Kingsway. As soon as he could afford it, he sent for his younger brother Gomer to come and help - another parallel with the Harmsworths.

The brothers soon sold *Advertising World* and in 1909 launched another magazine; this was *Boxing* and it was an immediate success. The print started at 100,000 and soon hit 250,000. The brothers began to make money and as they did so their horizons expanded again. Within a few years, shortly after the start of the First World War, they were in the market for a national newspaper. William Berry found it in the dining room of the National Liberal Club. He had gone there to lunch with his friend Jimmy White, a rather shady financier and boxing promoter who years later, totally bankrupt, was to commit suicide. (Berry went to his funeral.) Towards the end of their meal a publisher named West de Wend Fenton strolled over to say he had an option to buy the *Sunday Times*. Were the Berrys interested? White offered to help finance the deal and negotiations began.

The historians of the *Sunday Times* state that the owners of the paper at that time were Hermann Schmidt, a German financier who lived in Britain and was thus interned; Sir Basil Zaharoff, the legendary and secretive munitions dealer; Dr Jameson (of Jameson Raid fame) and Sir Arthur Steel-Maitland, MP, chairman of the Conservative party – a rather curious group, each presumably attempting either to promote or to defend some special interest of his own. Schmidt's interest had to be sold by the custodian of enemy property; the circulation was only 30,000 copies a week; and the other partners were ready to sell.

After complicated negotiations it appears that the newspaper passed to the Berrys for £75,000. They managed to raise the money

* Ewart was correctly spelt this time.

without borrowing a penny from White. The date was 6th June 1915. The editorial offices of the paper were transferred to the Ewart, Seymour offices in Windsor House, Kingsway, and some of the key men behind the success of *Boxing* were transferred too. The editor of the magazine became the chief leader-writer. The publisher of the magazine became publisher and circulation manager of the newspaper, and a senior compositor was trained up to become its manager, a penny pinching post he held for twenty-five years. In the best Berry tradition staffing was minimal, but the paper's fortunes were improving rapidly. Three years after they had bought it Beaverbrook offered to buy the *Sunday Times* for £200,000 as part of a deal he was putting together for Lloyd George which also involved the *Daily Chronicle*. Surprisingly, the Berrys at first accepted and then told him that the Liberal party which they still supported would not agree that they should sell to a Tory. So William Berry continued his work on the paper; he made typographical improvements which made it a little easier to read and he pushed more news into it, mainly obtained from weekend casual staff. As the profits materialised, so the ambitions of the older brother grew. First to be absorbed was the *Financier*. The next target was the *Financial Times* with its own printing press, the St Clement's Press. In October 1919 the Berrys offered the secretive financier Sir John Ellerman, who was the chief proprietor, a handsome sum (said to be around £225,000) for that paper; he took it. Then came *Kelly's Directories* because the firm owned a corner block in the Strand which was needed for the expanding business. This led to a most fruitful partnership with the owner Sir Edward Iliffe, younger son of William, founder of the Coventry publishing firm. Other acquisitions included a paper pattern business; the publishers, Cassells, who owned many more magazines; the *Daily Graphic*; and the weekly *Bystander*. After all this, in June 1921, William Berry ended up with a baronetcy. (Beaverbrook was quick to congratulate him: 'My dear Bill, I am delighted you have been made a Baronet but you ought to go to the Lords which is the real and rightful Newspapers Proprietors' Association.' Bill made it in 1929, as Lord Camrose, being raised to a Viscountcy in 1941.)

The buying spree was not over. Two years later the brothers tried to obtain the newspapers of Sir Edward Hulton, but Beaverbrook beat them to it (details in Chapter 5) and sold on to Rothermere. Within two years Rothermere had sold them most of the Hulton papers and plant in Manchester, such as the *Daily Dispatch* and

Sunday Chronicle, for £4 million cash and £1,500.000 in debentures. The Berrys got the money back putting the Hulton papers together with the *Sunday Times* into a new company called Allied Newspapers and floating that publicly. Still their expansion went on: Rothermere sold them the *Daily Sketch* together with the *Sunday Mail* in Glasgow. Soon they were being offered provincial papers all over the country, and they bought many of them, including properties in Aberdeen, Glasgow, Sheffield, Newcastle, Cardiff and Middlesborough. Finally Northcliffe's former secretary and confidant, Sir George Sutton, an executor of the will who was also chairman of Amalgamated Press, sold them that company, an amazing mix of some one hundred periodicals, encyclopaedias and other works, since he had to raise the money to pay various legacies. The Berrys asked Sutton to remain with the firm, but he preferred to stick with the Harmsworths.

Theirs was now an amazingly large publishing enterprise built up with surprising speed from a tiny base. Where Northcliffe launched publications, the Berrys preferred to buy, and then, with journalistic skill, careful, not to say stingy, housekeeping and steady nerve, build up more profitable businesses. The drive came from the elder brother, Sir William; the housekeeping was mainly the job of the younger brother, Gomer. Everyone described how good looking William was: 'As handsome as a Roman gladiator, with peculiarly searching eyes and of such commanding stature and presence that nearly everyone in the office trembled if they were summoned,' wrote Leonard Russell.[3] Another proprietor claimed 'he was that rare being: an imaginative Celt without nerves'.[4] A former employee said, 'He was the best of the lot for fairness, *firmness* and inspiration'.[5] Others add that he knew his own mind; he was lucid; he was 'scrupulously honest and laboriously just'; he had the outstanding characteristic of all good journalists, an almost insatiable curiosity. He was particularly insistent on wide and accurate news coverage and maintained a news tape in his office so that he could keep the news editor up to the mark. And if he was a redoubtable editor-in-chief he also acted, sometimes, as sub-editor-in-chief, always on the lookout for wasted words, wasted space, slack writing. While inclined to be peppery, according to W. W. Hadley, his first employer and later editor of the *Sunday Times*, he never raised his voice. He hated sensationalism and he refused to use such tawdry circulation aids as competitions for large prizes, free insurance or free gifts. He wanted his newspapers to sell on merit alone. He did not watch television when it emerged later.

There were one or two weaknesses in this formidable personality. He disliked giving publicity either to rival newspapers or to men and movements of which he disapproved. While there was no formal blacklist, the effect was the same. It may be that he was particularly anxious not to advertise *The Times*, but the ban went much too far. Then, with his obsession for quality, he would sometimes do other people's jobs for them behind their backs, and this could lead to confusion. His 'editors' had no authority over the news side; that was usually left to a managing editor. (It was not until the 1980s, under a new owner, that Max Hastings insisted that he, as editor, should be given overall control of the *Daily Telegraph*, and *he* soon had an editor-in-chief placed over him.)

Away from the office William Berry enjoyed his family life, with eight children. He bought and expanded a large estate at Hackwood Park outside Basingstoke. He almost always went bareheaded and he could walk twenty miles a day. In later years his greatest pleasure and extravagance was his 742-ton yacht *Virginia*, the largest in British ownership, with its crew of thirty-five. He became vice-commodore of the Royal Yacht Squadron and a regular attender at Cowes. While he lived frugally when young he later became a member of Churchill's Other Club and savoured the social round. He enjoyed boxing and the music hall, loved a wager and played canasta or backgammon.

When the offer of the *Daily Telegraph* came along in 1927 it was carefully considered for several weeks which, as his son, Lord Hartwell, has written, was for him a long time. He was reviewing what needed to be done. He was now forty-eight, an experienced publisher with a record of success behind him. He took the view that the *Telegraph's* problems arose not from the staff but from lack of organisation and poor equipment. There was no news editor or news desk; there was no cuttings library. The handful of special writers, usually in frock coats, produced their columns with careful penmanship. And at night the paper was edited by a night editor and five assistants who worked in dignified silence in a large club-like 'library' with horsehair sofas and chairs; the woman's page editor sat behind a curtain, and decorously went home early. There was no proper financial control. A large sum would be needed to modern-ise the machine room.

But . . . Sir William wanted to control a quality national

newspaper. Eventually he struck a deal with his brother and Sir Edward Iliffe in the billiard room of the Oxford and Cambridge Club – clubland strikes again. He would take forty per cent of the *Telegraph*; Gomer and Sir Edward would take thirty per cent each. The new owners took over on 1st January 1928.

The existing staff had been nervous and Arthur Watson, the managing editor, went to see the new editor-in-chief to elicit his views. Watson was told, 'There is nobody I wish to get on the *Telegraph* and there is nobody on the *Telegraph* of whom I wish to get rid.' On the eve of assuming control and, formally, at the invitation of Lord Burnham, Sir William then addressed the staff at a meeting chaired by Watson. He gave them the same message. He reported, 'Lord and Lady Burnham were both in tears . . . and a number of the staff were in the same condition.' Unsurprisingly, his reassuring words were very well received.

One senior appointment symbolised the Berry approach to change. Fred Lawson, Burnham's nephew, was general manager of the paper and he stayed on, later being promoted to the post of managing director as well as succeeding to his uncle's title. As Camrose was to write:

> He had been on the paper for a number of years and knew everything there was to be known about the *Telegraph*. Incidentally it used to be said that he was one of the few people who really knew their way about the old extensive but mystifying building and that when his uncle attempted to show visitors round he always lost his way![6]

Lawson was put in charge of the replanting programme and soon earned the complete confidence of the chief proprietor. Later he represented the paper on the NPA, eventually becoming its vice-chairman. Here he was perhaps less successful, for Cecil King summed him up as follows: 'Though a pleasant social figure, he was a major disaster to the industry. I remember saying of him that his idea of negotiation was to lie on the floor and invite the union general secretaries to kick him, which they willingly did.'

William Berry as the new editor-in-chief wanted no revolutionary changes on the paper. Everything was done very gradually. Almost his first move was to increase the number of pages with no increase in advertisements. He enlarged the staff, improved the news service and tightened up the subbing. He insisted on two columns of read-ers' letters. He published a woman's page every day instead of only once a week. Meanwhile a large scheme of rebuilding and capital re-equipment was progressing so that some two years after the take-over the grey antiquated and elongated appearance of the paper was eliminated by trimming two inches off the page size. In December 1930 Lord Camrose – after asking the chairman of the Conservative Party for consideration, he had been raised to the peerage the year before – took the bold step of slashing the price by half. Although Gomer had been improving advertising revenues this was still a gamble. But it paid off. Circulation, which had improved to 100,000 as a result of the changes already introduced, was doubled in three months and thereafter climbed rapidly. In six years the circulation had passed half a million.

Meanwhile Camrose had been fighting a rough battle on another front, in the provinces. Lord Rothermere had sold large parts of the Northcliffe empire to the Berrys; Sir George Sutton had sold Amalgamated Press to them; then Rothermere had sold them, in two slices and at a profit, the major part of the Hulton group. Finally, in 1927, Rothermere saw the Busy Bees, as the brothers were known,* directly challenging the supremacy of his beloved *Daily Mail* (which he had made even more profitable by accenting advertising at the expense of the editorial). It was too much for a Harmsworth to bear. In fact Beaverbrook was told in a private note from his manag-ing director that Rothermere was 'almost frantic when the Berrys got the *Telegraph* and had declared war on everything Berry'.[7] Rothermere was determined to make the provinces too hot for them and in 1928 published a massive three-and-half column announce-ment in the *Daily Mail* that he was setting up Northcliffe Newspapers Ltd, with a nominal capital of £7,500,000, to establish a chain of evening newspapers. He stated rather unconvincingly, 'Sir William Berry and his brother will be, I am sure, the first to admit the undesirability of any form of press monopoly, and to welcome exper-ienced and powerful competition.'[8] A map showed he was targeting several of the cities where the Berrys' Allied Newspapers had enjoyed a monopoly. In the event he started newspapers in Newcastle and Bristol. He bought newspapers in Derby, Swansea, Leicester, Gloucester, Leicestershire and Staffordshire together with a fifty per cent share of a newspaper in Hull. It was a real newspaper war.

* Inside their offices they were also known as Beri-Beri; apparently they did not like it.

The battle raged for nearly four years and then, in 1932, Rothermere had had enough. A deal was made much to the Berrys' advantage. The fiercest and most expensive battle had been in Newcastle. Rothermere closed his paper there while Camrose shut down in Derby and Bristol. Rothermere agreed to keep out of Sheffield, Cardiff and Aberdeen while Camrose let him have uninterrupted play in other parts of South Wales. Northcliffe Newspapers went into liquidation.[9] The Berrys wound up with ten daily newspapers, five evening newspapers, six Sunday newspapers, eighty weekly papers and periodicals, plus another eighty annuals. It was the biggest publishing enterprise in the country. It says much for Camrose's nerve and steadiness that he did not allow his struggle to protect the provincial group from the Rothermere onslaught to deflect him from what he saw as his main task: to rebuild the fortunes of the *Daily Telegraph*.

Nearly ten years after taking over the paper, the partnership was dissolved. There were too many sons to look after (no one mentioned daughters although there were quite a few of those too), and death duties could be a problem for a family business. Camrose had four sons; Kemsley (Gomer had got his peerage in 1936) had six; Iliffe had two.* Camrose retained the *Financial Times*, the *Daily Telegraph* and Amalgamated Press. Iliffe kept Kelly's *Directories* but sold most of his shareholding in the *Telegraph* to Camrose. Kemsley got the *Sunday Times* and Allied Newspapers (later to be renamed Kemsley Newspapers). Camrose was at first reluctant to part with the *Sunday Times*, but the second Lady Kemsley, the former Edith du Plessis, by all accounts a somewhat ambitious influence on her husband, insisted that the provincial chain was not enough without the Sunday. It was said that she wished her husband to cut more of an influential figure in London society and provincial newspapers were not the right base for her diplomatic dinners.

Within months Camrose was to secure a major success. The desiccated and ultra right-wing *Morning Post* had been losing money for years. Now its owners, a consortium led by the Duke of Northumberland which had been put together by the Conservative Central Office in 1924 to take it off the hands of the heiress Lady Bathurst, decided to sell. At one time Beaverbrook was sniffing

---

* Kemsley's sons were certainly looked after. Four had directorships with the firm, each with their own chauffeur-driven Rolls-Royce or Bentley. According to Roy Thomson (in *After I was Sixty*, Hamish Hamilton, 1975) the firm even employed a grand-daughter who had a company Jaguar.

around but the elderly editor, said Beaverbrook's informant, 'dreads being subjected to your discipline'.[10] Camrose snapped it up for about £150,000 in July 1937, and in October merged it into the *Telegraph*. ('Terribly sad that yr fine old true blue paper is going to those *rich* & colourless Camroses', wrote Margot Asquith to H. A. Gwynne who had been editor since 1911.[11]) The operation was skilfully managed. The *Post* had been selling around 100,000 copies; the *Telegraph* picked up ninety per cent of their readers.

The same year Camrose sued for libel. A former MP called John Beckett wrote an article for a scruffy fascist newspaper called *Action*, suggesting that Camrose was an international Jewish financier who had no sense of patriotism and who subordinated the public interest to his personal financial gain. The trial was interesting from three aspects. First, Camrose was asked in the witness box, 'Are you in any sense a Jew?' His denial was complete: 'No, in no sense whatsoever.' Secondly, Beckett implied that he had been given the information by Mosley who had ratted on him. 'When I discovered that, so far from the information my titled friend gave me about Lord Camrose being a Jew being true, he was a Welshman – if I may say so, he is an obvious Welshman – I did not want to go into the box to justify that.' The publishers of *Action* were defended by Gerald Gardiner, KC, later a Labour Lord Chancellor, who said that Beckett was solely to blame since Mosley had influenza when the article was written. Beckett was convincing when he said, 'The proofs were read, the article instructed and approved by a certain individual.' Later he added. 'I must say that I envied Mr Watson when he was in the witness box. His chief, at any rate, was man enough to say he was the chief, and did not get behind a £100 company in one instance, and send his typist into the witness box, in another, to say he had influenza.' Finally, the damages were enormous for those days: Lord Camrose was awarded £12,500 and the *Telegraph* £7,500.

With the split of their properties and the approach of war the two brothers began to reveal differences of style and differences of policy. Kemsley was a close friend of Neville Chamberlain and believed in a policy of appeasement. Sometimes he carried his beliefs to extremes. When he bought the *Sunday Referee* to merge it into the *Sunday Chronicle* he asked R. J. Minney, the *Referee's* editor, what features were pulling. Minney replied proudly that Genevieve Tabouis, the French political columnist and a stern critic of appeasement, was certainly worth 40,000 copies every Sunday. Kemsley replied curtly. 'I will not have that woman in my paper at any price.'[12]

News Chronicle
and Daily Dispatch

No. 35,648   MONDAY, OCTOBER 17, 1960   PRICE 2½d.

LAST-DITCH PEACE PLEA TO GAITSKELL

Shadow Cabinet will try to heal rift

By ARTHUR BUTLER

AN attempt to persuade Mr. Gaitskell not to lead MPs in an all-out fight against the Labour Party conference's unilateralist vote will be made at a Shadow Cabinet meeting this week.

If he rejects peace moves he may find a significant section of middle-of-the-road MPs and trade union leaders lining up against him, and Mr. Harold Wilson standing for the leadership in the name of party unity.

An alliance between such peace-seeking moderates and Left-wingers on the party's national executive could certainly put Mr. Gaitskell in a difficult position when the executive meets next week.

The first demand of the peacemakers is expected to be a cooling-off period of about six weeks pending a joint meeting between the re-elected Shadow Cabinet and the party executive.

Such a meeting would seek to reach a stand-still agreement to prevent the party breaking up on the defence policy issue—and certainly there will be strong opposition among the executive this week to Mr. Gaitskell's call for a spring conference to reverse the Scarborough defence vote.

An indication of how some moderate opinion is moving came during the weekend from Mr. Ness Edwards, MP, a former Postmaster-General, who said he could not support a leadership which regarded acceptance of conference decisions as a crime. He urged the Parliamentary party to avoid a fundamental

PRINCESS ALEXANDRA flew back to London yesterday after her successful tour of Nigeria—and the forecast is that it will not be long before she does another job as a royal ambassador overseas.

It was her first foreign tour as the Queen's special representative.

She toured all three

'Rain Princess' is home

regions of the new independent Nigeria where she was called "The Rain Princess " because she insisted on driving in open cars in the rain so that everyone could see her.

The Princess was greeted by her mother and the Duke of Kent when she landed at London Airport (above) yesterday.
● After an overnight journey in the royal train from Perth, the Queen and Duke of Edinburgh arrived back in London yesterday at the end of their Scottish holiday.

CHURCHES PRAY FOR MISSING BOY

News Chronicle Reporter

PRAYERS were said in Worcester churches yesterday for an eight-year-old boy who has been missing from his home in the city for five days.

While the prayers were being offered, police searched the banks of the River Severn and dragged a deep, swiftly running brook, but no trace of the boy, Roy Alan Hines, was found.

Roy was last seen crossing the Severn Bridge on Wednesday afternoon. He had been to see his school play football and was assumed to be on his way to his home in Raleigh Close, Worcester.

Hates the dark

He never reached home, and since then more than 1,000 schoolchildren have been questioned and a 1,000-acre council estate has been searched.

Though Roy's photograph and description have been posted in every public house in the city, no one has reported seeing the lad.

Mr. Ronald Hines, Roy's 31-year-old father said last night: " I feel something must have happened to my son. He would not play out at night on his own if he could help it. He hates the dark."

A police spokesman said: "At the moment there is nothing to suggest foul play, but the longer the boy is missing the greater are our fears for his safety."

Car plunges 40ft. over parapet

A DRIVER escaped death twice when his car plunged 40ft. over a parapet yesterday.

He survived the fall. An eight-foot spike impaled the car and missed him by inches.

Roland Lambert, 30, of Ivanhoe Road, Thornton, Yorkshire, was taken to hospital with head injuries.

To our readers

A statement about the future of the News Chronicle, which has been the subject of many ill-informed rumours, will be made shortly.

The Exchange Telegraph News Agency reports:

MR. JOHN COOPE, managing director of the News Chronicle and The Star, said last night: "There are about eight different rumours and I cannot make any statement about any of them.

"It would be most unwise to say anything at the moment. Certainly there will be no statement today."

Mr. Coope added that the next meeting of his board of directors would be on Wednesday. This would be their monthly meeting.

Rumours about the future of the News Chronicle were discussed yesterday by the federated house chapel, representing the journalists and printing unions, but no statement was issued.

Today there will be a conference between the management and representatives from nine printing unions, the Amalgamated Engineering Union and the Electrical Trades Union.

Tidal wave kills 3,000

DACCA, East Pakistan, Sunday.—About 3,000 people have been killed in a cyclone which hit the Ganges Delta area this week after the worst tidal wave in living memory, according to official reports here today.

The 70 mph winds ripped across the Bay of Bengal and East Pakistan, leaving a trail of corpses and wrecked villages.

Today's first detailed reports said about 80 per cent. of the huts in the path of the cyclone were ripped up as the storm lashing for six hours across the Chittagong Burisal and Noakhali regions.

The tidal wave which followed the storm is believed to have washed a large number of bodies into the sea. Other bodies of fishing boats were capsized and harbour lighters had their cargoes tossed into the boiling seas.

Jeep tour

The Governor of East Pakistan, Lieutenant-General Azam Khan, is touring the affected area in a jeep supervising relief to stricken people.

The area hit by the tidal wave is about 290 miles east of Calcutta and near the mouth of the River Ganges, which has been reported swollen for the past week following torrential rain.

Farther up the Ganges floodwaters were earlier reported swirling in the main streets of Lucknow. Normal life for the 700,000 inhabitants was almost at a standstill in the worst floods in the city's history.

Indian Air Force helicopters and transport aircraft helped in evacuation and dropped supplies.—Reuter.

Rates plan dropped

A proposal to publish a "black list" of rates defaulters has been abandoned by Lenden and Winstre Urban Council, Essex, on legal advice.

LATE NEWS

The Daily Telegraph
and
Morning Post

TO-DAY'S WEATHER:
Thundery; rather warm

BROADCASTING:
Page Twelve

No. 25,691 Daily Telegraph
51,562 Morning Post

LONDON, FRIDAY, OCTOBER 1, 1937

LONDON LATE EDITION

ONE PENNY

Merging newspapers does not always work, but *Morning Post* readers loved the *Telegraph*. Above is the first joint issue. The merger of Kemsley's *Daily Despatch* into the *News Chronicle* was a disaster, for the Tory readership of the *Despatch* was appalled when the *Chronicle* opposed the Suez adventure. The upper picture shows the ultimate result – the last edition of the *News Chronicle*.

The Berry Connection 43

Meanwhile the editor of the *Sunday Times*, now none other than the ageing W. W. Hadley who had given William Berry his first encouragement to go into journalism, saw Chamberlain every week. Chamberlain used his friends badly, one day giving them a written total denial of any differences between himself and his Foreign Secretary, Anthony Eden. The *Sunday Times* published a story under the heading, 'A POLITICAL CANARD Premier and Mr Eden IN COMPLETE AGREEMENT'. A few days later Eden resigned from the Cabinet. Kemsley pursued his desire for appeasement so far that, accompanied by Lady Kemsley, he had an hour-long talk with Hitler only six weeks before war broke out. He was pursuing a plan floated for propaganda purposes by the German press chief, Dr Otto Dietrich, suggesting an exchange of articles in British and German newspapers. Nothing came of the project.

Kemsley had been overshadowed by his abler brother for too long by the time he gained editorial control of Allied Newspapers and the *Sunday Times*. It was perhaps because he longed for more public recognition of his merits that during the war Allied Newspapers became Kemsley Newspapers and soon every title, including the *Sunday Times*, had to carry the words, 'A Kemsley Newspaper'. Lord Camrose, who never referred to Camrose newspapers, commented laconically, 'He is, perhaps, more a believer in personal journalism than I am.'

There were other problems. Gomer was insufferably pompous and his ambition to run a 'serious' newspaper led to a desire to avoid controversy and disclosure. He was vain. When he travelled, someone nearby would be carrying a briefcase labelled VISCOUNT KEMSLEY. The lift at his private entrance to Kemsley House had to be opened five minutes before he was due to arrive. His car was a high-bodied Rolls-Royce. He wore a black coat and striped trousers with striped black silk tie adorned with a pearl tie pin. Formal titles had to be used in the paper, presumably so that the common herd would realise that he had been elevated to a rung above the mere barons. Nor was his judgment of talent always perfect. Indeed Leonard Russell commented, 'Left to himself he could have been an outstanding collector of men on the way down.' Nor was the influence of his sons regarded as altogether benign.* Further, his attention was so focused on his Sunday treasure that he grossly

* A private note from E. J. Robertson to Beaverbrook in December 1949 said that one of them was 'wrecking the outfit by his arrogance'. He added, 'Papa doesn't seem able to control "the boys".'

neglected other parts of his empire and contraction became the order of the day. The *Daily Graphic* was sold, and so was the *Daily Dispatch* despite the fact that the circulation of the *Dispatch* was rising. (Kemsley reckoned he would make more money leasing the presses to the *Mirror* and *Pictorial*.) The *Empire News* folded and so did the *Sunday Chronicle*. Then when Cecil King bought Kemsley's Glasgow papers, one of his shrewdest purchases for IPC and a source of grief to the Tory chairman, Lord Woolton, who wanted them kept in the Conservative fold, he discovered just how slack the Kemsley management had become. The glass panes in the roof over the Glasgow garage of the Kemsley papers had been leaking and for six months letters requesting authority to put the matter right had been sent to the London headquarters. No reply had ever been received. In addition a weekly report had been sent on the progress of the papers. No comment was ever made.

Nonetheless the progress of the *Sunday Times* under Kemsley's surveillance was remarkable. When he took over the circulation was 263,000; in 1959, when he sold out, it was 885,000. How far this was due to Denis Hamilton, a remarkable and inspiring editor and editorial director, and the people Hamilton picked, and how far to the constant attention Kemsley gave to it may be debated. But Kemsley should not be totally derided; nor should it be forgotten that he earned the affection of those who knew him and his highly conservative ways.

No one could ever accuse Camrose of being a sloppy manager, and the war put his skills to the severest test. Newsprint rationing was of course the order of the day, and penny papers (of which the *Telegraph* was one) were restricted first to six pages and then, in 1941, to only four. Camrose did not believe that he could produce a quality paper on that basis. First he reduced the weight of the paper he had been using. Then he increased the price of the paper to 1½d. Finally he began to cut the sale so that he could print six pages most of the week. Eventually he cut back the *Telegraph's* circulation by more than 250,000 copies a day. It was all worthwhile in the end, for in April 1947 the sale hit the million which old Mr Levy had dreamt of nearly a century earlier. That figure was not sustained owing to new restrictions on dollar costs and the consequent fresh curtailment of newsprint supplies, but it was finally secured in 1953.

Camrose had become one of Winston Churchill's most intimate friends. It was Camrose who immediately after the war organised a group of rich men to make the generous gift of his beloved Chartwell to Churchill. And it was Camrose who, with the help of Emery Reve, Churchill's pre-war literary agent, handled the placing of the serial and book rights of Churchill's war memoirs throughout the English-speaking world. He sold the American serial rights to Henry Luce of *Time-Life* for $1,150.000 while the book advance produced another $250,000 from Houghton Mifflin. Camrose meanwhile paid another £75,000 for the British serial rights and Cassells, his own publishing firm, got the British book rights. It was a very good deal for Churchill who received the money as a capital sum, and a pretty good one for the *Telegraph*, too.

Of course Churchill was paid in this way to cut back the tax payable on his memoirs. Camrose was equally concerned about the possible depradations of the Revenue on the fortunes of the family businesses, Telegraph Newspapers, the Financial Times Company and Amalgamated Press. During the war he had become very friendly with another of Churchill's closest friends, Brendan Bracken, who was the *de facto* chairman of the *Financial News* on behalf of the Eyre Trust. They had collaborated on a deal to raise advertising rates for the two financial papers. They also reached a private understanding that if either ever wanted to sell he would first offer it to the other. Shortly before the end of the war Camrose decided to sell and, true to the understanding, approached Bracken. (Gomer was not pleased; he reckoned that he should have had the option himself.) In fact Financial News Ltd did not really have the money that Camrose wanted for the paper but he made it as easy as possible for the merger to take place. Undoubtedly he really cared about the *FT*; before the war he had appointed his younger son, Michael Berry, to be managing director; on another occasion he had totally vetoed one pushy editor's suggestion that the *FT* should revert to white paper, giving the very sensible reason that young men travelling to the City liked to be identified by the colour as City types. Now, perhaps realising that his older son was not really interested in newspapers and that he needed Michael back at the *Telegraph*, he determined to concentrate on his main interests while ensuring that a strong financial paper survived. To help the *Financial News* raise the purchase price of £743,000 for his controlling interest he bought most of the *FT*'s investments which then financed the purchase of the *FN*'s copyright and goodwill for £280,000. He also bought the shares of minority shareholders in the *FT* at the same price he had been offered; he bought 50,000 *FN* shares himself; and he provided a three-month bridging loan. Not surprisingly he wound up in 1945 with a significant shareholding in the company. But later he regretted the deal, saying to one acquaintance that it was the greatest mistake he had ever made.[13]

Soon he also transferred 1,080,000 of his 1,200,000 shares in the family business to his two surviving sons in time to avoid death duties. But under the Articles of Association he remained chairman and editor-in-chief for life. Even so a paragraph in the Londoner's Diary of the *Evening Standard* published in January 1968 calculated that death duties paid by the Berry family over the previous nine years amounted to £1.9 million. A third son Rodney, had died at the age of only forty-six; death duties of £975,000 were paid on his estate of £1,300,000 Camrose himself, who died in 1954, left a net estate valued at only £1 million, but of that sum £610,000 went to the Exchequer. The family business was now under the control of Michael Berry with the second Lord Camrose in a supporting role. It remained intact, a family business, but it had been considerably weakened.

Stranger things were happening at the *Sunday Times*. Kemsley had always been prone to take impetuous decisions, and to press them through in a hurry. When commercial television was starting in 1955, Kemsley intelligently formed a consortium with an impresario called Maurice Winnick and the retailer Isaac Wolfson; they were awarded the potentially very lucrative franchise for weekend broadcasting in the Midlands and the North of England. But Kemsley's sons, who might have had to look after some of the business side, were cool on the project. Kemsley withdrew, and the consortium collapsed. A potential money-maker was lost.[14]

The man who most fully realised how much money could be made out of commercial television was, of course, Roy Thomson, the Canadian newspaper owner who bought *The Scotsman* and then formed the group which secured the franchise for Scottish television, the famous 'licence to print money'. Thomson was always on the lookout for newspapers he could buy and in 1959 arranged a lunch with Kemsley so that he could enquire about the prospects for a deal on the Aberdeen *Press and Journal*. Kemsley jokingly asked for a ridiculous price and the lunch did not go well. But seven weeks later Kemsley asked Thomson to come to London in a hurry. Kemsley offered to sell him the entire business, the *Sunday Times* included, for £15 million. After four weeks of secret discussions the deal was fixed at £5 million. (Further details are given in chapter 7.)

Thomson had got a bargain. But why did Kemsley do it? The influence of his children, some of whom had no great appetite for the business or had lost it, together with increasing problems on the business side and the looming threat of death duties, must have decided the matter. Kemsley was to confide to a friend that selling the *Sunday Times* was the greatest mistake of his life – an echo of his brother's remark on the sale of the *Financial Times*. But Kemsley's was the more serious error, for he was left with nothing to do for the rest of his life.

On his farewell appearance in the office he summoned Denis Hamilton and thanked him most warmly, as well he might, for everything Hamilton had done over the past twelve years. Then he gave Hamilton a 'souvenir' – a photograph of the cheque for £3.5 million he had received from S. G. Warburgs, Thomson's merchant bank – one of the strangest parting gifts in Fleet Street's history.

Notes:
1. There is very little written material on Lord Camrose. He did not approve of 'personal journalism'. This chapter is based largely on material contained in *The Pearl of Days*, the excellent history of the *Sunday Times*, written by Harold Hobson, Leonard Russell and Phillip Knightley, Hamish Hamilton, 1972. I have also drawn on *Peterborough Court*, the less forthcoming book about the *Daily Telegraph* written by the fourth Lord Burnham, Cassell, 1955.
2. *The Pearl of Days*, op cit.
3. *The Pearl of Days*, op cit.
4. Quoted in *The Financial Times, a Centenary History*, by David Kynaston, Viking, 1988, an outstanding account of how the *Financial Times* was transformed from a narrowly financial paper to a broad based international newspaper.
5. Quoted in *Double Harness* by Lord Drogheda, Weidenfeld, 1978. This chatty book is particularly good on Brendan Bracken's methods of working.
6. *British Newspapers and their Controllers*, by Lord Camrose, Cassell, 1947.
7. Note from E. J. Robertson to Lord Beaverbrook, 8th January 1929. Beaverbrook Papers, House of Lords Record Office.
8. *Daily Mail*, 13th February 1928.
9. *British Newspapers and their Controllers*, op. cit.
10. The informant was Brigadier Mike Wardell who later became general manager of the *Evening Standard*. See Beaverbrook Papers.
11. Quoted in *The Rise and Fall of the Political Press in Britain* Volume 2,

by Stephen Koss, Hamish Hamilton, 1984. Invaluable but excessively detailed.

12. See R. J. Minney's oral evidence to the Royal Commission on the Press, HMSO, 1949.
13. The story of Camrose and the *Financial Times* is based on the account in Kynaston, op cit.
14. The story is summarised by Denis Hamilton in his admirably dry account of Kemsley for the *Dictionary of National Biography*.

3
Lord Snow White and the Daily Herald

It is not enough to be busy ... the question is: what are we busy about.
Henry Thoreau

Julius Salter Elias, later Lord Southwood, was about the most ordinary fellow ever to run a large newspaper empire.[1] In his whole life he went abroad just twice: once to play golf at Le Touquet, and once to take a day-trip to Boulogne with his wife (but they didn't go so far as to leave the boat). He went to the Derby once but he did not gamble. He took virtually no interest in public affairs, preferring to concentrate on the business and nothing but the business. Tom Clarke described him as 'a little ginger-faced man with sharp eyes'.[2] He was very shy of women and often blushed in their company. He was absolutely appalled when, at a company function, the actress Fay Compton dragged him on to the dance floor and could not wait until, quite scarlet, he was able to retreat to his seat. He rarely drank wine, preferring water or grapefruit juice. Clear soup and rice pudding often figured on his menu.

He had an idyllically happy, though childless, marriage. His wife would wave him goodbye in the morning until his car was no longer in sight and she would help him off with his coat in the evening usually around nine or ten pm, having been warned when he finally left the office. After supper she refused to go off to her twin bed before her husband, however late he worked (and it was often after midnight before he was done). She would sit reading and writing letters, occasionally offering her views on the problems he was trying to solve or bringing a calming glass of hot milk when needed.

Every year they took a four-week holiday at the Grand Hotel, Eastbourne, where they liked to listen to the Palm Court orches-

49

tra, particularly if it was playing the Blue Danube. He rarely read books, apart from the Bible, but sometimes his wife read him extracts from the *Daily World*, an American religious journal to which she subscribed. He was never known to visit the theatre or an opera house. It was an intensely respectable, impeccably tedious life.

But Elias was a worker. He was born in 1873, the youngest of seven children. His father ran a small unprofitable business in Birmingham, making the jet jewellery that was quite popular at the time. But fashion changed and the family moved to London, at one time owning a newsagent's shop. When he was ten young Elias was delivering newspapers in the Hammersmith area. By the time he was thirteen his schooldays were over. Eventually he got a job as a clerk with a printing firm called the Carlyle Press but, after he had been there for five years, it went bankrupt and he was out of work for nearly a year. The family were short of money and sometimes this twenty-year-old youth had only a penny for food through the day. Finally, by sheer persistence, he got a job with Odhams, a family printing business in Covent Garden that had the contract to print the *Guardian Weekly* and the *Railway Times*. The firm was trying to expand and to succeed they desperately needed more orders. They found that the young clerk had extraordinary ability in this area and indeed was helpful in every way. Soon, at his own suggestion, he was appointed manager of a small subsidiary branch, initially 'for a few weeks'. He made such a success of it that within four years of joining the firm he was appointed a director.

Odhams was soon doing so well that the firm was able to buy control of other printers and was eventually able to take over a key site in Long Acre. Meanwhile Elias, working eighty hours a week or more, was tireless in finding new work for the presses and eventually persuaded the manager of the Hotel Cecil to let Odhams produce a little publication called *Table Talk* for their guests. It was his first effort as a publisher.

A much bigger job was on the way. In 1906 he obtained the printing contract for *John Bull*, the weekly penny magazine founded and edited by the notorious Horatio Bottomley with nearly £100,000 perhaps partly supplied by another city fraudster, Ernest Terah Hooley. Bottomley was a popular muck-racking journalist and MP, a super patriot and super scoundrel who, after many dubious financial escapades, finally went to jail for putting the proceeds of a bond-selling drive into his own pocket. As an editor he sounded off with jingoistic gusto under the general theme of

Politics without Party – Criticism without Cant
Without Fear or Favour – Rancour or Rant.

The board of the *Guardian Weekly* were appalled at the thought that the presses they used were also printing such scurrilous material. Elias reassured them with this accurate statement of his position, 'My purpose is to keep the machines going. I don't take sides.' But it soon became clear that if *John Bull* was to survive and ever pay its way Odhams would have to do more than just print it. They became its publishers too and took over the selling of advertising space. Elias was made the general manager and so took on responsibility for vetting the proofs for libel, a task he did not enjoy but conscientiously shouldered.

In his own horrible way Bottomley was an inspired journalist.[3] He posed as the champion of the little man, exposing scandals, attacking foreigners and pacifists, all done with bite and crude humour. 'Who are the two Front Bench men who are in the habit of coming down to the House in an advanced stage of alcoholic stimulation?' he would ask. His biographer wrote,

Almost every issue contained an attack on begging-letter writers, perverted schoolmasters, badly conducted mental homes, the neglect of patients in hospitals, or such savage judicial decisions as that by which a twelve-year-old boy who stole a piece of cod worth fivepence was sentenced to live for seven years on a training ship and to receive six strokes of the birch.[4]

(It reads like an excellent menu for a popular Sunday newspaper seventy years on.) Less appealing was Bottomley's habit of attacking some large concern like Harrods and dropping the attacks on being appointed a special investigator at, say, £500 a year.

By 1916 *John Bull* was selling 500,000 copies a week and by the end of the war it was up to 1,700,000. But the publishers' profits were erratic. To safeguard the business Elias felt it was necessary to expand the range of papers printed by Odhams, so he bought *Kinematograph Weekly* and *The Picturegoer*. The needs of the presses were indeed driving the whole strategy of the company. (A red light flashed in his office whenever the presses stopped.) With some reason Elias got more and more worried about what Bottomley was doing; he was drawn into a few of the endless law suits that occurred and must have had more than just a suspicion about some of the devices Bottomley was using in *John Bull* to step up the take. Eventually Elias had something like a breakdown and was away from the business for three months. When he returned expansion continued. He bought *Sporting Life*, the racing paper whose great rival was the *Sporting Chronicle*, Edward Hulton's first daily. He bought poster companies, launched *Ideal Home*, started fiction magazines and took over Debrett's. Finally he broke with Bottomley; it was only six months before the denouement. The charlatan's swindles were exposed; he was arrested, tried and jailed for seven years. The effect on the sale of *John Bull* was horrific. Circulation slumped from 2,000,000 to 300,000. Elias, who seemed amazingly calm in the general turmoil, did not lose his nerve. He secured new writers such as Arnold Bennett, Asquith and Field Marshal Lord Haig; he ran a big insurance scheme, supported by door-to-door canvassers. In two years the sale was back to a million. Later Lord Camrose paid Elias a remarkable tribute: 'Not one of us would have dared to attempt such a formidable work of salvage. Only Elias was capable of putting it through. It was a magnificent achievement.'

Soon another MP was in trouble. This was a Canadian speculator called Grant Morden who had bought *The People* for £160,000. Elias, who had purchased a large rotary machine that was used only once a week for *John Bull*, obtained more work for it by securing the printing contract for the Sunday newspaper, even though he had to subscribe £10,000 for debenture shares.

Hannen Swaffer was the editor but he was not a success. (He later complained that Morden had treated the staff as though 'we were a tin mine somewhere in Uganda'.) The paper's debts rose to nearly £250,000 and the sale would not go higher than 250,000. Elias arranged to take over the paper in payment for its outstanding debts. His appointment of Harry Ainsworth as editor proved inspired. A policy of sensational serials was instituted, covering such enjoyable topics as 'King Carol's Love for Madame Lupescu,' the 'Story of Nurse Edith Cavell' by a priest who had known her in Brussels, the cases of Marshall Hall, the famous KC, and the life of Lord Lonsdale, the racing peer. Elias read the lot, and marked the proofs if there was anything he did not understand or wished pointed up. (Ainsworth said he was a good judge of a human interest story.) Other editorial improvements included a new make-up with more pictures, more human interest stories and more sport. Then there were £1,000 prizes offered for crosswords and more prizes for football forecasts. Elias would not leave the editor alone, and insisted that he should be rung at any hour if there was some important development. He also worried about the editor's health. On one occasion when Ainsworth had a cold, Elias rang his wife and shortly afterwards a tin of Horlicks was on its way, by Rolls-Royce, from his home in Highgate to Ainsworth's office in Covent Garden. On Saturdays now Elias did not leave the office before eight pm.

In March 1925 Elias introduced an even bigger promotion; he offered free insurance to new readers, the first time a Sunday newspaper had entered the field. Next of kin of a registered reader were paid £1,000 if the reader was killed. For loss of limb or eyesight the reader could get £250. If totally disabled he got £3 a week for up to six weeks. Other benefits were added. There were plenty of canvassers to urge these advantages on potential readers and Elias cunningly first deployed them well away from London so that his rivals only heard about his new promotion weeks after it was well launched.

The other Sunday newspapers could scarcely compete anyway since the popular ones had vast numbers of readers already, and they could not offer free insurance only to new readers without giving mortal offence to existing ones. In eighteen months *The People*'s circulation had risen to a million. By 1929 it hit two million, and went on rising. No one was more pleased than Ainsworth; his salary was £35 a week plus a share in the profits as soon as sale exceeded 500,000. As a result he became the highest paid editor in Fleet Street and stayed on for years, even when the paper was really being edited by the so-called managing editor, Sam Campbell. By 1951, when *The People*'s circulation was more than five million, Ainsworth was still around.[5]

Of course the success of *The People* entailed more presses and they were only being used one day a week. At one time Elias thought he might secure the print contract for the *Radio Times*. Unfortunately for him Sir John Reith, head of the BBC, was married to an Odhams who was cousin of the head of the firm; of course the Scots Presbyterian in Reith could not abide anything that might look even remotely like nepotism. So Elias had to turn his mind in other directions; he had already been thinking about buying a morning paper. At one moment he thought seriously about purchasing the high Tory *Morning Post;* next he enquired whether the Liberal *Daily Chronicle* was available – there could scarcely be clearer proof that he saw himself as a printer and nothing else. He had not thought about the *Daily Herald* but the leaders of the Labour party and the TUC had been thinking about him, for they were distinctly impressed by the manner in which Odhams had transformed the fortunes of *The People.*

The Labour daily had been in trouble from the day it was launched in 1912 as a successor to a printers' news sheet which had been issued during their strike of 1911. With a capital of only £300 but with the presence of Ben Tillett and George Lansbury on the board it took a radical stance from the first, giving full support to strikes and to female suffrage and attacking the official Labour leadership for timidity. It barely survived until the war and then became a weekly, giving its full blessing to the Russian Revolution. In 1919 the paper was relaunched as a daily and Lansbury, the editor, gathered the most distinguished clutch of contributors journalism has ever seen, including E. M. Forster, Bernard Shaw, Siegfried Sassoon and Havelock Ellis. (Later Aldous Huxley, Rose Macaulay, Edward Garnett and Phillip Guedalla joined the team.) When the board doubled the price of the paper to 2d with negligible effects on sale even Northcliffe was impressed, saying, 'I thought I knew everything there was to know about the newspaper business, but these fellows have something I don't understand.' He called it 'The Miracle of Fleet Street'.

But the miracle did not produce sufficient funds to maintain its independence; the Labour party and the TUC had to be called in to help, with the TUC as senior partner. Such Labour stalwarts as J. R. Clynes and Arthur Henderson joined the board and Lansbury gave up the editorship. But there was no money for the free insurance schemes which other newspapers were offering and certain big advertisers refused to support it although some firms, such as Boots and Beechams, Lyons and Lever Bros, came in. The sale was less than a third of other popular papers, and well short of the paper's half million target. The Labour movement poured at least £250,000 into the paper between 1922 and 1929, money it could barely afford, but it was not enough.[6] One Welsh railwayman was reported as saying, 'Of course I vote Labour, but the *Express* helps me with the insurance, so I take that.' However much the *Herald* might pretend to scoff at papers which put insurance first and news next, purity of intention did not help sale. The *Mail* and *Express* were both spending nearly £1 million a year on insurance schemes and they were not doing it for charity; they were getting results. Further, both the *Express* and the *Mail* set up northern offices for editorial and production purposes, while the TUC was unable to fund such expansion. The *Herald*'s problem had still not been solved.

With control now firmly in the hands of the TUC, Ernest Bevin became the dominant figure in deciding what should be done. He took the sensible view that the TUC needed an outside partner. After first consulting the National Provincial Bank, he went to the Co-operative Insurance Society and the Prudential Assurance Company asking for a loan of £300,000, repayable over seventeen to twenty-one years. The CIS turned him down flat but the Prudential was ready to take it on provided the TUC guaranteed the interest payments by pledging affiliation fees for the appropriate period. However the General Council of the TUC decided that the terms were too onerous. Then Bevin turned to Odhams. In August 1929 Elias, who had needed little persuading about the size of the potential audience, took over commercial direction and financial responsibility for the *Herald* with fifty-one per cent of the shares in a new company called the Daily Herald 1929 Ltd. Political land industrial policy remained with the TUC. Neither the National Executive of the Labour party nor the Parliamentary Labour party were invited to nominate directors. But Bevin and Elias hit it off. 'I liked him,' said Bevin of his partner in the enterprise, 'I thought he was straight, a man on whose word one could instinctively rely.'

Both partners exerted themselves to the utmost to make their project a success. On no less than thirty-five consecutive weekends Bevin spoke at Labour rallies urging support for the party's paper. Other Labour leaders also rallied to the cause of what was called the 'Million campaign'. Meanwhile Elias, aided by the Odhams publicity supremo Surrey Dane, despatched his canvassing army of Labour supporters, 100,000 strong, to every corner of Britain. It was financially worth their time, for each new reader signed up for ten weeks was worth 1s 3d to the agent, although forty per cent went to the local Labour party funds. There was plenty on offer – a bigger paper with star writers such as Edgar Wallace, H. G. Wells, Hannen Swaffer and H. V. Morton, plus more sport and tempting insurance schemes and the choice of free gifts – either a camera or a writing set. On the eve of launch day for the Odhams-backed *Herald*, 17th March 1930, Prime Minister Ramsay Macdonald visited the office and composed a message of good wishes. They were fulfilled: circulation advanced from 250,000 to a million in one day. But the expected advertising failed to materialise. The three principal opposition papers were the *Daily Mail, Daily Express* and *News Chronicle*; they were selling 1,850,000, 1,690,000 and 1,450,000 respectively. The *Herald* was not yet in the big league.

Elias became obsessed with the need to sell more copies than the *Express*. The Labour party members had done their work; now professional canvassers were employed at a salary of about £3 a week plus commission to sign up more readers. The new incentive was free gifts and they poured out, soon matched from other newspapers. The *Herald* was losing £10,000 a week but Elias kept going; somewhere on the circulation horizon was the Holy Grail of bigger advertising revenue. He paid no attention to a demand from the president of the NUJ, who happened to be a *Daily Herald* sub-editor, that if economies were needed they should be secured by abolishing insurance and free gifts. But when, in 1932, the Council of the NPA demanded the abolition of free gifts, a limitation on insurance offers and restrictions on the number of canvassers, he agreed.

Within a year he had found a crafty way round the agreement. Odhams were book publishers and with their printing facilities they could cut prices to the bone. So the *Herald* began offering sixteen-volume sets of Dickens for eleven shillings plus ninety-six coupons from successive issues of the paper. The rival proprietors were absolutely furious but none was angrier than Beaverbrook. Eventually they arranged a meeting with Elias at the Savoy Hotel. To their surprise the *Herald* publisher agreed to end the book offers. But Beaverbrook wanted more; he demanded that the Dickens offer should be withdrawn *at once*. Elias refused, saying the *Herald* could not withdraw an offer that had already been made to the readers. (He would have lost money since the books had already been printed.)

'Elias, this is war – war to the death,' and here Beaverbrook drew an imaginary sword from its sheath. 'I shall fight you to the bitter end,' and with a flourish he ran it through. Elias affected to brush it aside, and departed.

A. J. P. Taylor, Beaverbrook's admiring biographer, says that in fact he enjoyed the contest, but it may have been difficult for his staff to perceive that emotion at the time. Beaverbrook derided his rival privately, first as Lord Snow White and later as Lord Blackout. Nonetheless he made quite a favourable judgment of his opponent. He told Elias's biographer, 'Don't make the mistake of underestimating his remarkable personality and character. It was not visible but it was there – flowing underground.'[7]

The brawl now broke out with renewed fury. Free gifts and unrestricted canvassing came back as if there was to be no tomorrow with the balance sheet. An issue of *The Economist*, published in July 1933, stated with a note of awe:

> There followed a phase of competitive insanity. Team on team of canvassers toured the country offering, in return for eight or twelve weeks' subscriptions, gifts whose costliness mounted every month. Toys, cutlery, cameras, hosiery, underwear and finally even mangles and complete tea-sets as lures to the prospective 'new reader', whose recruitment by the journal was the signal for instant counter-attack by its rivals.[8]

It was good news for readers ready to switch their favours around. Indeed it was claimed that an entire family could be clothed by subscribing to the *Express* for eight weeks.

The effect on the sale of the two principal warriors – the *Herald* and the *Express* – was as sensational as anything achieved in the early days of bingo. In the first months of 1933 they both added nearly 400,000 copies but it was the *Herald* which reached the two million mark first with the *Express* only a week or so behind. There was a permanent increase in national newspaper readership: by 1930 five national newspapers were selling a total of seven million a day; by 1937 the figure was eight and a half million. But the cost was appalling: *The Economist* calculated that the *Herald* was then paying £1 for each new reader. And the dreadful fact gradually emerged that the advertisers were still unimpressed. There may have been some political prejudice involved. There may have been, initially, a lack of sophisticated market research. But in 1936 an independent readership survey produced by the Incorporated Society of British Advertisers revealed the unwelcome truth: ninety-five per cent of *Herald* readers had an annual income of less than £250 compared with seventy-five per cent of *Express* readers and only fifty-seven per cent of *Mail* readers. Elias decided a new editor might help; he appointed his respected City editor, Francis Williams, perhaps for no better reason than the fact that Beaverbrook wanted him back. They did not get on. In fact Francis Williams, having accurately described his boss as 'kindly and benevolent, good to children and his employees and much dedicated to charitable enterprises for which he raised more than £20,000.000,' admitted frankly, 'I came to hate him more than any man I have ever known.' He added, 'Under his single-minded enthusiasm journalism almost ceased to be a profession and became an adjunct to a bargain basement.'[9]

The failures of the *Herald* were not all the fault of Elias's ultra commercial approach. In the face of Hitler's increasingly threatening ambitions Williams was, understandably, producing a very political but distinctly dull newspaper. While the *Express* was excessively optimistic ('Britain will not be involved in a war this year, or next year either'),* the *Herald* went too far the other way and was also notably short of human interest stories. By 1936 six out of the seven popular papers were devoting twice as much space to human interest stories and sport as to public affairs. The exception was the *Daily Herald* which devoted twenty per cent of its content to public affairs, a proportion said to be even higher than that of the *Daily Telegraph*.[10] Elias frequently sent Williams quite detailed criticisms of the paper. In July 1937 he wrote, 'I am thoroughly dissatisfied with the paper this morning – the worst we have produced in ages.' He went on to attack the choice of front page pictures: 'Why put funeral pictures on the front page; isn't the paper dull enough without them?' He attacked the layout of the feature pages: 'Compare the book pages in the *Express* with our page. The *Express* page is brightly presented, ours is as dull as ditchwater.' And he complained bitterly about the number of 'turnovers' from the front to inside pages. Williams regarded these notes as 'nagging' from someone who knew nothing about journalism. What he didn't know was that Harry Ainsworth sent Elias a written critique of the *Herald* every morning. On the other hand Elias, according to Williams, could not understand the need to 'waste money on foreign correspondents when he could get all the news from Reuters'. In May 1939 Beaverbrook gave his friend Lord Camrose a breakdown of the number of canvassers still employed by the leading popular papers: the *Express* employed 336, the *News Chronicle* 499, the *Mail* 761 and the *Herald* 1,056 – probably at least five times its editorial strength. That same year the *Express*, whose foreign service, under constant chivvying from Beaverbrook, was generally regarded as quite outstanding sold 2,400,000 a day while the *Herald* was still struggling to hold 2,000,000 and losing substantial sums of money.

The struggle was almost too much for Elias and in 1937 he had

---

* *Daily Express*, 30th September 1938. A. J. P. Taylor reports that Beaverbrook himself added the last four words.

another breakdown and was ordered to rest at the London Clinic. There he received a happy surprise: a letter telling him that he was being raised to the peerage. The honour was conferred by Stanley Baldwin on the advice of Ramsay Macdonald, probably in return for the *Herald*'s support of the government (and Labour party) line during the abdication crisis.

Lord Southwood liked being a peer – the first *Labour* press baron and by no means the last – but he still worried about the economic use of his presses. He tried to buy the Cadburys' *Star*, but was rebuffed because the directors realised that without their evening paper to share overheads the *News Chronicle* would be dangerously exposed. He was even ready to allow *The Star* to continue to be printed on the Cadbury presses. He was again rejected. So he proposed that Odhams should start an *Evening Herald*, but the war intervened before his plans could be brought to fruition.

However the war made his life much simpler in other respects. Stocks of the limited newsprint available were pooled and newspaper pagination restricted; the circulation war had to be abandoned in the face of the real war; gifts, insurance schemes, canvassing were all dropped. Newspaper sales were in effect stabilised. Even better, it suddenly became quite easy to make a profit on the *Herald*. Advertisers unable to buy space in their favourite papers were suddenly queuing up for what they could get in the *Herald*.

Southwood soon took advantage of the situation to remove Francis Williams (later Lord Francis-Williams and Attlee's press secretary at No 10). He did not like the bellicose tone of his editor's pronouncements for during the period of the 'phony war' he believed that if Britain did nothing to hurt Hitler, then the Germans would do nothing to hurt us. When early in 1940 Williams wrote in his weekly signed column that there was a need to organise pockets of resistance behind enemy lines and to train men to set up underground forces in occupied territories Southwood killed the column. The policy directors, says Williams, were ready to support him, but the appointment of the editor was a matter for the full board on which, of course, Odhams had a majority. Much to Williams's surprise, he was then offered the job of editorial adviser at a higher salary.

'I am sure we can come to understand each other,' said the little man. 'You know we don't want to make the war any worse.' Williams declined the offer; Percy Cudlipp, brother of Hugh, was appointed his successor and lasted twelve years. He was soon to learn that Southwood's aversion to stirring things up was as strong as ever.

Soon after his appointment Cudlipp wrote a tough leader urging the immediate resignation of Neville Chamberlain. He was scanning the proof when Southwood came on the phone and said, 'I see you are attacking the Prime Minister, Mr Cudlipp. You have attacked him in rather strong words. Do you think it is right to attack him quite so strongly when the country is at war?' 'Yes, I do,' said Cudlipp. 'I see,' said Southwood. 'Still, I think the article would be improved if you made just one little change. At the end of it you say, "It comes to this: Chamberlain must go". Might I suggest altering that to, "It comes to this: Mister Chamberlain must go"?'

The war did in fact become quite a lot worse, particularly for Odhams. A bomb fell on the plant one night, killing thirty-five people in the shelter, destroying three large rotary presses and causing severe damage to the warehouse and machine room. South-wood was on the south coast when the bomb struck and made frantic efforts to get to London, eventually hitching a ride in the cab of a train engine. Since the composing room was undamaged it was possible to continue the setting of the *Herald* and *The People* while the papers were run off elsewhere. Curiously, Odhams were never able to secure any compensation for the damage.

During the war Southwood's genius for fund-raising found full scope. He started a Penny-A-Week fund for the Red Cross; by the end of the war he had raised £17 million. It is not surprising that he was given a Viscountcy in 1946, this time by a Labour government. He was also a major benefactor to the Great Ormond Street Hospital for Sick Children; he became chairman of the governors and helped to raise £1 million for it. For the local St Martin's Northern School he paid for an annual outing to Bognor as well as Christmas parties where all the children were given the presents they had asked for. Eventually he was appropriately named School Patron.

He raised very large sums for worthy causes but he amassed no great fortune for himself. He could have arranged to buy shares in Odhams on favourable terms and, considering what he did for the firm, he was entitled to them. But he did nothing of the kind. He just put his money in the bank; he did not even invest it. When he died he left only £101,412 5s 11d net.

On the human level he was an excellent employer. He always wanted to know whenever a member of the staff was ill so that he could take practical steps to help if the wage-earner was out of action. He continued to pay men's wages if they died. He helped Bottomley when he was in prison and afterwards, even though Bottomley launched a magazine called *John Blunt* as a rival to *John Bull* (with disastrous results for Bottomley; it soon folded). He even paid some of Bottomley's funeral expenses. He seems to have had a genuine sympathy for the underdog. At the Grand Hotel, Eastbourne, he discovered that what a violinist in the Palm Court orchestra really wanted to do was grow tomatoes; Southwood set him up with some land at Polegate in Sussex and frequently visited him there. During the war he had a flat in Brighton and invited his ex-chauffeur, with his wife, to stay there when the driver was on leave from the army. 'We were treated wonderfully,' said the driver.

His door was always open to the union officials particularly to George Isaacs, then the general secretary of NATSOPA,[11] and quite early in his career he had so impressed Isaacs with his fairness that he was asked to arbitrate in a union dispute. Subsequently he was made an honorary member of the union. When Beaverbrook asked him to print the *British Gazette* during the General Strike, first a knighthood and then a baronetcy were dangled before him if he would agree, but he refused to contemplate the use of blackleg labour in his works. Instead, it was thought that production of the strikers' paper, the *British Worker*, may have been helped by reels of paper left in the street on Elias's instructions. At the NPA he seems to have been in favour of settlements rather than confrontation but he was no exception there.

As a newspaper publisher he was a disaster for both Odhams and the industry. The magazine selling techniques he and Ainsworth applied so successfully to *The People* were unsuitable for a national daily, but few realised just how catastrophic they were at the time. He managed to fool even that astute publisher Lord Camrose who said, 'He is the greatest organiser Fleet Street has ever known. He spends money like a drunken sailor but he always seems to get results.' The immediate results were high sales based on give-aways and the like, not journalism, coupled with barely supportable losses. The long-term results could be seen after the war when both the *Express* and the *Mirror* reported sales more than double that of the *Herald*. But it was the *Mirror*, then a punchy, raucous, radical tabloid, which eventually captured the ground which the *Herald* should have secured. Everybody blamed the poor old TUC for the failure of the paper, but it was primarily the management's inability to understand that the journalistic quality of the paper mattered even more than circulation gimmicks which led eventually to the death of the whole enterprise. By the time in 1961 when Cecil King's Mirror Group took it over the paper was virtually beyond hope.

Odhams had always been a rather eccentric organisation in some ways. W. J. B. Odhams, the son of the founder, believed that a palmist had forecast the firm's success in buying their much-prized site in Long Acre. Elias, a most meticulous and tidy character, was quite excessively superstitious. He would not take big decisions on a Friday. He could not bear any designs that contained a peacock; his loving wife once bought him a carpet with what she believed was some heraldic design in it, but when Elias arrived home he glanced at it and said, 'It looks like a peacock to me' and had the carpet returned next day. He disliked green intensely, so that his wife could never wear a green dress, and he would not keep pennies in his pocket.

After his death the board of Odhams was bereft of its leader. But A. C. Duncan, chairman of Odhams from 1949 to 1960, was a Spiritualist, his co-director Harry Ainsworth was also a Spiritualist and Hannen Swaffer was another. They decided to keep in touch with Southwood through a medium. Duncan was much impressed by the fact that Southwood introduced himself as 'Julius', saying 'we have no lords here'. He told Duncan 'you have got to take risks'.[12] But for practical guidance all they could glean was that the *Herald* worried him. Even beyond the grave, apparently, Southwood, for all his practicality and common sense, could not see that *he* was the real problem.

Notes:
1. Elias's character is tactfully described in *Southwood* by R. J. Minney, Odhams, 1954. Minney was commissioned to write the life by the directors of Odhams. A less favourable view of Southwood's life and character is given by Francis Williams in *Dangerous Estate*, Longman, 1957, and in *Nothing So Strange*, his autobiography, Cassell, 1970. Other useful sources are the monographs on aspects of the *Herald* written by Huw Richards in *History Today*, December 1981, and in *Journalism Studies Review*, July 1983.
2. *My Lloyd George Diary* by Tom Clarke, Methuen, 1939.
3. Bottomley was not a modest man. During his wartime recruiting drive he circulated a brochure about himself. The text included this passage:

Who is Mr Bottomley?
He is the finest orator in the kingdom;
He is the first lay lawyer in the land;
He is our best recruiter;
He is a fine sportsman;
He is a great financier;
He is a fearless politician.
There are many people who think Mr Bottomley is the greatest man in Britain today.
Quoted in S. T. Felstead, *Horatio Bottomley*, John Murray, 1936.

4. *Horatio Bottomley* by Julian Symons, Cresset Press, 1955, an entertaining account of his journalism, his law cases, his betting and his entourage.
5. Robert Edwards gives these details in his enjoyable and well-honed, if not always accurate, reminiscences entitled *Goodbye Fleet Street*, Cape, 1988. Ainsworth was also paid during the war for editing *John Bull*.
6. Huw Richards has pointed out in a letter to the author that the Labour party stopped contributing funds in 1926, so the main source of funds was the TUC.
7. Quoted by R. J. Minney, op cit.
8. *The Economist* of 15th July 1933, quoted by Huw Richards in *Journalism Studies Review*, op cit.
9. *Nothing So Strange* by Francis Williams, Cassell, 1970.
10. Estimated by James Curran and Jean Seaton in *Power Without Responsibility*, Routledge 1981.
11. Then the National Society of Operative Printers and Assistants.
12. Verbatim record in *At Your Peril* by Hugh Cudlipp, Weidenfeld, 1962.

4

The Cocoa Press is Swallowed

We know what happens to people who stay in the middle of the road. They get run over.

Aneurin Bevan

The death of the *News Chronicle* in October 1960 created a colossal storm. It had been formed by the merger of the *Daily News* and the *Daily Chronicle* only thirty years before, and had, for those three decades, nurtured the hopes and dreams of every liberal and many others too. Suddenly it was no longer there. Associated Newspapers emerged as the buyer and folded it into the *Daily Mail* of all papers, while the evening *Star* was absorbed by the *Evening News*.

Many years later veterans of the paper had still not quite overcome their feelings of shock, betrayal and anger at the closure. It was partly the secrecy of the deal, done with the best of motives; partly the feeling that it was not really necessary; partly the silencing of a liberal voice. Lady Violet Bonham-Carter spoke for many when she wrote to her friend Lord Layton, a key member of the management team:

> You must (of course) realise the pain and utter bewilderment which the tragedy of the *News Chronicle* has brought to those who have given it their unswerving love and loyalty for countless years. Not only the fact of its death – but the manner of it – has shocked thousands who did not share its ideology and looked to it for light and leading and the expression of their faith.

Many, less intimately concerned than members of the Liberal party, were also worried by the silencing of an independent newspaper following so closely on the closure of Roy Thomson's *Empire News*. There were plenty to point out that there must be something wrong with Fleet Street if newspapers with circulations of more than a million could not pay their way; production costs and restrictive practices had clearly got out of hand. In the end the Conservative government of Harold Macmillan decided to set up another Royal Commission to look into the state of the press and appointed Lord Shawcross, the former Labour Attorney-General, to the chairmanship.

Yet the most curious aspect of the collapse of the *News Chronicle* and *The Star* is that virtually every other newspaper publisher wanted to save either one or both of them. They knew all about production costs and union problems. But only Lord Rothermere's Associated Newspapers, which eventually won with its '1925 Plan' (so-called after the price they offered of £1,925,000), wished to swallow them both.

First of the publishers to suggest a deal was that obsessive printer, Lord Southwood, who had tried to buy *The Star* in the late 1930s and, as the last chapter showed, was even ready to allow the printing to remain with the *Chronicle* presses – an early proposal for contract printing in Fleet Street. Then there was an approach from Lord Beaverbrook. During the war he had employed Walter Layton, former editor of *The Economist* and later chairman of the *News Chronicle*, as a senior official on his staff first at the Ministry of Supply and then at the Ministry of Production. (He had also dealt with him before the war as a fellow newspaper controller, enrolling him as an ally, for example, over the handling of Edward VIII's relations with Mrs Simpson.) He seems to have respected his editorial talents if not his managerial skills. He was probably aware that relations between Layton and Laurence Cadbury, the principal trustee, were uneasy and that Layton nourished dreams of buying out the Cadbury family. In 1952 he wrote to Layton:

If you want to buy those papers I would be glad to provide money for you. The basis of the arrangement I would suggest would be as follows. The policy of the paper and also the production of the news pages would be entirely your responsibility. And I would not interfere. The business side would rest with me . . . We will make a community of interest between the *Express* and the *News Chronicle* which will be publicly declared . . . but the community of interest would be for business and management only.[1]

Layton first replied by stressing his age, then sixty-eight, and the fact that the Cadburys showed no wish to sell, but said he would consider the offer carefully. Finally he turned it down, apparently on the grounds that their policies on Europe were too far apart. Later Beaverbrook told Brendan Bracken of his proposal and added a detail that he had omitted to spell out to Layton, 'I will put in an editor and also Tom Blackburn to manage it.'[2] Perhaps Layton was right to turn down the proposal after all.

Cecil King was another publisher who was interested. Owing to Layton's mounting involvement in the Council of Europe – from 1949 to 1957 he spent nearly a third of every year abroad – Laurence Cadbury took over the chairmanship of the Daily News Ltd (which owned the *News Chronicle*) in 1950. Laurence (the eldest son of Elizabeth Cadbury, second wife of George Cadbury who had taken the family into newspapers) appointed an able general manager, Frank Waters, a former Marine colonel and rugby international who had been lured from *The Times*. But Waters soon found that Cadbury had difficulty delegating and in 1954 was attracted by an offer from Cecil King, chairman of the Mirror Group. Later King told the second Royal Commission on the Press[3] of what followed.

'Cadbury said [to Waters], "What can I offer you to induce you to stay?"'

'Waters: "A deal with the *Mirror*, the only people who can save us." '

Cecil King went on to tell the Commission that he then had some talks with Laurence Cadbury about the possibility of acquiring an interest in the Daily News Ltd. (There seems little doubt that he was attracted at the possibility of taking over *The Star* as part of the deal.) 'Then Mr Waters went away on holiday to the South of France* before joining us, and contracted polio and died. So I was left with these negotiations and no Waters.' Eventually he suggested that Cadbury should give him a two-year management agreement for the *News Chronicle* with an option to purchase it. He told Cadbury that he thought the *News Chronicle* had gone down so far there was only a fifty-fifty chance of saving it but he would like to save it. 'I would throw everything the *Mirror* had into the fight to save it.' (He was thinking of turning the paper into a *Daily Observer* according to the diary kept by Waters.) Cadbury turned down the idea; Layton was apparently doubtful about the deal and indeed appeared to forget all about it since he told the Commission that 'not one of them [the publishers] was ready to tackle the problem of the *News*

* Cecil King's memory was at fault. Waters went on holiday to Majorca where he contracted polio. He died in the Paris flat of the *News Chronicle* correspondent, Geoffrey Hoare. See Koss, op cit.

Chronicle or thought they could keep it alive as a separate newspaper'. However Cadbury did offer King the possibility of buying an interest in *The Star*. 'So I said Yes, we would be interested in considering an investment in *The Star*, and to that letter I never had a reply. And that is where our negotiations ended,' Cecil King told the Commission. Cadbury was asked why he had not replied, and he responded by talking of the disruption caused by a newspaper strike and other pressing calls on his time. It is possible however that the healthy profit of £253,000 made by the *News Chronicle* in 1953 (more than double the sum realised in the previous year)[4] had given Cadbury a false sense of security.

Roy Thomson was another publisher to take a look. He told the Royal Commission that he had been approached before it was known the papers were going out of business. 'I seriously considered it, discussed it and I wanted to take it . . . We came up against the fact that if I could not make it go and I had to close it, in two years I would have faced redundancy problems of £2 to £3 million. I would have taken it had there been no liability to face in connection with redundancy and . . . it would have been running today.' With his usual disarming frankness Thomson added, 'I could not afford to gamble £2 to £3 million. They paid out £2 million [the redundancy pay-out was less in the end], and you know everyone is hollering blue murder that they did not give them enough.'

Yet another proposal was discussed with the board of Odhams: the possibility of creating 'an independent journal of the Left'. By May 1957 Odhams had already sunk something like £2,000,000 in the *Daily Herald* and were trying to escape from the political tie with the TUC. It seems that the Odhams directors saw a link with the *News Chronicle* as a possible way out of a crippling burden on their finances. Nothing came of that proposal either; Frank Cousins, the Transport Union's leader, persuaded the TUC not to relinquish editorial control of the *Herald*, their only loyal support in the press. The difference in political outlook made any thought of a merger impossible.

Finally it was said that Frank Packer, the Australian media magnate, was ready to pay £10,000 for an option to buy at £2,500,000. He got no reply either.

Adding to the problems of the troubled papers was the increasing lack of sympathy between Laurence Cadbury and Walter Layton. It was Henry Cadbury, Laurence's older stepbrother, who, in 1927, had asked Layton to join the firm as financial and policy adviser, but Laurence also admired Layton, having been taught by him at Cambridge. Laurence eventually became chairman of the trustees, the real owners, and Layton became chairman of the Daily News Ltd, the holding company which managed the two papers. Tension was inevitable as the editorial drift of the papers was to the Left while Laurence moved to the Right. The trustees felt, with reason, that they carried the ultimate responsibility, while Layton enjoyed all the prestige. Finally, Layton was given a peerage in recognition of his high-powered role in the wartime civil service while Cadbury, who had been head of a supplies mission to Moscow, did not even get a knighthood. It was not the last time in Fleet Street history that jealousy over honours would cause serious problems.

Yet if Beaverbrook, Cecil King and Roy Thomson all believed there was a good chance of saving the *News Chronicle*, disagreements in top management should not have been enough to kill it. There were clearly other factors and some of them went back to the very origins of the paper.

In the mid-nineteenth century the Quaker, George Cadbury, with his elder brother Richard, had saved the family cocoa and chocolate business from bankruptcy with total self-sacrifice and drive. To economise he gave up tea and coffee and newspapers and was spending for 'travelling, clothing, charities and everything else £25 a year'. Gradually the firm emerged from the financial shadows and began to make money on a substantial scale. George Cadbury's interests centred on Birmingham and he bought four weekly newspapers with the aim of raising civic and moral standards in the city. With the outbreak of the Boer War, which he regarded as a mine-owners' war waged for financial interests, he began to focus on the wider national and international scene. Very few newspapers were opposing the war and first Cadbury paid for a special train to bring copies of one of them, the *Morning Leader*, to the north, then he put in £20,000 to secure the future of the *Daily News* and to influence its policy against the war. Advertisements fell right away and the existing syndicate of owners began to break up. Under the urging of Lloyd George, Cadbury decided he had to buy them out and put his own man in charge; this was Thomas Ritzema, a North Country journalist with Liberal views. Cadbury laid down there should be no betting news or advertisements; Ritzema put a bar on liquor advertisements. The sale of the paper, under this rather puritan regime, rose sharply – from 30,000 to 80,000 – but the losses were running at £20,000 to £30,000 a year. The price was cut to ½d; the Cadbury family moved in: one son took over from Ritzema and another became chairman. Printing started in Manchester as well as London and the sale rose to 400,000. The losses continued. Then the owners of the *Morning Leader* and *The Star* said they wanted to sell as well. After much heart-searching and with the help of the Rowntrees, the other big Quaker family in the cocoa business, George Cadbury went ahead with the purchase saying, '*The Star* with betting news and pleading for social reform and peace was far better than *The Star* with betting and opposing social reform and stirring up strife with neighbouring nations.'[5] He was of course bitterly attacked for hypocrisy but he had not built up a vast business from scratch without a character of rugged strength. Bottomley's description of him as 'a serpentine and malevolent cocoa magnate' was so misjudged that it missed the target completely. Eventually, in 1911, George Cadbury handed over his controlling shares to the Daily News Trust, accompanying the deeds with a lengthy letter setting out his quite saintly philosophy:

> I desire, in forming the Daily News Trust, that it may be of service in bringing the ethical teaching of Jesus Christ to bear upon National Questions and in promoting National Righteousness; for example that Arbitration should take the place of War, and the Sermon on the Mount, especially the Beatitudes, should take the place of Imperialism and of the military spirit which is contrary to Christ's teaching that love is the badge by which Christians should be known.

Among other policy pointers he also wanted to tax land values, to cut defence spending, to ensure that it was the wealthy, not the poor, who paid for that spending, to move towards the acquisition by the state of all minerals below the surface and of all monopolies which could be better administered by the community for the welfare of all. That kind of idealistic purpose was rarely echoed by later generations of newspaper publishers.

While the *Daily News* pursued Cadbury's brand of independent Liberalism there were two other Liberal papers: the *Westminster Gazette*, a morning newspaper owned by the Asquithian Lord

Cowdray,* and the *Daily Chronicle* which was firmly in the Lloyd George camp. They were both losing money. It was only a matter of time before further mergers occurred and in 1928 the *Daily News* merged with the *Gazette*; the combined paper was said to hold a sale of 900,000. Walter Layton now emerged as the key figure at the *Daily News*. He had refused to become its editor in 1926 because he did not wish to give up being editor of *The Economist*, but had accepted the seat on the board offered by Henry Cadbury charged with responsibility for editorial policy and an investigation into the newspaper's finances. Layton was known for his intelligence, kindness and courtesy and his willingness to listen. But he had never been a man of enterprise or drive. Unfortunately his spoken utterances were woolly to the point of incoherence, he frequently seemed quite unable to make up his mind while he reviewed, with goodwill, charity and a liberal spirit, all the possible options. His silences and his perfectionism were legendary. As a civil servant he had been masterly at presenting a written analysis and he seems to have been an able negotiator, though a poor chairman. He was intensely serious, disapproving of drink, altogether too academic and hesitant to be a dynamic publishing entrepreneur.

Layton soon heard that the much peddled *Daily Chronicle* was up for sale again. It had changed hands several times since 1918 when a syndicate had bought it as their contribution to the Lloyd George Fund. By 1930 it was in receivership, part of the over-stretched United Newspapers group, and Layton was able to secure a merger.

Control of the new combined paper, the *News Chronicle*, lay with five trustees. They were Laurence Cadbury, chairman of the Daily News Ltd; Walter Layton, chairman of the News and Westminster Ltd, the company set up after the *News*'s merger with the *Gazette*; Lord Cowdray, vice-chairman of the News and Westminster Ltd; Bernhard Binder, an accountant who was now chairman of United Newspapers; and Jack Ackerman, managing director and vice-chairman of United Newspapers. It was an interesting group which might have had a very different complexion for only a few months earlier Henry Cadbury had written to Layton saying that Lord Cowdray and his friends would be acquiring full control of the *News* and

* Cowdray's father had been mortally offended by Lloyd George who had suggested to Northcliffe during the 1914–18 war that he might take over the Air Ministry which was then occupied by Lord Cowdray. Northcliffe had promptly printed news of the offer, and his refusal, in the *Daily Mail*. Cowdray never forgave Lloyd George – and who can blame him? His son carried on the feud.

Star. Obviously George Cadbury's sons were extremely reluctant newspaper publishers, but it seems that Layton persuaded them that the deal to absorb the *Chronicle* would make it all worthwhile. Although the Daily News Ltd had only thirty-six and a half per cent of the new company, the three Liberals were in control. Financially the deal was equally satisfactory, for the new paper, now selling 1,400,000, was in profit for the next twenty-five years. Before long the Cadburys were able to buy out the other shareholders on the basis that the *News Chronicle* was worth £1 million.

Layton, in full editorial control, was moving the paper further to the Left than other members of the board were happy to accept. (On Cowdray's death in 1933 his brother Clive Pearson upheld the family interest in the paper and protested vigorously at its Labour sympathies, with spasmodic support from Binder and Ackerman.) Layton was indeed a Liberal – he had been chairman of the Executive Committee that produced the famous Liberal *Yellow Book* in 1926 – but Liberal politicians of those days were in an even greater muddle than usual, being divided between those whose allegiance was still held by Lloyd George, the National Liberals led by Sir Herbert Samuel and the independent remnants of Asquithian Liberals. When Tom Clarke, former protégé of Northcliffe, left the editorial chair in 1933,* Layton appointed the Marxist Aylmer Vallance in his place. Frances Stevenson, Lloyd George's mistress and later his wife, noted in her diary[6] for 10th March 1934 that the Laytons had come to dinner and were very dismissive of the Liberal Party.

Layton and indeed all the management of the *News Chronicle* are inclined to go Labour. D. [Lloyd George] had already told me of a talk he had had with Vallance in which the latter gave a hint of a combination and understanding with the *Herald* on a progressive policy. And a young friend of ours who has got a job as leader-writer on the *Chronicle* was told that his line was to be 'half-way between Maxton and Samuel'.

Later Layton told Lloyd George that he wanted to expand the News group by founding a Sunday paper operating on an 'advanced

* He was too independent for Layton and was eventually given the nudge to go. Beaverbrook had earlier offered him twice his current salary to join the *Express*. See *My Lloyd George Diary* by Tom Clarke, Methuen, 1939.

progressive policy', with Elias having a large share in the management. 'Would D. put money into the scheme? D. said he would.'

How far Layton kept the Cadburys informed about these ambitions is obscure. But they had not forgotten their father's Liberal beliefs even if they did not share them, and they did not like the drift of Layton's opinions. Vallance was however producing a serious paper with plenty of international news fronted by Vernon Bartlett whom he hired as diplomatic correspondent, improving city coverage through the recruitment of Paul Bareau and Oscar Hobson and giving full value to the work of A. J. Cummings, the political columnist who at one time had nursed ambitions to become editor himself. Unfortunately Vallance had a weakness for making love in the office after hours – it was said that 'even Arthur Cummings's sacred desk was violated' – and this incautious activity tended to reduce his authority on a Quaker-owned paper. Layton, emerging from the editor's office one day after catching him *in flagrante delicto*, muttered sadly, 'And they didn't even stop when I came in . . .' Vallance also made all too plain where his sympathies lay when he applauded lost Liberal deposits at an election night party in November 1935. So Layton sacked him and he went off to be Kingsley Martin's deputy at the *New Statesman*. Fewer desks, but perhaps a more congenial atmosphere.

The new editor was Gerald Barry, another socialist and a close friend of Herbert Morrison. Barry proved a brilliant editor. Leaders were still controlled, if not written by Layton, but the paper entered a golden period, happily symbolised by Barry's recruitment of Vicky, that gnomic genius among cartoonists.[7] Vicky had only recently come to Britain; his style was still unformed; his knowledge of English politics and English culture was minimal; his true abilities could only be surmised. 'His English was then almost as funny as the cartoons he brought under his arm,' said Barry. But the editor spotted his talent, paid him a retainer and set him on a learning curve of Dickens, *Punch* and Lewis Carroll. English pursuits such as football at White Hart Lane, the dogs at White City, the Derby at Epsom and debates in Parliament – all had to be studied. And then his cartoons had to be polished too. Barry's tuition was richly rewarded in later years. The team also included such outstanding writers as Ian Mackay, the industrial correspondent whom Barry encouraged to develop into an idiosyncratic diary writer and essayist ('Away from home,' said Mackay, 'the first thing I do is to send for the morning's newspapers so that I can start the day at least knowing what town I'm in'); Richard Winnington, cartoonist and film critic; and William Forrest, foreign correspondent, while, of course, A. J. Cummings and the city staff continued. With such a brilliantly talkative and opinionated group of characters in the office there was no shortage of spark and spirit. Indeed an exceptionally happy atmosphere prevailed and journalists were ready to accept lower salaries than they might attract elsewhere because they liked Barry and they liked the paper.

Although Layton and Barry were quite friendly, the editor was frequently maddened by Layton's hesitations and suppressions. Layton believed in 'responsible journalism' and of course this phrase frequently means a disposition to leave out anything that might be regarded as rocking the establishment boat. So he suppressed news of a leaflet issued by Henlein, the Sudeten German leader, which gave a specific timetable for Hitler's conquest of Europe because it came to the *News Chronicle* office just as Chamberlain was setting off for his third trip to Munich. He also suppressed a tough article by Forrest critical of appeasement policy and he tried to kill an article by Vernon Bartlett on the sell-out of the Czechs at Munich, but eventually agreed to publication after pressure from Barry and other members of the staff. As for the *News Chronicle*'s opinion of Munich, Layton came into the office on the day 'peace in our time' was announced and according to Ivor Bulmer-Thomas, leader-writer at the time, 'We discussed and discussed from every angle, while edition after edition went out without any leader on the subject and when it did appear, in the latest editions, it was too indecisive to have any value.'[8] Layton was even urging the formation of a national government led by Halifax and including Lloyd George.

When the war began Layton was given nothing to do until Churchill succeeded Chamberlain (characteristically Layton would have preferred Lloyd George). Then he was appointed Director-General of Programmes at the Ministry of Supply, so he gave up the chairmanship of the Daily News Ltd to Laurence Cadbury, relinquished his salary of £7,500 a year but kept a healthy commission on the number of copies sold. He stayed in touch with the paper, maintaining a direct line from his flat to the Bouverie Street offices and, at least nominally, was consulted on major policy.

Laurence Cadbury did not care for Barry, and the editor clearly resented his conservative proprietor. If Cadbury wished to change some leading article Barry would apparently retire to the lavatory, proof in hand, knowing that Cadbury, who was still in charge of the chocolate factory, had to catch an evening train back to Birmingham. When Cadbury had gone Barry would emerge and run the uncorrected leader in the paper. Eventually Cadbury made an effort to extract Robin Cruikshank from the Ministry of Information so that Barry could be replaced, but the Minister, Brendan Bracken, would not play. So the uneasy partnership continued.

In 1944 Layton, not in the best of health, decided that his main work at what was by now the Ministry of Production had been completed and that he should enter the public debate on post-war aims and reconstruction. So he resigned from the civil service and, apparently without demur on the part of Cadbury, resumed as chairman of the Daily News Ltd. Fairly soon after the war the elaborate quadrille that ended in the ritual extinction of the *News Chronicle* was begun. Cadbury, Layton, the editor and the staff began a stately dance of death. Circulation was falling and the tide of complaint from the Cadbury family was rising. Layton was now spending more time in the Lords and in nursing the European Movement. Barry left the paper in 1947 to run the Festival of Britain, an idea from his excellent deputy, Ralph McCarthy that he had promoted to the full. According to Cadbury's evidence to the Royal Commission, Barry left only after he had been told that his supersession was imminent. But Barry had been trailing his coat for some time. He complained to Tom Hopkinson,[9] 'He [Layton] wants to decide everything of importance and a great deal that's unimportant too. I'm left as a kind of dignified office boy.' One night when he was out enjoying a good dinner at the Café Royal Layton came into the office and altered several paragraphs of the leading article. When Barry eventually returned, he was furious. 'I'm the bloody editor,' he roared, 'he's only the chairman', and he restored the original leader.[10] The appointment of Robin Cruikshank was made soon after this incident.

Cadbury was basically a rather conservative and mean-minded businessman who had inherited the responsibility of newspaper ownership from his father; he was too weak to oust Layton but not big enough to support his chief executive either. So there was carping from the sidelines and nothing very constructive besides. Editorially he was timid beyond belief. A features treatment on entertaining at home illustrated an elegant dining room with, in the background, a bottle of wine. It was removed because Cadbury insisted the wine could not appear in the Birmingham edition as his mother, Dame Elizabeth, would have been shocked to see the *Chron-*

icle 'publicising alcohol'. (She was nearly ninety at the time.) He was also very stingy. When Ian Mackay, that warm-hearted soul, died at the end of a Labour party conference in Scarborough, I learnt that the *News Chronicle* had sent his widow the railway's bill for transporting the body back to London. Although only a junior editorial executive on another paper at the time, I was so outraged that I wrote Cadbury a pained note. There was no reply, although in time the bill was paid by the office. And when Vicky left the paper Layton said the firm would like to give him a parting present: was there anything in particular he would like? Vicky, grateful for the gesture, said he had always cherished the hope of visiting India. Layton accepted the idea – and Vicky was presented with a *one-way* ticket to India.[11]

Cruikshank's appointment signalled a swing to the Right, with the editorial staff believing that Cruikshank's American wife was playing too large a role in policy-making. Some of them found him a 'disastrous editor', lacking in guts.

While Vicky owed so much to Barry and found him a totally sympathetic editor, Cruikshank in contrast emerged as unresponsive and jittery about his cartoons. When Vicky brought them in for the editor's approval Cruikshank used to writhe with anguish as he looked at them and eventually would expostulate that they were 'stretching things a bit'. Eventually, on grounds of taste, he killed one of Vicky's more savage jabs at Wall Street (the cartoon showed investors jumping out of their skyscraper windows), and Vicky decided that the moment had come to make a move. In 1952 he went to the *Mirror*. Even though James Cameron, one of the outstanding reporters of his day, had joined the staff, the editorial rot was starting and the situation was not helped by the sudden death of Ian Mackay.

In 1950 Layton handed the chairmanship back to Cadbury but remained on the board. Cadbury attempted to strengthen the managerial structure by recruiting Frank Waters. In the relatively short time before his death Waters became convinced that the *News Chronicle*, even though it was still in profit, could not long survive as an independent newspaper; circulation was falling and as paper restrictions were relaxed advertisers found it possible to buy space elsewhere. So Waters began his talks with Cecil King. Meanwhile Layton, when he was not abroad on his European concerns, was scouting round Fleet Street looking for help and Cadbury was becoming more depressed. Both Layton and Cadbury were now in their sixties; Layton had been born in 1884 and Laurence Cadbury in 1889. Layton's wife was in poor health – she eventually died of cancer in 1959 – and Layton was deeply concerned, spending more and more time at home with her, and after her death writing an unexpectedly moving memoir of their courtship, their love and their life together. The trustees' editorial problems were soon redoubled for Cruikshank's health began to fail and in 1954 he had to resign the editorship. Layton, who had been complaining about indecision at the top, now resumed his membership of the board and in effect took charge for a time although Cadbury remained chairman.

After some debate about age and experience the board accepted Layton's advice and appointed Michael Curtis, a young leader-writer who had helped Layton draft one of his innumerable manifestos. Curtis wished to move the *News Chronicle* up-market, with a firm Liberal posture, towards a tabloid format based to some extent on the *Evening Standard*. But Cadbury, perhaps influenced by the advertising department, wanted a higher circulation figure and a more popular paper. Layton, typically, came down in the middle with another of his beautifully written memoranda and so there was little change.

Then Layton scored another little coup. Kemsley wanted to close down the *Daily Dispatch* so that he could use the presses for more lucrative printing contracts, and in November 1955 Layton was able to buy it. The circulation was 463,000 and the *News Chronicle* held on to 300,000 of them – a welcome addition in the numbers game but events soon revealed that they were not natural *Chronicle* readers. The *News Chronicle* now had the longest imprint in Fleet Street; it read '*News Chronicle*, incorporating the *Daily News*, the *Daily Chronicle*, the *Daily Dispatch*, *Westminster Gazette* and *Morning Leader*. Printed by the Daily News Ltd and published by News Chronicle Ltd.' But the reinforcements did not stay long for in the summer of 1956, after Nasser's nationalisation of the Suez Canal, Curtis and the *Chronicle* were among those who bitterly attacked Eden's bungled invasion of Egypt. The new readers, many of them working-class Mancunians, fell away in droves. Cadbury was appalled; Layton backed the editor.

The paper's situation was now getting desperate. By July 1957 Layton was telling friends that the papers were 'hanging on by their eyebrows'[12] and talks with other newspaper publishers were in full spate. Curtis took the view that if a merger with the *Herald* was impossible the price of the paper should be increased by a 1d to 3d, the format changed to tabloid and the contents gradually made more serious in approach. While he was away on holiday in August the directors turned his proposals down flat.

Curtis was furious: he wrote to the board, 'If this is really the board's intention – knowing how strongly I feel on the subject – I must presume that they no longer have any confidence in my judgment – a sentiment which in the circumstances can only be mutual.' Cadbury asked him to resign at once and Curtis wrote to Layton, still seeking some support for his proposals and adding, 'So long as Laurence remains in command I am certain the paper is doomed to die . . .' As the directors had already decided to hire as managing director and chief executive one John Coope a former *Mirror* executive whose services were suddenly available, Layton felt unable to support Curtis any further and the editor left, eventually finding employment with the Aga Khan.

Layton took refuge in a long memorandum to Cadbury, saying that he wished to resign from the board but first the price should be increased by ½d to 2½d and secondly the assets of the company should not be pledged against overdrafts to an extent that would threaten the company's obligations to its pensioners. In fact he never did resign and the definitive negotiations now began between Coope for the Daily News Ltd and R. A. Redhead for Associated. These culminated in an option to sell the two papers for £1,925,000 plus ten shillings for each new reader gained by the *Mail* over 300,000. Although the option was dated March 1959 it was renewed every three months until the final closure.

Rumours of the *News Chronicle*'s difficulties were now all over Fleet Street. On three separate occasions the editorial staff went to see the directors to express their concern at what they saw as the policy of lethargic drift at the top. They claimed they had been met with indifference and had apparently been regarded as 'agitators'. James Cameron, their star reporter, was so disillusioned that he resigned, together with Douglas Brown, a political columnist. (Cummings had retired in 1955.) The acting editor appointed to succeed Curtis was Norman Cursley who had been assistant editor. He did not command much confidence. Senior Liberals became more and more worried. Frank Byers, later Lord Byers, went to see Cadbury who said, 'No comment'. Mark Bonham-Carter saw Layton twice, and got nowhere. Jo Grimond tried to see Cadbury and failed.[13]

Meanwhile losses were mounting; the two papers lost £300,000 in the first nine months of 1960. Since 1957 the *News Chronicle* had lost 257,000 readers and *The Star* some 170,000. A new go-ahead advertising director, Noel Holland, was increasing revenue on *The Star*; in the first six months of 1960 it was up by fifty per cent on the same period in 1958. But he found the *News Chronicle* an intractable problem; the market research which the paper had exploited so successfully in its editorial columns showed a collapse of its readership among women and there was a shortage of young readers too. Nonetheless he was able to show a small increase in the *Chronicle*'s advertising revenue in 1960. It demonstrated what an energetic man could do. Even so *News Chronicle* paging remained persistently below its rivals; it was estimated that just to match their sizes would cost some £4,000,000.

Many felt, with Michael Curtis, that a price increase was the answer. Giving evidence to the Shawcross Commission on the Press, R. A. Redhead of Associated Newspapers said he had discussed price with John Coope, 'and he thought that the *News Chronicle* would lose the magic million, and it would have a bad effect on advertising'. Max Aitken of Beaverbrook Newspapers said that in 1959 the *Evening Standard* had suggested raising the price of *The Star* and *Standard* by 1d, 'and they [the *Chronicle* and *Star* management] turned us down'. The reason was later revealed by Cadbury who said, 'We had discussed with them [Associated] in the past putting up the evening paper [*The Star*] and they were very much against it.' The fact is that the existence of the 1925 Plan hamstrung the *Chronicle* board. Their general manager told the Commission, 'We had this basic agreement with Associated and could not very well have made such a fundamental decision without their consent.' The directors were terrified that this final escape route would be closed if they annoyed Associated. There was however widespread suspicion that other publishers, including Associated, were putting the squeeze on the *Chronicle* by delaying a price increase – a suspicion that was reinforced when cover prices went up a few months after the closure. The Shawcross Commission 'having anxiously studied all the available evidence' said the suggestion 'could not be substantiated'. It was a generous conclusion, for Roy Thomson said without equivocation that at that time 'some newspapers deliberately held back their selling price to embarrass their less successful rivals'.[14] None the less a price increase alone would not have been enough. As Cecil King said, 'The argument which you read every now and then about how the *News Chronicle* would have been saved by a higher price is wrong. It would not. It is taking a drowning man and pushing his head under water. It would make a little more money for a short time, and kill him.'

Why had they not accepted the Curtis plan to go tabloid? A most extraordinary explanation was given to the Commission: 'We had an unsuccessful experience in changing size in *The Star*. It was turned from a tabloid before the war to a full sized sheet which proved a failure and it returned in due course to the smaller size.' To suggest that such a lunatic experiment as making a commuters' paper into a broadsheet was a good reason for refusing to modernise the *Chronicle* shows how pathetically feeble the management of the paper had become.

In the last two years of the *News Chronicle*'s existence the chief aim of the management seems to have been a worthy effort to obtain enough money for the pensioners and compensation for the staff. For this reason the existence of the deal was kept a deadly secret, for Associated could obtain full value for their money and the extra payment activated only if other newspapers had no inkling of the date and nature of the merger. So it was not until five pm on Monday, 17th October 1960, that unions and staff were told that publication of both papers was ceasing at once. As a result many never got the word: Alan Dent, the drama critic, first knew what had happened when the *Daily Mail* came through his letter box in the morning; the crime reporter got the message when he tried to draw £5 expenses for a trip to the Yard. Among journalists there was much bitterness at the closure and disgust at the compensation terms, fixed at one week's pay for every year of service in addition to holiday payments due. Cadbury's remoteness did not help; he did not even write a letter to the staff, preferring to make statements to the *Daily Mail*, a newspaper which probably reflected his views rather more closely than the *Chronicle*. It was also noted that the Daily News Ltd had retained its lucrative shares in Tyne Tees Television, an investment that Layton had persuaded Cadbury to make. And there was particular bitterness that it was the *Daily Mail*, a strong supporter of Suez, which took over. Cadbury said the two papers had so much in common 'in the integrity of their reporting and honesty of outlook'. The staff did not feel that way; as James Cameron wrote in his local paper, the *West London Observer*, in its closing days the *News Chronicle* was 'a potential war horse ridden by grocers'. There was even greater fury when a shareholder, son of a former editor of *The Star* who had 50,000 shares, succeeded in halting the payout to the staff on the grounds that the rights of shareholders had been infringed. In the end £900,000 or some eighty per cent of the original sum was made available to the staff, but compensation terms had been cut still further; they eventually worked out at four days' pay for every year of service. It was another indication of faulty managerial planning.

It is true that the company suffered an appalling run of mortally bad luck: there was the death of Frank Waters, the ultimately fatal illness of Robin Cruikshank. Perhaps even more significant, as Laurence Cadbury sadly told the authors of *The Last Days of Bouverie Street*,[15] was the death of his eldest son, Julian, in a motoring accident in 1950. Julian was to have become head of the chocolate interests and then his second son Adrian, better known in the 1980s as Sir Adrian Cadbury, chairman of Cadbury-Schweppes and a highly successful industrialist, would have taken over the paper and perhaps led the fight to restore the *Chronicle*'s fortunes.

Unfortunately might-have-beens cannot resurrect dead newspapers. Admittedly the *News Chronicle* was past its best when it died. Even James Cameron admitted that 'towards the end the *News Chronicle* may have been insecure, indefinite, compensating for vigour here by fatuity there'. And R. A. Redhead told the Shawcross Commission, 'I do not think [closure] could be blamed on the management. I think one should put the blame on the fact that the paper did not appeal. The *Chronicle* had long-winded stories, a lot of politics, a tremendous number of features and very bad news coverage.' It is just as well to remember that the large staff of journalists (300 for the two papers) were not blameless.

Yet the judgment of their peers was that management was to blame. Lord Rothermere told the Shawcross Commission: 'The management of the *News Chronicle* made a lot of mistakes.' He suggested that they had been over-optimistic after the war and spent £2 million on machinery they did not need. 'They would have been very happy to have had one of those in the bank when they got into trouble.' Cecil King talked of 'incompetent management'. And Beaverbrook said, 'It had no management. It passed from one weak management to another weak management with divided counsels. It had no will to survive.' He was in his eighties when he said that, and the Shawcross Commission asked him to expand on what should have been done. He explained that the management should have built up 'the advertising side and the circulation side; making economies; taking advantage of situations that develop; making the paper feel the effects of vigour, drive and energy all the time. This is what

ABOVE Alfred Harmsworth in 1896, the year he launched the *Daily Mail* at a half-penny. 'We've struck a gold mine!' he said. He was made a baronet in 1904, a baron in 1905, and became a Viscount in 1917.

TOP RIGHT Northcliffe towards the end his life when he was vainly struggling to keep his weight down. Little can be seen of the youth whom a barrister once described as 'having the face and figure of a Greek god'.

BOTTOM RIGHT Wickham Steed, editor of *The Times*, and Northcliffe visit the United States in 1921. A tremendous scandal exploded over a fake interview with Steed involving the King's views on Ireland. Northcliffe stayed loyal to Steed at the time but later schemed unsuccessfully to force Steed's resignation.

TOP LEFT Laurence Cadbury, the man who killed the *News Chronicle*. He was better at making chocolate than publishing newspapers. And politically he was moving to the Right while Layton, his editorial director, was moving Left. It was not a happy partnership.

TOP RIGHT Viscount Southwood of Odhams Press. A printer who was drawn into publishing by his need to keep the presses running, he started the big canvassing wars which, at ruinous cost, led to a permanent increase in newspaper circulations.

BOTTOM LEFT A portrait of Lord Camrose who, with his less talented brother Cromer Kemsley, built up one of the biggest publishing empires of his day. Later, for family reasons, they split and Kemsley took the *Sunday Times* and the provincial chain.

makes a newspaper, and the spirit of it. Like many other businesses it wants leadership and they had no leadership.'

It might be more accurate to say that the leadership had lost its way completely. Idealism had gone out of the window and now neither the directors nor the editor knew which way to go. There was neither conviction nor dynamism. Succeeding to the fine traditions of the *Daily News* the paper wobbled between trying to find an audience 'entirely in the comfortable classes' and deserting 'principles and good taste' to build a mass circulation. It was too late when the board learnt that they needed a little less idealism and a little more attention to profit. Only George Cadbury had known how to mix the two.

Notes:

1. The letter is quoted in *No Ordinary Press Baron, a Life of Walter Layton*, by David Hubback, Weidenfeld, 1985. This kindly biography by a family friend may err on the side of charity, but it is a prime source of light on the reasons for the *Chronicle*'s death, and I have relied on it throughout this chapter.
2. Quoted in *Beaverbrook* by A. J. P. Taylor, Hamish Hamilton, 1972.
3. Oral evidence, Royal Commission on the Press, 1961–62, HMSO, Cmnd 1812.
4. Note from E. J. Robertson to Lord Beaverbrook in Beaverbrook Papers.
5. Quoted by A. G. Gardiner in his *Life of George Cadbury*, Cassell, 1923.
6. *Lloyd George – a Diary*, by Frances Stevenson, Hutchinson, 1971.
7. A detailed account of Vicky's life at the *News Chronicle* appears in *Vicky*, by Russell Davies and Liz Ottaway, Secker and Warburg, 1987. Essential reading for Vicky's admirers if a little heavy-handed at times.
8. Letter quoted by David Hubback, op cit.
9. *Of This Our Time, a Journalist's Story*, by Tom Hopkinson, Hutchinson, 1982.
10. Tom Baistow, foreign editor of the *News Chronicle*, to the author.
11. Reported by Louis Heren, then *The Times* correspondent in India, to whom Vicky showed the ticket.
12. Note from Tom Blackburn to Lord Beaverbrook, Beaverbrook Papers, 15th July 1957.
13. Letter from Lady Violet Bonham-Carter to Layton, quoted by David Hubback, op cit.
14. Quoted by the Printing and Kindred Trades Federation in evidence to the Shawcross Commission.
15. *The Last Days of Bouverie Street* by George Glenton and William Pattinson 1963. This book by two members of the editorial staff gives a graphic and naturally indignant account of the death throes.

5
Beaverbrook

*If Max gets to Heaven he won't last long. He'll be chucked out for
trying to pull off a merger between Heaven and Hell – after having
secured a controlling interest in both places, of course.*

H. G. Wells

Beaverbrook[1] had a short attention span, ravenous curiosity, demonic
energy, an observant eye and an impish sense of mischief and fun
that occasionally spilled over into malice. Boredom was always
threatening and had to be forcibly repelled. He had a prodigious
memory; with its aid he was a superb raconteur and vivid chronicler
of events. As an outsider on the British social scene he nurtured a
fierce contempt for tradition and enjoyed the company of rebels. He
was thus marvellously equipped to be a popular journalist, and he
was indeed the very best.

In his youth he read Stevenson, Scott and, he claimed, a little
Thackeray, but the main literary influence was the Bible which he
certainly absorbed into his innermost heart. By the time I worked
for him after the war he seemed more interested in the possession
of books than in reading them. Indeed I never saw him read a book;
the floor of his room would be littered with crumpled newspaper
and magazine cuttings which he had skimmed and tossed aside,
while a few would be carefully placed on his lectern for further
action – praise, criticism or enquiry.

That was one clue to his extraordinary grip on his newspapers.
'The Principal Reader' made his views known about every aspect of
the business except the sports pages which, in my time at least, he
left alone. If he had a complaint he would usually let the editor
know. If he wanted to praise someone, he would frequently get
through to the writer direct. Sometimes he would send a note of
praise while complaining to the editor that the subject was 'old hat'
or the article was too long. If he wanted to be flattering he was well

aware that few writers believed their work was unworthy of the most fulsome commendation.

In a previous book[2] I tried to describe him:

At his best he was like a conspiratorial gnome, eyes full of mischief in a grinning, deeply furrowed face. Sitting in the sun with right leg crossed over his left thigh and a panama hat tilted over his head, he would speak in a soft, chuckling, almost caressing Canadian twang, of some new story he had heard, some new policy he liked, or some new talent he had found and wished to be employed.

He was always encouraging to new talent. For example Peter Howard, at one time a leader-writer and later a leader of Dr Frank Buchman's Moral Rearmament movement, wrote, 'Beaverbrook took immense trouble over me. His instruction in the art of journalistic writing was unflagging, vivid and beyond price.'[3] Tom Driberg said much the same thing: 'He experiments. He nags. He gives a writer no peace until what he wants is produced.' And James Cameron used to tell the splendid story of how he had been working on the *Daily Express* for some time when he wrote an article on Malta entitled, 'YOU CANNOT EAT THE GEORGE CROSS'. He was summoned to see the Principal Reader at Arlington House, and when he arrived it was clear that Beaverbrook had forgotten why he was there. Then Beaverbook picked up a cutting of the article which happened to be lying on a little table and told him to read it out loud. Cameron did so, feeling more and more pleased as he read on. Beaverbrook was delighted. 'Take it with you and study it. *That's* the sort of article we want in the *Express*', and Cameron was ushered out. So Cameron was not only praised for his article but given another delicious story for his rich repertoire as well.

Yet Beaverbrook, born William Maxwell Aitken in Maple, Ontario, in May 1879, originally became involved with newspapers purely as a sideline to his political ambitions. He had made a fortune in Canada, some said by dubious means although the evidence now seems pretty unconvincing. He began with such harmless enterprises as a bowling alley where, it was said, he allowed customers a free bowl if they could beat him. (He became so proficient that they rarely succeeded.) His first major money-making activity was to buy out for cash a business that could be made more profitable by good management. As a highly persuasive bond salesman operating at first in Nova Scotia he then sold the company's preference or debenture shares carrying a fixed rate of interest – usually four or five per cent – but kept for himself and his associates the ordinary shares in that company, for which he paid nothing. As the Canadian economy was expanding fast the ordinary shares soon started paying good dividends and he would then be able to sell them at a handsome price. The buyers of his bonds were perfectly happy; they got what they had paid for – namely a fixed income. Aitken, using this technique and with the backing of his first hero John F. Stairs, the leading financier of Nova Scotia, made money fast. He was a dollar millionaire by the time he was twenty-eight. He then moved to Montreal where eventually he put together a massive cement merger, followed by a successful steel merger. The pace at which he was moving and the substantial profits he was making ($2,000,000 on the steel deal alone), coupled with his refusal to bail out a shaky cement company controlled by the grand old man of Canadian business, Sir Sandford Fleming and his family, led to increasing criticism of his methods from the Flemings and their friends in the Liberal party. But his financial standing with the banks was high.

At this time – it was July 1910 – he and his wife set out for London to expand his burgeoning financial empire still further. Some of his City friends encouraged him to enter Parliament; for a rich man, able to finance his own campaign, there were few problems. John F. Stairs, so important in helping Aitken get started in his financial operations (he died suddenly in 1904), had been chairman of the Conservative party in Nova Scotia, and led Aitken into that party as a fervent supporter of Joseph Chamberlain's doctrine of Imperial Preference (which meant imposing tariffs on goods entering from foreign countries while allowing goods from the Empire to enter freely or at a preferential rate).[4] In London Aitken soon became friendly with the man who would become his second hero, Bonar Law, who was Canadian born and of Scots descent. Apart from that they could not have been more dissimilar. Bonar Law appeared as taciturn and pessimistic as Aitken was outgoing and optimistic. Yet soon financial dealings (which proved highly profitable to Law) and political interests drew them ever closer together. Law found something irresistibly engaging about the exuberant go-getting storytelling young Canadian financier. His sister Mary initially resisted the Aitken charm, but capitulated when Law, a widower, said, 'Do let me like him.' When she died she left Aitken money in her will and made him her executor.

Eventually Law, who wished to fight a seat held by a Free Trader, was offered one at Ashton-under-Lyne. He didn't want it and suggested Aitken instead. The constituency complied. After initial hesitation Aitken accepted and won the seat from the Liberals at the general election of December 1910 with a majority of 196 out of a total of 7,892 votes cast. Aitken's election campaign had been fortified not only by the presence of his attractive and charming wife Gladys but also by quotations from friendly articles he had planted in Canadian newspapers. Less than a month later he was on holiday in Monte Carlo when the editor of the *Daily Express*, the American R. D. Blumenfeld, approached him with a hard-luck story. The paper was in severe financial difficulties as the original founder, Arthur Pearson, was going blind and had withdrawn his financial support. Conservative party backing was available but Blumenfeld did not wish to accept it since he was a supporter of Tariff Reform and he could not trust the Conservatives to back it. Blumenfeld had pledged his own resources to keep the *Express* afloat and was now running out of money; he was faced with a large bill for newsprint. Bonar Law had suggested he should seek Aitken's support, so Blumenfeld rushed to the South of France. Aitken had already witnessed the value of skilful press propaganda in his own election campaign and as a rising young politician saw the benefit of making friends with a national newspaper editor. He took Blumenfeld back to the Hotel de Paris and at once gave him a cheque for £25,000 as a personal loan.

He seems to have obtained full value for money. As early as November 1911 Balfour's secretary was noting, inaccurately, that 'Aitken, the little Canadian adventurer, practically owns the *Daily Express*'. He added that as a result the *Daily Express* had run Bonar Law for the last two days for all its worth.[5]

Beaverbrook continued to 'run' Bonar Law, and his friend first became leader of the Conservative party and then Prime Minister. 'Between us there was absolute trust,' he told me many years later. 'I have never done a twist or turn in relation to him.' (This suggested there were few politicians of whom he could say the same thing.) 'I gave him the news – and it was reliable. For at that time I was in as great receipt of custom as anyone in England.' On Churchill's advice he had studied Burke and there found a passage which he copied out and learnt by heart: 'The world is governed by go-betweens. These go-betweens influence the persons with whom they carry on intercourse by stating their own sense to each of them as the sense of the other; and thus they reciprocally master both sides.'

A year after his loan to the editor of the *Daily Express* Aitken again took a financial interest in a newspaper. Probably prompted by the Conservative party and certainly with their help, he bought a London evening newspaper called *The Globe* from one of Northcliffe's younger brothers. Hildebrand Harmsworth, who had himself bought it for £75,000 seven years earlier and then lost £80,000 keeping it afloat.* He took no part in running the paper which, from his viewpoint, was designed to provide a job for Blumenfeld if the *Express* failed. Of the £40,000 purchase price Aitken provided only £15,000 of his own money; the rest came from party sources. A few years later he claimed to have paid Dudley Docker, a Birmingham industrialist, £5,000 to take it off his hands. Aitken now became a knight, after the honour had been offered by the Conservative chief whip 'for the purpose of rewarding [him] for services to come' – clearly financial services, among them helping to keep friendly newspapers alive.

The troubles of the *Daily Express* continued and Blumenfeld had to swallow his scruples about party subsidy. There were complicated negotiations and two rivals schemes of reconstruction. A plan backed by Conservative party headquarters which would have led to the reduction of Blumenfeld's influence was discarded and in the end it appears that the Conservatives accepted an alternative scheme under which they bought £10,000 worth of *Express* shares which, to conceal their direct interest, were held by Sir Max Aitken and two others. The next step is obscure. According to the historian A. J. P. Taylor, Aitken craftily made a further investment by providing a £40,000 first mortgage on the plant which gave him a prior claim on the assets. He did not tell the party about this arrangement; it may have been this type of hidden deal which led Asquith, the Liberal premier, to tell Winston Churchill, then a Liberal MP, 'Aitken is quite impossible. I take it that his Canadian record is of the shadiest . . .'† Aitken added one condition for the mortgage, namely that the *Express* would print paragraphs about him which could usefully be reproduced in the local papers circulating in his constituency. It is significant that the papers relating to this first serious investment in the *Daily Express* were filed in boxes marked 'Ashton-under-Lyne'. As Taylor concludes: 'Thus, Aitken's associ-

* Although Hildebrand later took life very easily, living in a Brighton hotel and wearing gym shoes for comfort, he left more than £1,500,000 when he died of cirrhosis. He was given a baronetcy by Lloyd George in 1921, allegedly at the request of Lord Rothermere who rather liked Hildebrand's son.
† Asquith had been briefed by the Governor-General of Canada who was passing on the attacks made by Aitken's political and business enemies in Canada.

ation with the *Daily Express*, which later shaped his life, began as a by-product of his constituency propaganda.' It also arose out of his interest in the political influence of the press which, at that time and indeed later, he may have been inclined to over-rate.

The next stage of Aitken's gradually developing relationship with the *Express* came when, owing to continuing financial problems, it was necessary to appoint a receiver. The chief of the Tory Central Office suggested that Aitken and his colleagues should appoint three Conservative MPs to do the job, but Aitken pointed out that the mortgage holders had a prior claim to make the appointment. Only after the Tory chief had agreed and Aitken, as mortgagor, had appointed his good friend Blumenfeld, the editor and general manager, as receiver did the full extent of Aitken's interest become known, to the marked annoyance of Conservative headquarters. Combined with Aitken's influence over Bonar Law which led J. L. Garvin, editor of *The Observer*, to describe him as 'The Hermit Crab, always putting himself into the other man's ear and swaying in his sinister, insistent way as he likes that strange unfixed feeble mass of timidity and ambition' the incident may have added to the tally which later caused Lord Camrose to remark, 'The Conservative party loathe him so.'[6] Indeed a chairman of the Conservative Party during the 1940–45 war went so far as to say he was 'a man utterly and completely untrustworthy, a crook of crooks, without principle or conscience.'[7]

That was in the future. Aitken finally gained complete control of the *Express* in November 1916 when the largest private shareholder, George Lawson Johnston (his fortune came from Bovril; he was later knighted and finally ennobled as the first Baron Luke), sold him his non-dividend bearing ordinary shares in return for interest bearing preference shares. The price was only £17,500 but Aitken also assumed responsibility for the paper's debts. There was no public announcement at the time as Aitken, now a baronet, was heavily engaged in the plot to destroy the Asquith government. In fact he did not take active command until the war was over; in September 1918 it was announced that he was chairman and head of affairs at the *Daily Express*.

By then he had spent more than £80,000 supporting the paper by one means or another and his influence with Blumenfeld was generally acknowledged. But the *Express* had merely survived; it had not prospered. After the war he put in another £200,000 and began to make it the most successful paper of the inter-war period. He had considerable advantages: he was already a multi-millionaire and his fortunes did not depend on the success or failure of a newspaper. He had consulted Northcliffe about buying the paper. 'How much are you worth?' asked Northcliffe. 'Over $5 million,' said Aitken. 'You will lose it all in Fleet Street,' said Northcliffe; but he was wrong and later urged his colleagues to watch Beaverbrook carefully. Aitken also moved easily in political circles and, quite apart from Law, cultivated the friendship of such influential figures as Churchill and F. E. Smith (as Lord Birkenhead Lord Chancellor in the Coalition government). He became a peer himself at the end of 1916 (despite objections from King George V) – a step he later bitterly regretted since he was now removed from the House of Commons, the real power centre of politics, and pretended he had been bounced into it.[8] With his money, his harsh humour and his impish charm he cut quite a social figure; his many amorous liaisons, which he made little attempt to conceal even from his loving and tolerant wife, added to his circle. (Rebecca West fell in love with him and wrote an unfinished novel about their affair which she sensibly did not publish; it was exhumed after her death.[9] Tallulah Bankhead was another conquest.) Leading literary figures such as Rudyard Kipling, his literary tutor, Arnold Bennett and H. G. Wells were often at his table. And he could write effectively too as his wartime despatches from the front, where he had been appointed official Canadian Eye Witness, had demonstrated.

As soon as the war was over he launched the *Sunday Express*; it made economic sense to use the presses seven days a week and he believed that the launch cost would be small. Blumenfeld told him that it would cost no more than £20,000. In fact it cost him more than twenty times that sum and it was not until he found John Gordon, a dour Scot with the gift of expressing the prejudices of his readers in the most forthright terms, that the paper began moving out of the wood. Then, in 1923, through his friendship with the dying Sir Edward Hulton, he was able to outsmart the Berry brothers who wanted the Hulton chain in London (the *Evening Standard* and the *Daily Graphic*), and Manchester (the *Sporting Chronicle*, the *Sunday Chronicle* and the *Manchester Evening Chronicle* plus the *Daily Dispatch*). First he suggested to Rothermere that he should buy the chain on behalf of the Harmsworths. Then he walked from his home at Cherkley to Hulton's house which was also near Leatherhead. He said he would buy the papers for £6 million with an immediate deposit of £1 million. He left the cheque by the bedside and with Hulton's written acceptance of the deal in his pocket hurried back home. Hulton's family were furious when they discovered what had happened and rang the bank to see if Beaverbrook had the money.[10] The bank said he had no account with them. Within twenty minutes there was another call to say the cheque would be honoured. Beaverbrook had telephoned his friend Reginald McKenna, chairman of the Midland Bank, who agreed to honour the cheque. Only then did Beaverbrook reveal the identity of the real buyer, Lord Rothermere; for Hulton would not sell his group direct to Rothermere as he didn't like the Harmsworths. Beaverbrook took control of the *Evening Standard* as his percentage on the deal. In addition the close links between the Express Group and the Mail Group were fortified. Rothermere already owned a forty-nine per cent interest in Express Newspapers and Beaverbrook had 80,000 shares in the Daily Mail Trust. Rothermere now took a forty-nine per cent interest in the *Standard*, and Beaverbrook gained a further 40,000 shares in the Daily Mail Trust, giving him about six per cent of his highly prosperous rivals. The deal was much to Beaverbrook's advantage for the Trust was paying out substantial dividends while Beaverbrook was ploughing Express Newspaper profits back into the business. So Rothermere was financing the *Mail*'s principal rival and getting back nothing in return. However, by selling on most of Hulton's papers to the Berrys he made a profit of about £1,800,000, and the Berrys later sold off most of those properties for some £2,400,000 more than they had paid.[11] So everyone was happy except Hulton's heirs. The financial links between the Rothermere group and Beaverbrook continued until 1933.

In time Beaverbrook realised that Blumenfeld, although an excellent and respected editor of the old school who knew many of the political leaders and whose views on Tariff Reform were similar to his own, was too serious a figure to produce the kind of lively paper he had in mind. So he appointed the Canadian Beverley Baxter, often derided as 'the piano-tuner' because in his youth he had sold pianos in pursuit of an original ambition to become a concert pianist. Blumenfeld was not too distressed – in fact he remained nominal chairman of Express Newspapers Ltd until his death in 1948 – and told his son, later Sir John Elliot,* that Beaverbrook was 'the most gifted natural journalist he had ever met, not excluding Northcliffe'.

* Beaverbrook believed that the son would have a big career in journalism and that John Blumenfeld should therefore change his name to something with a more English sound. The father agreed. But the career in journalism did not take off and Sir John Elliot made a successful career elsewhere, fetching up as chairman of London Transport. He wrote the biography of Beaverbrook in the *Dictionary of National Biography*.

Beaverbrook started the *Sunday Express* immediately after the first world war. He was told by Blumenfeld, then the editor of the *Daily Express*, that it would cost £20,000 to launch. He had to draw £2m from his Canadian funds before success was assured.

Baxter and Beaverbrook hit it off splendidly for a time and the *Express* carried an air of knowing sophistication that reflected their joint interests in parties, gossip and intrigue.

Baxter wrote an account of Beaverbrook at work that carries complete conviction.

> Secretaries darted in and out like minnows in a torrent. Three telephones sprang into life and never paused a moment for breath. In the centre of it all, creating the energy which he exhausted, was this strange buoyant, fascinating figure, chuckling, roaring, winking, frowning, talking while he signed letters, issuing instructions, gossiping like a spinster, buying, selling, interviewing his interviewers, wheedling, terrifying and enjoying himself enormously.[12]

Beaverbrook was *having fun*.

The capacity for sheer devilment and enjoyment at the top was one reason why the Beaverbrook press was able to capture the services of so many exceptional writers and cartoonists. From Dean Inge to Alan Moorehead and Leonard Mosley, from Arnold Bennett and James Agate to Sefton Delmer and James Cameron, from Strube and Low to Osbert Lancaster and Vicky, they were all aware that their work was being watched and savoured by the Principal Reader. Sometimes they detested his politics and flaked off, but the basic creed of the *Express* permeated the paper; it was stated by Beaverbrook in 1922: 'More life – more hope – more money – more work – more happiness'. It was not a bad prospectus.

In a well-known phrase Beaverbrook told the first Royal Commission on the Press that he ran his newspapers 'purely for propaganda, and with no other purpose'. He qualified this later by saying that to make propaganda the paper had to be successful, in other words circulation should be strong and the balance sheet healthy. The propaganda he dispensed ranged from Empire Free Trade to protection for British agriculture and, later, the Second Front, and the anti-Common Market campaign. Between the wars he carried his Empire Crusade to extreme lengths, filling his papers with propaganda, suppressing the views of those who did not agree with his policy, running anti-government (and anti-Baldwin) candidates, stumping the country and preaching his creed to bemused audiences. By the time I worked for him (after the Second World War) he liked to lament what a failure he had been. But at one moment in 1931 Baldwin, his principal opponent, had actually decided to resign, only to be saved by the failure of the Empire Free Trade candidate sponsored by Beaverbrook and Rothermere to defeat the official Conservative (Duff Cooper) at a by-election in the constituency of St George's, Westminster. It was two days before the poll that Baldwin delivered his devastating blast at the press lords 'aiming at . . . power without responsibility – the prerogative of the harlot throughout the ages' – a phrase now attributed to Kipling who had fallen out with Beaverbrook over Home Rule for Ireland. So Beaverbrook came fairly close to success. He was however happily aware that in newspaper terms his causes were often quite popular *'and'*, he once told me about the Common Market with a mischievous grin, 'no one else is taking our line'.

His streak of iconoclasm could also be very appealing. As Michael Foot wrote,[13] 'One partial explanation of the devotion he could excite in the most unlikely quarters derived from the nature and scale of his "emotional radicalism".' Indeed Tom Clarke, an independent observer, wrote of Beaverbrook in the 1920s that 'he was as conscious of inequality and as sympathetic to the working man as any social reformer I have met'.[14] His gaiety was equally important. He never seemed to take politics too seriously; for more earnest politicians this showed how cynical he was. During the turmoil in 1963 over the succession to Macmillan as Prime Minister he used to sing over the telephone in an appalling croak, 'We'll sow the seeds of discord' to any tune that came into his head – he was too fond of singing the corniest songs.

He was far from being a routine Conservative. After the First World War he was not only in favour of an Excess Profits Tax but also of a tax on war fortunes. He was strongly critical of the attempt, backed by Churchill, to support the Russian counter-revolutionaries. He believed in Home Rule for Ireland. He bitterly opposed Lloyd George's efforts to support the Greeks against the Turkish onslaught in 1922 on the grounds that Britain's commitments in the Middle East should be reduced to the minimum. He favoured the abolition of a hereditary House of Lords. After the General Strike of 1926, in which he sympathised with the miners while fighting the strikers, he proposed a form of merger for the mines, a forerunner of nationalisation. While genuinely respecting the Queen he scoffed at the institution of monarchy. (' "Holy cows" may still be necessary in India,' he told Sir John Elliot, 'they are an anachronism in Britain.') He nourished a deep dislike of the British public school system, and favoured co-education – quite an advanced thought for a Victorian son of a Canadian manse. And he had no worries about changing his mind: 'Nothing is so bad as consistency,' he said, adding that the policy of great nations was often diverted into wrong courses by the memory of old speeches.

Beaverbrook had just arrived for a long visit to the United States when the storm finally broke in England over Edward VIII's love for Mrs Simpson. At the King's request Beaverbrook had helped to trim British newspaper coverage of the Simpson divorce case to the minimum; now he was asked to return at once to give the monarch further counsel. Since the Prime Minister was Baldwin, with whom Beaverbrook had a long-standing and bitter feud ('We battled for the soul of Bonar Law,' said Baldwin explaining the origin of the dispute), Beaverbrook abandoned his plan to stay in Arizona. He told reporters the sea voyage had done his asthma so much good that he was going to breathe some more sea air on the return voyage. When he got back Beaverbrook was appalled to learn that the King had already put forward his proposal for a morganatic marriage, for that in itself implied that the King accepted Mrs Simpson could never be Queen. The only newspapers to back the King were the *Express*, the *Mail* and the *News Chronicle*. Since Dominion opinion was also

Daily Mirror

No. 2   NEWS BULLETIN.   One Penny
Thursday, May 6th, 1926.

London "CARRIES ON"

"Carrying On" described the situation on the second day of the Strike. Apart from a few minor incidents general calm prevailed throughout the country and the public cheerfully and helpfully shouldered the inconveniences which the strike brought in its train. Londoners were wonderful and the manner in which transport difficulties were overcome, despite midday gloom, was admirable.

ARRESTS IN POPLAR.

On Tuesday evening excitement ran high in Poplar and Canning Town. Three arrests were made at Poplar and two arrests at Bow.

When the crowd became aggressive a number of police baton charges were made. Numerous casualties occurred and the injured were taken to Poplar Hospital which is opposite Blackwall Tunnel. The injuries were mostly of a head character.

The Rioters' objective appeared to be the prevention of the passage of cars and one motor car was wrecked. Where drivers had no passengers the vehicles were allowed to proceed, but cars containing girls and others returning from work were stopped and passengers were forced to proceed on foot.

SIX 'BUSES ATTACKED.

Six 'buses were attacked and disabled by strikers at Hammersmith. One arrest was made.

STOCK EXCHANGE.

Stock Markets steady at lower level. War Loan 99⅜. French Franc 153½.

WARSHIPS LANDING FOOD.

Two warships, H.M.S. Ramilies and H.M.S. Barham landed food supplies, mainly yeast, at Liverpool.

"THE BRITISH GAZETTE"

The first number of the Government's newspaper "The British Gazette" — four pages of seven columns, printed back and front — was published by His Majesty's Stationery Office, price one penny, for distribution by the Civil Commissioners whose districts cover the whole country.

It included a "Reply to strike-makers' plan to paralyse public opinion", which points out that silencing the Press would result in "rumours poisoning the air, raise panics and disorders, and carry us all to depths which no sane man would care to contemplate"

LIGHT AND POWER.

Members of the Electrical Trades Union in the London Power stations ceased work.

There is no likelihood of power or light being cut off in London. The Government have an adequate supply of volunteers to maintain services in the event of other Unions coming out.

> ### OUR LEADING ARTICLE.
>
> The people expect the Government not to fail in its duty. If the Cabinet surrenders, democratic government will be for ever impossible in this country. The nation is firm. It is calm and confident. There must be no provocation. Let us all pursue our daily tasks tranquilly, helping each other, offending nobody.

PRINTERS RETURN TO WORK.

Compositors, printers and stereotypers returned to work and the "Sheffield Telegraph" and "Sheffield Independent" published again at midnight.

At Rugby the compositors including a labour official returned to work declaring that the strike was unconstitutional.

OFFICER DRIVES TRAIN.

When a train with troops and sailors leaving Portsmouth had left Fratton, the first station out, the driver left the engine. An officer on the train stepped into the cab, examined the levers and drove the train on.

STRIKE BREVITIES.

Mr. Baldwin presided over a full meeting of the Cabinet.

All news messages are from Reuters and other agencies.

Eight London Theatres have closed. Others may do so.

Deliveries of letters are being made in London daily at 9 a.m., 11 a.m., and 4 p.m.

There was a heavy supply of meat at Smithfield.

Worthing market gardeners pooled lorry resources to take produce to London.

During the General Strike most newspapers struggled to maintain independent publication as this example of the *Daily Mirror* shows but Churchill wanted a monopoly for his British Gazette. His attempt to requisition *Daily Express* supplies of newsprint led to the biggest-ever row between him and Beaverbrook.

strongly against the proposal the battle did not last long. When the King said he wished to abdicate, Beaverbrook told Churchill, 'Our cock won't fight.' Baldwin made a masterly speech in the Commons, and was able to retire a year later with his reputation at its highest. 'I've never had so much fun in my life,' Beaverbrook concluded.

This brief account focusing on his newspaper activities would be incomplete if it excluded any reference to his work at Churchill's side during the Second World War. The crisis of the Battle of Britain when he was charged with remedying the shortage of fighter planes brought out his greatest qualities: unremitting energy applied to removing any bottlenecks, total commitment to spurring on – by exhortation, by praise, by violent condemnation - all those who were producing them. ORGANISATION IS THE ENEMY OF IMPROVISATION was his cry. The Ministry of Aircraft Production became a whirlwind of action and enterprise run as Beaverbrook's private fiefdom. (He drew no salary, used no official cars, paid for many of the staff from his own pocket; even half the typists were being paid by the *Express*.) 'He's done miracles,' Churchill told the editor of the *Manchester Guardian*. And it was true.

Yet before the war Beaverbrook had proclaimed himself a Pacifist. 'In modern war,' he broadcast in 1934, 'all nations are defeated.' While urging stronger defences he believed in 'Splendid Isolation' with no European alliances. The doctrine led the *Express* to proclaim, 'Britain will not be involved in a European war this year, or next year either', the last four words being added by Beaverbrook who certainly believed there *would* be war, but hoped Britain would keep out of it.

After John F. Stairs and Bonar Law, Churchill was the third hero of his life. Once, well after the war, when I had been summoned to see him at Arlington House he took a call from Lady Churchill who wanted him to go and cheer up her bedridden husband in Hyde Park Gate. He rose at once, ordered the Rolls to the front door and we were on our way in five minutes.

'During the war,' he told me as we sped down Piccadilly, 'I was proud to receive a call from Churchill. He was carrying the burden and if I could help him to any degree I would hurry round. It was an honour to be in his company. Now he is old and sick but if he calls I am again proud to respond on the instant. I have not forgotten what we owe him. I will not fail him now.'

None the less when Churchill's leadership was being most savagely attacked during 1941–2 the mirage of a summons to take over supreme power did seem to haunt his dreams. Beaverbrook wrote at least fourteen letters of resignation while in office, some of them undoubtedly of a tactical nature, to gain a departmental point. Others were part of his ongoing battle with Ernest Bevin, then Minister of Labour, over the control of manpower for aircraft production factories. There were others, born of frustration (which quickly led to crippling asthma) and concealed ambition. Finally when the immediate aircraft production problems had been resolved and he had been appointed first Minister of Supply and then Minister of Production he resigned again after an ill-tempered row with Attlee. His health had been undermined by strain, overwork and arduous journeys under difficult conditions, including the historic first mission to Moscow with Averell Harriman which he conducted with consummate success. Significantly, his resignation took effect just four days after the fall of Singapore. Churchill offered other jobs but in the end had to accept the resignation on grounds of health.

Beaverbrook now took his campaign for a Second Front on to the platform and into the leader columns, knowing that he had the full support of President Roosevelt; perhaps he was still wondering if a Commons revolt would overthrow the Premier. But Churchill's position became impregnable when he persuaded the Americans that the Mediterranean Front should take priority and so the Second Front had to wait. In September 1943, after Churchill had told him in confidence that the Second Front would be opened the following year, Beaverbrook was back in his role of confidential adviser as Lord Privy Seal, without a seat in the Cabinet. Harry Hopkins remarked that Beaverbrook was however in the real Cabinet of the men who saw Churchill after midnight. In that role he continued to press for all possible assistance to Russia – he published some glowing assessments of Stalin's character – and equal status with the United States. Beaverbrook is thus unique among newspaper publishers in attaining considerable triumphs in two careers outside the newspaper field - finance and politics. It gave him a perspective on events that no other contemporary could rival.

After the war it was back to his newspapers. The *Daily Mirror* soon passed the sale of the *Express*; it was brilliantly and freshly edited; it had been eagerly read by the troops and it profited from the post-war leftward swing in British politics. Nonetheless the prosperity of the *Express* was at its highest. The superb technical skills of Arthur Christiansen, who had succeeded Baxter as editor in the 1930s, combined with his proud and arrogant team of journalists, curiously incestuous in their love of each other and of their editor, produced a sparkling newspaper that Christiansen reasonably regarded as 'a university for the masses'. Christiansen had no political views of his own; he simply echoed his master's voice. 'I was a journalist, not a political animal; my proprietor was a journalist *and* a political animal,' he wrote in his autobiography.[15]

The end of their association was sad: Christiansen had a heart attack in 1956 while staying with Beaverbrook in the South of France. After a long interval during which the job was kept open for the editor I was invited one Friday to take 'a walk in the park with the Lord'. He told me in confidence that Christiansen's health was no longer reliable; he was out and his place would be taken by the managing editor, Pickering (now Sir Edward and at the time of writing executive vice-chairman of Times Newspapers); I was to become managing editor – in effect the editor in charge of production – and to start on Monday. It was a dreadful job for which I was quite unsuited but, naturally, I accepted. Everything seemed to go reasonably well on my first day. Next day, to my astonishment, Christiansen turned up in the office and took over the morning conference, kindly welcoming me to the staff and asking for my views on the political situation. No one had dared tell him that he was no longer editor. As soon as the conference was over I steamed upstairs to see Max Aitken, Beaverbrook's son and co-chairman; he was not there. In fact he was at his house on the Cherkley estate. (He told me later that as soon as he heard Christiansen was in the office 'I ran to the bottom of my garden'. He was so much braver in the air than on the ground.) My next call was on the other co-chairman, Tom Blackburn (later Sir Tom). I explained that I had come over to the *Express* as a Number Two, not Number Three. If Christiansen was staying I was going back to the *Evening Standard* where I was very happy as deputy editor. Meanwhile I returned to the editorial floor and there was Christiansen, shirt unbuttoned to the navel, wandering around caressing his buddies and assuming that normal service would soon be resumed. Beaverbrook hated sacking people he knew and in the end Blackburn was deputed to offer Christiansen a lush panelled office at the *Standard* and some grandiloquent title such as editorial consultant. No one could believe that Christiansen had gone, especially his secretary who refused to handle my telephone calls in the secretaries' outer office until Christiansen had told her himself. There was a sad epilogue: Beaverbrook and Christiansen met to say farewell, for Christiansen was

not happy with his sinecure. They both wept. Then Beaverbrook
escorted Christiansen to the lift. As it was about to descend he said
his final farewell, 'Well, goodbye, Chris. Sorry to see you going
down.' Not even a generous settlement could make up for that last
cruel clout. Christiansen later wrote to Beaverbrook saying he 'must
come home [to Beaverbrook] as soon as I can'. But then he wrote
saying he was advised he couldn't do it. Presumably his financial
settlement was for loss of office. Christiansen finally died in 1963.
The discards of journalism, however gifted and financially secure,
sometimes find it exceptionally hard to adjust to a life without the
daily 'fix' of excitement.

Towards the end of his life Beaverbrook became increasingly
enchanted with the writing of books, or 'chronicles' as he preferred
to call them. During the 1914–18 war, due to the encouragement
of Arnold Bennett, he had produced an account of how the Asquith
government had been brought down. This was originally drafted as
early as 1917 by a secretary called Maurice Woods who was adept
at writing in Beaverbrook's staccato style. The title was 'History of
the Crisis'. But Beaverbrook later bought, begged, borrowed (or
otherwise obtained) more documents and letters of the period while
he continually revised and reshaped the work. It was finally published
in two volumes as *Politicians and the War* in 1928 and 1932.[16] But
it was not until 1956, with the publication of *Men and Power*[17] dealing
with the events of 1917 to 1918, that his talents as an author were
widely acclaimed.

Before the first narrative opens he gives thirty-four brief biographical sketches. Some of the comments catch the exact flavour
of Beaverbrook's conversation at its best:

Curzon changed sides on almost every issue during his long
career. Often undecided whether to desert a sinking ship for one
that might not float, he would make up his mind to sit on the
wharf for a day . . . House [President Wilson's confidant] walked
delicately. Everything was done softly. He had a rare capacity for
gaining confidences, which he always passed on to the
President . . . [Haig's] diary is a self-revealing document: frank,
truthful, self-confident and malicious. His spear knew no brother.
With the publication of his Private Papers in 1952, he committed
suicide twenty-five years after his death.

Beaverbrook was compared with Tacitus, Creevey, Aubrey. The

Sunday Times said of *Men and Power*, 'It deserves to rank as a classic'. But it was the historian A. J. P. Taylor's praise which gave Beaverbrook the greatest pleasure and encouragement; later they became close friends.* Beaverbrook, who had been so nervous about the book's reception that he had restricted the first printing to 3,000 copies, was astounded and enchanted. 'It was a new event in my life. I was fascinated by the spectacle of success in a world that was not mine,' he told an interviewer. He completed several more books of which the most important was the *Decline and Fall of Lloyd George*, but his plans to write 'The Age of Baldwin' and a book about Churchill were never taken beyond the planning stage.

On the eve of his eighty-fourth birthday I interviewed him about his historical methods. He told me that after his secretaries had gathered all the relevant material together with the notes on particular events which he had scribbled or dictated at various times, he would consult his Timetable, particularly the diary of his own engagements. Then his extraordinary memory came into play and he could vividly recall dinner parties, conversations and other events he had witnessed. When a chapter was nearing completion he began the process to which he attached greatest importance; he called it 'balancing'. The aim was to inject a little more sparkle and liveliness into what might otherwise have been too dry. It was like dropping a tablet of Eno's Fruit Salts into a glass of tap water. It must be said that not every piece of 'balancing' had complete historical authenticity. Even Taylor, his greatest fan, had to include 'romantic imagination, instances of' in the index of his biography. Nonetheless the books convey the flavour of the period, the personalities and the discords with quite exceptional intensity. 'In ten years' time,' Lord Beaverbrook said to me with some satisfaction, 'if I'm remembered at all, it will not be for my newspapers. It will be for my books.' In fact he is remembered as one of the most extraordinary, gifted and complicated figures among the whole bizarre gallery of newspaper publishers. His final farewell, delivered at the magnificent birthday dinner which Lord Thomson of Fleet gave him at the Dorchester just a fortnight before he died, was etched in the memory of everyone present. He had spoken throughout his speech of how he had always

---

* Beaverbrook repaid his debt to Taylor by writing the introduction to *A Century of Conflict, Essays for A J P Taylor*, edited by Martin Gilbert, Hamish Hamilton, 1966 – two years after his death. His chapter is headed 'The Man Who Likes to Stir Things Up'. He concluded, 'I am proud to write this introduction, even though I shall not be in a position to read it when it is published.'

been an apprentice. Then he concluded, 'Here I must say, in my eighty-sixth year, I do not feel greatly different from when I was eighty-five. This is my final word. It is time for me to become an apprentice once more. I have not settled in which direction. But somewhere, sometime soon.'

Unfortunately he will not also be remembered as an ideal husband and father. His treatment of his wife was quite appalling. When his mistress moved into Cherkley his wife finally moved out. She died of cancer in her forties, and for a time Beaverbrook was stricken with remorse. His daughter Janet stood up to him with a mixture of tears and cunning. 'I gave as good I got,' she wrote in her charming autobiography. But Max, her elder brother, 'learned just to do what he was told'; he became, she thought, a 'yes man' to their father, and 'imitated his moods and mannerisms'. Peter, the younger brother who later died in a yachting accident, 'developed a habit of retiring into himself and saying nothing'. Beaverbrook genuinely loved his elder son and was noticeably edgy during the Battle of Britain until Max's nightly call came through, but in later years, as guests at Cherkley could see for themselves, treated him far too often as a rather clumsy servant. The second Lord Rothermere told Cecil King that he was with Beaverbrook once when he 'held forth on the inadequacies of his son Max' and Max was present. He certainly discussed with me (and no doubt with others) whether Max or Vere Harmsworth (later the third Lord Rothermere) would make the best of their inheritance and did not give the impression that he had much confidence in Max. It was not the treatment designed to inculcate much self-confidence.

He made things worse by frequently announcing that he was withdrawing from active control of the *Express*. As early as 1928 he was saying, 'I can conceive and create but I cannot conduct . . . So on the very last day of November I said goodbye to the *Daily Express* office for ever.' In June 1929 when his son was nineteen he announced publicly that he had transferred his shares in Express Newspapers to his son Max; they would be held in trust until Max came of age. In fact he transferred his shares to a private company in which he held 5,000 voting shares and Max was given 35,000 non-voting shares. At some later stage he bought back the non-voting shares; he made a similar arrangement for his younger son but did not buy back his shares, presumably because of Peter's death.

The following year he said that his association with the *Daily*

Express was at an end; he heard nothing from 'them' and gave 'them' no assistance. In 1931 he was planning to transfer control of the *Evening Standard* to his son Peter (not to Max), but this was blocked by the Daily Mail Trust which still possessed an option to buy the *Standard* if he ever wished to sell it. In 1936, just before he was summoned back to England by King Edward VIII, he said he was going away for a long time. Three years later he planned to sell the papers to their staffs. After the war, to escape crippling death duties, he really did transfer his voting shares to the two Beaverbrook Foundations. Beaverbrook however was chairman for life with Max to succeed him. He also devised the curious scheme by which Beaverbrook Newspapers had two chairmen: Blackburn was chairman of the company and Max was chairman of the board. Real power remained of course with the chairman of the Foundations. ('Some chairmen are more equal than others,' Blackburn commented to me ruefully.)

Max did once turn on his father when he complained that he and Blackburn received nothing but criticism. He wrote a pained but skilfully phrased letter:

> When you used to work at the office with your coat off you drove everyone hard but you also made them laugh and feel they were 'on the sunny side of the street'.
> This is still necessary and some of it mus come from the master however far away he may be.
> Therefore I hope you will continue to hold us by the hand each and every day and beam an occasional smile our way.

Max made his point and Beaverbrook tempered his criticisms accordingly. But Max failed in his battle to persuade Beaverbrook to invest in commercial television. A long exchange of memos in the Beaverbrook Papers shows that Max constantly pressed his father to get involved with an application to share in one of the many franchises which were then being distributed. Equally E. J. Robertson, the dour Canadian who ran the business side of the group with devotion and complete control until felled by a stroke,[18] was blocking any dissipation of effort and resources. He was probably doing so under instruction; I recall that Beaverbrook was even consulted about raising the price of coffee in the *Express* canteen. It should also be remembered that Beaverbrook was a very conservative financier. At one stage he had acquired the Colonial Bank in the

City. Later he sold it to Barclays; one of their executives reported that he was an excellent banker 'but rather too orthodox'. He did not like borrowing money and all the newspaper properties were freehold. At one stage even I suggested that we should get into television. 'Ah no, Mr Raabertson won't allow it,' he said. And that was the end of the matter. The result was that he again stopped his son from exercising any initiative. It was not good training for a publisher.

Beaverbrook was of course quite maddening in many ways. He could keep a confidence most faithfully; his political career as a go-between would never have succeeded if he had published everything he knew. But he could not always be trusted. One very minor example: he wrote to me once saying he had destroyed a letter I had sent him about evidence I was due to give in a libel case. The letter is still in the files. Some observers found him positively evil, among them Cecil King and Lord Reith. Malcolm Muggeridge who was fascinated by him said, 'I feel sure he was someone who'd sold his soul to the devil.' Cripps said, 'The way Beaverbrook turned his bright young men into drunkards was done out of sheer sadism.' (I saw only one man who was destroyed by too much success, and too much drink, too soon; I think he had a self-destruct mechanism in him anyway.) Harold Macmillan gave a fairer verdict, saying Beaverbrook had a streak of vindictiveness and even cruelty. 'But he was equally capable of extraordinary kindness. While I served him and until the end of his life I received from him nothing but kindness. Perhaps I was fortunate but that was my experience.' Beaverbrook was also a foul-weather friend. If anyone of his friends or of the staff known to him was in difficulties and asked for help, his response was immediate.

The reverse side was the fury with which he responded to any personal slight, occasionally leading to vendettas of the most unpleasant kind. The worst of these concerned Mountbatten. I could never understand the origin of his dislike of Lord Louis, which was shown by repeated harping on the failure of the Dieppe raid at a time when Mountbatten was chief of Combined Operations. Even in 1958 he was directing his son to print statements in the *Daily Express* saying, 'DON'T TRUST MOUNTBATTEN IN ANY PUBLIC CAPACITY'. Sometimes Beaverbrook suggested the pro-blem lay in the British withdrawal from India at a time when Mountbatten was Viceroy and deeply involved in the final nego-tiations. But his daughter, Janet Kidd, reports, 'By far the most likely reason for their feud was that Father found a stack of passionate love letters Lord Louis had written to Jean Norton [Beaverbrook's long-time mistress].' That was the dark side of Beaverbrook's character, and it is the principal blot on his record as a newspaper publisher.

But unlike most other major publishers this century Beaverbrook was not in the business primarily to make money. In January 1948 he sent a message to E. J. Robertson:

> I don't care whether you make money or not. All I want to see, Mr Robertson, is a great newspaper, strong in reserves and so completely and absolutely set up in finance that no other newspaper can ever challenge us. Even after you and I have laid down our task, Mr Robertson.

Yet it was only thirteen years after his death that Beaverbrook Newspapers was in such heavy debt and facing so many financial problems that a take-over of some kind seemed the only solution. After frantic negotiations with a variety of interested tycoons who included Rupert Murdoch, Lord Rothermere, Sir James Goldsmith and Victor Matthews (later Lord Matthews), deputy chairman of Trafalgar House, Sir Max Aitken obtained the agreement of the board and a majority of the trustees (who held the final power) to sell the group for £14.6 million to Trafalgar House. Sir Max, who had suffered several minor strokes and was far from well, had certainly endorsed a number of management errors, notably a very expensive replanting programme, and the editorial direction of the *Daily Express* had been extremely uncertain, symbolised by a dazzling kaleidoscope of changing editors and editorial strategies. 'The *Daily Express* is the milch cow that feeds us all,' Beaverbrook said to me once. 'If it falters for one minute, instant action must be taken.' The trouble was that too many instant decisions were taken, only to be reversed with equal speed. Soon it was the *Sunday Express* that became the milch cow under the implacable editorship of John Junor who was knighted in 1980.

Unhappily for Sir Max, his father had left him an inheritance that was rotten at its roots, the production base. The Beaverbrook doctrine of high wages had been carried too far. As a politician Beaverbrook was a conciliator, a fixer, a go-between. He preferred peace to war, compromise to conflict. It was just the same in Fleet Street. Cecil King wrote:

For seven years I was chairman of the NPA and for many years before that had been a member of the council representing my newspaper. The perennial problem before the London newspaper publishers was uneconomically high wages and massive over-manning. As the print unions always acted together, the only way the proprietors could hope to stand up to them was to stand together also. But whatever pledges were made or undertakings signed, when the crunch came it was the *Express* that broke the united front. At an earlier stage in the history of the *Express* Beaverbrook calculated that he could afford to meet the extravagant demands of the unions while his rivals could not, but of course in the end the *Express* finances were as embarrassed as everyone else.[19]

Cecil King is not an altogether impartial witness. At one time he said that if he saw Beaverbrook approaching his house, he would set the dog on him. My own impression is that whichever newspaper group felt strongest, or sometimes the weakest, was likely to make its own deal. Nonetheless the indictment is relevant to the plight of the group after Beaverbrook's death.

There was another difficulty. Beaverbrook had resisted his son's earnest efforts to get into commercial television, so his group depended almost entirely on the newspapers for its profits. If newspapers hit a bad patch there was no other area of the business to support the core. Beaverbrook himself had always been able to rely, in the last resort, on his own fortune to support his British newspaper enterprise. At one stage he drew at least £2,000,000 from Canada to help him with the launch of the *Sunday Express*. But by the time of his death his Canadian fortune was being used to support his many charitable activities there, mainly connected with the University of New Brunswick, and on his death was absorbed into his Canadian Foundation. In Britain his voting shares in the company were given to the two Beaverbrook Foundations with the twin objects of preserving control from death duties and ensuring that the basic policies of the group remained unchanged. Other family legacies meant that there were no hidden reserves. Sir Max was quite wealthy, but one of his principal assets was the block of voting shares he owned himself (and for which he eventually received £1,200,000). There was no escape.

As Sir Max left the *Express* building after the sale to Trafalgar House he was asked what would his father be saying if he was still alive? 'I think he would have sold up long before,' he replied.[20] He may have been right about his father in old age when the writing of books seemed almost as fascinating as running newspapers. But a Beaverbrook in his forties or fifties would never have got there in the first place.

Notes:
1. The essential source on Beaverbrook's life is of course A. J. P. Taylor's *Beaverbrook*, Hamish Hamilton, 1972. A labour of genuine love, it is perhaps elaborately defensive at times, but it is brilliantly written with complete mastery of the voluminous documentation available. There are innumerable sidelights on Beaverbrook in many volumes of reminiscences and biography. Apart from authors already quoted I particularly recommend Hugh Cudlipp's *Walking on the Water*, Bodley Head, 1976, James Cameron's *Points of Departure* (2nd edition), Oriel Press, 1978, and *The Beaverbrook I Knew*, edited by Logan Gourlay, Quartet Books, 1984. For a close-up of Beaverbrook in the last three years of his life there is nothing to beat *A Little Nut-Brown Man* by C. M. Vines, his former secretary, Leslie Frewin, 1968. But his daughter Janet Kidd's *The Beaverbrook Girl*, Collins, 1987, is the most intimate, revealing and affectionate of them all.
2. *Pressures on the Press, An editor looks at Fleet Street*, André Deutsch, 1972.
3. From *Innocent Men* by Peter Howard, Heinemann, 1941. (Earlier Peter Howard had been co-author with Frank Owen and Michael Foot of the anti-Munich pamphlet, *Guilty Men*.)
4. The policy had been launched by Joseph Chamberlain in 1903. It was hoped that the Empire countries would reciprocate. Of course the tax on foreign goods really meant foreign food stuffs; hence the attacks on 'food taxes' or, as Northcliffe called them, 'stomach taxes'.
5. Sanders to Balfour, 10th November 1911, Balfour papers quoted in Koss, op cit.
6. Quoted by Lord Moran in *Churchill, The Struggle for Survival*, Constable, 1966. Camrose was saying that it was 'a tragedy' Beaverbrook had been Churchill's first visitor after his stroke in June 1953.
7. Sir Thomas Dugdale, later Lord Crathorne, quoted in Collin Brooks's Diary. See Koss, op cit.
8. For a full description of what actually happened and why Beaverbrook may have concocted his story, see A. J. P. Taylor, op cit, pages 121–127.
9. *Sunflower* by Rebecca West, with an illuminating Afterword by Victoria Glendinning, Virago Press, 1986.
10. Private information.

11. The complicated, and lucrative, financial aspects of the deal are clearly set out in a Penguin Special on *The Press* by Wickham Steed, 1938.
12. From *Strange Street*, by Beverley Baxter, Hutchinson, 1936.
13. In *Debts of Honour*.
14. *My Lord George Diary*, op cit.
15. *Headlines All My Life* by Arthur Christiansen, Heinemann, 1961.
16. They were republished in one volume by Collins, 1960.
17. First published by Hutchinson in 1956, later republished by Collins.
18. Robertson had promised his wife to take her on a cruise to Australia, where he was due to preside over a meeting of the Commonwealth Press Union. Before leaving he needed an operation to remove a kidney stone. He went straight from his office to the hospital as he did not wish to miss the boat. He had the stroke while doctors were operating. He then lived for five years, unable to speak.
19. From 'The Evil Adventurer' by Cecil King in Logan Gourlay, op cit.
20. Quoted in *The Fall of the House of Beaverbrook*, by Lewis Chester and Jonathan Fenby, André Deutsch, 1979.

6

The Prudent Prince of Publishers

Take care of the pence and the pounds will take care of themselves
William Lowndes

On New Year's Day 1964 Roy Thomson, the barber's son from Toronto, attained his long proclaimed ambition: the Honours List revealed that he had become a peer of the realm. He was probably worth at least £100 million with television companies, radio stations, newspapers, magazines, printers, book publishers and travel companies scattered over the globe. (His oil interests came later.) At the age of sixty-nine he still arrived every day at eight forty-five am in his new Snowdon-designed office at the *Sunday Times*. But next day he was late; it was unheard of. He was still not there at nine forty-five am. His secretaries were getting worried. Finally he bustled in shortly after ten. He had been queuing in the street at Burberry's sale and was delighted that he had bought a £75 cashmere overcoat for £40. He told his staff that anyone who didn't buy at a discount or the sales needed his head examined.[1]

Thomson, with his habitual honesty, admitted that he was 'rather stingy'. But the stories of his continued frugality are almost mind-boggling. Summoned from Scotland by Lord Kemsley for an urgent interview he and his managing director took an overnight train to London. They arrived in time for breakfast before the meeting. But instead of going to the Savoy Hotel where they had rooms booked. Thomson led his managing director to a lorry-drivers' cafe in Covent Garden where he was evidently regarded as a regular; they had an excellent breakfast for 3s 6d. Then Thomson went on to see Kemsley who asked £15 million for all his papers.

Four years later Thomson bought Thomas Nelson, the Edinburgh publishers. He was ready to pay £2,600,000 but Gordon Brunton (now Sir Gordon), who had joined the organisation from Odhams,

106

persuaded him the business was worth only £1,750,000 and that was the figure finally agreed. So Brunton had saved him £850,000.* 'I'll buy you supper for that,' said Thomson – they had soup, spaghetti with meat balls and tinned fruit salad at a local caff. Thomson later reported gleefully that it was Brunton who paid the bill of 11s 4d.

Thomson also economised on travel. He flew Economy Class across the Atlantic. To save petrol and the driver's overtime he frequently travelled to and from his home in Buckinghamshire by Underground with the office Rolls for the journey between Gray's Inn Road and King's Cross. The fact is he hated to spend money, particularly on himself. For instance, one visitor to his home found him gazing myopically – he was very short sighted and wore pebble spectacles – at a tiny television screen. Asked why he didn't buy a set with a decent sized screen, Thomson explained, 'But the Japanese *gave* this to me. It's free.' His suits were notoriously shiny; for a date with royalty a visit to the cleaners was enough.

Later it was well known in his office that where money *had* to be spent, the boss frequently preferred to be left in ignorance of the details. Eric Cheadle (now Sir Eric), as deputy managing director of the Thomson Organisation, organised the magnificent banquet at the Dorchester Hotel that Thomson gave to celebrate Lord Beaverbrook's eighty-fifth birthday. There were 658 guests, lavish food and drink, Mounties especially flown in from Canada and a forty-five foot panoramic picture of Beaverbrook's birthplace. The cost was enormous, but Cheadle never told Thomson how much it was, and Thomson never asked. Brunton had a major row with Thomson soon after his appointment; it was about salaries and pensions. He told Thomson there had to be higher salaries and a pension scheme. Then he suddenly saw a side of Thomson he had never seen before. 'NO!' said Thomson. 'I don't believe in them. We don't have them in Canada. People should pay for their own pensions from their salaries.' Brunton replied, 'Not on the salaries you're paying.' But Thomson was adamant; he would not change his mind.

Next morning Brunton's buzzer sounded; Thomson wanted to see him. He had been thinking over what Brunton had said. 'You're right,' said Thomson. 'Do what's necessary, but don't tell me what it costs.' And the subject was never mentioned again.

Again while Thomson would watch the overall editorial budget

* There is some dispute about the exact amount saved; Thomson's own book puts it at £600,000.

he preferred not to hear the details. 'It hurts me to find out,' he said. 'These writers get paid so damned much, I'd rather not know.' Harry Evans, the editor of the *Sunday Times*, was never known for tight financial controls, but one morning in Florida having breakfast with Thomson he was roundly 'roasted', not for spending a fortune on some big feature, but for buying both the *Wall Street Journal* and the *Miami Herald* to read over breakfast.

If Thomson's thriftiness in later years sometimes seemed a little too extreme, it all stemmed from the bitter experiences of his twenties and thirties. Twice his business had failed. 'I don't like spending money,' he told his Scottish friends, the Stevensons, 'I've been hungry.' His father was an amiable but not very successful barber who had a slight weakness for drink; his mother had worked in a hotel owned by her aunt. There had never been much money at home. But Roy was determined to make plenty; when he was only seventeen he told friends that he would be worth a million dollars by the time he was thirty. He started work first as a clerk and then as a salesman, impressing his employer enough to get the job of branch manager. Amazingly, when he was twenty-five and had saved $15,000, he decided he wanted to be a farmer and bought more than 600 acres in Saskatchewan. It look less than a year to convince him that it was all a terrible mistake. He sold up without too heavy a loss and went back to Toronto where he and his brother Carl decided to invest their money in a business selling and distributing spare parts for motor cars. It was apparently doing well, reaching an annual turnover of some $70,000 in 1924, when the gap between getting paid by garages and having to make prompt payments to suppliers suddenly threatened bankruptcy. The partners were just able to avoid the worst, but Thomson decided to leave the Toronto business in the care of his brother and brother-in-law and to start up in Ottawa, 200 miles to the east. His new firm was slow to get going and he accepted a franchise to sell radios. There seemed to be a limit to the potential of the business and so he took the advice of the radio manufacturer to go north, to a small town called North Bay on Lake Nipissing, Ontario. It was bitterly cold during the winter, and the Thomsons were living in a wooden frame house which had no central heating. Thomson was now thirty-five and very far from being a millionaire. But he was popular; he was a tremendous salesman; he never stopped working; and he never lost the belief that he would be rich one day.

There was however a distinct difficulty about selling radio sets in

Northern Ontario. The big depression had started, and, even worse, radio reception was terrible. Roy Thomson then produced the simple idea that was to lead to riches: he would start his own radio station in North Bay. He had no licence, no money, no premises, no equipment and no staff. He found that a local lumber and paper company had the licence; they let him have it for a year at the cost of a dollar, and if the company did not want it back after that year it was his. He persuaded the local theatre to let him have backstage space for his studio in return for free advertising slots. He bought a second-hand transmitter for $500, to be paid in three months, and two $80 valves on the same basis. He borrowed an ingenious engineer, one Jack Barnaby, to make everything work (which Barnaby did with the aid of jam jars, electric irons, chicken wire and a mighty gift for improvisation). After seeing what Barnaby could do Thomson persuaded him to quit his $45-a-week job in Toronto and accept $25 a week (which he didn't always get on the due date) in North Bay. Meanwhile Thomson was out selling time, at five dollars a spot. He badly needed the money because he reckoned that he owed something like $30,000.

In March 1931, after a grand Inaugural Dinner, Station CFCH went on air. The broadcast material was pretty amateur, with music from the local record shop in exchange for free 'spots', local choirs singing for free, weather forecasts produced by the announcer looking out of the window, news received from Toronto in morse and then decoded. But the station kept on air until the generator broke down. Then Thomson went to the Nova Scotia Bank and raised a $1,000 loan to buy a new and more powerful transmitter. He still asserted he would soon be a millionaire, even in a newspaper interview. His wife Edna, with a growing family, was in despair. 'What a crazy thing to say,' she said. 'We can't even pay for the milk.'

But Thomson was just beginning. With the help of Barnaby and another bank loan he opened up a second radio station, this time in Timmins, a gold mining town some 200 miles to the north-east of North Bay. The programmes were equally unpolished, the staff equally lucky to get paid on time, but it kept going. The next station was at Kirkland Lake, 200 miles to the north of North Bay, but only fifty miles from Timmins. Here Thomson was able to find the financial backing from Kirkland Lake itself and the station was soon on air.

Meanwhile Thomson had bought his first newspaper. It was the *Citizen* of Timmins, which happened to be housed in the basement of the building where he rented his broadcasting studio. The price was $6,000 – but Thomson only put down $200 with the rest paid at the rate of $200 over twenty-eight months. It was another transaction on credit. Thomson had always been fascinated by newspapers, even buying as many as he could find on his New York honeymoon and spreading them out in the bedroom. He soon moved to expand the business; he renamed the paper *The Press*, turned it into a daily, and bought new machinery. Finance was partly provided by local citizens and partly by another bank loan, this time from the Dominion Bank, as the Nova Scotia Bank did not believe he could make the paper pay. Then he leased a fourth radio station at Stratford, between Detroit and Toronto, again with borrowed money. He was soon able to sell that station at a good profit, thanks largely to the work of Jack Kent Cooke who, for a time, became Thomson's closest friend and partner. Cooke was a tremendous salesman and a fantastic radio manager; he was also such good company that Thomson saw even less of his wife and family than before. Thomson and Cooke became partners on a two shares (for Thomson) to one (for Cooke) basis and prospered considerably. In fact by 1944 Thomson was out of his financial difficulties and asked virtually any fellow publisher he met whether he was interested in selling. He had picked up four more newspapers in Southern Ontario for around $850,000, with a bank loan of $375,000 and a mortgage from the vendors for the rest. As usual he was paying his staff minimum salaries, but at least they were now paid regularly. If anyone wanted a rise they had to go elsewhere to get it. Then after the war he got the offer of two more newspapers; to buy them he needed another loan of $750,000, but this time the Bank of Nova Scotia refused, pointing out that he already owed them $500,000. Thomson crossed the road to the Royal Bank of Canada which, after looking at his books, gave him the money and took over the existing loan from the other bank. Then, with professional help, he went to the public and raised a million dollars in debentures.

Thomson went on buying and borrowing, improving the titles he had bought, raising the profitability of his radio stations and gradually becoming a much better known figure in Canada. But between 1949 and 1953 three events occurred which led him to leave Canada and start afresh in England. First his close buddy, Jack Kent Cooke, made a big deal for himself in which Thomson had no part. Thomson was stunned; he felt totally betrayed by his best friend, and the partnership, after dragging on for a while, was dissolved. But there were no more visits to burlesque theatres and baseball games, no more private jokes, a lot less fun all round. Then his long-suffering wife, who had never lost her faith in his ability, but saw her husband completely wrapped up in his business and felt he could at least ease up as they had enough money now, died of cancer. Only then did Thomson realise how important she was in his life, even though she had never played any public role. 'At such a time a man realises what he has suffered and neglected while he went in blinkers about his business,' Thomson wrote years later in his autobiography. Finally Thomson stood for the Federal Parliament as a Progressive Conservative, fought a good campaign, hinting that he might be of use in the Finance Ministry, and was defeated largely owing to the unpopularity of the Conservative leader, George Drew. It was significant that he would not order any of his newspapers, even the local one, to support his candidature.

During the campaign Thomson had received a letter from Scotland in answer to one of the many flies he had cast, 'Do you want to sell?' A share in *The Scotsman* was available. If he had won the election he could never have taken it up. As it was he felt a degree of disenchantment with Canada, and a degree of ambition to own a newspaper that was more than the sixteen very local dailies he had collected in Canada. So he flew to Edinburgh where two of his executives had been looking at the books for several days. It emerged that his ancestral ties with Scotland – his great-great-grandfather, a master-carpenter, had emigrated to Canada from Dumfriesshire in 1773 – were important in persuading the owning family to consider him as a buyer; Sassenachs had been ruled right out. The company, which owned the loss-making *Edinburgh Evening Dispatch* as well as *The Scotsman*, had an overdraft of £500,000 and was losing money. But in 1953 Thomson agreed to pay £393,750 for eighty per cent of the ordinary shares, while two Edinburgh insurance companies put in £150,000 for preference shares. Thomson's money once again came from a Canadian bank loan. (Thomson shrewdly made the president of the bank, also of Scots ancestry, a director of *The Scotsman*.) He also agreed to move to Edinburgh, leaving his son Kenneth in charge of the business in Canada, and never to sell *The Scotsman* to an Englishman. At the last moment Thomson, for the first time in his life, suffered 'grave doubts about the step I was planning to take'. He left the negotiators and took a walk down Princes Street. Finally he decided to go ahead. Soon he was jubilant. Travelling round Edinburgh (naturally by tram – the fare was only

2d) he realised the company had far more property than it needed and that could be sold to pay off the debts. He told friends in Canada that while his deal valued the company at only £775,000 the property alone was worth £1 million. To move the company into profit was more difficult. The staff were opposed to change. The editors were opposed to change. The people of Edinburgh said they did not want change.

None the less, changes there had to be if the losses were to be cut. Not all of them were successful at first. Thomson picked the wrong editor, from the pop end of Fleet Street, for the *Edinburgh Evening Dispatch*; he picked the wrong publisher from Canada; and he cut back the staff which, while necessary, made him even more unpopular. But he persisted: the editor of the evening paper found his contract was not renewed; the editor of *The Scotsman*, whose hostility to Thomson had been unremitting, eventually fell ill and had to retire. Thomson's new appointments were much better; he persuaded James Coltart from Beaverbrook's Scottish office to join him as managing director and Coltart persuaded Alastair Dunnett, then with a Kemsley paper in Glasgow, to edit *The Scotsman*. Coltart became Thomson's closest colleague in Britain; he liked figuring out balance sheets as much as Thomson, he was trustworthy, and his wife, too, had just died of cancer. He was also a fervent supporter of Moral Rearmament but that didn't worry Thomson who regarded it as an irrelevance. Dunnett proved a brilliant editor and the paper began to make progress at once, particularly when the small ads were removed from the front page and replaced by news. (With a typical salesman's touch Thomson gave a series of lunches, starting at the Festival Hall in London, to announce the change and to herald the growing importance of Scotland. He was never stingy where necessary publicity was concerned.)

But Thomson was not popular in Edinburgh society. Although people liked his frankness and his lack of pretension, he wore the wrong clothes – double-breasted blue suits with red socks and brown shoes; he drank the wrong drink – orange juice, not Scotch; he had the wrong attitude to fishing – if he wasn't *certain* to catch salmon, he saw no point in trying; he hired the wrong driver, a German whose wife acted as his housekeeper and cook; and of course he was thought to be wrong when he sold the property he didn't need. Thomson's one society friend was Sir Edward Stevenson, Queen's Keeper of the Purse in Scotland; but the snobs even sneered at that. And his somewhat patronising attitude to Britain was wrong too, in

Beaverbrook, here in his 40s, arrives in the United States. He was enjoying social life as much as political intrigue. His attitude was reflected in his remark about novelist Arnold Bennett, 'How I loved my Arnold, and how he loved my champagne!'

RIGHT Churchill and Beaverbrook on HMS *Prince of Wales* off Newfoundland for the signing of the Atlantic charter. Beaverbrook's influence as an international go-between was at its highest.

Beaverbrook, flanked by his son, Max Aitken, is greeted by his host Lord Thomson at his 85th birthday dinner. His speech concluded, 'It is time for me to become an apprentice again. I have not settled in which direction. But somewhere, sometime soon.' He died a fortnight later.

LEFT Lord Thomson starts the presses rolling in January 1962 for the first issue of the *Sunday Times* colour magazine. When he saw it, he said, 'My God! This is going to be a disaster.'

Hugh Cudlipp (left) and Cecil King at an IPC shareholders' meeting shortly after Cudlipp had secretly organised King's dismissal from the chairmanship. They had formed a great publishing partnership until King became convinced that the Wilson government was ruining Britain.

Lord Matthews toasts the birth of his baby, the *Daily Star*, in February 1978. He preferred to give the over-manned Express group more work rather than hand out redundancy notices; but it was an expensive decision.

Jocelyn Stevens in 1978 when he was managing director of Express Newspapers. His advice was decisive in persuading Sir Max Aitken to sell to Trafalgar House. Later Trafalgar fired him. Sometimes unpredictable he was immense fun to work with. The author remains his devoted fan.

the eyes of the snobs and the nobs. 'There must be something wrong in this country,' he was quoted as saying, 'when a fellow like me can make so much money so quick.'

It is therefore not so surprising that when Thomson, who believed that newspapers and television should profit from each other just as years earlier he had believed in the synergy between local newspapers and local radio, sought support for his bid to secure the franchise for Scottish television, he found few ready to invest even modest sums of money. Of course the London companies, which had begun on a fairly extravagant basis, were losing money, but Thomson was convinced from his Canadian background that it was only a matter of time and sensible housekeeping before the profits began rolling in. He did his best to persuade the leaders of Scottish society to join him in the enterprise but it was very tough going. In his book Thomson happily listed some of the people he approached; they ranged from dukes and earls to MPs and businessmen. The few who were ready to gamble included Lord Balfour of Inchrye who was ready to invest £10,000 but in the event was asked for only £2,000; two thirds of that sum was debenture money which was soon repaid. The happy peer was left with about £650 in ordinary shares which were worth nearly £150,000 when the company went public. Jimmie Logan, a Scottish comedian, was ready to subscribe £1,000 but was only asked for £400; after repayment of £300 debentures his £100 worth of ordinary shares multiplied to £22,000. Quite a good joke at the expense of the dukes. Sir Edward Stevenson was in for £2,400, with Thomson's bank ready to stand by him with the money if needed. Since the prudent Scots were so reluctant to support the venture far more equity than expected – some eighty per cent – was left in Thomson's own hands.

Thomson then began setting up Scottish Television for transmission. He took over the Theatre Royal, Glasgow, from Howard and Wyndhams, one of his backers, for £105,000. In a tough negotiation with Lew Grade and Val Parnell he beat down the price of the networked programmes he needed. He cut his accountant's spending budget in two. He was enraged at the labour demands of the unions, vastly in excess of real needs, crying, 'It can't take three Britons to do the work of one American.' And he protested furiously that a lunch-time quintet was being used when one Wurlitzer organ would have saved four fees each day. Told that none could be found, he had one shipped from Canada to make his point. Aided by an upturn in advertising, he was soon able to tell *Time* magazine that his

Scottish television station was 'just like having a licence to print your own money'. His own book put an exact figure on it: 'During the eight years we had an eighty per cent holding in Scottish Television until ITA forced us to reduce our holding first to fifty-five per cent and then to twenty-five per cent, our share of the company profits ran to £13 million.'

Meanwhile this extraordinary man had his eye on a higher prize: he wanted a peerage. A few years earlier he had confided in at least one Canadian friend that he wanted a knighthood, and that with *The Scotsman* he might get it. Under the guidance of Alastair Dunnett he had been giving some money to well chosen charitable projects in Scotland and his public image had been improving. He was now well known for his candour and quotability. He could no longer be dismissed as 'a little guy, owns a lot of little newspapers', as Beaverbrook once said.

Privately he was the same as ever: a simple man, courageous, totally honest, pretty insensitive, driven by a mixture of pride, acquisitive self-interest and perhaps a desire for public recognition of what he had achieved starting from nowhere. With his thick glasses, shambling gait and shiny suits, he never pretended to be grander than he was, introducing himself everywhere as, 'The name's Thomson. Call me Roy.' At home, if he was not entertaining, he could be quite lonely at the weekends. He devoured paperbacks – Westerns and thrillers – signing them when he'd finished so he wouldn't waste time reading them again. Lunch might be just a ham salad washed down with a glass of water. Economy began at home. He really couldn't wait to get back to work. He was ready to ask advice on the simplest questions of etiquette: how to address a bishop, what whisky to serve, what to call people with Scottish titles. There was always one area where he needed no advice and that was figuring. The *Dictionary of National Biography*[2] described him as 'a self taught genius with a balance sheet, who could discern trends, strengths and potential weaknesses within seconds'.

He was not a saint. His biographer, obviously writing with Thomson's full approval, says of his Timmins days that he was 'strangely careless, indeed alarmingly frank, about his own occasional and brief affairs with local women'. And however distinguished the company, he liked to gather a group of men together and regale them with what a fellow guest described politely as 'men's room humour'.[3] (Frank Giles who was deputy editor of the *Sunday Times* during

Thomson's regime said he had three typed collections of jokes, 'tellable in any company, slightly risqué and downright filthy'.⁴)

The real breakthrough for Thomson came with that sudden telephone call from Kemsley. Only seven weeks earlier Kemsley had asked a ludicrous price for one of his Scottish papers. Now, amazingly, Kemsley himself came on the line to ask Thomson to get down to London in a hurry, and once there had offered to sell him the whole Kemsley group, including the *Sunday Times*, for what amounted to £15 million. When Thomson said he couldn't afford that kind of money Kemsley indicated that the merchant bankers could find a way, and almost hurried him out of the office.

The merchant bankers were up to the challenge. The key to their solution was found first in persuading Kemsley to drop the price of his million shares to £5 million and then to arrange a reverse takeover whereby Kemsley's first bought Scottish Television, paying with 2 million shares, plus £1 million and £500,000 debentures. Then a new class of shares was created with a thirty per cent dividend guaranteed which raised the value of each share from around £2 to £5. With Kemsley's shares Thomson then had a total of three million shares and hence voting control. All he needed was one more loan, this time of £3 million. He got it from the National Commercial Bank of Scotland. And so Thomson became the owner of three national Sundays, thirteen provincial dailies, several weeklies and a provincial Sunday. He became by this masterpiece of negotiation, carried out in the utmost secrecy, one of the biggest newspaper owners in the country.

When he finally took over he first asked for the executive salary list and then he asked who had company cars. The salaries shook him, but he was particularly surprised to find that all the Berry directors had Rolls-Royces with their own chauffeurs and, sometimes, other cars for their families as well. That soon stopped. And although he had agreed to keep the Berrys as directors for another two years they soon resigned when they discovered that their responsibilities had been taken over by an executive board chaired by Coltart. Few other executives left for although Thomson felt the firm had been 'too benevolently run' he realised that in general the editorial and management staffs Kemsley had recruited were 'excellent' and the paper on the whole was in a sound condition.

A nasty shock was coming. Michael Berry, Kemsley's nephew, whose *Telegraph* presses had been printing the *Sunday Times* (after all it had been a Berry family business for thirty years) gave six months' notice to terminate the contract, clearly with the aim of starting his own Sunday paper. There was no way in which the *Sunday Times* could install presses to print itself in that length of time. But with that failure of managerial acumen which foreshadowed later difficulties for the *Telegraph*, Berry's lawyers had failed to spot that the contract had been amended by his uncle to allow twelve months' notice. The difference was crucial and was extended a further four weeks by delays in the *Telegraph* office in acknowledging the existence of the supplemental agreement. As a result, when the contract finally came to its end, the *Sunday Times* was able to continue printing at Gray's Inn Road without interruption, and Michael Berry was often to rue the day that he had started his own Sunday paper. He was however right to realise that Thomson would eventually withdraw from the contract since the *Telegraph* presses were limited to forty-eight page issues and that was not enough for the expanding requirements of the *Sunday Times*.

Thomson's next big move forward was the launching of the *Sunday Times* colour magazine. Beaverbrook had nourished a similar plan for the *Sunday Express*, but the economics for a free magazine with a print run of more than 4,000,000 did not seem to make sense at that time. Thomson knew that Sunday supplements paid off in Canada and thought something similar but perhaps a little less garish would make profits in Britain. There were trade unions to placate, newsagents to appease, staff to be recruited, advertisers to woo. When the first magazine emerged in February 1962 Thomson was appalled and cried, 'My God! This is going to be a disaster.'[5] It was indeed a paltry and disappointing production, unworthy of its brilliant editor Mark Boxer, savaged by the other publishers (led by Lord Beaverbrook) and without much support from advertisers. Once again Thomson showed his courage; he would not contemplate closure. It is true that the magazine had increased the sales of the *Sunday Times* considerably, but the losses were piling up and eventually reached nearly £1 million. Something was needed to give it a push. The marketing department came up with a bright idea after a brainstorming session in a riverside pub: a tycoons' trip to Moscow. Thomson gave them a week to find out if it was practicable, and they were lucky to find enthusiastic support from Intourist. The trip proved an amazing success, culminating in an invitation for Thomson to meet Khrushchev which resulted in worldwide exposure of Khrushchev's desire for détente and equally worldwide exposure for the *Sunday Times* colour magazine. Any idea that Thomson might close the magazine was finally squashed. It was a success from then on. The magazine established a brilliant style of its own, subsequently much imitated. Advertising picked up at once *and* – even better from Thomson's viewpoint – the visit had been free. Intourist picked up the hotel bill, and the Aeroflot flight was covered by a couple of contra pages in the magazine.

The one professional disappointment in Thomson's life at this time, apart from the lack of a peerage (and after he had taken British citizenship that came through on the recommendation of Harold Macmillan to his successor, Sir Alec Douglas-Home), was that he did not own a national daily. He told John Freeman on a *Face to Face* interview that he owned a total of ninety-five newspapers and forty-two magazines world-wide, and that some forty newspapers were in Britain. But there was no national daily. He had considered taking over the *News Chronicle* as we have seen, but the cost of funding pensions and making provision for redundancies in the possible event of failure was too much. He had been invited to merge with Odhams which would have given him control of the *Daily Herald* as well as *The People*, but the deal had been frustrated by a heavy take-over bid from Cecil King of the Mirror group. He had also suggested to the second Lord Rothermere that he would be glad to take over the *Daily Mail* should the Harmsworths wish to relinquish control; nothing came of that either.

The big prize was, of course, *The Times*. The paper was clearly in trouble. Circulation was static; advertising was thin; management was inert. The *Telegraph* was forging ahead. Thomson himself had delicately sounded out Lord Astor, the principal proprietor of *The Times* (he had bought the shares on Northcliffe's death) who was living in tax exile in the South of France. Denis Hamilton, Thomson's ambitious editorial chief, had suggested a merger to Gavin Astor and to other *Times* executives. There was only a negative response.[6] Then *The Times* attempted to save itself with an ill-judged campaign aimed at 'Top People'; the circulation went up, but not enough to allow an increase in advertising rates. Now the merchant banker advising *The Times*, Sir Kenneth Keith, indicated that they were ready to talk. Sir William Haley, chief executive and editor of *The Times*, believed the paper needed an injection of at least £4 million, and Cecil King had told *Times* executives that Thomson was the only man who could save them.

The scheme eventually put together was designed to safeguard the editorial independence of *The Times* and to ensure that any losses incurred fell solely on Thomson and his family. A new company, Times Newspapers, took over the *Sunday Times* and *The Times*. The Astors would retain a fifteen per cent holding in that company. A new board would have four Astor nominees and four Thomson nominees; there would be in addition four independent national directors whose approval was needed on any fundamental issues. Kenneth Thomson would become joint president and Denis Hamilton would be editor-in-chief and chief executive. It was a most extraordinary deal for, in effect, Thomson was guaranteeing the survival of *The Times* while accepting that he had virtually no control over its contents. Even so the government set up a Monopolies Commission enquiry which, after further explanations, cleared the merger with one dissentient.

Thomson had other commercial successes; he started Yellow Page telephone directories in Britain; he went into the package tour business; he launched the *Family Living* magazine for sale at check-out counters in supermarkets; and he made a highly profitable investment in North Sea oil. The strength of Thomson was revealed when the package tour business was in trouble. The company had gone into it, after careful study, because the organisation needed more profits to help with the re-equipment of some of their provincial plants and because they had unused marketing skills in the business. Everything worked out well at first; and then price-cutting began and Thomsons started to lose market share. Most of the board felt they should get out of it for the best price obtainable; Brunton did not. The problem went to Thomson who took two days to study the papers. Thomson's decision was absolutely clear: 'We're bloody well going to stick it and we're going to make a success of it . . . My gut feeling is that this is the way to do it.' Perhaps his one failure was an attempt to ring London with a string of profitable local newspapers, but that was the fault of union bickering, not of any lack of perception on his part. It is an astonishing record and belies Cecil King's savage remark that Thomson 'made a minus contribution to Britain. The only contribution Thomson has made is to his own bank account.'[7]

Apart from a very early foray into local politicking in Timmins Thomson never used his newspapers for political propaganda. In this respect he was the reverse of the traditional British press baron from Northcliffe to Matthews. It was in 1951, when his Canadian newspaper group was beginning to attract criticism for its constant expansion, that he bought space in the Toronto *Globe* to publish his editorial 'Creed' as a lengthy advertisement. Later he had the essential part of the Creed printed on a card which he always carried with him. It read:

> I can state with the utmost emphasis that no person or group can buy or influence editorial support from any newspaper in the Thomson group. Each paper may perceive this interest in its own way, and will do this without advice, counsel or guidance from the central office of the Thomson organisation.
>
> I do not believe that a newspaper can be run properly unless its editorial columns are run freely and independently by a highly skilled and dedicated professional journalist.
>
> This is and will continue to be my policy.

The original advertisement also included the statement. 'It has often been asked "Why does the Thomson company buy newspapers?" My answer to that is to say the business I know best is the publishing of newspapers.'

Since the Creed was published there was no known instance of Thomson breaching that undertaking. On the contrary there are many examples of how he honoured it. At the time he was being considered for the peerage he wanted so badly the *Sunday Times*, under the editorship of Harry Evans, quite frequently criticised the Conservative government of Harold Macmillan. Thomson wrote in his own book, 'The editor of the *Sunday Times* never heard a word of reproach from me; I would have bitten my tongue first.' Just when his hopes of a peerage were rising Macmillan resigned and the *Sunday Times* strongly attacked the choice of Sir Alec Douglas-Home to succeed him. Again he made no complaint. Harry Evans himself wrote later[8] that if Thomson was attacked over some policy advocated by one of his newspapers he would produce his card from his pocket and say, 'You wouldn't expect me to go back on my word, would ya?'

Of course if Thomson believed the editor was professionally below standard he was ready to sack him. He fired the editor of the *Edinburgh Evening Dispatch* and did not renew the contract of his successor. And it was not long after he took over the *Sunday Times* that H.V.Hodson was replaced by Denis Hamilton. But these moves did not jolt the principle of editorial freedom. John Freeman, in the celebrated *Face to Face* interview, tried to nail Thomson over editorial support for segregation in his Florida newspapers. Thomson was quite unperturbed. He said they didn't take a very good line. 'They reflect the communities in which they operate . . . It's as they see it, and I can't interfere with them.'

He was also splendidly robust if his newspapers were publicly attacked. When the *Sunday Times* was preparing its articles exposing the Philby scandal and Philby offered his own book to the *Sunday Times*, the Foreign Office were kept informed. George Brown, the Foreign Secretary, attended a dinner being given by Thomson for a group of visiting American businessmen and rounded on his host in quite brutal terms. 'It's about time you shut up,' he cried in his curious whine. 'Some of us think it is about time we stopped giving the Russians half a start on what we are doing, and, my dear Roy, I ask you and the *Sunday Times* to take this into account and for God's sake stop.' It says a lot about Thomson's character that he simply remarked to the Americans, 'We don't always take George very seriously and now you have a very good picture of the man who is Foreign Secretary of this great country.'[9]

The *Sunday Times* in particular flourished under his policy of benign neglect. Hamilton had recruited a brilliant staff during his period in the chair, and Harry Evans built on that foundation. Some of the campaigns and exposés run during that period have become classics of English journalism; among them, the thalidomide campaign to ensure adequate compensation for the victims, the exposure of the damage done by Philby over his many years as Russia's agent in the British secret service, and the long battle to pin down responsibility for the crash of the Turkish Airlines DC–10. Against this record few would now agree with the adverse verdict of an otherwise witty and discerning critic that 'Thomson's papers remain too inoffensive, too balanced. They are the journalistic equivalent of airline food'.[10]

Thomson regarded his editorial self-denial as the only practical way in which to run such a large and disparate group: it allowed him to concentrate on figuring and strategy. If he had been immersed in policy decisions he might not have had the time and energy to enter so many new and very profitable fields. But his doctrine never quite took root in this country. Prospective publishers find that playing around with editorial matters provides them with half their fun, and, of course, it may provide a quick route to a peerage as well.

Another aspect of the Thomson approach had much more lasting effects on British newspaper publishing. This was the introduction of transatlantic methods in the selling of classified advertising. The attitude of most advertising managers had been to wait for requests for space to come through; there was a little persuasion, but not too much. It was thought the existing customers would not like to be pressured. An American advertising consultant called George Pappas, summoned by Thomson to train his British staffs, soon changed all that. He hired large teams mainly of young girls and trained them to *sell* advertising; he coached them to canvass from prospective advertisers; he trained them on the appropriate sales pitch for each situation; he coached them to persuade advertisers to take bigger spaces by providing them with prompts which might make the advertisement seem more attractive; he encouraged series bookings with special discounts, such as five advertisements for the price of four; he encouraged them to persuade firms to regard appointment advertising as a form of corporate image building; and above all he encouraged a spirit of intense competition within each office, aided by special bonuses and other incentives. Some of the Thomson offices did not want to know, but they soon fell into line. The techniques were rapidly adopted elsewhere. I recall that when the *Evening Standard* appointed a Thomson-trained classified advertising manager called Colin Owen-Browne, the retiring manager forecast doom and disaster. In fact our classified advertising pages shot up from some two pages a day to sixteen or more and the profitability of our paper was transformed. The distressing aspect of the intense training and sales techniques employed was the strain on the staff, leading to exceptionally high turnover. But the results were phenomenal, and the long-term benefits particularly to quality newspapers were enormous. No doubt someone else would have introduced these methods sooner or later, but it took a Canadian, with comparative budget figures for his newspapers in the United Kingdom and Canada, to see what was needed and to take action. 'What he [Pappas] taught may ultimately have saved *The Times*,' wrote Thomson; 'it certainly saved several other papers throughout the country from going down.'

When Thomson had achieved so much, both personally and for the newspaper industry, it is bizarre to record that within a mere five years of his death the jewel in the splendid crown he had left to his son – Times Newspapers – had been sold off. What was the reason?

Thomson had left the organisation in excellent shape at the time of his death. Trading profits in the year after his death were the highest in the history of the company; the *Sunday Times* had made nearly £2 million; regional newspapers contributed £9.6 million; other publishing activities chipped in £8 million; the travel business produced £4.1 million. *The Times* had lost £900,000 which was an improvement of more than £600,000 but that did not appear in the Thomson Organisation accounts because they were met by the Thomson family. Thomson had never believed in confrontation with the unions. Back in 1932 when the installation of transmission equipment for his second radio station – in Timmins – was halted by the local electricians' union he agreed that a local electrician could accompany his two experts and be paid full union rates for doing nothing. Again, while he was appalled at union manning levels for Scottish Television he accepted them. He would bargain very hard with union leaders, but he worked with the unions and not to overthrow them. If anything he was too generous. In one negotiation to reduce manning he said, 'Well, let's work on the basis of a dollar for you, and a dollar for me.' After that concession the management kept him away from union leaders, who never forgot the remark which was constantly being quoted. The unions were therefore strongly entrenched in Times Newspapers when, on the advice of Denis Hamilton, then the chief executive as well as editor-in-chief, and Marmaduke Hussey, the managing director, he agreed that *The Times* should leave its home near Blackfriars and move next to the *Sunday Times* in Gray's Inn Road. On the surface the move had everything to commend it. The old site would be freed and a capital gain secured; the presses would be used full time; many services could be shared. Hamilton was also dreaming of developing *The Times* as a seven-day-a-week newspaper in the manner of the *New York Times*.

Unfortunately each newspaper deeply resented the change and many of the worst characteristics of each were transferred to the other. There was tremendous jealousy and dislike on both sides. The *Sunday Times* production men were paid very highly for short weekend shifts; *The Times* men wanted parity or as near as they could get to it. The *Sunday Times* editorial staff was very highly paid and rather arrogant. *The Times* editorial staff was underpaid but regarded themselves as superior; they resented the patronising manner of their colleagues. The clerical staffs were up in arms at the suggestion that libraries and other functions should be combined, leading to loss of jobs. The speed with which Gray's Inn Road had had to be equipped for full production when the *Telegraph* printing contract was terminated had led to a production line that was less than perfect; seven-day-a-week working meant that maintenance became even more of a problem. Add the fact that the organisation was known to be immensely wealthy from its oil and television interests and here was a situation that was quite ideal for union activists, of which Times Newspapers had its full quota.

Thomson had promised the Monopolies Commission that if the profits of the *Sunday Times* were not enough to cover losses on *The Times*, then he and his son would use their own money to make it up. But after Thomson's death in 1976 the mounting production hold-ups of the Sunday paper, often due to inter-union disputes in the press room, were cutting into profits and the new Thomson board decided on a showdown, leaving Times Newspapers executives headed by Marmaduke Hussey to handle the details. Unfortunately the objectives of the operation were too broad: the management was looking first for manning cuts, secondly for a new disciplinary procedure and thirdly for the acceptance of 'new' technology. It was too much to expect to get the lot in one negotiation, and Hussey, who enjoyed good relations with the national officers of the print unions, did not seem to realise the clout of the London branches and chapels. After the breakdown of negotiations Times Newspapers stopped publication, hoping to break union resistance. After an eleven-month stalemate and the loss of £46 million, for the building had to be maintained and many salaries paid, there had been an inconclusive deal and then massive production losses continued.[11]

To the utter dismay and chagrin of Denis Hamilton, no longer chief executive but still editor-in-chief, *The Times* journalists, led by a highly intelligent but somewhat ruthless left-winger called Jacob Ecclestone, went on strike in August 1980 (nine months after the resumption of publication) to press their claims for a twenty-one per cent pay rise. Hamilton subsequently claimed[12] that this strike, taken after they had been paid for eleven months during the stoppage, persuaded him to telephone Kenneth Thomson in Canada and urge him to get out of Times Newspapers. Since Hamilton had in effect been the keeper of the covenant, there can be no doubt that his advice carried weight. Indeed Lord Thomson of Fleet confirmed[13] that while the general intransigence of the unions was the 'key factor' in determining the family to walk away from Times Newspapers, the strike by the National Union of Journalists was 'the last straw and more than any other single development brought to a head our decision to sell'. Lord Thomson added, 'I was devastated that,

Thursday November 30 1978

No 60,472

Price fifteen pence

THE TIMES

Last-ditch Commons move to avert 'Times' suspension

As it became clear last night that this was likely to be the last edition of 'The Times' for some weeks, the Commons decided to hold an emergency debate today on the imminent suspension by the management of 'The Times', 'The Sunday Times' and the three supplements. Lord Thomson of Fleet, president of Times Newspapers, said there was no intention of closing permanently.

Ministers hold out little hope

LONDON: THURSDAY NOVEMBER 30 1978   8p

Evening News

BRITAIN'S BIGGEST EVENING SALE

LATE EXTRA

LORD THOMSON

We can't allow the papers to be slowly bled to death—Lord Thomson

THE TIMES NIGHTMARE

Evening STANDARD

MIDDAY

London. Thursday November 30, 1978
Price: Ten pence

Presses silent after issue No. 60,472

TIME RUNS OUT AT THE TIMES

The suspension of publication in November 1978 was intended to break union power, but the management muddled its tactics. After losses of nearly £50 million publication was resumed and so were the obstructive practices of the unions. Kenneth Thomson had had enough and soon sold out to Murdoch.

LONDON
TUESDAY
MAY 3 1966

THE TIMES

NO. 56,621

PRICE 6D.

✦✦✦ LONDON EDITION

London to be new H.Q. for Nato

Mr. Thomson to pursue talks with allies today

FROM OUR DIPLOMATIC CORRESPONDENT

London will be the new headquarters of the North Atlantic Treaty Organization. This is the firm conclusion of Nato experts directly concerned, although they emphasize that no final decision is likely to be announced until the spring meeting of the organization, which opens in Brussels on June 6.

This conclusion of the experts is based on a study of the possible alternatives and supported by some leaders of British Ministers most closely involved, notably Mr. Michael Stewart, the Foreign Secretary, and Mr. George Thomson, who was recently given responsibilities which make him in effect Minister for Europe and Nato.

The alternatives before Nato have throughout been limited to the United Kingdom or the Benelux countries, but neither the Netherlands nor Luxembourg has a suitable site to offer.

Tho has limited the choice to London or Brussels for conceivably. Antwerp, which has the advantage of being an American supply line to Germany. However, London is favoured as being much the better centre for air communications with the other Nato capitals.

There is already a communications system from London with the Supreme Allied Commander, North Atlantic, and through the Channel Command across the Channel, and in many ways London is said to be the most convenient centre.

MR. LODGE HAS TALKS WITH THE POPE

FROM OUR CORRESPONDENT

ROME, MAY 2

Mr. Henry Cabot Lodge, the United States ambassador to Vietnam, had a 45-minute meeting with the Pope today. The conversation, which was carried on in French without interpreters, is thought to have dealt with the efforts to end the war in Vietnam. No official statement was issued.

The Pope recently said that efforts were still being made by Vatican diplomatists to achieve peace in Vietnam and that such efforts would continue.

It is thought possible that the two men talked about the new Canadian proposal for negotiations. Mr. Lester Pearson, the Canadian Prime Minister, said today that a cease-fire should begin without preliminaries, and should be followed by a gradual and parallel withdrawal of North Vietnam and American troops while the two Vietnam Governments negotiated peace.

The withdrawal and subsequent elections would be supervised by an international group. Canada is a member of the Vietnam International Control Commission, with Poland and India.

WASHINGTON, May 2—Mr. Bill D.

First of visits

The Belgians, though prepared to offer a site, are not pressing their claims, and M. Harmel, the new Belgian Foreign Minister, is likely to make this clear when Mr. Thomson visits him in Brussels today—significantly this is the first of several visits which Mr. Thomson is to make to Nato capitals.

After this talk M. Harmel is expected to consult with his Benelux colleagues in the special committee which they set up between themselves after the French decision to withdraw from the Nato organization.

The relocation of the Council will be further discussed on Friday and Saturday when Signor Fanfani, the Italian Foreign Minister, visits London. Italy acts as rapporteur for the sub-committee of the Fourteen on relocation. The others (with their rapporteurs) are:—Military consequences of the French decision (United States). Reorganization (Britain).

MR. BROWN AT PRE-BUDGET CABINET

FROM OUR POLITICAL CORRESPONDENT

The Budget Cabinet meeting at 10 Downing Street yesterday lasted two hours and 15 minutes. Mr. Brown attended for the first time since he left hospital, and he led his colleagues know that he meant to plunge into work without delay.

The only Cabinet Ministers absent were Mr. Stewart, Foreign Secretary, who was in Strasbourg, and Mr. Greenwood, Minister of Overseas Development, who was in Stockholm.

There is no doubt that a decision in principle has been reached by the Cabinet on the findings of the Kindersley review body on doctors' and dentists' pay, but no date has been given for a Government announcement or for publication of the Kindersley report to the Prime Minister.

BRITISH MOVE ON

Mr. Callaghan, the Chancellor of the Exchequer, at work in his study at No. 11 Downing Street, yesterday. With him are Mr. G. Mackenzie, his Parliamentary Private Secretary (left), and Mr. P. Vinter, Third Secretary.

Labour M.P.s want better deal for coal

Minister umpire on rival claims

FROM OUR POLITICAL CORRESPONDENT

Behind-the-scenes pressures on Mr. Marsh, the new Minister of Power, to give the coal industry a more hopeful future within the Government's national plan are now going to be felt by Mr. Cledwyn Hughes, the new Secretary of State for Wales, and Mr. George Thomas, his Minister of State. After a meeting at the Commons the Welsh group of Labour M.P.s have invited both Welsh Ministers to face their questions and demands in a private discussion.

The pressure is also being brought to bear on Mr. Wilson and Mr. Brown in the Commons. Mr. Lee Abse, Labour M.P. for Pontypool, has put down a question asking for the creation of an interdepartmental committee of the Ministers of Power and Labour, the Board of Trade and the Welsh Office charged with the task of ensuring no pit

Marsh have many more millions of pounds a political commitment to coal would involve.

Looking ahead, the gas interests of course would like to be able to take advantage of any large-scale find of natural gas on the Continental shelf. But when the Ministry of Power ask how certain such a large-scale find may be the answer comes that there is no certainty yet to be had. Mr. Marsh and the Government in all their fuel policy planning are bedevilled by the familiar political problem of making fateful decisions where some of the essential factors can be only guessed at.

Costs Compared

Sir Henry Jones has categorically asserted that making gas from coal is

Strike by seamen to go on

The National Union of Seamen yesterday unanimously decided to support the executive council's decision to call a strike on May 16 over a pay and hours claim. Delegates stood and applauded the decision at the union's annual conference at Worthing.

Mr. F. B. Bolton, president of the Chamber of Shipping of the United Kingdom, said last night that the strike would be disastrous for the nation as well over 90 per cent in value of Britain's external trade goes by sea.

He added: "The effect on imports would be less immediately apparent, but nonetheless, devastating over a fairly short period, for a nation so dependent on imports, including the whole of our oil supplies."

Mr. Ford Geddes, chairman of the Shipping Federation, said: "The strike is a critical one for a country like Britain. It is to try to enforce demands that would cost 17 per cent. We have gone a long way to try to meet the demands of the N.U.S. It is out of the question to concede the claim in full."

Conference report, page 14.

12,000 WILL BE LAID OFF

COVENTRY, MAY 2

Twelve thousand workers employed by Standard Triumph International in Coventry, Birmingham, and Liverpool will be laid off tomorrow because unofficial strikes by 60 Coventry machinists have stopped supplies of cylinder heads and blocks. Three factories in Coventry will close tomorrow and only about half the 9,300 people laid off will be able to restart on Wednesday.

The strikers, who caused 6,500 to be laid off for two days last week, are in dispute over piecework prices and did not work on Friday and today.

The company said that provided they restarted tomorrow it would meet the trade unions on Thursday.

DEATH SENTENCE ON BRADBURY

FROM OUR CORRESPONDENT

JOHANNESBURG, MAY 2

Lawrence Bradbury, 33-year-old British immigrant, was sentenced to death today at the Rand Criminal Sessions for the murder of Mr. Thomas Waldeck, a wealthy mining prospector.

BIG DOLLARS SALE BY BRITAIN

$83m. U.S. oil shares released

From Our City Editor

The British Government have agreed to sell a further $83m. (£29,700,000) of the official portfolio of dollar securities, which in March stood at £180m. after the Treasury had liquefied a large portion in order to bolster sterling area reserves. The proceeds, though, will not be reflected in the gold and foreign currency figures to be published today.

The Ham Oil and Chemical Corporation has agreed to buy 1,242,824 shares held by the Government in the Amerada Petroleum Corporation, one of the larger domestic oil producers in the United States. It is not known whether this block, representing nearly a tenth of the issued capital outstanding, is the full extent of the British official interest.

Taking Friday's closing price on the New York stock exchange, $66¼, the transaction would be worth over $83m. Since it has been rumoured for some time that the British Government had a substantial stake in the corporation, tending to depress the price, the shares quickly rose on the news to $72¼.

Amerada's main interests are in the United States, but there are others in Venezuela, Libya and Canada. The group has an explorative company in the United Kingdom.

Print inquiry by Ld. Cameron

From Our Labour Staff

Lord Cameron, the Scottish Lord of Sessions, is to be chairman of an inquiry into the problems associated with the introduction of web-offset printing techniques. The inquiry has been set up by Mr. Gunter, Minister of Labour, and as well as looking at general problems it will also inquire into disputes at Southwark Offset Ltd., London, and the Co-operative Press, Manchester.

Talks continued throughout yesterday in an unsuccessful attempt to find a solution to the manning problems at Southwark Offset. Because of the dispute the £2,250,000 plant was closed last Friday and 350 employees were dismissed. The talks will be resumed today.

THE TIMES WEDNESDAY MAY 11 1977

UNIQUE RECORD IN THE TIMES

MOMENTOUS EVENTS OF NEARLY 200 YEARS

THE THUNDERER IN THE MAKING

Compiled by Eric MacHardy

Today's issue of The Times is the 60,000th since publication began in 1785.

During the intervening span of nearly 200 years the momentous events in Britain and abroad have been recorded day by day, and fortnight leading articles, which earned the paper the title of The Thunderer, have denounced injustice and incompetence. The files provide a unique record of a period crowded with dramatic moments of history.

To mark the occasion selections from the files are reprinted here in the vertical style of the Bill page familiar to readers from 1932 to the late 'sixties.

STORMING OF THE BASTILLE

FEROCITY OF PARIS MOBS

Monday, July 20, 1789.—Rebellion and civil war in France. The disputes which have for some time past convulsed this neighbouring kingdom have at length been brought to a crisis which no man could have foreseen or supposed.

The minutes of what Paris has been doing for some days are truly horrid, and have turned the...

EXECUTION OF LOUIS XVI

EFFORT TO SEIZE BODY

Thursday, January 2, 1793. Paris, Sunday noon.—Yesterday the drum was beaten throughout the several sections ordering the citizens to signify there wishes for the death of Louis XVI. The drum was followed by a great number of horse and foot...

DEATH OF NELSON IN BATTLE

FRENCH FLEET DESTROYED

GLORIOUS VICTORY AT TRAFALGAR

London, Thursday, November 7, 1805.—The London Gazette Extraordinary, Wednesday, November 6. Dispatches, of which the following are copies, have been received at the Admiralty this day at one o'clock a.m. from Vice-Admiral Collingwood, Commander in Chief of his Majesty's ships and vessels off Cadiz.

The Waggoners, a picture taken on February 18, 1931, at Ribbesbroough, Kent, by a staff photographer. It was published as a half-page in The Times and is typical of the pictures which appeared daily on the back page at that time.

NAPOLEON ROUTED AT WATERLOO

ARMY FLEES IN CONFUSION

'GREATEST' SCOOP OF ALL

INITIATIVE BY THE TIMES

TREATY OF BERLIN

THE PANIC AT BULL'S RUN

GRAND ARMY BURLESQUE

PRESIDENT LINCOLN SHOT

ASSASSINATED IN THEATRE

REBEL CONSPIRACY

THE TIMES WEDNESDAY MAY 11 1977

CHANGES AT TURN OF CENTURY

BRITAIN'S DOMINATING NAVAL POWER

DEMAND FOR POLITICAL RIGHTS

At the turn of the century Britain emerged from the Victorian era a dominating naval power with a vast empire. Exciting scientific discoveries and inventions promised great industrial progress, and a growing awareness by the people of their rights brought demands for social and political advancement.

BLUNDERS OF THE CRIMEA

SICKNESS AND HARDSHIP

HAUNTING SCENE

GOSPEL OF HATE BY LENIN

BOLSHEVISM'S WIDE IMPACT

FIRST ATOMIC BOMB ON JAPAN

HIROSHIMA ATTACKED

"RAIN OF RUIN"

RALLYING CALL TO BRITAIN

BLOOD, TOIL AND TEARS

MAN STEPS ON THE MOON

GIANT LEAP BY MANKIND

A WATCHING WORLD

After prolonged debate *The Times* finally succumbed to front-page news in May 1966, and ran a campaign that it was the 'Top People's' paper. Circulation rose but so did losses. Three months later discussions opened with Roy Thomson. As one of the world's newspapers of record it had every reason to celebrate its 60,000th issue in May 1977.

having supported the journalists throughout the whole period of suspension, the journalists would strike the newspapers. That was the final discouragement.'

Times Newspapers had lost £72 million since Thomson took over *The Times* and there seemed no prospect of any adequate return on the investment of so much money and effort. At his father's wish Kenneth Thomson had for long been in charge of the Canadian and American organisation. He was married to a Canadian and preferred living there. While devoted to his father and anxious to carry on with Times Newspapers he clearly felt there was a limit to the money and time he should spend on such a fruitless task. His father had seen the publication of *The Times* as a privilege and an honour; the son could see it only as an affliction and a penance.

Towards the end of his life Thomson confided to his biographer that he had only two loves in his life – 'my family and my business'. He went on, 'If I *had* to choose between the two ... well, I don't know, I'd probably choose my business, because my family can now look after itself.' So he might have approved of his son's decision, but it is still shocking that a prize he fought so hard to get was sold so soon in acrimony and dismay. The blame must lie primarily with the senior management of *The Times* – Denis Hamilton for the move of *The Times* to Gray's Inn Road and Marmaduke Hussey for mishandling the negotiations with the unions – but also with those union leaders who were too blind to realise that they were digging their own grave. Thomson had left a rich and powerful organisation which continued to prosper but the jewel in his crown was soon adorning the head of a very different character indeed.

Notes:
  1. The story is told in *Lord Thomson of Fleet*, by Russell Braddon, Collins, 1965. This remarkable biography, written with Lord Thomson's full co-operation and with the help of his family and friends, is *the* essential source for Lord Thomson's life and business deals. It is supplemented by Lord Thomson's own partial autobiography, *After I Was Sixty*, Hamish Hamilton, 1975 – a typically frank account of his outstanding business record in Britain including the take-over of *The Times* which represented the summit of his achievement.
  2. The *Dictionary of National Biography*, 1970–80. Thomson's entry was written by R. A. Denniston and Denis Hamilton.
  3. Private information.
  4. Frank Giles gives an enjoyable portrait of Thomson in his engaging book of reminiscences, *Sundry Times*, John Murray, 1986. He was

rather shocked that in China when Thomson was introducing his party which included his son, then aged forty-nine, he would add, 'and this is my son Ken, who doesn't do anything'.

5. See Godfrey Smith's obituary notice of Mark Boxer in the *Sunday Times*, 25th July 1988.
6. In 1966 the *Financial Times* had also suggested a merger. Haley, the editor of *The Times*, accepted the idea that he should be chairman of the new combined paper. The *FT* would have been the predominant force with Gordon Newton of the *FT* in the editor's chair, but *The Times* title would have been retained. However the merger terms were unacceptable to the Astors; they would have accepted 12.5 per cent of the new paper. Pearsons, owners of the *FT*, wouldn't go over 8.25 per cent, the figure recommended by their financial advisers. Some of the Pearsons board were cool on the idea. The story is clearly told in *The Financial Crisis* by David Kynaston, Viking, 1988.
7. Report in the Toronto *Daily Star* 5th November, 1956.
8. *Good Times, Bad Times* by Harold Evans, Weidenfeld, 1983.
9. See *The Pearl of Days*, by Harold Hobson, Leonard Russell and Phillip Knightley, Hamish Hamilton. 1972.
10. *The Life and Death of the Press Barons* by Piers Brendon, Secker and Warburg, 1982.
11. The whole dreadful story is brilliantly and dispassionately told by Eric Jacobs in *Stop Press*, André Deutsch, 1980.
12. In a conversation with the author.
13. In a letter to the author dated 17th June, 1988.

7

The Man who would be King

The hope I dreamed of was a dream,
Was but a dream; and now I wake,
Exceeding comfortless . . .
Christina Rossetti, 'Mirage'

Cecil Harmsworth King[1] was a boss of bosses. As chairman of the
International Publishing Corporation, in 1968 he controlled the
publication of some 300 titles every year including such national
newspapers as the *Daily Mirror* and the new IPC *Sun*, formerly the
Daily Herald, together with best-selling women's magazines such as
Woman, with its circulation of 3,300,000, and *Women's Own* not far
behind. There was a large book division which incorporated the
recently acquired Hamlyn Publishing, and there was a vast printing
division with some twenty plants scattered over Southern England.
There was a substantial shareholding in Associated Television and
twenty-eight per cent of Reed Paper which gave effective control.
There were 28,000 employees and the company was among the top
twenty business corporations in the country.

King was aloof, autocratic, intelligent and vain. Some members
of the board had become increasingly disenchanted with the strident
vendetta he was conducting against the Labour premier, Harold
Wilson. After all, the *Mirror* newspapers were meant to support the
Labour party and yet week after week they sought to undermine the
leader's position. Other members of the board were more concerned
that their chairman was so obsessed with exercising the political
clout of the *Mirror* that he was neglecting the urgent task of knocking
the vast conglomerate into slimmer, more efficient shape, and without his authority they couldn't get on with the job themselves.

It was the more political group, led by the deputy chairman of
four years' standing, Hugh Cudlipp (now Lord Cudlipp), and Ellis
Birk (whose wife Alma had three times been a Labour candidate
and had just been ennobled by Harold Wilson), which took the

initiative. Ellis Birk was the goad, Cudlipp the organiser. Under the company's articles of association the chairman could be removed by a majority vote, but the agreement of *every* other member of the board was needed to remove a single director. There were two technocrat directors who had been rapidly promoted under the aegis of King – one was Frank Rogers, the managing director later knighted, and the other was Don Ryder (later Lord Ryder), managing director of the Reed Paper group, who had been appointed to the board by Cecil King despite misgivings by other directors. Further, Paul Hamlyn, the largest shareholder in the company whose publishing firm had been acquired for £2,250,000 four years earlier, had only joined the board at that time. It was not certain how any of these three would react to the suggestion that King should be forced off the board.

The first and crucial move was to ascertain the views of the managing director. Without his agreement – and he was seen as one of 'King's men' – the coup was impossible. Frank Rogers was in Kyoto, Japan, attending a newspaper conference. On returning to his hotel one day in May he was handed a grubby piece of paper with a handwritten message asking him to ring 'Mr Pickling' as soon as possible at a Glasgow number. This 'Mr Pickling' was Edward Pickering, who, on leaving Express Newspapers, was employed by Cudlipp and was now a director of IPC. When Rogers got through to Glasgow Pickering at once turned the call over to Hugh Cudlipp. The question was broached immediately: would Rogers support a move to oust King from the chair?

Earlier in the year Rogers had convened a three-day conference of his executives at the Carlton Tower to consider where IPC should be heading over the next five years. King had spoken to the group one evening after dinner, rather badly reading out a script which seemed entirely new to him, and interjecting 'whatever that means' after two particularly obscure sentences. In the question-and-answer session afterwards, his comments had appeared quite out of sympathy with what the rest of the group were trying to do. Further, Rogers and some of his colleagues had been attempting to persuade the chairman to rationalise some parts of the company; they felt there were too many companies with their own directors; there was too much money wasted; there was an urgent need for reorganisation and more modern methods of management. Yet they felt that whenever they attempted to raise these matters they were treated to another long monologue on the iniquities of the Wilson administration, the subject which by was then obsessing their chairman. And the financial results due to be announced shortly were worrying. So Rogers, despite his affection and respect for King, was ready to join the firing squad and told Cudlipp so accordingly. A few days later, immediately after his return from Japan, he invited Cudlipp to dinner and the plot advanced.

Later in the week a meeting of directors (apart from the chairman) was held at the registered office of the company in Orbit House, Holborn Circus, while Cecil King and his wife Dame Ruth were supping peacefully and unsuspecting on the ninth floor of the *Mirror* building opposite. The arguments were now well rehearsed, but was there unanimity? Each director was asked to speak in turn. Frank Rogers was the first. But it was Paul Hamlyn, who owed least to King, who fought the hardest to save him. He was not a company man; he had built up his own business before being 'seduced' by King who had told him, 'I want you, not your company'. As a result of the take-over of his company that followed he owned ten times as many IPC shares as all the other directors put together, which gave him a certain independence. He was not impressed by the calibre of the people King had picked. 'Too many were second-rate people he felt safe with and as the company became enlarged they were incapable of running it,' was his judgment years later.[2] Hamlyn had been summoned back from Australia where he was drumming up business for the publishing division; after a thirty-six hour flight he was exhausted but he did not like what was being done to the man he 'adored'. He tried to persuade Ryder to join him, but Ryder refused; perhaps he had his own ambitions. In the end Hamlyn, who had been appalled by a visit paid by King to Mosley in Paris in pursuit of his ambition to form a national government, succumbed to the united pressure of the other directors. 'I felt pretty ashamed,' he admitted later. So he put his name to the letter which invited King to resign on grounds of age and stated that the directors felt that 'your increasing preoccupation and intervention in national affairs in a personal sense rather than a more objective publishing sense has created a situation . . . which is detrimental to the present and future conduct of the business of IPC'. The crunch came in the terse statement, 'It has been decided that you should retire immediately as chairman.' The letter informed King that Cudlipp had been elected chairman. A formal request for his resignation, signed by all the directors, was enclosed. The unanimity of the document made it ineluctable.

The following morning at eight fifteen am when King was shaving in the bathroom of his lovely Wren-designed house on the banks of the Thames at Hampton Court, a worried company secretary rang the front-door bell and delivered the letter. King came down to read it in his dressing gown. Some eighty minutes later he was in his commodious office at the *Mirror* building. He sat at an octagonal writing desk made up of two antique tables in a room comfortably furnished with Chippendale armchairs, an oak-panelled sideboard, bookshelves with rare books on Africa and, on the floor, expensive rugs and an Iranian prayer mat. The coal fire, installed at considerable expense in the modern office building, was unlit.

King buzzed Cudlipp on the intercom and said, 'I understand you wish to see me.' A few minutes late Cudlipp, Ryder and Rogers assembled in his office. The atmosphere was tense and frosty. It was again suggested that King should resign. He refused, saying it would look 'as if he had been caught with his hand in the till'. Rogers said that all his colleagues held him in esteem and affection. They had done what they thought was right for the company and its shareholders. King remarked that it was a odd way of showing it. Ryder said, 'This is in no way a revolt led by Hugh against you.' King replied, 'I think we have had enough insincerity for one morning', and suggested he should leave in two or three months. The directors withdrew to consider the suggestion but they knew very well that if King was around for another two months he would work to divide the board and would succeed. After all most of them were terrified of him. They wrote to say that it was the unanimous view of the directors that the original letter 'could not be revoked or altered in any way', and that an announcement would be made later that day.

King rang his son Francis, who was a director of Fleetway, a magazine subsidiary of IPC, and told him 'I want you to be the first to know I've been sacked.' Francis said he was very sorry but asked, courageously, was his father really surprised? 'Why do you say that?' King asked. Francis explained that as his father had chosen to resign from the board of the Bank of England owing to his involvement in political activity it was not altogether surprising if the directors of a public company also felt it was inappropriate for their chairman to be so heavily involved in a political campaign. 'They never told me that,' said King.

King was not going to allow the board the satisfaction of breaking the news and telephoned ITN and the BBC which interrupted the afternoon's racing to put out a news flash. Soon he was being interviewed. 'Fleet Street is a bit of a jungle,' he said. 'It's not played like an old-fashioned minuet, is it?' (He must have recalled an earlier reference to the jungle: 'Fleet Street is a jungle,' he had said. 'I shall survive. A man of my ability will keep his head above water.'[3]) Of course he was in a good position to know since he had given his predecessor Harry Guy Bartholomew (better known as 'Bart') exactly the same treatment seventeen years before. But the manner of his dismissal rankled severely. 'On no single occasion has any director expressed any dissatisfaction with my conduct in the chair . . . The thing was just a conspiracy of a particularly squalid kind . . . if they called a board meeting and had said to my face they wanted a new chairman, there was nothing I could do except accept the position.' In fact he had to accept the position anyway but unlike Bart he did not find solace in a bottle of whisky shared with a doorman, he retreated with all guns blazing.

Later only one director went to see him in an office Ryder had given him in Reed House: it was Paul Hamlyn. Cecil King swivelled his chair round so that his back faced his visitor and said nothing. Hamlyn stood there for nearly an hour and finally said, 'Look, Cecil, this is as difficult for me as it is for you.' Their friendship was resumed.[2]

The day after King's dismissal IPC cut its dividend from twenty-one per cent to eighteen per cent. Profits had fallen from £14 million to £9.4 million. The printing business was losing £2 million; the launch of Cudlipp's *Sun*, an ill-fated attempt to transform the TUC-ridden *Daily Herald* into a profit-making middle-market paper, had cost £1.75 million. Refusal by the Prices and Incomes Board to sanction a price increase by the *Mirror* had proved costly, while devaluation had considerably increased the cost of newsprint. The *Financial Times* commented, 'IPC has proved an unrewarding investment over the last five years. At 17s 6d it stands in line with its 1963 peak though the shares have been as high as 22s 6d in the meantime.' For a Harmsworth it was a mortifying conclusion to a brilliant newspaper career.

By his own account King had a really miserable childhood. His father, married to Geraldine, Northcliffe's sister, had achieved reasonable distinction in the Indian Civil Service and on retirement became Professor of Oriental Languages at Trinity College, Dublin. Rothermere, working through Beaverbrook to Lloyd George, obtained a knighthood for him as a favour to Geraldine. He was short-tempered, throwing a leg of mutton out of the window when he didn't like it; he showed no interest in his children; and, according to his son, had been totally squashed and 'devitalised' by his wife.

Geraldine was a monster. Cecil King wrote many years later, 'I have never been sure in my own mind whether at bottom she was an evil woman determined to destroy me, or a violent and selfish woman quite indifferent to the threat she presented to a very sensitive, emotional child.' He harped on his mother's behaviour, saying that he knew she would destroy him if he let her. There was some pent-up violence in her. Sometimes she would beat him with a walking stick, and then come to the bathroom later to inspect the weals. But Geraldine suffered two dreadful sorrows during the war: one son was killed at Ypres and the youngest boy was drowned crossing the Irish Sea on his way to school after his boat was torpedoed. The death of Luke, her first son, shattered Geraldine and drove her nearly insane with grief. Cecil had to be with her every hour. But he had to conceal his true thoughts, learn not to develop any emotional feelings for his mother, learn, he wrote, 'to be invisible'. King had to endure two other harsh blows; his childhood sweetheart died of a brain tumour at the age of fifteen, and his sister died in the post-war flu epidemic.

He read voraciously, particularly the classic novelists, Thackeray, Dickens, Jane Austen, Scott, and thus developed a wide general knowledge. But Winchester was a torment. 'I hated almost every day of my time at Winchester,' he wrote. When life at home was such a fierce strain it was 'the last straw' to suffer life at a boarding school where conformism reigned and it was almost impossible to be alone. He also found he had such a towering temper that unless he learnt to control it he was likely to kill someone. He learnt.

When he was seventeen he was back in Ireland and the scenes of violence during the Easter Rebellion made a deep impression on him. He wrote fifty years later that he was then cured of 'the comfortable feeling so prevalent in England to this day that riot and commotion, let alone civil war, could not happen here'. Matters improved when he went to Oxford. That was bliss because of the privacy he could secure by 'sporting his oak'.

The senior uncles were already taking an interest in his career; naturally that meant the family business – newspapers. Even while he was still at Oxford Northcliffe ordained that he should do a stint as a reporter on the *Daily Mail*. Later he had a short spell on *The Times*, attending the leader-writers' conference. Then, when

Northcliffe's health failed, Rothermere took a hand and sent him off to to the Glasgow *Record* where, over a ten-month period, he worked in every department. then it was back to the *Mail* where he fetched up in the promotions department. He learnt two things there. From Sir Andrew Caird, the managing director whom King described as 'a mean penny-pinching Scotsman', he saw that cutting out extravagance could 'cut the heart out of a newspaper'. (Beaverbrook once rebuked me for saying that some proposed overseas project would cost a lot of money, 'You can't run a good newspaper without extravagance, Mr Win*tour*.' It was the same message and it still holds good.) And when Uncle Alfred died he saw how much the whole group depended on his drive and inspiration. Uncle Harold, for all his business sense and family feeling, simply lacked the touch.

When King was twenty-six Uncle Harold made him a director of the Empire Paper Mills, sent him round the world and then pushed him into the *Daily Mirror* as assistant advertisement manager. At that time Rothermere owned some eighty per cent of the Daily Mirror and Sunday Pictorial companies which themselves held seventy per cent of the Daily Mail Trust. King was therefore the highly privileged nephew of the boss whose own two sons had been killed in the war – a blow from which Rothermere never quite recovered. Three years later, in 1929, 'after much importuning,' wrote King, he was made a director of the Mirror company. His speedy promotion was not popular with his colleagues and, although a director, he was not shown the financial figures. (He persuaded the company secretary to let him have them on the quiet.) Rothermere had appointed a nonentity called John Cowley as chairman. Cowley at one time had been a £1-a-week cashier at the *Evening News* and had made himself useful to Rothermere; indeed King says that he would do anything that Rothermere told him to do, 'however foolish or dishonest'.

At this time Rothermere was immensely wealthy, but he was not really interested in newspapers apart from the money they could make and the influence they commanded (before the days of television and radio). As a result the *Mirror* was not well managed. The true circulation figure was at least 200,000 less than the million sale which was claimed and it was going down at a dangerous rate – 70,000 a year. There was no advertising staff and no budget for advertising sales. It was now that Cecil King began to show his quality as a newspaper manager. Although the youngest he was much the ablest member of the board and he initiated a number of editorial moves which transformed the *Mirror* from being a rather second-rate right-wing tabloid to supremacy in its market as a brash left-wing radical anti-establishment newspaper which enjoyed a particularly close rapport with its predominantly working-class audience.

First he secured the departure of a cricket-loving editor – a former schoolmaster and county cap – called Brownlee. Then he formed an alliance with Bart, an unpleasant, uneducated but brilliantly creative tabloid journalist who became editorial director of the *Daily Mirror*, while a man called Cecil Thomas did the chores as editor. For his pains Thomas was bashed over his head with an eight-foot balsa wood plank by the intolerable Bart, who had at one time been manager of the *Mirror* process department. Bart liked spying on his colleagues, opened their letters and listened to their telephone calls. He was a petty tyrant of the worst kind, firing people for no reason and insisting on ludicrous measures of secrecy about his plans. But he gave the paper sledge-hammer headlines in type one inch deep, brilliant pictures and strips, short punchy stories, but more important still, vitality, heart, toughness and an instinctive affinity with the reader. It is impossible to overrate Bart's creative contribution to the revival of the *Daily Mirror*.

King's next major achievement was to appoint Hugh Cudlipp, later his principal ally and later still his principal executioner, as assistant features editor. (Cudlipp had been working on the *Sunday Chronicle* but applied for the *Mirror* job because Kemsley himself would not allow the editor to offer him more than a ten-shilling rise; he would have stayed for a sovereign.) While King supplied political guidance, Bart stoked up the furnace and Cudlipp, soon promoted to be features editor, introduced 'Live Letters', plenty of controversy and a breathless daily column by the young Godfrey Winn. 'We were the first newspaper to deal frankly with the subject of birth control,' King wrote later, 'and the first to publish pictures of curvaceous ladies in bathing dresses.' That was daring enough for those days.

Rothermere himself made two typical contributions. In 1934 he was going through a Fascist phase and wrote an article for the *Mirror* which urged readers to 'Give the Blackshirts a helping hand' and provided addresses where they could join up. (King and Bartholomew, for all their anti-establishment views, went along with the proprietorial edict, apparently without protest.) The following year, taking his usual despairing view of the outlook, Rothermere sold to the public virtually all the Daily Mail Trust's shares in the Mirror and Pictorial companies as well as his personal shareholding. John Cowley remained chairman and everything appeared to continue as before; but the two papers were in reality no longer under proprietorial control. King was the only blood-related link to the Harmsworth uncles who, mostly titled, were now aiming at respectability, however ineffectually, and disliked the rumbustious paper which had contributed substantially to their fortunes. And so did his mother.

The *Sunday Pictorial* was the next problem. Its circulation had dropped from more than 2,400,000 in the mid–1920s to less than 1,400,000 in 1937. Under pressure from King, chairman John Cowley agreed to offer Bart the editorship of the *Pictorial*, but Bart was so insulting to him that he wouldn't do it. So King became editorial director and offered Cudlipp the editorship. Bart was first incredulous that Cudlipp should accept and then furious. He had informed King that he would do his best to 'ruin' any member of his staff who accepted a job on the *Pictorial*, and after Cudlipp's appointment barred King, a director of the company, from the editorial floor of the *Mirror*. But the *Pictorial* began to pick up at once. The circulation rose by 400,000 over the next three years.

On Saturday nights King took Cudlipp off to the Martinez Restaurant in Swallow Street where they shared a couple of bottles of claret and gradually developed a friendship which became, for a time, the most formidable partnership in Fleet Street. The repressed, intelligent and solitary figure of King found in Hugh Cudlipp, an ebullient, highly talented and self-confident Welshman, some key to a normal relationship. Indeed Cudlipp claims to have 'introduced King to the human race'.

Some people had little respect for King. The Wykehamist Cabinet Minister Dick Crossman said, he was 'a great big beefy rather silly fellow who lives in Chelsea, is a Wykehamist but is otherwise insignificant'. Hugh Gaitskell, the Wykehamist Labour party leader, was more astute. He described him in conversation as an 'unlikely combination of Northcliffe and a Wykehamist . . . very able but . . . very isolated[4]'. The isolation was very real and was partly due to shyness. (Once at a film premiere Hamlyn, who was sitting quite close to King, tried to speak to him several times; King stared straight ahead. Next day Hamlyn asked if he had offended King in some way; why hadn't he responded? King replied, 'I couldn't say *anything*.* The isolation was also due to King's genuine feeling that he was rather a superior person. But in his early days with the company he tried to convey a sense of humility and, while his views were of the Left, he did not attempt to throw the political weight of the newspapers around as his uncles had done. Some believed that his first wife, Margot, a daughter of the Regius Professor of Divinity at Oxford, urged him to keep out of politics. But his tongue could be blistering. Apart from contemptuous assessments of most of his fellow publishers he never saw any need to be polite to bores or boors. One evening he was sitting next to the wife of a former colonial governor. She held forth at length on the iniquities of the press and eventually wound up saying, 'All newspaper publishers are crooks.' King replied tersely, 'All governors' wives are tarts.'

Unlike his Uncle Harold, King professed that he was not interested in the possession of money at any time. His rich uncles had shown him that wealth guaranteed neither happiness nor security. All the same, he had excellent taste in antiques and left more than £1 million when he died.

As the influence of his first wife waned his egotism waxed. His autobiography contains these statements:

> I have a greater gift of foresight than anyone I have met ... My judgment is very good and over a wide range ... some have thought me the best talker in London ... I am regarded by my colleagues as a master of timing ... The fact that I am a good judge of people has helped me enormously in my career, and partly explains why I am such a good administrator.

King would have regarded such boastful self-assessment as a completely objective account of his talents, and the fact is that until the last few years of his reign at IPC he had a lot to boast about. Frank Rogers, now chairman of EMAP, the highly successful media group, has told me that in his experience King's judgment was superb. Chosen to take over the management of the group's Nigerian interests, Rogers was given a complete briefing by King on how to handle a rather tricky situation; he followed his instructions carefully

* On another occasion Hamlyn was entertaining Allen Lane, founder of Penguin Books, in the directors' dining room and asked King to look in. King arrived and stood in silence. Lane, to break the silence, looked out of the window and said, 'Isn't that St Paul's?' King agreed that it was, and again lapsed into silence. There was no further attempt at conversation.

THE DAILY MIRROR, Friday, December 11, 1936.

Daily Mirror

No. 10306   Registered at the G.P.O. as a newspaper.   ONE PENNY

LATE LONDON

EDWARD VIII'S RADIO FAREWELL TO-NIGHT

THE NEW KING ARRIVES IN HIS CAPITAL

London Cheers George VI

Edward VIII will broadcast to the Empire and the world to-night as Mr. Edward Windsor, a "private individual owing allegiance to the new King."

This will follow the signing of his abdication papers and the succession to the Throne of his brother, the Duke of York, who will be 41 on Monday.

The time has been fixed tentatively for 10 p.m. During the evening Edward VIII is expected to leave the country.

THE capital welcomed its new King — who will reign as George VI—for the first time just before midnight when he arrived back at his home at 145, Piccadilly, after dining with his brother at Fort Belvedere.

A crowd of 20,000 which had waited for hours burst into wild and prolonged cheering.

The King's arrival was so sudden that his car was caught up in the home-going theatre traffic.

Two taxis barred his entrance into his home, and though hundreds of police struggled wildly, they could not keep the surging crowd back.

People ran shouting round the royal car waving their hands, hats and handkerchiefs in the King's face.

Tired and Pale

He sat well back in his car, looking tired and pale. Obviously he was moved by the tremendous demonstration and he smiled wanly and bowed once or twice.

After being held up for quite five minutes in the crowd the car edged its way into the courtyard.

When the King stepped from the car there was more tremendous cheering. By this time the crowd was quite out of hand and swept right up to the railings of the house.

Further police were rushed to the scene and they helped to restore order.

After the King had gone indoors the great multitude stood outside and sang the National Anthem and 'For He's a Jolly Good

(Continued on back page)

Britain's new King, the Duke of York, arriving home at 145, Piccadilly, last night, after dining at Fort Belvedere with his brother. Huge crowds gave the new Monarch a great welcome to his capital. (See back page).

Picture pages are 8, 12, 14, 16, 17, 19 and 28.

The *Daily Mirror* appeared to cover the Abdication as well as anyone, but the editor was in the dark about what was going on behind the scenes. Cecil King decided that he must become better informed. His growing interest in politics led ultimately to his downfall.

and as a result made a considerable success of the enterprise; his success there formed the basis of a glittering career in publishing. On questions of 'foresight' King's record is perhaps less convincing. In his 1966 Granada lecture on 'The Future of the Press' King stated, 'One deduces from Dr Abrams's* findings (into newspaper reading booklists) that popular newspapers will follow their present course of becoming increasingly intelligent and less ideological.' He had not foreseen what damage the less intelligent and more ideological *Sun* would do to the *Mirror* in the next decade.

King's good judgment was of little value to a popular paper unless someone was able to light the fireworks with pictures and text. In Bart and Cudlipp he had two real explosives experts. It was Bart who was the first to show a picture of Mrs Simpson at the time of the abdication crisis under the headline:

THE KING WANTS TO
MARRY MRS SIMPSON:
CABINET ADVISES 'NO'

It was typical of the stranglehold the old guard still held on the *Daily Mirror* that Bart kept the story out of the paper until not only Cowley, the chairman, but Cowley's son had left the building. But while Beaverbrook and Rothermere's son, Esmond, were advising the King and other newspapers were in close touch with Number 10, the Mirror newspapers were left reading agency copy. King 'vowed never to be caught in the dark of some crisis like this ever again.' That was sensible enough until he decided to take a hand at creating his own crises.

During the war King played a somewhat equivocal role in the Mirror group's battles with the authorities. When Churchill became Prime Minister he was deeply irritated by any attacks on his conduct of the war and his selection of Cabinet Ministers; indeed he grew to regard the *Mirror*'s criticisms as subversive and malicious. Of course the criticisms of the 'brass hats' and 'dope survivors' was one reason (apart from the strip cartoons of Jane) why the paper was so popular with the troops. But for Churchill, leading the country's ruthless battle for survival, they proved almost unbearable pinpricks. In June 1940 Cecil King had gone to see Churchill at Number 10. (Churchill had been writing for the *Sunday Pictorial* before the war.)

* Dr Mark Abrams was a leading market reseach expert. His findings were influential at IPC.

He knew that Churchill was irritated by calls that Chamberlain should resign from the government and, according to his own diary, said, 'I had come to find out exactly what he did want us to do'. It was an odd approach for a supposedly highly independent newspaper publisher. Churchill gave a long explanation of his reasons for keeping Chamberlain in the Cabinet and indicated that this was not a time for political bickering. That meeting passed off peacefully. But in October Cudlipp wrote in the *Sunday Pictorial* that Churchill had written in his book *The World Crisis* that in wartime decisions must be clear-cut and ruthless. 'Churchill you have warned yourself,' Cudlipp concluded. Combined with criticisms of Home Secretary Sir John Anderson, the muddle at Dakar and continuing attacks on some members of the recently reshuffled Cabinet, this brought about an official threat of compulsory censorship covering both news *and* views. First a delegation from the Newspaper Proprietors' Association was summoned to see Attlee and warned accordingly. Then the principal offenders, in the shape of King and Bart, called on Attlee, the deputy Prime Minister, to hear the details from him. They found him in a Whitehall air raid shelter and quite unable to produce specific examples of what the Cabinet did not like. 'Obviously,' said King after the meeting, 'we shall pipe down for a few weeks.'

Further exchanges followed. Churchill's personal private secretary wrote to King complaining about one 'offensive' and 'inaccurate' story in the Cassandra column written by William Connor (later knighted) and another which he found 'dominated by malevolence'. After King's reply, in which he explained that the first story had been described as 'apocryphal' and that the aim of the other was simply to bring younger men into the Cabinet, Churchill wrote back at length to say he found 'a spirit of hatred and malice against the government' in the columns of the two newspapers, and he believed this could in the long run encourage 'naked defeatism'. King answered, '. . . if you consider we have gone beyond what should be permissible in wartime we should, of course, meet your wishes in so far as we conscientiously can'. Churchill saw him at once and a further exchange of letters followed. King concluded, 'I had assumed that if anything published by us should cause you serious annoyance you would send a message through one of your secretaries asking us to be more moderate . . . The staff have had their instructions and you may have already noticed a marked change of tone.' After such a climb-down, the exchange ended on a friendly note.

While King may have issued instructions, the key figures at the *Daily Mirror* paid little heed, and the War Office began to complain that constant sniping at the 'brass hats' was undermining morale. Churchill demanded an enquiry into the ownership of the paper in the ludicrous belief that some hidden aliens might be in control. But in March 1942, after the loss of Singapore, the *Mirror* published a cartoon by Philip Zec showing an exhausted sailor adrift on a life raft in the middle of the Atlantic over a caption (supplied by Cassandra) saying, ' "The price of petrol has been increased by one penny" – Official.' The intention was to emphasise the heroism of the sailors and the need to avoid waste, but it could also be taken as an attack on petrol profiteering. Both Churchill and Bevin were absolutely furious. Bevin, Minister of Labour, asked Morrison, Home Secretary, 'How was he to "press" people almost into the merchant navy if they were then to see the suggestion that they were being "pressed" to put the price of petrol up for the owners?'[5] It was Beaverbrook who persuaded his colleagues that a stern warning was preferable to suppression. Morrison then summoned the editor and chairman to the Home Office. Bart came instead of the chairman. After implying that the *Mirror*'s line of criticism was close to fifth column activity and amounted to unfair criticism, Morrison reminded them that he had closed down the *Daily Worker* a year before, and it would be a long time before it opened. 'And that goes for you, too. You might bear that in mind.' No further warning would be given. Later that day Morrison made a statement in the House, clarifying the threat to use the Defence Regulation 2D ('which authorises the suppression of a newspaper that systematically publishes matter calculated to foment opposition to the successful prosecution of the war'). Most newspapers and some MPs were appalled. Both sides backed off; William Connor joined up, the war began to take a turn for the better and no more was heard of suppressing newspapers for vigorous criticism of the war effort. The episode did not affect the growing popularity of the *Mirror*, which was now on its way to overtake the *Express* at the top of the market. In January 1934, when the *Mirror* reached the pit of its circulation, it was selling only 732,000 against the *Express* at 1,710,000. By 1941 the *Mirror* sold 1,686,000 and the *Express* 2,511,000. (Newsprint supplies were then pegged.) By 1947 the *Mirror* had increased to 3,742,000 while the *Express* was still just ahead at 3,880,000. Two years later the *Mirror* finally put its nose in front with a circulation of more than 4,000,000.

Towards the end of the war John Cowley died. King naturally felt he was the best fitted to succeed as chairman, but the job went to Bart who was by far the senior director, having been appointed by Northcliffe as long ago as 1920. King became vice-chairman for the *Sunday Pictorial* and another man, John Coope, was vice-chairman for the *Daily Mirror*. Eventually Bart was able to get his revenge on Cudlipp for leaving his *Mirror* to edit the *Sunday Pictorial*. A failure to carry a report from King himself about riots in Enugu was the pretext for dismissal. Cudlipp was immediately hired by Beaverbrook, with the prospect of succeeding John Gordon as editor of the *Sunday Express*. But over the next few years Bart's drinking became worse and he was usually incoherent by nine thirty am. Eventually King organised a putsch and after gathering the opinions of his co-directors told Bart that he had to go. Bart was at first incredulous that Sylvester Bolam, whom he had appointed editor of the *Daily Mirror* in 1948, had turned against him and then subsided in whisky-sodden tears. The removal of the chairman was an ominous precedent.

The Mirror group now entered its most fruitful period. King at once persuaded Cudlipp to rejoin him, now as editorial director of the two papers. Their partnership worked exceptionally well. 'There is no policy committee,' King told the Shawcross Commission, 'There are only two of us – Cudlipp and myself.' He added that he saw Cudlipp nearly every day. King gave Cudlipp every encouragement. Having found him and promoted him, he now delegated to him, subject only to King's litmus test of *Mirror* journalism – whether or not a story was intelligible to a busdriver's wife in Sheffield. Stunts and shock issues were the order of the day and the circulation hit 5,000,000. King supplied the ballast and Cudlipp was the powerhouse. While King's view on political matters normally prevailed, there were occasions when contrary opinions were adopted as the right line for the *Mirror*. Sydney (later Lord) Jacobson and Connor would not allow the *Mirror* to advocate hanging as King wished. Further, Cudlipp and Jacobson opposed Eden's unilateral intervention over Suez, again against the wishes of King. The *Mirror*'s opposition to the Suez invasion cost 90,000 readers, and was then somewhat muted. But in general these were the years when Mirror Newspapers were riding high and King began talking about them as 'my newspapers' as well as 'my editors'.

It was about this time that Dame Ruth Railton, who married King in 1962,* appeared on the scene. Apart from being a professional musician and founder of the National Youth Orchestra, she claimed considerable psychic powers and King was fascinated since he had been intrigued by the subject of extra-sensory perception for several decades. In his book *Without Fear or Favour*[6] King reported how his wife had once held up an aeroplane at Heathrow so that they could catch a flight, and that her only comment was that as a child she could always stop a train. He gave other examples of her psychic or telepathic experiences. Perhaps more importantly Dame Ruth clearly believed that Cecil King was a most wonderful man. It was said that she sometimes slept on the floor at the foot of his bed.

Anyway it was in 1959 that King decided to widen the base of the business. Michael Berry (later Lord Hartwell) wished to sell Amalgamated Press, the magazine company which published such titles as *Woman's Weekly* and *Woman and Home*; it also included two subsidiaries, the Kelly-Iliffe *Directories* and Imperial Paper Mills which King reckoned were worth more than he paid for the whole. With profits of around £1 million a year, King believed the company was a snip; that the marketing skills of the Mirror group could be applied successfully in the magazine field, and that the main board directors were able but had been doing the same thing for too long. It would benefit the group if they were stretched in a new direction.

Others felt that the company had been insufficiently researched. The titles were waning in popularity, and few were the leaders in their own field. Promotion costs were getting bigger all the time, and advertisers were beginning to become more selective. Certainly Odhams, the other big magazine publishers with newspapers, bill-posting and printers also in the group, were also looking for partners by 1960. One suggestion was that Roy Thomson's organisation should take over the newspapers so that Odhams could concentrate on the magazines, which now included Newnes and Hultons, and printing. But when Thomson put his proposition to the Odhams board, it was turned down. The next move came from King who spoke to the chairman of Odhams, Sir Christopher Chancellor, at a Christmas party given by the second Lord Rothermere, 'Why do we go on battling with each other with the women's magazines? If you stop one of yours, I'll stop one of mine.'

This suggestion was pursued at a lunch when the idea was thrown out that Odhams might take over Fleetway at a price of £10 million.

---

* She had taken the surname of King some years earlier.

That price was too high for Odhams, so King then proposed a merger through an exchange of shares. In answer to a question from Chancellor he said he was not planning a take-over 'yet' but he did not want to wait too long for an answer to the merger proposal. Chancellor became convinced that a take-over was what King had in mind, and went back to Thomson. In three days an agreement had been reached for Odhams to take over Thomson, paying Thomson with thirty-nine per cent of Odhams shares which, he thought, would be enough to give him control; a new company would be formed with Thomson in the chair and Chancellor vice-chairman.[7]

When King saw Thomson saying on television that no one could afford to make a counter-bid he felt 'that was a bit too much, so I reached for the telephone' and two days later bid 55s 1½d for Odhams shares which were then valued at 40s on the market. The Labour leadership was appalled at the idea of both daily newspapers friendly to the Labour cause being under the same control and extracted two crucial concessions from King and Cudlipp; first Cudlipp stated that no amalgamation of the *Mirror* and the *Herald* would ever take place while Odhams remained under the Mirror group's control; secondly, he stated that the *Herald* would be kept alive for seven years whatever happened. They also said that the then editor of the *Herald*, John Beavan (later Lord Ardwick), would remain. Thomson did not believe in entering auctions, he preferred friendly take-overs; and so he retreated to the South of France. King improved his offer to 63s, worth about £35 million, and the Odhams board finally succumbed. The Labour politicians decided to accept the change as gracefully as they could, 'in order not to bitch up our relations with him [King] too badly', as Gaitskell said.[8]

King's critics believed that, after his initial mistake in buying Amalgamated Press, he was right to try to swamp that error by grabbing Odhams, despite all the political disadvantages and the costs involved. But then he failed to grasp hold of the vastly increased business. It was a huge group to digest. It needed rationalisation – trimming back the overheads and all the little empires that had existed in Odhams, firm action to make the whole into a homogeneous company.

Another mistake was for King to become too involved in Reeds, the paper and paint company. He became executive chairman and, although he brought in Ryder as managing director, he had less time for the publishing scene he knew best.

His final fatal blunder was to succumb to his uncles' disease of megalomania. It is easy to understand why he felt so despairing of his country. High-minded and reflective, he had lived through two European wars. Two brothers had been killed in the first. The wealth of Britain had been dissipated in the next. The old gang of politicians, he felt, had failed to respond to the yearnings of the young and the needs of the time as Kennedy had in the United States and, in his own way, Khrushchev had tried in the Soviet Union. He had played the major role in creating the *Mirror* as a newspaper of authority. He felt convinced that his abilities were underrated by politicians in general and by Harold Wilson, the Prime Minister in particular.

In 1964, when Labour won the October election with massive support from the *Mirror* newspapers, Wilson invited him to lunch at once and offered him a life peerage and junior office at the Board of Trade. Neither was anything like enough for King. His uncles had been viscounts; the Berrys were viscounts; Southwood had been a viscount; Cowdray was a viscount. He felt that to be a mere life baron was below his rightful station: he preferred to continue as Cecil Harmsworth King. Wilson explained that he was pledged not to introduce any hereditary peers, but King would not be mollified. As for junior office, it was not worth considering. Wilson tried on at least two other occasions to placate King. In August 1965 Wilson again offered a peerage and the job of Minister of State at the Board of Trade with responsibility for the export drive. And in 1967 Wilson made much the same offer with a Privy Councillorship thrown in. King turned him down again. Eventually, in 1967, Callaghan made him a non-executive director of the Bank of England; he became a member of the Coal Board and vice-chairman of the National Parks Commission. He still felt under-valued. His autobiography concludes with a quotation from a letter written by Herbert Asquith to a Mrs Horner in 1892:

Do you remember the Theban, somewhere in Herodotus, who says - that of all human troubles the most hateful is to feel that you have the capacity for power and yet you have no field to exercise it. That was for years my case, and no one who has not been through it can know the chilly paralysing deadening depression of hope deferred and energy wasted and vitality run to seed. I sometimes think it is the most tragic thing in life.

This then was the underlying emotion which lay behind so many of his activities in the 1960s.

As a newspaper publisher he felt himself 'duty bound' to take a deep and sustained interest in public affairs. 'I myself regularly see the party leaders, trade union leaders and back-benchers,' as well as hearing the views of journalists. He told his audience at the Granada lectures in 1966, 'The need is, I believe, to steer clear of purely personal idiosyncracies. The publisher must smoke out the bees in his own bonnet.'[9] That was an aim he completely failed to achieve. He became more and more apocalyptic in his vision, convinced that Wilson was interested only in parliamentary manoeuvring and that Britain was heading for bankruptcy, leading to mounting disorder. At some stage he stopped listening to what people were telling him, and began telling them what he thought. Cudlipp later wrote that the problems which arose from King's 'personal intervention did not surface until 1964'. Others would say that this growing frustration became evident somewhat earlier. Indeed Hugh Gaitskell, who had been strongly opposed to the acquisition of the *Daily Herald* by the Mirror group, saw in King 'too much of his uncle Alfred' as early as 1961.

King's solution for Britain's difficulties was simple: form a national government in which he and other businessmen – the name of Lord Robens, chairman of the National Coal Board, kept cropping up – would play a major part. In February 1968 Tony Benn, then Minister of Technology, had lunch with King who held forth at length about the gravity of the financial crisis. He believed that a coalition government was necessary. Wilson would be swept away; nobody believed a word he said. After disparaging virtually all the leading politicians of the day, he indicated that Denis Healey might be the man to lead the new government, and told Benn, 'there may well be a larger part for you to play'. Benn concluded that King was really 'slightly unbalanced'.[10] The following month King met the group's editors; they heard his doom-laden scenario 'in embarrassed silence' which he probably interpreted as assent. (On another occasion he had said he always found it very difficult to know what the other man was thinking.) King then persuaded Cudlipp to arrange a meeting with Mountbatten whom Cudlipp knew reasonably well. Mountbatten had previously had a rather woolly conversation with Cudlipp about the country facing disaster and imminent collapse under the Labour government; he suggested there should be 'something like the emergency committee he ran in India during the war'.

Daily Mirror

5d. Friday, May 10, 1968 • No. 20,022

DISASTER AT THE POLLS FOR LABOUR

The Tories storm to victory in thirty towns

—SEE BACK PAGE

ENOUGH IS ENOUGH

By Cecil H. King
Chairman of the International Publishing Corporation

THE results of the local elections are fully confirming the verdicts of the opinion polls and of the Dudley by-election.

Mr. Wilson and his Government have lost all credibility: all authority.

The Government which was voted into office with so much goodwill only three and a half years ago has revealed itself as lacking in foresight, in administrative ability, in political sensitivity, and in integrity. Mr. Wilson is seen to be a brilliant Parliamentary tactician and nothing more.

DECLINE

If these disastrous years only marked the decline of Mr. Wilson and the Labour Party, the damage to our political self-confidence would be serious enough, but the Labour Party came into power with such high

CECIL H. KING, Chairman of the International Publishing Corporation. The Corporation publishes the Daily Mirror, the Sunday Mirror, the Sun, The People and the Daily Record and Sunday Mail in Scotland.

Continued on Page Three

ELECTION—LATEST

TORIES	1322 net gains
LABOUR	1184 net losses
LIBERALS	7 net losses
INDEPENDENTS	11 net losses

King showed his famous onslaught on the Wilson Government to Cudlipp, his deputy chairman and to the editors. Cudlipp suggested only minor amendments. The editors thought he had gone over the top, but King thought they agreed. His article precipitated the moves leading to his dismissal.

Amazingly enough Mountbatten thought the person to rally the country should be Mrs Barbara Castle. Cudlipp attempted to disabuse him of any idea that Barbara Castle could save the country and reported the conversation to King.[11] So King had some reason to believe that he and Mountbatten were thinking along the same lines. At this second meeting Mountbatten was accompanied by Sir Solly (now Lord) Zuckerman, then Scientific Adviser to the Cabinet (Mountbatten had told Cudlipp that Zuckerman was 'disaffected'.) King trotted out his now well-rehearsed scenario of a crisis of confidence arising which would lead to the disintegration of the government, rioting in the streets, the need for involvement by the armed forces and wound up with the question: would Lord Mountbatten agree to be titular head of a new administration in such a crisis? Cudlipp later reported that this was too much for Sir Solly who rose and said, 'This is rank treachery. All this talk of machine guns at street corners is appalling. I am a public servant and will have nothing to do with it. Nor should you, Dickie.' He then left and Mountbatten, quickly agreeing with him, brought the meeting courteously, but swiftly, to an end.

Two days later, on 10th May 1968, the front page of the *Daily Mirror* was dominated by the stark headline 'ENOUGH IS ENOUGH by Cecil H. King, chairman of the International Publishing Corporation'. The article stated: 'Mr Wilson and his government have lost all credibility and all authority. The government... has revealed itself as lacking in foresight, in administrative ability, in political sensitivity, in integrity.' As an example of the manner in which Cabinet reshuffles were used instead of action, King pointed out that there had been four Ministers of Education in four years and three Ministers of Fuel and Power in three years. The real punch followed: 'We are now threatened with the greatest financial crisis in our history. It is not to be removed by lies about our reserves, but only by a fresh start under a fresh leader.' The article concluded that it was up to the Parliamentary Labour party to 'give us that leader – and soon'. Cudlipp had certainly seen and agreed with the gist of the article although he had struck out the word 'monthly' before 'lies' and had also suggested that King should at once resign his directorship of the Bank of England. King later claimed that the editors subsequently saw his article and approved it. It seems likely that again their 'approval' was muted in the extreme. Indeed Sydney Jacobson, then editor of IPC's *Sun*, rightly suggested that it would rally the ranks behind Wilson. But it was

Ellis Birk, the director with closest links to the Labour party, who reacted most strongly; he was 'hopping mad'. The plot to remove King from the board then took on its own momentum.

There is a postscript to the story. In 1975, seven years after he had been deposed, Cecil King was invited to speak to an informal dinner party of students at the Army Staff College. They hoped to hear some diverting comments on the state of Fleet Street. Instead King reviewed the state of the country; one institution after another was dismissed as bankrupt of leadership. King concluded that only the armed services could save the country from chaos. A reporter who was present wrote after King's death, 'I had no doubt I was listening to a treasonable attempt to suborn the loyalty of the Queen's officers. And neither did they.' King was subjected to questions which 'began as hostile and grew increasingly derisive'. King 'became defensive, then irritable and finally silent'. Then he rose and announced 'I want to go home' and left the room, unescorted, to find his chauffeur.[12] It was a sad finale to King's attempt to run Britain the Harmsworth way.

Notes:
1. Cecil King wrote an extraordinarily vivid account of his own life, embellished with frank accounts of his amazing uncles, in *Strictly Personal*, Weidenfeld, 1969. He later published a number of diaries which revealed that confidentiality had little meaning for him. His editorial colleague and successor Hugh Cudlipp was almost bewitched by him and wrote a number of accounts of King's character and career. The calmest assessment is given in *Walking on the Water*, Bodley Head, 1976. It is interesting to contrast this with his more adulatory article, 'The Seeker after Knowledge', published in *Fleet Street*, Macdonald, 1966 – two years before the coup which displaced King. The authentic voice of King can also be heard in the oral evidence to the Shawcross Commission on the press. I have drawn heavily on these books and checked them out with some of the participants.
2. In an interview with the author, 8th September 1988.
3. Quoted by Hugh Cudlipp in 'The Humble Seeker after Knowledge', a chapter in *Fleet Street, the Inside Story*, published by Macdonald, 1966.
4. Both remarks quoted in Koss, op cit.
5. Quoted in Koss, op cit.
6. Sidgwick and Jackson, 1971. I am indebted to Lord Cudlipp for drawing my attention to the reference.
7. From *After I was Sixty*, by Lord Thomson.

8. P. M. Williams, *Gaitskell*, Jonathan Cape, 1979.
9. *The Future of the Press* by Cecil King, MacGibbon & Kee, 1967.
10. From Tony Benn's *Office Without Power* Political Diaries, 1968–72, Hutchinson, 1988, an extract published in *The Guardian*, 29th April 1987.
11. A memo from Hugh Cudlipp to King was found in King's papers, now held by Boston University. See, 'Mountbatten proposed emergency government', report by Charles Bremner in *The Times*, 29th April 1987.
12. 'The day Cecil King talked of treason', by John Keegan, Defence Correspondent, *Daily Telegraph*, 21st April 1987.

8
Victor Matthews

Ev'n victors are by victory undone
John Dryden, 'To John Driden of Chesterton'

Victor Matthews[1] was the most unlikely newspaper publisher of the century. He was fifty-eight when, as the new chairman of Beaverbrook Newspapers, he walked under the shiny gilt and silver ceiling of the *Daily Express* entrance hall in Fleet Street, passed the Epstein bust of Lord Beaverbrook, rose by lift to the third floor, and took charge. Northcliffe and Camrose started in journalism during their schooldays; it was a family business for Laurence Cadbury; Southwood worked in a printing firm before he was twenty; Beaverbrook and Thomson both came to the business in their thirties, and that seemed pretty late. But the deal which brought Matthews into the control of a major newspaper group had first been proposed less than six weeks before. He had delivered newspapers as a boy around St Paul's Road, Islington, but had never even dreamt of running one.

It is true that he had often been in the black glass structure before, but as a building contractor, and that was his original skill. Brought up by his mother, after his father mysteriously disappeared shortly after the First World War, he had been through a Church of England elementary school and, after a spell of unemployment, got his first job as a 25-shillings-a-week office boy in the tobacco company producing Kensitas and du Maurier cigarettes. Money was short – his mother was 'in the credit business' and owned some small houses in Islington. The half-crowns (12½p) he got for delivering newspapers helped to balance the family budget. He was good at football and his first big thrill was playing on the Arsenal ground with other boys from Islington; he even thought of playing professionally but perhaps he was not fast enough. Shortly before the Second World War began – he was twenty – he joined the Royal Naval Volunteer Reserve at HMS *President* on the Embankment; he had hoped to get into the RAF but their waiting list seemed too long. He soon found himself, as an ordinary seaman, launched on some of the more dangerous Combined Operations. He took part in their first raid – on the Lofoten Islands; he helped evacuate the RAF from Dunkirk; he took part in the Dieppe raid; he even sailed to Bayonne near the Pyrenees in a fruitless attempt to blow up some German ammunition dumps. No one could say he had a sheltered life; he suffered miserably from seasickness and says frankly, 'I hated every minute at sea.' By the end of it all he was married and had won promotion – to the rank of able seaman.

He became a trainee with Trollope and Colls, the city building firm, and eventually emerged as a contracts manager. He reckoned the firm was rather like the civil service; salaries were on the low side but the job was safe. He remembered the massive unemployment of the 1930s and initially he put job security first; his wife Joyce, always an important influence on his life, felt the same. When he was twenty-eight he took out a ninety-five per cent mortgage on a semi-detached house in Southgate, raising the £140 deposit with some difficulty; three years later he bought his first car, a pre-war Morris.

Some time later he began to notice that the specialist sub-contractor with whom he did business not only ran bigger cars but had twice as much money to spend. Envy spurred ambition. He took the decisive step: he left Trollope and Colls and, in the hope of getting a share of the action, moved to Clark and Fenn, a specialist contracting firm run by a man called Victor Hosp who was the first to recognise Matthews's potential. There he began to develop a major interest in acoustic tiles; he had them made, he sold them and he supervised their installation. Before long he was installing acoustic ceilings all over London: the Marks and Spencer building in Baker Street, the BBC Television Centre, the US Embassy, and finally, the prestige job to top the lot, the Science Museum in South Kensington. He was careful to insist on first-class workmanship and soon the acoustic business was making more money than all the rest of Clark and Fenn. After three years the firm went public, but Matthews was left out of the deal. Disillusioned, he told Hosp he was going. But in 1960 Hosp helped Matthews buy a small building firm called Bridge Walker which had an annual turnover of £250,000. Three years later Matthews had increased turnover to more than £3 million and bought back Hosp's half-share of the business.

Following the bad winter of 1962–3 when building projects throughout the country were held up, a new bank manager took over Matthews's account and put the squeeze on Bridge Walker. After Westminster and Country Properties had offered to buy the firm with a view to extending its contracting activities Nigel Broackes (now Sir Nigel), then the managing director of Trafalgar House, who had been impressed by the extensive work done on flat conversions for him under Matthews's supervision, came up with a rival offer. The financial value was the same: Bridge Walker's shares were worth £130,000, but Westminster wanted guarantees about profits on existing contracts and Trafalgar did not. Matthews sold forty-nine per cent of his business. Then he and Broackes set up a new house-building company together and eventually Trafalgar bought the remainder of Bridge Walker for shares. On paper Matthews was now a millionaire. He was given a five-year contract and decided that he would retire at the end of it. In truth a famous business partnership had been born; Trafalgar House grew and prospered.

Within six months the Ideal Building Corporation (originally New Ideal Homes) which built some 2,000 houses a year came on the market and was snapped up, followed by the take-over of Trollope and Colls for £14 million. It was typical of Matthews that when he went back to his old firm as chairman after the take-over he should describe it as 'one of the worst moments of my life – all those people looking at me and wondering whether to call me "Vic" or "Sir" '. Other major acquisitions included Cementation, the international civil engineering firm, for £17 million; the Cunard shipping line, which included the *QE II*, for £ 26.5 million; and the Ritz Hotel for £2.7 million. Usually the main strategic thrust came from Broackes; Matthews's role was to go into the firm as chairman and sort it out. At one time he was chairman or director of nearly 200 companies. At Cunard he sold two out of four passenger ships, made 700 seamen redundant, and completely refitted the *QE II*, including new de luxe penthouses. At the Ritz he gave every waiter a new uniform, refurbished the ground floor, introducing a row of shops on Piccadilly, modernised the bedrooms and let the basement to Mecca as a casino, all at a total cost of around £5 million.

So Matthews had an outstanding track record as a manager. But in 1977 he had to decide whether he wished to manage Beaverbrook Newspapers as well. Over the years the Trollope and Colls arm of Trafalgar House had been used by Beaverbrook Newspapers on many projects and Matthews knew the top men well. In 1975 he mentioned to Peter Hetherington, at that time financial director of Beaverbrook Newspapers, that if the group ever needed help to escape unwelcome attentions from a predator he should remember Trafalgar. The following year Matthews told Jocelyn Stevens, the vigorous and sometimes volatile managing director of Beaverbrook, that Stevens should contact him if he needed help. At that stage Matthews had an investment of perhaps £2 million to £3 million in mind.

By 1977 Beaverbrook had an overdraft of some £14 million and the company was barely able to find the interest payments of nearly £2 million a year. Although the property was unencumbered British banks were unwilling to lend any more money, partly because of the poor reputation of Fleet Street for profitability and partly because of the tight voting control exercised by the family through the Beaverbrook Foundations. (Eventually an American bank provided £5 million, urgently needed to fund newsprint purchases.) Stevens and Hetherington then followed up the suggestion from Matthews and showed him the figures; he asked them to put forward a proposal but nothing happened, for Stevens had re-opened secret talks with Associated with a view to merging the two evening papers the *Evening Standard* and *Evening News* and setting up a jointly-owned 'Black Glass' printing operation to print all the Associated and Express titles.

Discussions about co-operation between the two newspaper groups had been continuing, hesitantly and erratically, since 1971. The Harmsworths and the Aitkens had never been natural partners since those happy days when Beaverbrook and the first Lord Rothermere each had shares in each other's companies. Indeed on one occasion Max Aitken had driven his boat on to a sandbank rather than return to London for talks with Vere Harmsworth. But towards the end of 1976 the talks took on a new urgency. The financial plight of Beaverbrook Newspapers was becoming really serious; meanwhile, although Associated Newspaper profits were in much better shape, the losses of the *Evening News* were mounting. Then at one of the annual Boat Show luncheons held by the group in January Sir James Goldsmith, chairman of Cavenham Foods, announced that he had bought thirty-five per cent of Beaverbrook Newspapers non-voting stock; he was now by far the largest individual shareholder and, despite the fact that his shares carried no votes, was universally regarded as a possible predator.* If an additional spur to continuing the talks with Associated was needed, it was provided by the illness of Sir Max Aitken; he had a number of strokes which led to his confinement in King's College Hospital. On his release he was clearly operating at a lower level of capacity, for in April 1977 when he was still convalescing at home, he sanctioned an inept attempt led by Hetherington, with the support of his son Maxwell Aitken, to expel Stevens from the managing directorship, and, when Stevens complained, reversed his position. Only a chairman not making any real sense could have made *both* decisions. Then there was a well-informed leak in *The Times* about the possible closure of one of the London evenings. Suddenly everything got rather hectic.

As the negotiations with Associated continued Sir Max became more and more unhappy. Returning to the office from his convalescence, he called me over from the *Evening Standard* building in Shoe Lane (I had resigned as editor on reaching the ago of sixty and was now chairman; Simon Jenkins was editor). Sir Max told me. 'I do not want to sell the *Standard*, and particularly not to the Harmsworths. Do I have to sign? Is there any alternative?'[2] This was the green light for some frantic scouring of the horizon for alternatives. At first the only serious proposal came from Goldsmith, later in association with Tiny Rowland.[3] It was enough to delay signature of the Associated deal. Meanwhile there had been a fortunate meeting between Evelyn de Rothschild, a Beaverbrook director, and Matthews at Sandown Park; the interest of Trafalgar House was canvassed again. A follow-up meeting on Derby Day, 1st June, took place at the Trafalgar offices. After further discussions Broackes, who had earlier been approached by Simon Jenkins, a doughty fighter for his paper, decided that Trafalgar House would benefit from diversifying into the communications area and took Matthews out to lunch at the Ritz with a view to persuading him to take on the *Express*. He subsequently described Matthews's state of mind at the time as 'morbid and morose', and needing a fresh challenge, a view deeply resented by Matthews, although it was clear that the

* Most of these shares had previously been held by Rupert Murdoch, after passing through the hands of Sir Max Rayne the property magnate. Rayne had been involved in a complicated scheme, backed by Lord Goodman (who was Sir Max Aitken's personal legal adviser and friend) to maximise the property potential of the group. Goodman explained this scheme to a sceptical Beaverbrook board and said, at one point, that it was to 'Sir Max's advantage'. At this stage John Junor cuttingly interjected, 'Which Sir Max?' The scheme was dropped.

burden and boredom of chairing twenty-four subsidiary board meetings every twenty days was becoming a tedious grind; he was talking of retiring, even emigrating. It was a good lunch and at one stage Matthews asked, 'But who's going to run it?' Broackes replied. 'Why you are, Victor, of course.' With the aid of a second bottle of wine Matthews agreed to take on the job and so another press baron was born. On Matthews's insistence the partners agreed first that the newspaper group should not be integrated into Trafalgar – there was too much danger of industrial cross-infection; and secondly that Matthews should run it alone. Broackes and the board of Trafalgar would remain in the background.

The bid was then constructed; Trafalgar agreed they would go up to £15 million. Neither a late bid for management control by Murdoch (fortified by a cheque of £1.4 million for Sir Max's personal shareholding) nor the possibility of a rival offer from Associated prevailed at the final decisive meeting of the Beaverbrook trustees. On the advice of Jocelyn Stevens Sir Max accepted the Trafalgar offer, even though he received less money for his own shares;* a majority of the trustees agreed. Only his wife Lady Aitken and his children voted against, believing that the Beaverbrook Group could still survive independently.

Within minutes of hearing that the Trafalgar bid had succeeded Matthews was speeding from the Berkeley Street headquarters of Trafalgar House to Fleet Street in his Rolls-Royce TRA 1, accompanied by a BBC television team and explaining his admiration for Lord Beaverbrook and his belief in Britain. 'I am just like any other chap that we see walking across the street who has got to the top. If that can happen in a straightforward ordinary way, by hard work, then I am very anxious to maintain that.' Matthews subsequently explained that he had expected the media fuss to die down after a fortnight. It never did because he believed that a policy of avoiding media enquiries could be counter-productive, rarely refused to pick up the phone when asked for a comment, and was usually good for a printable quote.

It was easy to underrate Matthews. Meetings often began with a ramble round the links or a description of the most recent failure of his expensive racehorses. An hour or more might go by before we turned to the business in hand. At first he freely admitted he knew nothing about newspapers. He was an *Express* reader who

---

* He received £1,218,523, or £181,477 less.

hankered after a return to the broadsheet formula. He hated the Hickey column and would have eliminated it if he could have done it without damage to circulation. His views about politics were ortho-dox Conservatism added to an adamant determination to curb union power. The editor of the *Daily Express* often fared the worst, as his colleague Simon Jenkins later reported: 'Matthews would delight in pouring out home-spun wisdom, at considerable length, often at the busiest time of the day.' But he was remarkably shrewd and he insisted on accurate up-to-date financial information. He demanded and carefully scrutinised weekly sheets showing actual earnings, not nominal rates (they were often very different) in every department of the paper, both in London and Manchester, together with expla-nations of any unusual variations. They covered every class of employee from cleaners to chauffeurs, from linotype operators to electricians. Almost at once the plague of little local payments auth-orised at a low level to soothe some chapel grievance, real or imagin-ary, was cured. Nor was he easy to fool. One evening when I went to see him I remarked that he was looking pretty exhausted, 'Yes,' he said, 'it's very tiring, trying to hear what people are not telling me.'

Sir Max was given the honorary title of president, but Matthews soon removed young Maxwell. He left the editorial staff intact with one exception. He had announced on arrival, 'The paper that is not doing as well as it should is the *Daily Express* and we are going to concentrate on it.' To the *Financial Times* he added, 'It's the same story as any other business. You have got to get the product right.' And *The Guardian* readers were told there had to be an increase in *Daily Express* circulation. He did not feel that Roy Wright, the current editor who had presided over the recent transformation to tabloid format, had the popular touch he was seeking and asked me to suggest someone who might broaden the paper's appeal. I con-sulted my friend Harry Evans, then editor of the *Sunday Times*, who said he had heard good things about Derek Jameson, the northern editor of the *Daily Mirror*. We met, and I thought he was well worth producing to the chairman. Lunch was arranged the very next day in the Presidential Suite of the Bristol Hotel, then owned by Trafal-gar and next door to their offices. Jameson's anecdotal style, cockney beginnings and total self-confidence in his own talents seemed to cast a spell on Matthews. I soon felt as surplus to the lunch as a mother-in-law on a honeymoon and left them still talking long after the meal was over. Jocelyn Stevens was invited to breakfast with

Jameson the next morning so that he could make his own judgment but had scarcely sat down when Matthews arrived, congratulated Jameson on his appointment and began discussing when the announcement should be made. The new editor was only a partial success for reasons which will be explained later.

Within a month Matthews faced his first real challenge and won a highly significant victory. He had asked for three months of industrial peace when he took over. The engineers gave him six weeks. They were already paid £140 for a four-day week with a nominal thirty-five hours on days and thirty hours on nights; now they demanded as much money as the highest paid printers, namely £250 a week, an increase of more than seventy-five per cent. They probably did not expect to get as much as that but in traditional fashion they wanted 'money on the table' to sweeten the negotiation. Matthews refused to pay it, so they held a meeting during working hours to press their claim and failed to return to work when instructed to do so. That type of bloody-minded and anarchic behaviour was all too common in Fleet Street at the time, and so was Matthews's response: they were given an ultimatum to return to work or be dismissed. They ignored it and removed essential equipment from the foundry – clips, bars and rings. Production was impossible. It was nothing less than sabotage and it hit the real money-maker of the group, the *Sunday Express*. Matthews was in a cold rage; he already considered the pay of the engineers 'totally obscene; they do half the work and get double the pay of engineers in the building industry'. Now they added theft to their crimes. First he threatened to move the entire production of the *Express* to Manchester on a permanent basis, and underlined the reality of that threat by printing an extra two million copies there and obtaining distribution throughout Southern England apart from the London area. (Two hundred and forty warehousemen were sacked for not handling the print which had been brought down.) Then he called in the police and it was soon evident that some engineers, who were unpopular enough among their colleagues, might go to jail. The industrial mood was getting uglier. A fire began in the publishing room; next day two editorial cars had their windscreens broken. Matthews had the *Express* building in London protected by barbed wire to prevent further sabotage.

Matthews then produced a front-page leading article for the *Daily Express*, written by Jameson, headed 'WE SHALL NOT BE MOVED'. The key passage read:

Far too many within the industry have cashed in on the vulnerability of newspapers in a shrinking and highly competitive market. Fleet Street has become a jungle where anyone who dares to oppose excessive and often outrageous demands does so at the eternal risk of instant stoppage and imminent bankruptcy . . . We shall not be moved.

It was not the first time a newspaper publisher had talked tough; but Matthews acted tough too.

At this stage the powerful figure of Reg Birch, the Maoist national organiser of the engineers' union, entered the scene and imposed some discipline on his chapel. (He possessed the ultimate sanction of withdrawing their union cards and abandoning them to the police if they failed to submit to his authority.) Matthews's conditions seem relatively mild but they amounted to a total change of climate: no unauthorised tea breaks, no absence from work without authority, no chapel meetings during working hours, full contract working to be guaranteed, a one-third cut in staffing to be examined and, above all, 'the right of management to manage'. Reg Birch signed; the engineers and warehousemen were reinstated; and the production workers at the *Express* knew they had a boss who would not stand any more nonsense.

Matthews summed it up: 'You don't realise how bad it was in there. It was like a no-go area in Belfast. Until the police got back into those areas you didn't realise law and order existed.' Matthews's belief in the law and readiness to use it marked the beginning of a new era in Fleet Street but at the time few of us realised just how far reaching the change would be.

In November there was another dispute in Fleet Street and Matthews again called in the law, but this time the battle took place in the courts and not in the plant. There was a dispute at the *Daily Mirror* which halted production. Matthews wished to increase the *Express* print by 200,000, to take advantage of the extra demand. Bill Keys, secretary of the general distributive and production workers' union SOGAT, refused to allow it; he was only following past practice in Fleet Street which had previously been accepted by the publishers. Matthews was outraged. 'The trouble with Fleet Street is that the proprietors have always given in to the unions,' he said. 'It is an intolerable interference with the right to manage by a union which is not in dispute with us or with any other company. They are trying to tell us what we can or cannot do.' He went to the

High Court to obtain an injunction to stop the restriction but his application failed. A day later he won in the Appeal Court, where Master of the Rolls Lord Denning said that Keys's instruction was a plain inducement to his members to break their contracts of employment and was not in contemplation, or furtherance, of an industrial dispute. Keys submitted to the ruling of the court. It was another turning point.

Two further instances of court action followed in 1979 and 1980. First the High Court granted an injunction to compel the NUJ to handle Press Association copy which it was boycotting as a gesture of sympathy with journalists striking in the provinces. Neither the *Express* nor the PA were involved in the dispute. The Court of Appeal upheld the injunction. The following year the *Express* won an injunction to prevent production workers from stopping newspaper production as part of a strike against government policies. The use of legal means to corral industrial action in Fleet Street was one of Matthews's greatest triumphs; he showed the way for others to follow. The passage into law of Jim Prior's Employment Act, 1980, which withdrew immunity from civil action for those engaged in secondary picketing away from their place of work, was particularly significant for Fleet Street, but Matthews had used the law even before the new Conservative labour legislation was passed.

With stricter industrial and financial discipline, some trimming of costs, a fall in the price of newsprint and improvement in advertising volumes, Matthews could see that Beaverbrook Newspapers was moving from loss to profit. The change was symbolised in February 1978 by a return to the name of Express Newspapers and by some rather woolly dreams of a new 'popular' evening newspaper and perhaps a new Sunday paper as well. 'Fleet Street is not over-manned,' Matthews told the *Sunday Times*, 'it is under-worked.' It was an admirable thought but it led him to make what emerged, to my mind, as a serious mistake.

Walking back from a meeting at the Newspaper Publishers Association in Bouverie Street, he complained to Jocelyn Stevens that while the *Sun* was off the streets the *Daily Express* picked up plenty of sale but as soon as it was back the paper lost the lot. If the big money lay in the *Sun*'s territory then he wanted a newspaper in that market. After frantic activity an announcement was made, in September, just twelve weeks later, that the *Daily Star* would be launched from Manchester in November making use of existing *Express* staff to a large degree. No less than eighty-six out of 165

Express journalists employed in Manchester were shifted to the new paper; the London bureau was staffed with twelve journalists from the *Express*. The theory was fine; the motives were splendid; but there was absolutely no evidence that a market existed for another popular paper either among readers or among advertisers. In fact the *Daily Star* never shook the grip of the *Sun* and the *Daily Mirror* in the mass market. I wrote a memo suggesting that if the *Daily Star* was a success it would hurt the *Express* but that failure was more likely.

Another error followed. Everyone agreed that Jameson was better suited to editing the *Daily Star* than the *Express*. But he emerged from the meeting with Matthews intended to transfer his undoubted talents to the sole benefit of the *Daily Star* with a new and additional job; he stayed as editor-in-chief of the *Express* as well as editing the *Star*. His hypnotic qualities had worked again. Stevens protested and later reported that he was told, 'You should be pleased. I've got two editors for the price of one.' Soon Jameson was spending less and less time in Manchester and more and more time on radio and television, his real love, where his ready wit and extravagant persona blossomed with growing success.

For the first few weeks it looked as if the *Daily Star* would prove a success. 'It's pure magic,' said Jameson, whose belief that such a quality resided mainly in the ample display of 'tits and bums' was soon tested to destruction. Matthews told me that he was going to frame my warning memo and hang it on his office wall 'to show just how wrong the experts can be'. After a few weeks that threat was heard no more. The sale of the paper slipped below the magic million. Within a year Broackes and Eric Parker, the accountant who later succeeded Matthews as chief executive at Trafalgar, were becoming increasingly uneasy about the financial drain. There was a tense meeting and Sir Francis Sandilands, one of Trafalgar's senior outside directors, was brought in to give a view. 'It was touch and go,' said Matthews later, but Sandilands backed his hunch.[4] Although his freedom was slightly circumscribed (the monthly figures submitted to Trafalgar showed exactly how much money the *Star* was costing) he would not abandon his child. He claims however that instead of going 'hell for leather' with the launch of bingo in the *Daily Star* he went more gently 'because of the monthly figures'. As it was, the bingo-assisted sale of the *Star* touched 1.9 million and *The Sun* fell as low as 3.2 million before Murdoch realised the sales potential of bingo and adopted it as his own. It was an expensive operation for Express Newspapers. According to a columnist in the *Sunday Times* the accounts for the *Daily Star* up to the end of 1986 showed accumulated losses of £58 million; the writer described it as 'one of the biggest disasters Fleet Street has ever known'.[5] In the end salvation came from an unexpected source, but not for several years, during which the losses were mounting. (Matthews believed that during his period as chairman the net losses amounted to no more than £20 million, including start-up costs; the figures quoted by the *Sunday Times* were 'management accounts' and included notional rent, etc.) Most of the *Express* staff benefited from a hand-out known as *Star* money, paid for their kindly co-operation in allowing the new newspaper to use *Express* facilities; but the *Express* went into profit because the *Star* now shared the overheads, particularly after some of the print was transferred to London. Indeed the *Star* is now so built into the financial structure of Express Newspapers that some observers claim it could not be closed without disastrous effects on the whole group.

In the New Year Honours List, 1980, Matthews became a peer, an honour that was well deserved for beginning to bring some reality into Fleet Street industrial relations. But it was not much good for the *Daily Star* where a new editor, the Australian Lloyd Turner, had been given the brief to run a newspaper that was left of centre and aimed at the young 'factory-gate reader'.[6] One day, Jocelyn Stevens was led to believe, Mrs Thatcher happened to meet Lord Matthews socially and commented on the attitude of the *Daily Star* towards her government. [Matthews later denied this story completely and said he had never discussed the *Star* with Mrs Thatcher.] In any event Stevens was told to instruct Turner not to attack Mrs Thatcher. Stevens argued in vain that this involved a fundamental change of policy. Unlike Roy Thomson who prided himself on leaving his editors alone, Matthews believed they should all sing basically the same tune.

The next major development involved the closure of the *Evening News* with redundancies amounting to £6 million paid by Associated Newspapers and an agreement that Associated would take fifty per cent of the Evening Standard Co Ltd (ESCO), the company that owned the *Evening Standard*. The paper would be printed under contract by Express Newspapers. The *Evening News* had been losing increasingly large sums, leading to a total loss of some £38 million. Internal forecasts at Associated showed that annual losses were likely to hit £20 million a year within five years. The *Evening Standard* had suffered from the battle to the death and, although it had been profitable, was forecast to lose more than £1 million that year. Owing to the intense competition between the two evenings, advertising rates could not be raised to economic levels, and cover prices were kept down.

The initial negotiations were conducted secretly between Eric Parker for Trafalgar House and Mick Shields, the brilliant managing director of Associated. In my view Associated got an even better deal than they deserved. They obtained what amounted to an option to buy Trafalgar's fifty per cent if Trafalgar ever wished to get out; they got a blocking veto on various reserved subjects such as price and title (although Matthews retained the casting vote); and the chairmanship would alternate between the groups when Matthews left. A minor aspect of the understanding was that I should resign the editorship; Vere Harmsworth had not forgotten an attack I made on him at the height of one of his previous attempts to obtain the *Standard*.[7] As I had already resigned the editorship voluntarily some years earlier, believing that it was a job for someone under sixty, I had no problem about resigning again, particularly as everyone else on the editorial staff kept his job. It was however an unpleasant surprise that Matthews agreed that Louis Kirby, editor of the *Evening News*, which I did not regard highly, should be given the chair at Harmsworth's request. I protested strongly, to no avail. So did Stevens, who says he told Matthews that the appointment was 'akin to appointing Goering, on VE Day, to command the RAF'. Matthews replied that editors were not important.* (Someone must have responded to my reservations in the end, for when the *Evening Standard* was threatened with competition from the ill-fated *London Daily News* Kirby was transferred and another editor appointed in his place.)

Yet was the deal really necessary? The *Evening News* was losing so much money that it was hurting Associated Newspapers and, while kept alive by prodigious infusions of cash, it was hampering preparations for the launch of the *Mail on Sunday*. As Matthews realised later, it was possible that Harmsworth would have admitted defeat quite soon and then Express Newspapers would have emerged as sole owners of the monopoly evening paper. As it was, Stevens, with the help of the accountants, screwed a monstrously lucrative printing contract out of the wretched ESCO and of course the *Standard*'s

*According to a reliable source Matthews told Harmsworth, 'I don't care a bugger who the editor is.'

losses were eliminated, but half the profits of the monopoly evening soon went to Trafalgar House, not to the Express group. For when Matthews wished to float off Express Newspapers from Trafalgar (as I explain shortly) ESCO could not be included since, under the contract, this would have involved a change of ownership and thus triggered Associated's option. Harmsworth was of course unyielding on the point. In consequence ESCO remained within Trafalgar, an unnecessary and bothersome increment to the property, engineering and shipping group and one which they were glad to sell to Associated (for £20 million) when Matthews stepped down.

While Matthews was chiselling away at costs in the *Express* building he was pressing a much more interesting scheme at the headquarters of Trafalgar House. Under the Finance Act of 1981, de-merger arrangements for subsidiary companies from their parent became possible. Matthews believed that what was happening in Fleet Street was 'dragging down' the Trafalgar share price, a key element in any take-overs. Further, as chief executive of Trafalgar House, he felt in a false position where the interests of the Express group and those of Trafalgar House did not necessarily coincide. De-merger plans were put in hand and again Stevens was sceptical; he did not like them. Although he was forecasting reasonable profits of £6.5 million for the year ending September 1981, he was worried about the declining sale and ageing readership of the money-spinning *Sunday Express* and resisted suggestions that the profits might be higher. He believed that a change of editorship was desirable, while hoping that Sir John Junor's well-read JJ column could be retained. He was worried that if Express Newspapers became independent and the *Sunday Express* was weakened much further the group would again become vulnerable to take-over. Matthews took the view that Stevens was 'frightened out of his life' by the proposal to float off. 'That was why he had to go,' he said later. However, Stevens believes that his dismissal was triggered by a management buy-out proposal he himself put forward with the support of Graham Sherren, head of the Morgan-Grampian magazine subsidiary; the proposal had not provided for Matthews to continue as chairman – a studied slight.

It had always been a source of some surprise that Stevens had got on so well with Matthews; they were total opposites. Stevens was outgoing, energetic, highly social, a life-enhancer, full of jokes, capable of inspiring people – and, occasionally, driving them to despair and sometimes departure – totally devoted to the Express group, perhaps too often involved in late-night sessions with union leaders to complete a deal, but highly visible, on top of his job, and caring more than he always let on. Matthews was an equally hard worker, with much wider experience in industry, but rather lonely in Fleet Street, suspicious and often pessimistic, but very tough when hard decisions had to be taken, loquacious but quite skilful at media interviews. They were both rather pleased with themselves and with what they'd done starting, in one case, near the top, and the other, near the bottom. But it was a partnership that had worked very successfully until the 'float' came up.

Stevens had been forecasting that he might be sacked, but he didn't really believe it was going to happen. He was summoned to the Berkeley Street headquarters of Trafalgar House and was confronted by what amounted to a kangaroo court of Broackes, Parker and Matthews. There he was charged with down-grading the profit forecast without proper consultation and told he had to go. Back in the office he was close to tears. Curiously enough it was an asset to which he was among the first to draw attention that eventually made the 'float' a roaring success. One day he had mentioned to Matthews that Reuters, the international news agency, was beginning to make profits owing to its development of computerised financial news and pointed out that the *Express*, through its membership of the NPA, was one of the owners. Matthews, he says, asked him not to bother him with trifling detail when there were more important matters to discuss. Indeed Matthews had not wished to pay the *Daily Star's* full subscription to the NPA. In the end he agreed to pay the smaller subscription for its Manchester office.

Meanwhile the 'float' went ahead. Trafalgar shareholders got one 20p Fleet Holdings share for every four Trafalgar shares they held and on 5th March 1982, the day the company was floated, Matthews bought 750,000 Fleet shares to add to those he already held. Subsequently the share price fell below 15p; nonetheless the profits up to September 1982 were less than £3 million but more than the final prospectus forecast. Then profitability started to improve; Morgan-Grampian, the magazine company which had been bought for £20.5 million by Trafalgar in 1977, was now part of Fleet Holdings and provided a stabilising element to the accounts.

Soon Matthews, now completely awake to the immense potential value of Reuters, began agitating for a public flotation. The agreement of all the parties was needed, but the pressure of ready money for the asking was growing. In 1981 Reuters' profits had risen from

£4.1 million to £16.4 million and were doubling up. While Matthews supplied the push, the new managing director of Fleet, a burly skin-diving accountant called Ian Irvine, worked out the details with the other parties. In the end Fleet proved to be one of the biggest beneficiaries with more than nine per cent of the shares which eventually proved to be worth at least £130 million.

With Stevens gone it was not surprising that Christopher Ward, his nominee (and mine) as editor, was soon joining the long list of ex-editors of the *Daily Express*. Sir Larry Lamb, former editor of the *Sun*, had suggested himself and Matthews, still looking for a magic formula to increase circulation, thought that Lamb, with a proven record of hyping sales, might provide the answer. Asked about the change, he said, 'Editors are like football managers. Unless they produce results, they have to be changed. It is very hard making a judgment on anybody until they work for you.' Lamb was given a vast promotional budget for the 'Millionaire's Club', a ludicrously profligate form of bingo, but after an early spurt, the trend turned down again. (The effect of the Millionaire's Club was blunted because both Robert Maxwell and Rupert Murdoch poached the same idea. Soon the popular newspapers were back to playing bingo for more modest sums.) Lamb did not improve his relations with Matthews by producing as a front page 'splash' a highly slanted imaginary speech by Arthur Scargill, the miners' leader. Matthews agreed to print Scargill's rebuttal, Lamb offered his resignation (which Matthews refused), and eventually Scargill's piece appeared. The episode did not help the rehabilitation of the *Daily Express* at all.

By August 1983 Fleet shares were priced at £1.22, six times their original value; a month later annual profits of £9.5 million were announced. They went on rising. For the year ending June 1984 they had risen to £22.1 million, of which Morgan-Grampian contributed nearly half. By now it had become clear that the Fleet shares provided the only practicable entrée into the national newspaper scene, plus an attractive share of the Reuters' fairy gold, and a variety of predators were eyeing the company. Among the first to emerge was Robert Holmes à Court, the Australian entrepreneur on whom fortune was smiling at that time; he picked up more than five per cent in 1983.

Matthews did not wish to cede control and started looking for a large acquisition which might provide the elusive third arm for Fleet Holdings. One day a luckless director of TV-AM, desperate to find some additional funding for his station as the banks would lend them no money, called on Matthews in his Fleet Street office and made his pitch. Having heard him out Matthews said, not unkindly, 'If they have to send someone like you to see someone like me, the company must need us badly.' Fleet made an investment of £4 million in TV-AM, ultimately securing a thirty-one per cent stake in the company (worth £34 million in 1988); Matthews joined the board and introduced proper financial controls. But it was not the big deal that would frighten off a bidder. Eventually the financial scouts brought back word of two possibilities. The first was to purchase the classified magazine *Exchange and Mart*. Matthews turned it down as he felt the price of £63 million was too high. (It was bought by United Newspapers.) The second was an American magazine company; but this time Matthews's advisers – both the managing director, Ian Irvine, and the chief executive of Morgan-Grampian, Brian Rowbottom – told him that it was too expensive. Matthews took their advice, and later regretted it. 'If I had been younger' (he was sixty-five at the time), he said later, 'I would have gone ahead and we might have been bid proof.'

The truth was that Matthews had already thrown away his guarantee against take-over. When Fleet Holdings was floated off, Trafalgar House retained £15 million worth of convertible loan stock which, in the event of a hostile take-over could be converted into forty per cent of the ordinary shares, enough to make Fleet completely bid proof. But sometime in 1983 Fleet paid back the £15 million and cancelled the loan stock. Matthews and other senior executives of Fleet were enjoying their independence from Trafalgar and were increasingly worried that as Trafalgar saw Fleet's profits rising it might seize the chance to convert into ordinary shares and would then again be in the driving seat. So Matthews went to Trafalgar and offered them a profit of £7 million on their £15 million stake if they would cancel the loan stock. By now Trafalgar did not wish to relinquish their holding. So Matthews had to tell their executive board that 'nearly every one owed their job to me' and he asked them to return the favour by giving him back the loan stock. His appeal was successful; then he really was on his own.

Meanwhile a larger and larger block of Fleet shares was whizzing round a group of players in a fevered and high priced game of 'pass the parcel'. From Holmes à Court some ten per cent went to Robert Maxwell who could hardly hope to bid himself once he had gained control of the Mirror Group in June 1984. An Egyptian player in the shape of Dr Ashraf Marwan, a friend of Lonrho's Tiny Rowland, briefly took a hand. But when in January 1985 Maxwell sold his stake, now up to 15.76 per cent, to United Newspapers for £30 million the identity of the ultimate predator became clear.

Matthews entered into talks with Aitken Hume International, a financial services group run with intermittent success by two other shareholders in TV-AM – Jonathan Aitken, Beaverbrook's great nephew, and Timothy Aitken, Beaverbrook's grandson; the object was 'to explore possible ways in which the two companies might form a mutually beneficial association'. But while the Aitken family might have provided for a family succession in Fleet the two sides really had little in common apart from their interest in TV-AM where the Aitkens held a private shareholding. The talks came to nothing.

In February 1985 Fleet's half-year profits showed still further growth. As the *Financial Times* commented, 'In more normal circumstances, Fleet's trading for the last six months of 1984 would in itself give it the makings of a fairly reasonable defence showing a 42 per cent increase in trading profits'. But the market capitalisation was still barely double the value of its stake in Reuters. By March United Newspapers' stake had reached 20.1 per cent and an investment group run by David Stevens (now Lord Stevens), chairman of United Newspapers, owned another 3.5 per cent. He announced that he would make a take-over bid as soon as clearance was received from the Monopolies Commission.

Matthews did his best to maintain the independence of Fleet Holdings, but although the City institutions were sympathetic to his plight they warned him that if Stevens offered enough money they would have to take it. A good profits record was not sufficient defence against a bidder prepared to pay over the odds to win control. By October the battle was over, with United raising their offer to £3.75p a share cash – nearly twenty times their original value. 'When I arrived,' said Matthews, 'the Express could not sign a cheque and be sure that it would not bounce. I leave a secure financial company that is making profits.' It was an amazing achievement and Matthews was certainly entitled to take a measure of pride in what he had done. He also took away £8 million personal profit from the transaction. Added to his Trafalgar shareholding and a very useful association with the Barclay brothers, his total fortune in 1988 was estimated by *Money* magazine at £19 million.[8] To safeguard it from the tax man he retreated to the Channel Islands, played golf and, with occasional sorties to the mainland, watched racing on television to see how his expensive string of horses, now trained by his son, were faring. His period in the spotlight was over.

How had he done it? 'I was there. I was pushing and listening and taking a view,' Matthews said later. 'There is no magic formula. You need hard work and determination. You have to get on or you get out.' While Express Newspapers launched the *Daily Star* and the profitable *Sunday Express* magazine under his chairmanship, as well as introducing bingo, an unmatched circulation builder at the time, Matthews tended to view journalists with suspicion and some dislike. He was offended by investigative journalism, loathed gossip columns, and seemed to feel he was personally responsible for everything that appeared in Express newspapers. 'By and large,' he said on taking over, 'the editors will have complete freedom as long as they agree with the policy I have laid down.' Unfortunately he never had the gift of handing out a few words of praise for work well done on the pages of a newspaper. 'You'll only hear from me if something goes wrong,' he would say. 'If you don't hear anything you can assume you are doing all right. Praise is not my style.' Journalists have aspects of showbiz about them, and they sometimes need a shot of flattery. His occasional meetings with editorial staffs failed to reveal much understanding of what they were trying to do. As a result Matthews never gained particular affection among the editorial staffs although, in the end, he won their respect and there was sadness at the loss of Fleet's independence. Nor did the *Daily Express*, to which he gave so much attention, improve under his command, veering direction almost as much as it had in the past. (It is only just to report that he was a very fair employer and showed much personal generosity to me, offering a well-paid sinecure on my retirement from the group.)

His two really big achievements for the newspaper industry were the break-up of the Reuters Trust into a public company, and his employment of the law in securing a greater measure of industrial discipline. Once seized of the value of the Reuters shares he was unrelenting in his pursuit of the money. The 'sacred breed of newspaper proprietors' all owe him a debt of gratitude for pressing the case so strongly. His own respect for justice was deeply offended by what he discovered in Fleet Street. His sense of fair play and decency and genuine horror at the rackets reported to him might have seemed naive to industry habitués but they supplied the motive force for a far tougher attitude to union arrogance than had ever been seen before. The unions did not realise it at the time, but the days of their absolute dominion over the production process were numbered. A one-time building contractor from Islington had rumbled them.

Notes:
1. There is no biography of Lord Matthews. There are many references to him – some rather ungracious – in *A Growing Concern* (Weidenfeld, 1979), the autobiography produced by Nigel Broackes, chairman of Trafalgar House, apparently as a counter to the massive publicity Matthews was receiving. There is also a fairly sharp section about Matthews in *Newspapers, The Power and the Money* by Simon Jenkins (Faber Paperback, 1979), written after Jenkins had left the editorship of the *Evening Standard*. The battle for control of Beaverbrook Newspapers is brilliantly and sometimes hilariously described in *The Fall of the House of Beaverbrook* by Lewis Chester and Jonathan Fenby, Deutsch, 1979.
2. Sir Max was not in good health which may explain why this normally direct and likeable man was beginning to say different things to different people. According to Chester and Fenby he was saying a fortnight later to David English, editor of the *Daily Mail*, 'I want to get back to deal with him [Harmsworth]. He understands newspapers. The others don't.'
3. The heiress Olga Deterding expressed an interest in the *Evening Standard* and I visited her to find out if she was serious. She was – until Jocelyn Stevens frightened her off. Her fortune was not as big as had been rumoured.
4. In a conversation with the author, June 1988.
5. Ivan Fallon in the *Sunday Times* of 6th September 1987.
6. See article by Jocelyn Stevens, 'Where Victor Went Wrong', *UK Press Gazette*, 28th October 1985.
7. I was speaking at the annual lunch of the Automobile Association in May 1977 and had intended to make only a light reference to our problems but Vere Harmsworth in trying to defend the *Daily Mail* from an attack by the Prime Minister, James Callaghan, on the fake Leyland letters in the *Mail*, had dragged in the appointment of Callaghan's son-in-law Peter Jay as our Ambassador in Washington. I said in part, 'Why is Mr Vere Harmsworth chairman of Associated Newspapers? Why is he in a position to squander millions of his shareholders' money in an effort to force the *Evening Standard* out of business? Why has he been able to sell his evening paper at an uneconomic price, to offer cut rates to advertisers who switch from the *Evening Standard* to his own paper, to start up costly and uneconomic ventures in the suburbs, and to maintain an uneconomic circulation area – all, I believe, with the aim of compelling his competitor to surrender?

   'May I suggest that the only reason why Mr Vere Harmsworth is chairman of Associated Newspapers is that he is the son of the second Lord Rothermere. And the second Lord Rothermere had the job because he was the son of the first Lord Rothermere. And the first Lord Rothermere had the *Daily Mail* because he was the brother of a real newspaper genius, Lord Northcliffe.'

There was a splendid row after that. Sir Max Aitken was very cross and rebuked me at a board meeting. Harmsworth wrote a savage letter to *The Times* pointing out that he had asked me to chair a selection meeting of Simon Jenkins and Louis Kirby, editor of the *Evening News*, to pick the staff of the new joint paper and accused me of 'hysterical utterances'. (Fortunately for me there were two inaccuracies in his letter.) But the staff of the *Evening Standard* were delighted.

8. *Money* magazine, March 1988. The magazine was later bought by Stonehart Publications and incorporated in *Family Wealth*.

9

Rothermere – The heir who flourished

With a good heredity, nature deals you a fine hand at cards; and with a good environment, you learn to play the hand well.

Walter C. Alvarez

One Saturday afternoon early in 1971 a dozen journalists headed by the editor of the *Daily Sketch*, David English (now Sir David), were planning, in the utmost secrecy, the new tabloid *Daily Mail*. They had been holed up in an over-crowded room in Carmelite House off Fleet Street since nine am. Various layouts had been prepared for discussion with Vere Harmsworth, who was then deputy chairman of Associated Newspapers although he would shortly become chairman in succession to his father, Esmond, the second Lord Rothermere. The two senior managers of the *Mail* – John Winnington-Ingram and Bert Irvine – were also present. Harmsworth had made quite a few typographical criticisms and suggestions and the editorial team were kept busy producing new sets of layouts. Suddenly at three thirty pm when the team were producing yet another set someone said, 'God, we ought to have a break'. English replied, rather crisply, 'We've got no time for a break.' Harmsworth sensibly remarked, 'We must have sandwiches', and looked around the room. A couple of the younger subs, knowing their place, said they would go and get them.

At this point Harmsworth signalled the beginning of a revolution at Associated. 'No,' he said. 'We are certainly not sending out any journalists to get sandwiches. You are far too valuable and there is far too much creative work to do. The management have just been standing here. *They* can get the sandwiches.' Turning to Winnington-Ingram he ordered, 'Sandwiches for everyone.' Winnington-Ingram promptly relayed the order to Irvine, thus craftily establishing his ascendancy over Irvine who had previously been regarded as his

172

equal. Irvine, muttering obscurely, went off and returned with a vast parcel of sandwiches which kept everyone going until late in the evening.

The journalists were thunderstruck: the *managers* getting sandwiches for the *journalists*! They could scarcely believe it. They knew then that a momentous upheaval was about to shake Associated Newspapers. Northcliffe, the founder of the *Daily Mail*, was above all a journalist; under his regime journalists were pampered and cosseted and loved – well, most of the time anyway. They were given high salaries, lavish expenses and sat in comfortable offices with coal fires while the management were hidden away upstairs in cold, poky and uncomfortable rooms.

As Northcliffe lay dying he forecast that his brother Harold, the first Lord Rothermere, would ruin his papers by meanness and his 'tendency to panic'; he was not far out. Under the Rothermere regime the editorial/management precedence was reversed. Management were put on top, profits came first, editorial space was squeezed to allow more advertising, editorial expenses were cut and the little comforts of life were that much harder for journalists to come by. Esmond was an excellent businessman, but never very comfortable with journalists; when he succeeded to the title in 1940 the management stayed on top. Vere Harmsworth, although he had been through every department of Associated Newspapers, from postal bargains to circulation, from production to labour relations, with the one exception of editorial, really liked the company of journalists, sought them out, had drinks with them and enjoyed talking with them.

He gradually came to the view that bad management was possibly more dangerous for newspapers than bad editors and further, that bad management could destroy good editors. Reflecting on the past of the family business, he felt that the *Mail* had declined since the 1920s and 1930s because it was management-led while the *Express* had been editorially led by Beaverbrook. So as he assumed power it was his considered resolve to make the editorial more powerful than the management and to stop management interference with editorial affairs. His demand to the senior managers that they should get the sandwiches was thus a reflection of his basic publishing philosophy.

Students of form noted several other changes as Vere took over the chairmanship. Esmond had been noted as a stickler for the hierarchy. If he came on the telephone a special operator would sometimes announce, 'The Lord Chairman wishes to speak to you.' In conversation the staff always addressed him either as 'Lord Rothermere' or, more often, 'Sir'. Company cars were strictly graded according to seniority. If a member of the staff was summoned to see him in the afternoon, it was noted that he had a tray with a teapot, biscuits and *one* cup from which he would drink. He shrank from direct involvement with difficult personal interviews, so he instructed his managing director to fire Guy Schofield from the editorship of the *Daily Mail*; later the same managing director was given the job of firing Mike Randall from the same job.

Vere's approach was very different. 'Call me "Vere" ', was the first instruction many people received, and if anyone saw him in the afternoon there were *two* cups on the tray with slices of cake and biscuits. He was generous where his father had been careful. He was so rich himself that he was almost separated from reality by wealth but he believed in paying talent handsomely. It was said that the late Mick Shields, his brilliant managing director, earned as much as £500,000 a year; Shields certainly enjoyed the use of a company Rolls-Royce. Further, thanks to share options and high salaries, he may well have created several millionaires among the salaried staffs of Associated Newspapers.

His charm was accentuated by a rather quizzical approach to life. He would gaze at people with one eyebrow half-raised and the other eye only half-open. His marked sense of humour could have a touch of menace in it. He had a genuine interest in Eastern mysticism and the occult. One day during lunch with his editors he had steered the conversation round to Buddhism and was warming to the idea of reincarnation. Stewart Steven, editor of the *Mail on Sunday*, suggested that if the theory were true Vere should be very worried for he might come back as an Untouchable sweeping the streets of Calcutta. Vere shot back, 'Yes, and you should be careful or *you* could be an Untouchable sweeping the streets of London.' He did in fact take quite a serious interest in the paranormal; Patric Walker, the highly paid astrologer who lives on Rhodes, furnished with a company car, became a close friend and adviser.

Arguments with Vere could also present problems. He liked arguing, said some observers, but he liked to win the day. One new management accountant engaged him in debate about accounting, seemed to know all the answers and contradicted the chairman. Shields observed, 'The chairman is many things, *but* he is never wrong. That man is finished.' And he was.

It was also part of Vere's character that he should get to know the journalists who worked for Associated. So it was that when English was working on the *Sketch* in the 1950s first as features editor and then as assistant editor, Harmsworth, the newly appointed manager, had met him and they had hit it off quite well. He kept in touch when English moved to the *Sunday Dispatch*. When that paper was merged into the *Sunday Express*, English, now in the New York office, was offered a job on the *Mail* as late night reporter in London. He reckoned that was a pretty insulting offer and refused. In fact he had decided to stay in the States and was on the point of joining the *Washington Post* when he received a call from Lord Beaverbrook, who clearly had also been watching his work with interest. Beaverbrook asked English to join the *Express* as New York reporter and soon promoted him first to be the New York columnist, then the White House correspondent and finally Chief of Bureau.

After Beaverbrook's death English was recalled to London and soon promoted to be associate editor of the *Daily Express* under Derek Marks. At first the large and genial Marks, who was much better at unravelling the secrets of the Conservative party than coping with the politics of editing the *Express*, did not warm to the slighter, more thrusting English whom he suspected of being after his job. But after that bumpy start they settled down quite well and English happily produced the paper while Marks had more time to pursue his political contacts.

For eight years Harmsworth had been the only person in Associated Newspapers who saw English from time to time and knew what he was doing. He now persuaded his father that English should be offered the editorship of the *Sketch* which was already in serious trouble. Sir Max Aitken was appalled at the idea of losing English and did his utmost to persuade him to stay. He even offered English the editorship of the *Daily Express* – but at some vague future date; he would not give a firm commitment. It was a decision that had fateful consequences for Beaverbrook Newspapers. Aitken's regard for Derek Marks was too great for him to contemplate removing his friend from the editor's chair at that moment although he came to that painful step before long. He could not possibly have realised it at the time, but his honourable and characteristic loyalty may well have cost him his inheritance. For English, the ablest tabloid journalist of his generation, preferred to accept the editorship of quite a small newspaper to a promise of future preferment on one of the largest. Although Aitken later made several attempts to find a new editor for the *Express* – he twice went back to English, but it was too late – he was never able to discover anyone who could edit the paper half as well as English could have done.

Harmsworth and English working together developed into a publishing partnership that rivalled, and in some ways transcended, the relationship between Beaverbrook and Christiansen. Although unsurpassed as a newspaper technician, Christiansen was Beaverbrook's political poodle as I saw for myself at a meeting of the Express Group's so-called policy committee, chaired by E. J. Robertson, the managing director. When some new development of Beaverbrook's anti-Common Market campaign was adumbrated, I heard Christiansen declare in all sincerity that 'a policy of such grandeur and insight and authority could have been formulated only by Lord Beaverbrook'. It would surely have been impossible for the sharp and sophisticated David English to utter such pompous and inflated sentiments. Further, English was given more power than Christiansen ever possessed. In effect, as he has said, he became the marketing manager of the *Mail*. He had the power to alter, on a day-to-day basis, the advertising/editorial ratio to accommodate a big story or serial, and he could influence the promotional spend on a big story. Since he was also made responsible for the overall revenue on the paper he obviously used this power with considerable care.

The first test of the new partnership came when Harmsworth took the crucial decision to close the *Sketch* and to change the broadsheet *Mail* into a tabloid. It was his decision alone and he had pondered it deeply. The *Daily Express* was riding high with a circulation of some 3,500,000, just about double that of the *Mail*. He took the view that the *Mail* had become a 'me too' paper. The editorial staff were always watching what the *Express* was up to; they were not thinking for themselves. (According to Mike Randall, Harmsworth himself was not immune to the plague of *Express*-watching. The most frequent user of the office intercom was Harmsworth, he wrote. 'His opening remark was always the same: "Did you see that marvellous story about such-and-such in the *Express* this morning? Why wasn't it in the *Mail*?" '[1]) It was necessary to raise morale in some way. It was also vital, as Harmsworth later explained,[2] for the *Mail* to be visibly different from the *Express*; it was necessary to 'twist the market' in a new direction. Although he had supported the absorption of the *News Chronicle* at the time, he now felt it had been a profound mistake, producing an unacceptable hybrid in an effort to hold the *Chronicle* readers just as the *Chronicle*'s absorption of the *Daily Dispatch* had also proved disastrous. A further factor had been his sense that the *Mail* and the *Sketch* seemed like

A Harmsworth family portrait. Northcliffe (on the left) did not think much of his brother Harold Rothermere (right) as a newspaper publisher, but relied on his financial stewardship. Harold's son Esmond (centre) was elegant and civilised but had little of his uncle's flair and passion.

The second Lord Rothermere in 1955. He was a touch austere for a publisher. If an editor was asked to see him around teatime there was only one cup – for the chairman. He was a successful financier, like his father, but shunned difficult decisions.

Sir David English, *Daily Mail* editor since 1971. His decision to accept the editorship of the *Daily Sketch* in 1969 rather than the promise of the *Daily Express* at some future date was crucial in swinging the *Express-Mail* battle Harmsworth's way.

Robert Maxwell at the launch of
Joe Haines biography of himself
in February 1988. Maxwell has
no inhibitions about self-
publicity, so the British Printing
Corporation has become the
Maxwell Communications
Corporation, housed, of course, in
Maxwell House. And here we get
three impressions of him for the
price of one.

Three media moguls meet at the
annual general meeting of
Reuters in 1987. The third Lord
Rothermere listens impassively
while Robert Maxwell expounds
some new thought about the
international media world while
Rupert Murdoch listens with
apparent scepticism.

two seperate halves of the same paper. A final factor was that in the *Evening Standard* of that time he saw 'the idea for the *Daily Mail*'.[3]

The conversion took place in May 1971 and it was by no means an instant success. The circulation of the *Mail*, far from showing any increment from *Sketch* readers, actually fell by nearly 100,000 to 1,613,000 and there was heavy pressure to make changes. It was nearly eighteen months before the tide turned. Ten years later English reported:

> The initial lean period tested the nerves of all involved . . . That we are in such a buoyant mood today is due to one man – Vere Harmsworth. Only Vere argued for holding steadfastly to our course. To change would be crazy and self-destructive, particularly when the worst was over. 'Stay with it and you will succeed.' So we stayed and we did.

A major factor in the paper's ability to survive a difficult period lay in the drastic programme of redundancies which was enforced. There had been 650 *Mail* editorial staff and 180 *Sketch*; this was cut to a total of only 320. The axe work was carried out by Howard French, then editorial director of Associated. His letters of dismissal, naturally known as 'French letters', were taken to their unfortunate recipients by English. It was the period of Butch Cassidy and the Sundance Kid. Gallows humorists on the editorial floors referred to 'Butcher Harmsworth and the Redundance Kid'. From being an over-padded staff the *Mail* took on a slimmer and altogether tougher look. There were altogether 1,700 redundancies at Associated Newspapers; it was strong medicine.

Harmsworth showed further courage in countermanding his managers' nervous decision to cut paging during the summer advertising drought. He insisted not only on restoring normal paging but in policy paging to show the outside world no sign of weakness or decline, and he made a point of appearing in the Press Club, then just off Salisbury Square, to have a drink with the somewhat shaken staff and to encourage them in the belief that the *Mail* was on the right track. In later years he would say that the successful realisation of the change and its eventual triumph was 'entirely due to the genius of David English with the inspirational support of the late R. M. Shields, together with John Winnington-Ingram', but the chief credit undoubtedly belonged to the man who insisted on change, and saw it through.

Just as Cecil King had been resented in his early days at the *Mirror*, Vere Harmsworth's introduction to the *Sketch* was not universally welcomed by other managers, hence the easy nickname of 'Mere'. He had been educated at Eton where he was already marked out as an eccentric and then took a less conventional course to the athletically minded Kent School, Connecticut, where he did not stay long. He was called up for the army and served as a private for two and a half years, including a spell in the Middle East. It was a period that may have given him an insight into ordinary people normally denied to the very wealthy.

His first civilian job, at the age of twenty-two, was in a logging camp belonging to the family firm of Anglo-Canadian Paper Mills in North Quebec. Two years later his father saw to it that he was thoroughly trained to be a publisher by putting him through the works of Associated Newspapers and by the time he was thirty he was appointed to his first solid job as manager of the *Daily Sketch*, Associated's ailing tabloid. He was known as quiet and amiable, a bit of a humorist, quite cultivated but markedly eccentric – a man who, like his father, enjoyed comfort, but unlike his father was willing to tolerate uncomfortable journalists if they had the talent to support their moods. One thing was clear: he bitterly resented suggestions that he was uninterested in publishing. In 1962 he brought a successful libel action against the *Investor's Chronicle* whose newsletter had said, 'He is believed to have little or no interest in the newspaper world'. He won £2,000 which he gave to charities. In 1973 he secured an apology and costs from *The Times* for a savage article by Bernard Levin about the closure of the *Sketch* entitled 'Profit and Dishonour in Fleet Street'. In 1978 he won another libel case when it was suggested that 'he was waiting for the *Express* to die and that he was unable to reach a firm decision'.

His father gave him two gifts of the greatest importance: first, he settled £2,750,000 on him in 1957, the year of his marriage to the actress Beverley Brooks, so he need never worry whether his inheritance was safe; and, secondly, of even greater importance, he was allowed to learn from his own mistakes. While across the street Beaverbrook was virtually hounding his son, Esmond Rothermere was supportive and understanding. After his father's death in 1977, Vere said his father had supported his decision to turn the *Mail* into a tabloid. 'This decision, which was mine, must have caused him many anguished hours of doubt in the early days. Nonetheless he supported me loyally and totally, never wavering.' When his father had succeeded to the title a friend observed, 'Esmond Harmsworth does not really know anything about the newspaper business and probably cares less, although he works hard at it.'[4] In fact the elegant and civilised Esmond was not at all a successful publisher himself, but he certainly knew how to make one. He also left family control of Associated Newspapers quite intact; a family trust controlled 49.95 per cent of the shares. His son made that control absolute in 1988 by buying out the rest.

Yet at one moment it had seemed that there might be no *Mail* for Vere to inherit. For some years talks had been proceeding between Marmaduke Hussey, then managing director of Associated Newspapers, and John Coote, managing director of Beaverbrook Newspapers.[5] Coote wished to instal new presses in the black glass building that housed the *Express* but had problems finding the money to pay for them, and Hussey controlled two newspapers – the *Mail* and the *Sketch* – that were clearly in trouble. The plan was to merge the two middle-market papers, and perhaps the two evenings as well, print them on the new *Express* plant, free Associated's property for development and reap fat profits. It was a manager's dream. At the beginning of 1971 a meeting of principals was held in Warwick House, Esmond Rothermere's London home; inevitably Lord Goodman, Sir Max's friend and legal adviser, was there with him. Verbal agreement was reached on a deal setting up a new joint company which would own the titles of the *Mail* and *Express*, the *News* and the *Standard*. (The highly profitable *Sunday Express* was to have remained outside the new company.) Mergers would have followed. Rothermere was going on safari for six weeks and the agreements were to be signed on his return. As soon as Vere heard about the proposed deal he protested violently that he was being deprived of his inheritance. Next day Rothermere, who was seventy-two, told a board meeting of Associated Newspapers that he was retiring as chairman of the company and handing over to Vere. 'Some will no doubt say that I should have done so before,' he said. 'Others will no doubt say I have done so too soon.' Meanwhile at Beaverbrook Newspapers Jocelyn Stevens, then managing director of the *Evening Standard*, was persuading Sir Max that Beaverbrook could go it alone and had no need for the Coote-Hussey deal.

Harmsworth's very first act as chairman was to replace Hussey, whom he regarded as perhaps too prone to usurp the role of the proprietor. Vere hated the thought that the family newspapers should be merged with their rivals and distrusted the man who had been negotiating their fate without him. Indeed he distrusted all managers. Once at a boardroom lunch he was giving, a senior management executive engaged the guest of honour, the Italian ambassador, in a discussion about the problems of the South Tyrol; the executive mentioned that he had been talking recently to the Austrian ambassador about the same subject when that ambassador had been staying with him for the weekend. The lunch proceeded frostily and afterwards a furious Vere demanded to know what the executive thought he was doing in entertaining an ambassador at home.

'Well, we met him and got on quite well, so we asked him to stay for the weekend,' said the executive mildly.

Vere, still in a rage, replied, '*Management* don't entertain ambassadors. Proprietors do because they are interested in power; editors do because they have to know what's going on. But *management* have no right to have ambassadors to dinner.' He added dismissively, 'Anyway ambassadors aren't interested in ink and paper and printing.' To emphasise that the place of management was 'below stairs' that executive was banned from boardroom lunches for a year.

In the Northcliffe tradition of keeping 'ferrets' Vere liked to have some 'loyal' executives who would keep him informed of the state of office politics where an atmosphere of conspiracy and suspicion frequently reigned. The story was told that at one interview John Gold, then the editor of the *Evening News* but treated with some reserve because he was a friend of Hussey, looked carefully under Vere's desk as if searching for hidden 'bugs' before he sat down.

'Why do you do that?' asked Vere.

'Well, you told me to be suspicious,' replied Gold.

'You are always criticising me for being mistrustful,' said Vere. He paused and concluded, 'If you had grown up with my background *you* would be suspicious.' Gold never knew whether Vere meant that his family were still conspiring, or whether suspicion was a legacy of his upbringing; probably the latter. Ironically Vere sometimes looked under his desk for bugs, and had his office electronically 'swept' at least twice.

The new managing director was the vibrant and aggressive figure of Mick Shields,* who having lost out to Hussey in the management power struggle under Esmond, had then been despatched away from

---

* Shields also had experience of a 'loyal' character reporting on him to Vere. He was furious and complained bitterly to Vere about the use of such people. 'Those are only my watchdogs', said Vere. 'They must be the only watchdogs trained to bite members of the household,' said the sardonic Shields.

the main building to the salt mines of Harmsworth Investments. There he launched National Opinion Polls as an Associated subsidiary and bided his time. Meanwhile across the street, Aitken first promoted Stevens to be managing director of the *Daily Express* in 1972 and then managing director of all the group's newspapers fourteen months later. So both the managing directors who had arranged such a cosy and profitable alliance were removed. The battle between the Harmsworths and the Aitkens was to be resumed in earnest until the Aitkens left the blood-stained field.

Harmsworth had inherited another major advantage over his rival. Associated Newspapers held many profitable interests outside national newspapers. The provincial chain started by the first Lord Rothermere to attack the Berrys had been further developed; there were now some twenty provincial newspapers and most of them were profitable. Associated also owned investments in property, taxi cabs, Canadian pulp, pizza parlours and television. A further immensely profitable stake was taken in North Sea oil. Lord Rothermere's fourth wife, Mrs Mary Ohrstrom, was the sister-in-law of Frederic C. Hamilton, chairman of the big American oil company called Hamilton Brothers. Hamilton needed a British partner so that he could bid for licences to drill in the North Sea. It was natural that he should turn first to his wealthy and influential brother-in-law and the investment was made in the late 1960s. (Subsequently Paul Getty told Esmond Rothermere he was wasting his money: he would find no oil in the North Sea. As a result Associated came close to pulling out. Fortunately for their shareholders Shields persuaded Rothermere to stay in; that is what earned him his Rolls. Later Getty himself invested huge sums in North Sea exploration.) Associated's outside interests earned about a third of their profits. This gave Harmsworth time to get his act together while Aitken, pressured by the banks, sought instant solutions.

English set about producing a bright, newsy, high pressure, gossipy, quick-reacting, entertaining and somewhat cynical tabloid newspaper with strong feminine appeal, targeted especially at the middle classes of London and the South. After the initial doubts the paper's circulation began to rise and two years after the relaunch was back over 1,700,000. It became much admired in advertising circles. Higher revenues followed and have been sustained so that years later the *Mail* was still claiming to attract the highest display advertising revenue in the business. Harmsworth could now concentrate on attempting to stem the drain on his resources caused by the financial problems of the *Evening News*, Northcliffe's first newspaper. By 1974 its sale was dropping by about 50,000 a year and if anything the decline was accelerating. The *Evening Standard* with a smaller sale had a wealthier, more concentrated readership and was able to charge a premium rate for advertisers. The drive of Jocelyn Stevens and the advertising flair of Brian Nicholson had actually produced a profit of more than £1 million in 1972. But distribution costs for both newspapers were appallingly high and balance sheets for both were soon under pressure. In 1974 Harmsworth tried the tabloid treatment on the *News* with a new editor. It did not work. (Earlier he had told John Gold, the previous editor, 'You know, John, I have a concept for the *Daily Mail* but I don't have a concept for the *Evening News*.' It was the writing on the wall.) By the summer of 1975 Harmsworth was warning that major savings and economies would be necessary if the paper was to survive. By 1976 it was said that losses on the *News* were close to £4 million a year, so he was receptive to another approach from the new management team at Beaverbrook, suggesting a merged evening paper printed on the *Express* plant. Negotiations began, inevitably under the aegis of Lord Goodman, and produced a plan by which the *Standard* was to be sold to Associated for £7.5 million and a new merged evening paper produced at the *Express* plant.

As a director of the Beaverbrook group I had been kept informed of the outline proposals and had protested privately. Fortunately Sheila Black of *The Times* broke the story in April 1977 and it was then possible for Simon Jenkins as editor and myself as chairman of the Evening Standard Co Ltd to make as much public fuss as possible to protect the *Standard*. Naturally, the staffs of both newspapers became extremely unsettled about their futures. Eventually Harmsworth went so far as to propose, over a rather fraught lunch attended by David English and Louis Kirby, the editor of the *News*, as well as by Simon Jenkins and myself, that an advisory committee should be set up to choose the staff for the new paper and suggested they might well find that eighty per cent of the staff of the new paper should be drawn from the *Standard*. (The lunch was made all the more edgy by the fact that as Vere's wife and the normal staff were away, the meal was served by his chauffeur who sometimes dropped the odd semi-frozen chop into the laps of his guests.) He did not however go so far as to suggest that Jenkins should be the editor. By this time I was so wound up at any idea that the *Standard*, a paper I loved and whose staff I cherished, might die that I rejected all thoughts of compromise.* Ultimately however the fate of the paper rested with Harmsworth and Jenkins. If Harmsworth had offered Jenkins the editorship and Jenkins had accepted, the deal would have gone through. But Jenkins was offered only the deputy editorship which he refused. Meanwhile, spurred by the imminence of the deal, frantic efforts were being made, principally by Jocelyn Stevens, to discover some alternative method of saving the Beaverbrook group from bankruptcy. In the end, Trafalgar House bought the company outright and, as described in the preceding chapter, the unlikely figure of Victor Matthews emerged as the new press lord.

One of Harmsworth's strongest suits is the ability to take a long-term view. Less than three years later, having decided that the losses of the *Evening News* were no longer sustainable, he made that very different deal to close the *News* entirely at Associated's expense. (He did not shirk the painful task of dealing with the closure himself, flying back from Paris to attend the wake.) In return for the closure he got a half-share of the Evening Standard Co Ltd with the option to buy the remaining half if Trafalgar House ever wished to sell. Matthews was then sixty-one and Rothermere, who had succeeded to the title in 1978, was fifty-five. 'I knew that Matthews would eventually retire and that, when he did, Trafalgar House would be ready to sell,' he said later. His calculation proved correct. In December 1985 Associated bought the remaining half of the *Evening Standard* for £20 million – the paper that was so nearly closed now, as a monopoly, had a market value that was more than twice the sum fetched by the entire Beaverbrook group, property and all, some eight years earlier.

Vere Rothermere again showed his ability to plan ahead when he launched the *Mail on Sunday* in 1982. He had first suggested he would launch a new national Sunday 'probably in tabloid form' five years ealier. Beaverbrook executives were so worried about the threat to the *Sunday Express* at that time that they inserted a clause into the original draft deal over the *Standard* that Associated would not enter the Sunday market for at least three years. When that deal collapsed Rothermere had to concentrate on trying to pull round the ailing *News*. Foreseeing ever-increasing losses, put as high as £20 million a year in another five years, he made the deal with

---

* According to Chester and Lewis, op cit, Harmsworth told Stevens that he had never been spoken to like that before 'even by my father'. Stevens told the author that Harmsworth said 'Wintour treated us like niggers'. I *was* extremely steamed up.

Rothermere did not want to close the *News* in 1980 but its losses were becoming too big. His shrewd deal with Matthews for a half-share in the *Standard* freed staff and plant to launch the *Mail on Sunday* 18 months later.

Trafalgar, shut it down and prepared for the launch of his Sunday paper. Rothermere appointed Bernard Shrimsley, formerly with the *News of the World*, as editor. The management were determined not to spend even more money on a colour supplement and urged the incorporation of a Lifestyle black and white magazine inside the paper. Rothermere went along with their plan.

Seven weeks before publication English took the dummies to New York for Rothermere to see. The next evening they had dinner at the Hotel Carlyle; Rothermere said at once that the new paper would not work in this form and that English should take over immediately. English resisted; he said time was far too short for a change of course to be successful. Eventually Rothermere was reluctantly persuaded and the launch went ahead with Shrimsley still in the chair. As Rothermere had correctly forecast the launch was indeed a disaster. The paper was too dry, too cramped, far too unappealing. The target sale had been 1,250,000; within six weeks the figure was down to 700,000 and falling. The dinner at the Carlyle had proved even more expensive than usual.

Shrimsley was bundled out; English and some twenty *Daily Mail* staffers took over. English had refused to take the job unless the paper had a colour supplement. Since Rothermere had now seen some American research which showed that no Sunday paper could hope to succeed without a colour magazine, he was in complete agreement. The new staff were paid two salaries, their *Mail* salary and a *Mail on Sunday* salary as well. Eventually nearly ninety per cent of Shrimsley's men were fired and a new team recruited. The typography was transformed, the content lightened, many personal columns introduced and a livelier sense of entertainment percolated the pages. *You* magazine was soon added. Within five months English received his proper reward[6] and was promoted to the role of group editor-in-chief, while remaining editor of the *Mail*; Stewart Steven, one of his colleagues from the *Daily Mail*, was given the editorship. Rothermere's instincts had been right in the first place, and he had acted with decision to save his investment.

Rothermere is of course a strong supporter of Mrs Thatcher. 'Our readers are all Conservative,' he told an interviewer.[7] 'They're middle-class people and middle class people tend to support Conservative governments because Conservative governments look after the interests of middle-class people.' But he is less rigid about his support for the Conservatives than his father who laid down that 'the *Daily Mail* had to support the Tories not only in the leading article but also throughout the newspaper'.[8] Indeed when Stewart Steven said he wanted the *Mail on Sunday* to support the Social Democratic party, Rothermere gave him the all clear. By election time however Steven had changed his mind. 'I would have had a hard time from Vere if he hadn't,' admitted English.

When another challenge came along Rothermere responded more subtly. Robert Maxwell's decision to launch a quality London evening paper to be called the *London Daily News* directly threatened the profitability of the *Evening Standard* which had become distinctly lazy in its monopoly position. The editor of the *Mail on Sunday*'s magazine, John Leese, was soon appointed editor; he re-styled the paper, vastly enlarged the magazine features and revitalised the staff. Bert Hardy, the chief executive, polished up the *Standard*'s distribution system and dreamt up a stunning and expensive promotion, offering five free houses to readers. But it was Rothermere, visiting Tokyo at the time, who decided to re-launch the *Evening News*. It was not a very expensive operation since the paper could be distributed in the *Standard*'s vans and put together by an exiguous staff as a cut price product.

As an editorial consultant for Maxwell's paper I had originally put forward the *LDN* title which Maxwell had accepted with enthusiasm; Magnus Linklater, the editor, also liked it. Later I became convinced that it would be absolutely in character for Rothermere to attempt the spoiler of reviving the *News*. I argued strongly that we should drop the *LDN* title; research indicated that *The Londoner* would be quite well received and there were other alternatives of which I favoured '*The London Griffin*'. Maxwell's reply was, 'If he does [re-launch the *News*], it'll hurt the *Standard* more than it hurts us.' When news of the re-launch was confirmed, I reminded Maxwell of his statement. 'All the same,' he said somewhat ruefully, 'I wish he hadn't done it.' The *LDN* had many other problems, which I sketch in the next chapter, but the confusion over titles certainly did not help. Fairly soon after the collapse of the *LDN*, Rothermere closed the *News* which had a sale of only 30,000 at the time. It had done its job. The editor, Lori Miles, had been hired from *Chat* magazine and had been been highly feted on her appointment as one of the first women editors in Fleet Street. Lunched by such luminaries as Rothermere, Hardy and English, she had been naive enough to believe what they told her about the glowing future of the revived *News*. When it closed the shock was appalling and she was far from appeased by a generous pay-off. Like any other savage battle Fleet Street wars have their casualties too.

Some of Rothermere's attempts to play an even bigger role in the newspaper industry have been less successful. He tried to buy *The Observer* in 1976, but it went to Atlantic Richfield instead. Five years later he was a strong contender for Times Newspapers, much to the horror of his managing director Mick Shields. 'My God, what have I got to do to stop the chairman wanting to acquire more newspapers? We've only just paid off half the *Evening News* staff,' he told Harry Evans.[9] But Sir Gordon Brunton, chief executive of the Thomson Organisation, was strongly in favour of Murdoch's offer. Speaking of Rothermere's interest, he said, 'I can get more than double the money out of him. But they would be a disaster. And they won't give me the necessary guarantees for the production of *The Times*.' In fact Associated offered either £25 million for the *Sunday Times* alone or £20 million for the two papers. Years later Rothermere was still puzzled by the hostility his bid aroused, but admitted that he would never have been able to 'do a Wapping' like Murdoch since he did not have an alternative plant. One factor in Brunton's mind may have been Murdoch's up-front approach; he handled the deal himself, frequently phoning to get further details of the financial picture. Rothermere remained in Paris and the negotiations were handled by Shields.

He also attempted one or two forays in the United States. In 1977 he took over *Esquire* with Clay Felker, the former editor and founder of the highly successful *New York* magazine, and Milton Glaser, its designer. (They had just been ousted by Rupert Murdoch.) Rothermere was fascinated by Felker who was a brilliant talker, and paid him extravagantly. But Felker could not repeat his *New York* success and was removed. A new team took over and turned it round while Rothermere retained an interest, selling out two years later. He also bought control of New York's *Soho News*, a possible rival of *Village Voice*; but the *News* could never rival the *Voice* so he folded it, reckoning that a massive investment would be needed to get on anything like level terms. He was frequently reported to be considering the purchase of an American newspaper, but he soon realised the potential of controlled circulation magazines in the United States. In consequence Associated Newspapers North America (ANNA) has bought or launched a number of them, particularly in the legal field. In 1988–9 ANNA was said to be making some $15 million to $20 million a year, but Rothermere trimmed it down.

Rothermere has always looked on newspaper publishing as a serious profession. 'Newspapers and magazines need a certain type of publisher,' he has said. 'If he doesn't understand the business he won't succeed.' He added that publishers must have 'empathy' with journalists, i.e. the capacity for imaginatively sharing in their feelings or ideas. Publishers must also be ready to invest in their newspapers. 'Beaverbrook spent £200,000 on *A King's Story* for the *Sunday Express* and everybody thought he was mad, but he got it all back and more. Rupert spent a fortune promoting the *Sun* – and he made it the most profitable tabloid in the country.'

Rothermere never forgot Beaverbrook's success with *A King's Story*. Some years before the Duchess of Windsor died he told English that there must be letters and documents which would make another series and that he should get after Maître Blum, the elderly woman lawyer who was in charge of the estate. English first asked his Paris office to make contact; they could not even see Maître Blum. He then sent a senior features executive; he saw her but got nowhere. Finally English went himself and was able to take her out to lunch. After several meetings he realised that the only way to clinch the deal was to produce Rothermere himself; Maître Blum was flattered and the deal was made. Associated paid £400,000 which included Commonwealth rights; their net outlay was thereby cut to £220,000. Seven years after negotiations began 'The Windsor love letters' were published to coincide with the launch of *Today*. The series put on 400,000 in the first week and after three weeks 300,000 was still holding. The magic of the Windsors still exerted its hold on the British public as Rothermere rightly believed.

He has shown scorn for publishers with a less serene view of their work. Talking on Radio 4 shortly after the launch of the *LDN*, he said, 'A lot of people come into newspapers on an ego trip. I don't think that's good business and I don't think that's a good way of being a newspaper publisher. It's a profession and that's it. To be on an ego trip is very dangerous; you make bad judgements; you make foolish decisions; and you're very likely to end up making a total ass of yourself.'

Rothermere prefers to work largely in the background and seems happy for his editors to collect the accolades, even if some of the credit for their creative success stems from him. Success may have given him a certain arrogant assurance about his own judgment but a sense of humour helps to prevent it being over-bearing. 'Publishing is like presiding over a perpetual War Game between management and journalists,' he has observed with some satisfaction.

As umpire of Associated's War game, he directed the attention of the participants to the need for colour as early as 1984 when he wrote a note to his senior executives saying that any newspaper which did not have colour capacity by 1990 would be dead, long before Eddy Shah launched *Today*, the first colourful effort at a national newspaper. In fact it was Maxwell who was the first to introduce colour to the mass circulation tabloids, and Associated had to speed up the commissioning of their new plant in the Surrey Docks. Rothermere is spending a total of £275 million on his modernisation programme. He can well afford it. In the year he took over, Associated's pre-tax profits amounted to only £3.7 million on a turnover of £58 million. In 1987 pre-tax profits had risen to £57 million on a turnover of £581 million. And the ratio of profit to turnover had increased from 6.3 per cent to 9.8 per cent.

Only one question remained unresolved at Associated Newspapers as the year 1988 was drawing to a close. What happened next? Rothermere was beginning to talk of retirement. If that happened when he was seventy, his son Harold would still be well under thirty. Sir David English, now deputy chairman of Mail Newspapers and six years younger than his chairman, could act as Regent to the

Crown Prince for a while, but that would not be an easy situation. It seemed likely that even if Rothermere took himself off to that mountain top he said he would eventually inhabit, this subtle and successful publisher who enjoyed himself so much would not relinquish control entirely. But it would be for future generations to carry out that middle-market merger which had proved so elusive. Only next time – if there *was* a next time – the Harmsworths would call the tune thanks largely to the third Lord Rothermere, the man whose inheritance blossomed and fructified.

Notes:
1. *The Funny Side of the Street*, by Mike Randall, Bloomsbury, 1988.
2. In a conversation with the author, 7th September, 1988.
3. In a letter to the author dated 8th August, 1988
4. From the diary of Collins Brooks, quoted in Koss, op cit.
5. Full details are given in Chester and Fenby, op cit.
6. John Leese rightly claims credit for the success of the magazine. He chose the title, introduced part-work series and a cartoon section.
7. Raymond Snoddy, in the *Financial Times*, 6th June 1988.
8. Letter from Esmond Rothermere to R. Hammond, then managing director, October 1964, quoted by Randall, op cit.
9. See *Good Times – Bad Times* by Harold Evans, op cit.

10
Robert Maxwell

Only in constant action was his constant certainty found. He will throw a longer shadow as time recedes.

written of John Cornford

One day in February 1988 a party of six financial journalists flew from Heathrow to the port of Bastia in Corsica and were then transported by launch to Robert Maxwell's[1] handsome yacht *Lady Ghislaine*, named after his youngest daughter and owned by a subsidiary of Mirror Group Newspapers. They were accompanied by Ian, one of his sons; Peter Jay, his chief of staff; a merchant banker from Samuel Montagu; a handler and a secretary. Like their host they all padded about in stockinged feet for only the thirteen-strong crew wore deck shoes.

The ostensible purpose of the visit was to allow Maxwell to explain some details of his $2.35 billion (£1.37 billion) bid for Macmillan Inc, the US publishing house. In the air-conditioned saloon he explained that he was ready to discuss the price but he would not pay 'a stupid price'. In the end, after recourse to the courts, he got what he wanted for $2.6 billion (£1.47 billion). Most key members of the staff agreed to stay on; it was a major triumph.

But there may have been two other objectives behind this sudden outing for the journalists. First, Maxwell was taking some of the spotlight off his long-time rival Rupert Murdoch who earlier in the week had announced his agreement in principle to buy Walter Annenberg's Triangle Publications for $3 billion. (Ultimately Murdoch paid a little less – $2.83 billion, or £1.56 billion.) As Murdoch's *Sunday Times* was to reveal at the weekend Murdoch then controlled the second largest media empire in the world, judged by News Corporation's annual turnover of $4.8 billion; at that time Maxwell Communications Corporation's turnover, estimated at $1.60 billion, came only twenty-third. Secondly, Maxwell was trying to show that he had a strong management team ready to take over when he stepped down, as he declared, 'at the end of the decade'.[2] Maxwell told his somewhat sceptical audience, 'I wanted to prove that the MCC board was perfectly capable of mounting such a bid in my absence.' The fact that the yacht was linked to his office by fax and telephone, with direct lines to at least four merchant banks as well as another link to the *Daily Mirror* so that the publisher could see a proof of the front page just as soon as the editor, indicated that so far delegation was notional rather than actual.

Indeed anyone who witnessed Maxwell at full steam during the year of 1986, when he was sixty-three in June, would doubt that he could possibly hand over control and remain content. A large man in every sense of the word, his voice could vary from a sibilant to a shout; his face looked as if it had survived some bruising battles and, very rarely, showed utter exhaustion as great yawns shook the massive frame. But in general his energy – 'one of my greatest assets' – was absolutely phenomenal. He operated then from the ninth floor of the *Mirror* building. In his main office there was a substantial desk with a telephone console continually blinking and buzzing and a screen for market prices; nearby, a round table with six or seven springy tubular chairs and another console. Next door was the private dining room with seats for twenty at a pinch and another console on a small trolley. Beyond that was the private sitting room, complete with comfortable sofas and chairs, a chess set and another console. It was perfectly usual for three meetings to be in progress simultaneously. The dining room might hold a meeting with trade union officials; there could be an American print executive in his office; and a prospective recruit to his staff in the sitting room. Other people with appointments would be queuing up in the reception area while senior executives would be cajoling the appointments secretary to let them know when 'R. M.' would be free for 'just two minutes'. The reason for the log jam was simply that delegation was virtually non-existent. Written authority for every new car and every new position on his papers, whether for a secretary or a managing director, had to be personally initialled by Maxwell. Senior executives had authority to spend up to set limits without reference, but they used it with care. Virtually all important negotiations, whether with trade unions or printers or computer manufacturers, were handled by Maxwell himself.

At the same time he kept a careful eye on the stock market and would frequently be telephoned by stockbrokers or merchant bankers with information and suggestions for a deal. Those calls were always accepted. So were most others, among them a lengthy call from the Yorkshire Ripper's Polish mother-in-law who complained of local press harassment (not from the *Mirror*); Maxwell spoke to her at length in her native tongue and was pleased when she complimented him on his excellent Polish. And there would be a ceaseless barrage of business calls from overseas which Maxwell would field in whatever language was appropriate. As Joe Haines, his biographer and closest political adviser, has written, 'compulsive answering of every telephone call makes coherent discussion almost impossible'.

There were frequent internal meetings, but their timing was erratic. Ten or twelve people might sit around a table for an hour waiting for 'the Publisher' to arrive. With other appointments piling up, it was rare for lengthy consideration to be given to any one subject. Maxwell put on a bravura performance of a tycoon in action. The larger the meeting, the quicker the decisions seemed to come. The mood varied from benign to cruel. On one occasion there was a minor celebration. I was asked what I would like to drink. Was there any champagne, I asked. 'Champagne?' said Maxwell. 'We have champagne in spades.' And we did, but in large tumblers. On another occasion an expert was deemed to have blundered and to have ignored, or misunderstood, instructions. 'Watch my lips!' roared Maxwell, and proceeded to give the individual a furious and humiliating slating in front of all his colleagues. (The executive decided to leave not long afterwards.) At other times he might adopt an air of sardonic humour. 'What have these heroes been up to now?' would be the cry. It was fairly certain that the heroes would soon be dismissed, feeling that their breast plates were somewhat tarnished.

While the scene in those three rooms often looked like an over-crowded circus, the burly ringmaster was having a marvellous time. He was a one-man power house, at one time a coaxing persuader, at another a menacing bully. He could be monumentally vain; equally he could at times prove a bold and exciting leader of a team. He was a man of moods and until he actually arrived the mood of the day was totally unpredictable. The one constant factor remained his absolute command of the organisation. It is doubtful whether any other public company of comparable size in Britain was subject to quite such autocratic direction; certainly no other newspaper company operated in this manner. (Even Northcliffe listened to his brother Harold.) With such centralisation of control in the hands of this one man there were many delays and inefficiencies, last-minute switches of policy and ill-considered gestures. And yet, whatever the sceptics might say, the technique worked, most of the time. Mirror Group Newspapers, barely breaking even when Maxwell bought it from the nerveless hands of Reed International, was now making nearly a million a week. The printing business was flourishing on both sides of the Atlantic; Maxwell was the largest contract printer in Europe and the second largest printer in the US. Pergamon was the second biggest publisher of scientific books and magazines in the world. Large profits were being made on the stock market, and the business was still expanding. Important investments were made in satellite and cable; deals in the US, France, Spain, Israel, Italy and Japan were on the horizon. And Maxwell still had as keen an eye for money as ever. Driving one day to a meeting to discuss an important printing contract he said to his companion, 'Now what is our edge in this negotiation?' He was always looking for that elusive 'edge'. Again and again he would delay signing a contract until the very last moment, always hoping to achieve a better deal. It drove his staff to despair but saved money. His own fortune was almost beyond computation.* 'Money is no problem,' he would say and he certainly had a lifestyle to match.

Ludvik Hoch had travelled very far since his birth on 10th June 1923 in the obscure and poverty-stricken Ruthenian town of Solotvino,† then part of Czechoslovakia. It lay in the forests between the southern slopes of the Carpathian mountains and the River Tisza, a tributary of the Danube. The town included many races – Hungarian, Romanian, Polish, Ukrainian and Slovak – a record of the shifting history of the area. His family were orthodox Jews whose family language was Yiddish; they also spoke Ruthenian and some Hungarian. Memel Hoch, Maxwell's father and tall as his family name implied, was a farm labourer and very minor cattle dealer who was often away and often out of work; he made very little money and the family were usually hungry. For the first thirteen years of Ludvik's life they all lived in an earthen-floored room of their better-off grandfather's house. This grandfather was a dealer and trader from whom Ludvik imbibed the first rudiments of how to make a profit. But mother Chanca was the key figure. Intensely curious, a

---

* In 1988 *Fortune* estimated the Maxwell family fortune at $1.4bn, a satisfactory $100m more than Murdoch's personal pile.
† The name of the village varied according to the country which controlled it. Bower (op cit) calls it Slatinske Doly. Haines gives another five names for the same place.

constant reader of newspapers and books, she was ambitious for all
her seven children but particularly for Ludvik, or 'Laiby' as she
called him after another grandfather. At first she hoped he would
become a Rabbi and he was sent to an academy in a neighbouring
town for the study of rabbinical literature, later moving to another
academy in Bratislava. In the big city young Ludvik soon realised
that there was more to life than academic studies. He began dealing
himself, in cheap jewellery, and before long had cut off his corkscrew
sidelocks and abandoned his rabbinical ambitions altogether.

Hitler's subjugation of Czechoslovakia threatened the Jews of
Solotvino with persecution. The Hoch family agreed that their eldest
boy should go and look for work in Budapest, some 450 miles to
the south. The fate of that family in the Nazi holocaust was appalling:
both the parents, the grandfather, three of Ludvik's sisters and a
brother, all perished in the concentration camps. When Maxwell
was reminded of Eichmann (who had supervised the deportation of
the Jews from Hungary) during the libel case he brought against
Private Eye there was every reason for him to break down and sob.
'My family', he told the judge, 'was destroyed by Eichmann.'

The account given by Joe Haines of Maxwell's life in Budapest
is highly dramatic: recruitment into the underground, imprisonment,
torture, sentenced to death, escape from a one-armed guard, unman-
acled by a gipsy woman. It may even be true. What matters is that
young Hoch fetched up with a group of Czech soldiers who made
their way to France via Turkey and Syria and joined the Czech
Legion. Ludvik saw little fighting before being marched back to
Sete, east of Marseilles. Churchill arranged to evacuate any Czech
units willing to fight and Ludvik reached Liverpool in July 1940.
Czech Jews who remained in France were shot by the Gestapo; the
death penalty remained throughout the war for any who were captured while fighting for the Western allies – a compelling reason for
Ludvik Hoch's later changes of name.

There was almost as much anti-Semitism among the Czechs in
England as there was in Germany. Maxwell was discharged from
the Czech army and shortly afterwards applied to join the Pioneer
Corps, the only unit open to him. There he broke stones and built
roads and loaded ammunition trucks for nearly three years. 'One
thing was for sure,' said a nurse who helped to look after him when
he was recovering from appendicitis, 'he literally and absolutely did
not give a damn what anyone thought of him.' He learnt to speak
English (from a lady tobacconist in Sutton Coldfield) and read

voraciously. Later he fell in love with a widow in Cambridge who helped civilise and mature the raw Czech peasant; more importantly she introduced him to Brigadier Carthew-Yorstoun, who interested himself in the lad's welfare and had him transferred to a British infantry battalion stationed on the South Coast. By now Ludvik Hoch had changed his name to du Maurier (after the cigarettes he smoked) and was soon put in a charge of the sniper section of the battalion. The battalion landed in Normandy towards the end of June and du Maurier was soon in the thick of it, fighting so bravely that he was recommended for an immediate commission – without effect; perhaps it was unusual enough for a Czech to be in charge of British soldiers. The battalion suffered very heavy casualties and du Maurier, told to change his name to Jones in view of the risk of capture, was slightly wounded in the jaw.

A few months later he was in Paris on a week's leave and, through the good offices of Carthew-Yorstoun, met the sparkling and attractive Elisabeth Meynard with whom he fell in love at first sight. In December 1944 he proposed and reinforced his suit by telling her, 'I shall win an MC. I shall re-create a family. I shall make my fortune. I shall become Prime Minister of England. And I shall make you happy until the end of my days.' It was an extraordinary declaration from a man who was not even a British citizen at the time and showed the scale both of his ambition and of his imperious self-confidence. Betty was right in thinking that with this man she would never be bored. Her distinguished family at first looked askance at a man they regarded as a Czech adventurer; they were won over when first he was commissioned as Ian Robert Maxwell, a Scots name recommended by the inevitable Carthew-Yorstoun, and then, six weeks after his proposal, was awarded an MC for acts of reckless bravery in clearing a Dutch village near the River Roer. The citation is glowing with such phrases as 'powers of leadership of the highest order . . . showing no regard for his own safety . . . magnificent example and offensive spirit'. A month later Montgomery himself pinned on the medal. If Maxwell had not been stuck in the Pioneer Corps for nearly three years he would surely have risen much higher in the ranks of the army – *if* he had lived. Believing all his family dead (in fact two sisters survived) his treatment of Germans could be brutal.

At the end of the war Maxwell's gift for languages proved invaluable. While on intelligence work he was promoted Captain and offered a permanent commission. He turned this down but found the offer useful in obtaining British nationality. He was employed in a section of the Control Commission called Public Relations/Information Services Control; and was in charge of licensing and censoring the emergent press of Berlin. Because of the total devastation of Germany, a licence to print was useless without the means to print – paper, power, ink, machinery. Maxwell was clearly superb at getting newspapers off the ground. His particular pet became *Der Telegraf* which sold more than 250,000 copies a day. His technique was basically barter. Detlev Raymond, then trainee-editor of the paper and later employed by Maxwell in Britain, described how Maxwell ordered him to sell 20,000 cigarettes on the black market at Leipzig in the Russian zone. When Raymond protested that this wasn't part of his job, Maxwell replied, 'Now you shut up . . . Number one, this here is a democratic institution where I make all the rules and, number two, Leipzig has the only factory intact able to provide us with photographic emulsion to publish this goddam newspaper.' Maxwell identified closely with the newspaper. 'I did everything I could to help the paper,' he told the author.[3] 'I had a knack for journalism and a good nose for a story. The Foreign Office gave us political guidance; it was asinine and I ignored it.' He became completely hooked on the newspaper and later confirmed that his determination to get into newspaper publishing dates from that time, although he added, with a typical flourish, 'Being patriotic I wished to make my own small contribution to overcoming Britain's retreat from the world and newspapers could help.'

His reputation as a superb fixer and dealer became widely known. Another press officer called John Kisch worked in Dusseldorf and desperately needed a particular item to make his printing works operative. An army officer told him, 'There is only one man who can help you, a press officer in Berlin by the name of Captain Robert Maxwell.' After 'extensive haggling' Kisch got what he wanted.

Maxwell's ability to conjure up supplies led the leading German publishing family of Springer to complain to him that the newspapers were getting too much paper and the book publishers not enough. According to Haines, Maxwell refused to help them at that time; but Maxwell told me, 'I was also responsible for helping German publishers.' In any event he became friendly with the family and with Dr Tonjes Lange who had kept the firm alive during the war. Maxwell resigned from the Control Commission in March 1947 before his contract expired and started expanding a tiny import-export business called Low-Bell after the name of Lobl, the Czech who founded it. Maxwell was already a director of the company having described himself, rather prematurely, on the formal documentation in 1946 as 'a merchant'. It seems that Maxwell had realised that his contacts in Germany and his gift for languages might point the way to his fortune.

Seven months after he had left the Control Commission Maxwell was back in Germany, resuming his friendship with the Springer family and playing a major role in re-establishing their business. A document written by Lange in 1959 reviewed their relationship and stated:

> It was a time when there was no telephone and no petrol, and no spare parts for printing machinery, or other vital things that were needed for the revival of a business such as Springer-Verlag. Captain Maxwell always knew the answer, solved the problems ... it was largely attributable to him that the road to the reconstruction of the business was cleared.

The Springer business was in the production and distribution of scientific and antiquarian books and journals, many of the back-numbers being hidden during the war. There was a vast demand for these publications throughout the world, but distribution of single copies direct from Germany was forbidden by the Allies. Maxwell offered to handle the distribution worldwide. 'The drastic and successful methods invented by the British Captain (with an MC) produced unimaginably successful solutions to overcome those [post-war] conditions so we could start exporting again' was how the 1959 memorandum recorded his work. At the same time another company, Butterworth-Springer, was formed to develop British scientific publishing, using some of the Springer expertise in this field. In 1951 Butterworth's, feeling that the company was working more to Springer's advantage than their own, pulled out, selling the company to Maxwell for £13,000, which he borrowed mainly from Hambros Bank and relations in the United States. It was this company that he called the Pergamon Press after the ancient city in Turkey. Thus in the early 1950s Maxwell was running three businesses simultaneously – distribution, international dealing and publishing. The pattern of multiple activities was already established.

Growing success and, as ever, an excess of self-confidence* led him to make a major blunder: he agreed to take over from Pitmans the wholesale publishing business of Simpkin Marshall, which was intended to supply single copies of books to booksellers, being funded by extra discounts allowed by the publishers. He was right in thinking there was a need for such a concern but wrong in thinking most of the publishers would do much to help. He also made the mistake of obtaining too large a warehouse in the Marylebone Road which was costly to rebuild and costly to run. And he caused Simpkins to finance the British Book Center in New York to the tune of more than £100,000. The collapse of the whole venture in 1955 led to great bitterness in the publishing trade, for the books held by Simpkins were deemed to be part of Simpkins' assets, and not the property of the publishers. Maxwell, on the other hand, still believes that it was the publishers who let him down.

The liquidation of Simpkins encouraged Maxwell to give his full attention to Pergamon, which so far had been ticking over rather than expanding. He was among the first British publishers to realise the truly global nature of scientific discovery and the global interest in quite small pockets of scientific research; he was certainly the first to exploit that field successfully. With his vast enthusiasm, his charm, his ability to talk to most scientists in their own language, coupled with a growing understanding of scientific, medical and technological developments, he was able to multiply the number of journals immensely. He secured a valuable contract to publish a range of Russian scientific journals and later expanded in Eastern Europe. Although circulations might be small, subscriptions were paid in advance and there was little waste; it was a profitable and worthwhile business. Maxwell gained the respect and deep gratitude of many distinguished scientists for the work he started then. An extraordinary tribute was published (by Pergamon Press, of course) on the occasion of his sixty-fifty birthday and the fortieth anniversary of the foundation of Pergamon.[4] From all over the scientific world Nobel prize winners, professors, deans, doctors, authors and editors paid what were evidently heartfelt tributes to the encouragement and practical support they had received. Undoubtedly they took a view of Maxwell which was very different from that shared by some of the journalists who worked for him.

* Maxwell prefers to say, 'My problem is that I can never say "No". If I was a woman I would always be pregnant.' However it must be said that I have heard him say 'No', more than once.

Back in the 1950s he was also becoming more widely known in political and business circles and took steps to cultivate the leaders of the Labour party. Springer's decision to wind up his ten-year-old arrangement to distribute their books was a blow, but one which he could now survive without difficulty.

In 1959 he fought his first election campaign, owing his selection as Labour candidate for Buckingham partly to luck (the previous candidate had been injured in a car accident), and partly to sheer cheek (he had been a member of the party for only a year). He fought a vigorous campaign with spectacular support from his wife, but lost by nearly 2,000 votes after an odious smear campaign against him. He stuck to the constituency and was rewarded by winning the seat in 1964, but as an MP he was a flop. The House of Commons is a club and Maxwell is not a very clubbable fellow. Breaking all conventions he made his maiden speech on the very first day of the new Parliament, and then bombarded the House with his views (which tended to be to the right of the Labour party) on almost every subject that came up. He became distinctly unpopular. While Wilson and Crossman both respected his ability and Crossman skilfully made him chairman of the Commons Catering Committee, Wilson never offered ministerial office. Eventually Maxwell lost the seat six years later in a general swing against Labour, and redoubled his efforts to master that other well-tried method of exercising power and influence in Britain – the press.

In his first year as an MP he had interested himself in the fate of the *Daily Herald* and proposed an ingenious method for financing its losses. All trade union printing as well as publication of the *Daily Herald* should be centralised in one plant, erected with the help of a government subsidy and the profits, estimated at £750,000 a year, would be used to pay any losses on the paper. He also took an interest in the fate of the *Sunday Citizen*. In 1968 after Cecil King had published his broadside against Wilson, Maxwell attempted to secure the Co-operative movement's agreement to cede him the titles of *Reynold's News* and *Sunday Citizen* with a view to establishing a non-profit making Labour party daily. None of these ideas was taken any further, but they show that the idea of newspaper publishing was exercising magnetic appeal.

His first major chance of owning a national newspaper – the *News of the World* – occurred that same year. It was also the first time he clashed openly with Rupert Murdoch, and lost. There had been previous meetings when Maxwell offered to sell Murdoch fifty per cent of Pergamon Australia, which would have carried the right to sell Pergamon's encyclopaedias in that part of the world. Michael Richardson, then with stockbrokers Panmure Gordon and now managing director of Rothschilds, was in Australia at the time and sat in on a number of the meetings. He reports that at first the relationship between the two men seemed to be one of mutual admiration, even friendship. Murdoch may have realised that he had run up against someone whose ambitions and abilities could equal his own. Meetings continued in San Francisco and New York, but Richardson was conscious that Murdoch was becoming more wary and the outcome seemed less and less certain.

Murdoch certainly had reason to be wary of Maxwell as a poker player. They were both tremendous gamblers and one day, well after midnight, following a strenuous round of discussions, Murdoch suggested a game of poker with one or two friends he would round up. In the very first hand Maxwell, who played with great panache and skill as well as inordinate good luck, looked at his cards, put them face down and said, grinning broadly, that he didn't want any more cards. The other players thought he could be bluffing and kept raising the pot. Maxwell would do the same. He was very hard to 'read'. Eventually someone said they'd 'see' Maxwell. He laid out a full house and scooped up a lot of money. In a later hand he picked up his cards, said he wanted no more and again smiled broadly; the other players had no idea whether he was bluffing or not. He wasn't.

Next day Richardson went to lunch by the harbour and met a pretty blonde girl who said she was in a bad temper that morning. Her husband had been in bed with her the previous night when the telephone rang and it was Rupert saying there were a couple of Poms there really ripe for milking. She protested but her husband had appeased her by saying, 'I'll give you half my winnings.' He came back at six am; sleepily she asked him how it had gone. All he said was, 'You owe me A$22,000.' She was not pleased. The Australians were so upset that some of them flew to San Francisco for a return game. Once again Maxwell won heavily.

However he did not win the contract with Murdoch. The Australian made enquiries about the value of the encyclopaedias, and questioned whether Maxwell had the editorial staff to bring them up to date. In the end he refused to buy. 'I simply realised the deal was one-sided and I was pretty lucky to find out,' he said later. The abortive partnership did not appear to leave very friendly feelings behind: Murdoch newspapers in Australia began enquiring into the selling methods used to dispose of the encyclopaedias. Although their opening talks had been friendly enough, a degree of bitterness was creeping in.

The chance to control the *News of the World* had arisen because an eccentric and much married genius, Professor Derek Jackson, wished to sell his twenty-five per cent shareholding in the company. His cousin Sir William Carr, who had inherited the chairmanship and, with his family, controlled nearly thirty per cent of the shares, offered him only 28s a share. Jacob Rothschild, acting for the professor, started looking for other buyers. Word reached Maxwell who promptly offered 37s.

Sir William Carr was an alcoholic who was normally unfit for business after ten thirty am. The company, which also owned printing works and a golf club, supported his lavish lunches at the Savoy and the deals he made there.* He was appalled at the thought of losing control. The editor of the *News of the World*, Stafford Somerfield, wrote a notoriously repellent leader stressing Maxwell's Czech origins and socialist beliefs, declaring that the paper was 'as British as roast beef and Yorkshire pudding'. He concluded, 'This is a British newspaper, run by British people. Let's keep it that way.'

On the same day that all this patriotism was being paraded to smear someone who during the war had done at least as much as the editor to keep Britain free, Murdoch flew quietly into London from Australia. Tipped off by his London bureau which was under instructions to watch Maxwell, he had at once reckoned 'there was a place here for a white knight'. A savage battle for control began at once.

Maxwell raised his offer – a mixture of Pergamon shares and convertible loan stock, with a cash alternative. But at the same time Carr's merchant bankers, Hambros, allocated £750,000 to buy *News of the World* shares, allegedly on their own account but unquestionably with the object of supporting Carr. Hambros picked up ten per cent of the shares – a powerful reinforcement for Carr. Despite the near-breach of the rule that companies should not buy their own shares to frustrate a take-over bid, the newly-formed Take-over

---

* After one such lunch Randolph Churchill told me with astonishment that Sir William had agreed to pay his annual fee whether Randolph wrote the agreed number of articles *or not*. Presumably Sir William had meant that the fee would be reduced if Randolph failed to produce, but the lunch had gone on too long for such a sensible proviso to be clear.

Panel seemed powerless to do more than wring its hands. City commentators were virtually unanimous in condemning the Panel's inaction.

Murdoch had breakfast with Carr and the crucial deal was made. Murdoch would inject some of his scruffier Australian publications, including a Melbourne-based weekly called *Truth* and some local papers in Queensland and Victoria, in return for 39.7 per cent of the *News of the World* company. He would become managing director (the suggestion that Carr would be joint managing director was quickly dropped) and Carr would remain chairman. The deal would require shareholder approval, so Murdoch also began buying shares. He wound up with ten per cent. Eventually the Panel obtained the agreement of all the merchant banks involved that shares bought by them after Pergamon's original offer would not be voted. Hambros still went ahead with a special contract by which individual shareholders gave a blind pledge to give Hambros first refusal on their shares and to support the board in all its resolutions. Again the Panel remained silent.

Maxwell was aware that his chances were fading because the fight was not about the price; he was offering considerably more than the Carr-Murdoch deal promised for the shareholders. His problem was that he was opposed by a sick man who saw him as an unwelcome foreigner and a socialist as well as by City institutions who suspected and disliked his methods. He does not give in easily: he blasted Murdoch as 'a moth-eaten, empty-pouched kangaroo'; he sued Murdoch's *Sydney Daily Mirror* for $A1,000,000; other writs were scattered around alleging breach of fiduciary duty on the part of the board; and he contemplated a raid of his own. He investigated the prospects of putting together a bid for Murdoch's News Ltd. But he could find no opening. At the same time the Pergamon share price benefited when he arranged for a family company to buy 245,000 shares as a 'long-term investment', and later for his two bankers to buy another 215,000 shares. Both transactions were reported and did not infringe the code.

Haines reports that before the final showdown Carr met Maxwell at breakfast and asked, 'If you buy the company for cash, would you keep me as chairman?' (Obviously he was having some last-minute qualms about the Murdoch deal.) Maxwell said he would not. Carr reminded Maxwell that Murdoch was keeping him as chairman; Maxwell replied that Murdoch would take it away in six months. Carr enquired why Maxwell would not have him as chairman and

Maxwell replied that whenever he had a haircut at the Savoy Hotel on a Friday afternoon he would find Carr and his cronies still drinking triple martinis at teatime; he did not find that suitable 'training' for a chairman.

Murdoch and Maxwell both attended the company Extraordinary General Meeting in the Connaught Rooms to decide the issue. It was a big meeting, packed with *News of the World* employees some of whom had been given shares for the occasion. Maxwell, heckled and interrupted constantly, at least made it clear that the shareholders would be worse off if they accepted the Murdoch deal. (The value of the company fell by £1 million after the board's victory.) On a show of hands Maxwell was overwhelmingly defeated, but the detailed count was much closer – 4,526,822 to 3,246,937. Maxwell had won more than forty per cent of the vote. He congratulated Murdoch on catching a very big fish with a very small hook, and to a journalist commented on the universal condemnation of Hambros' tactics: 'I'm on the side of the angels. It's amazing.'

Murdoch ditched Carr after about six months. He had bought most of Jackson's shares and now had voting control. Carr had been ringing people in the office almost every day, said Murdoch later. 'The only person he never called was me.'[5] Carr's health was now failing and Maxwell sent him a friendly note. Haines reports a macabre ending to the story: before he died in 1977 Carr sent Maxwell a letter regretting that he had not sold the company to him. If Carr and Maxwell made it up in the end, the rivalry between Maxwell and Murdoch had scarcely begun.

It is impossible to understand Maxwell's life without realising that he is normally engaged in at least a dozen enterprises and activities on any single day. While he was bidding for the *News of the World* he was still an active MP, and he was still promoting the growth of the Pergamon Press and its associated companies. This brief account focuses on his connection with Fleet Street but it is impossible to omit some mention of the abortive Leasco deal, and the subsequent Board of Trade enquiry, for these events coloured the public perception of Maxwell, and also acted as a powerful spur to his later efforts to restore his fortune and his reputation.

He had acquired Chambers's Encyclopaedia when he bought the subscription division of George Newnes. In 1967 he added the New English Encyclopaedia to his properties. To run these concerns he formed a new company with the British Printing Corporation (which printed both sets of encyclopaedias) called International Learning

Systems Corporation and, fortified by optimistic forecasts of sales, launched a bid for Butterworths, the publishers. After a bitter battle he was rebuffed when Cecil King offered a higher price. It seems that a 'Maxwell factor' was hindering his attempts to expand. That may have been one reason why he initially welcomed the prospect of linking up with Leasco, a fast growing American computer leasing firm run by Saul Steinberg. After various meetings in 1969 Leasco agreed to make a £25 million offer for the company, buying the shares owned by Maxwell and his family for £8 million with a mixture of shares and cash; Maxwell would continue to run Pergamon and in addition would become deputy chairman of Leasco and head of Leasco in Europe. But the two partners soon fell out; Leasco became increasingly suspicious of the Pergamon accounts and forecasts; Maxwell became disenchanted with Leasco, believing that they were trying to buy Pergamon on the cheap. Eventually Leasco withdrew their bid. A beefed up Take-over Panel, now chaired by Sir Hartley Shawcross, investigated whether the withdrawal was justified and concluded that it was; they praised the 'energetic leadership' of Maxwell, cleared him of any suggestion of 'personal misconduct' but recommended that the Board of Trade should set up an enquiry to consider whether Pergamon shareholders had been kept properly informed. Meanwhile Leasco, fortified by its holding of thirty-eight per cent of the shares, decided to pursue its aim of controlling Pergamon. At a critical meeting of Pergamon shareholders Maxwell said he would buy all non-Leasco shares for 25s but the vote showed that the majority of institutions backed Leasco. The 'Maxwell factor' had struck again. He was voted off the board and Leasco took over with an independent chairman and a Leasco appointee as managing director.

There were two important results. First, since Leasco could not run Pergamon without Maxwell, Maxwell was able to buy the company back for little more than £1.5 million five years later. Haines reports he was nearly broke at the time, having spent nearly £2 million on lawyers' fees; the money was borrowed, says Haines, by an American lawyer acting for Mrs Maxwell's family. Secondly the inspectors appointed by the Board of Trade, after making a number of criticisms, affirmed that 'notwithstanding Mr Maxwell's acknowledged abilities and energy he is not in our opinion a person who can be relied on to exercise proper stewardship of a publicly-quoted company'. The judgment was fundamentally flawed since they had failed to put the broad outline of their criticisms to Maxwell despite a clear direction from Lord Denning that 'they must be fair'. Maxwell was deeply angered at what he saw then, and still affirms, was 'a great injustice, a great sin'. Recently he said, 'I was broke and bitter. Sometimes there is less justice here than in Russia. But I was not so bitter that I would give up my nationality, never so bitter as to abandon this country.'⁶ Much of what he has done in public life since that report can be seen as a re-assertion of his integrity and a determined bid to clear the slur from his name. He *says*, 'I don't care what the natives say about me or what they don't say. I don't have to be accepted and praised.' All the same he must have seen the newspaper world as a key to the public acceptance of his stature and his reputation.

Even while he was engaged in talks with Leasco he made another effort to buy IPC's *Sun*, Cudlipp's unsuccessful effort to revitalise the old *Daily Herald*. Maxwell realised that production costs were a major problem and was planning to move printing to the *Evening Standard* plant in Shoe Lane, which was of course unused at night. He was ready to pay £50,000 for the *Sun*'s title and scattered offers of the editorship round Fleet Street. But IPC preferred to hand over the title to 'leading representatives of the Labour party . . . Such a transfer would be more appropriate to a group of persons than an individual.' IPC then gave six months' notice of their intention to close down the paper. Meanwhile Murdoch announced that he was interested if the talks with Maxwell broke down. He helped the process along by talking in encouraging terms to the print union SOGAT, which responded by announcing that it had lost confidence in Maxwell. He also offered Harry Evans, then editor of the *Sunday Times*, adverse material on Maxwell provided the source was kept secret. Evans read it but was unimpressed. However even Maxwell could not maintain the momentum of his proposals in the face of such opposition when he was so deeply involved in the turmoil over the Leasco bid and he withdrew his offer for the *Sun* leaving the way clear for Murdoch. The Australian was able to buy the paper for an initial payment of only £75,000 and a maximum of £600,000 to be paid out of profits over a six-year period. So Murdoch had won again, and Cudlipp rashly concluded, 'This is obviously the end of Mr Maxwell's dream of being the proprietor of a national newspaper.' How wrong he was, but the blow to Maxwell's pride could not be concealed and again it was Murdoch who had come off best.

By 1974 however Maxwell was back in full control of Pergamon and looking for ways to re-enter Parliament. Despite the devastating and humiliating criticism of his conduct made by the Board of Trade inspectors he was shrugging off all his problems and rebuilding his business. He also became involved in another newspaper project: this was a guaranteed loser, the attempt to run a brand-new newspaper, the *Scottish Daily News*, as a co-operative. This arose out of the ashes of the *Scottish Daily Express*, a newspaper that had never made money since the day it was founded, largely because of the appalling lack of industrial discipline on the production line, over-manning and over-pay. A sizeable group of redundant workers decided they could run a successful paper if they were given some backing by the government and others. Because of Tony Benn's commitment to the idea of workers' co-operatives the government produced £1.2 million; Beaverbrook Newspapers helped them buy the old *Express* plant and gave them a loan of £725,000; the workers, with the aid of redundancy payments, produced £350,000 and Maxwell agreed to chip in £100,000.

Since they were still short of £25,000 he agreed to add that sum also on condition that the paper was run on a twenty-four-hour basis and that he should be publisher and co-chairman of the co-operative. Some said that the conditions were accepted simply to get the extra money and the leaders of the co-operative did not intend to meet them. In any event the twenty-four-hour concept was dropped and within a month Maxwell was deprived of executive powers. It is true that he was trying to run a £2 million company for an investment of £125,000 but no one else had any hope of making a success of the enterprise. When the paper was launched in May 1975 its sale soon fell to half the figure needed and advertising volume was negligible. Maxwell was re-elected to the council, but initially was only in charge of advertising and circulation. After a showdown meeting in July he won full executive powers, although still subject to the vote of the workers' council. The paper was relaunched as a tabloid in August and circulation rose but the losses, although trimmed, were continuing. The divisions within the co-operative were now becoming acute, with Maxwell using the tannoy to denounce 'the enemy in our midst'. While he announced publicly that 'we have no financial problems' he privately warned that the paper might be bankrupt within a week, but he still believed that loans could be raised on the firm's assets. At this stage the dissidents began talking. *Campaign*, the trade magazine, quoted the former chairman of the co-operative as saying the paper was 'finished'.

The *Sunday Times* ran a doom-laden article headed, 'How Maxwell Sabotaged the Workers' Dream'. The workers' council was furious, saying the allegations about the paper were 'unfounded, cruel and irresponsible'. The workforce voted 248 to eighteen urging Maxwell to stay, but he had had enough and resigned. The paper closed within six weeks of the *Sunday Times* article.

His next attempt to gain control of a newspaper came up against Murdoch for the third time. The second Lord Thomson of Fleet, sickened by the conduct of the trade unions at Gray's Inn Road, decided that he would get out of Times Newspapers. In October 1980 he said he would close the papers unless a buyer was found by the following March. Bids had to be made by 31st December. His spokesmen said that his decision would not be determined solely by the size of the financial package and that he wished to sell Times Newspapers as a whole; this knocked out the separate consortia being promoted by the two editors. Maxwell produced his bid, but it was not a simple cash offer. He would have leased the premises at an initial rental of about £750,000 a year; he would have paid £5 million in cash and in five years have started to pay off a £15 million loan from Thomson at the rate of £1 million a year or twenty-five per cent of the profits. It was all subject to satisfactory negotiations with the unions. Murdoch put in a notional bid of £1 million to keep his place at the table and then the real dealing began. Sir Gordon Brunton, chief executive of the International Thomson Organisation, disqualified Maxwell along with Sir James Goldsmith, Lonrho and the Aga Khan without giving any explanation. The only bidders who reached the shortlist were Murdoch and Rothermere. Brunton was decisive in his preference for Murdoch, and the union leaders again backed Murdoch (their members were making small fortunes from the *Sun*). It was Murdoch's biggest triumph in their continuing rivalry; he now had four newspapers, and Maxwell had none.

The year of Maxwell's defeat over Times Newspapers was also the year when the dice began to roll for him. Pergamon, back under his control, was prospering and gave him the money to buy a near-thirty per cent stake in the money-losing British Printing Corporation. Soon, with the backing of Lord Kearton, originally brought in by BPC to fend off the raider, and with financial support from the National Westminster Bank, he won full control. As a result of relentless hard bargaining with union leaders he put through a tough survival plan, closing plants, forcing redundancies, winning new business. By the end of 1982 profits had risen to £20 million; the rehabilitation of Maxwell as a man fitted to undertake the steward-ship of a public company was under way. He was even able to defeat SOGAT's London Machine branch which had a chapel at Park Royal, one of the BPC plants producing the *Radio Times*. After a bitter struggle to reduce costs Maxwell warned that he would shut it down completely if his survival plan was not accepted. There was always an element of mock theatre about Maxwell's threats; the union officials never knew whether to believe him or not. Bemused, the SOGAT men refused to meet his deadline. In the end Maxwell sent men with sledgehammers to wreck the presses. Further, the law ensured that SOGAT members continued to distribute the *Radio Times* printed in other BPC plants. As one trade union official said, 'It was the first loss in the London branches I could ever remember. It gave the employers heart . . . The unions were no longer invincible.' The victory sharpened Maxwell's yearning for a national newspaper; his ambition was soon fulfilled.

First however there was a fruitless flirtation with Tiny Rowland over *The Observer*. Rowland was in dispute with his editor and he hoped to use the threat of Maxwell to scare the editor and the independent directors on the board. Later that year, Maxwell, having been assured by Reed International that there was no prospect of his buying the Mirror Group, bought ten per cent of Fleet shares from the Australian Robert Holmes à Court. Maxwell has said that he never wished to own the *Express*; it was too Conservative. But the *News of the World* was Conservative too.

In fact his prospect of buying the Mirror Group had never been brighter. The board of Reeds had already sold him their Odhams printing operation and they liked the idea of getting out of any part of their business which involved confrontation with the print unions. Like Trafalgar House, they reckoned it was affecting their share price adversely. Further, Sir Alex Jarratt, the former civil servant who was chairman of Reeds, did not really like the *Mirror* as a newspaper; he had actually been booed at a public meeting for a *Mirror* story about the royal family and he did not like that one bit. Worst of all, the Mirror Group, with a turnover of more than £200 million, was barely making £1 million a year.

The solution dreamed up by Reeds was for the Mirror Group to be floated as a public company. The city editor of the *Daily Mirror* was asked to suggest some names for the chairmanship who would make a good impression in the City. He suggested, among others,

A young and much rounder Rupert Murdoch flourishes the Sydney *Daily Mirror* which he had just bought. It was May 1960 and his first big deal: he was not yet 30 and on his way. Eight years later he won control of the *News of the World*.

Rupert Murdoch at New Printing House Square as he looks over his latest purchase in 1981. He appointed Harry Evans (*left*), award-winning editor of the *Sunday Times*, to take over *The Times* from William Rees-Mogg (*right*), but their honeymoon was short-lived. Evans lasted just over a year.

Furious print workers try to pull down part of the perimeter fence at Wapping in March 1986. Their failure to stop the distribution of Murdoch's papers meant that they were losing the battle, and they knew it.

Eddy Shah, the eternal optimist, flourishes the first edition of *Today* in March 1986. 'We said we'd go on 4 March two years ago and we were an hour and a half late. I think it's bloody magic.'

Andreas Whittam-Smith, founder and editor of *The Independent*, sits by the first 400 copies delivered from the printers in October 1986. He had mortgaged his home to rent the paper's offices. He was entitled to feel happy. Soon he will be a newspaper millionaire.

Clive Thornton, chief general manager of the Abbey National Building Society, as an attractive candidate who had turned round a rather
stick-in-the-mud business and clearly had a good touch in dealing
with the media; his view was accepted without too much thought.
Jarratt pledged that the Mirror Group would not be sold to a single
bidder.

Thornton, who proved both vain and naive, was out of his depth.
Very properly appalled at the lush expenditure of executives and
equally shocked by print union practices, he began holding forth
about the need for agreement on non-replacement of staff, massive
re-equipment plans, new newspapers and worker participation. He
proved better at talk than at deeds. The City, instead of hailing the
new chairman, viewed him with increasing scepticism. The float,
originally estimated to raise £100 million for Reeds, was downgraded
to only £48 million. Four days after Reeds had agreed that there
should be a fifteen per cent limit on any individual owning shares
in the new company and when formal announcement of the float
was imminent, Maxwell, who was amazingly well-informed both of
editorial developments and of board room worries, announced a bid
of £80 million and said he might be ready to go higher. In the
interests of their shareholders Reeds had no alternative but to talk
to Maxwell. Leslie Carpenter, then the chief executive, had negotiated with Maxwell before and insisted on a cash deal. He pushed
the price up to £90 million net, twice the value of the float. (Maxwell
was short of the last £6 million which Reeds kindly lent him, soon
being repaid.) Meanwhile worried print union leaders were pro-
mising Thornton no-strike deals in a last desperate effort to keep
Maxwell out; it was too late. The journalists, roused by a spirited
address from Haines, condemned Maxwell's intervention and urged
Reeds to stick to their promises about flotation. It was another futile
gesture.

Maxwell had finally secured his national newspaper group, and it
was his own. There was no public shareholding involved. He was
convinced he had an absolute bargain. With the Reuters shares, the
Holborn Circus site, and a sizeable surplus in the *Mirror* pension
fund, he reckoned the newspapers were thrown in for nothing. After
a midnight visit to the *Mirror* building to celebrate his victory he
made his intentions known the next day. He would put the *Mirror*
'back where it belonged, ahead of the *Sun*'. In other words he would
get his revenge on Murdoch. But he was in too much of a hurry.
In his first six months he launched a mammoth bingo game with

DAILY Mirror

Saturday, July 14, 1984   FORWARD WITH BRITAIN ★   17p.

My Princess!

FORWARD WITH BRITAIN!

THE Mirror Group newspapers have changed ownership. Their policies will not change.

I am proud to be the proprietor of this group of publications which holds such an important position in the life of the nation.

I certainly hope to make the papers more efficient and thereby more profitable.

Modern

My aim is to earn the resources which will enable our newspapers to regain their rightful places as the leaders in their markets.

The Daily Mirror and I already have one thing in common. We have supported the Labour Party in every election since 1945.

THAT support will continue. But the Mirror has never been a slavish party paper.

It will not be a Labour Party organ now. We treasure our independence.

This newspaper will go on investigating injustices, opposing privilege and standing alone among the popular dailies as the voice of the sensible Left,

We stand for a modern Britain—a

by ROBERT MAXWELL
Publisher of Mirror Group Newspapers

country which truly needs modernising, with industry and trade unions alike prepared to face the hard facts of survival in the Eighties.

The Mirror has always fought complacency in every sector of public life whether it be in Whitehall or local government. Bureaucrats be warned!

But there is much to be joyful about in Britain today. There are great qualities which we alone possess, great achievements to report.

And even greater achievements to come.

I HAVE been in a position to buy the Daily Mirror.

But what I cannot buy is the loyalty of its readers.

That will have to continue to be earned.

To me the Mirror has always meant something special.

I believe it means something special to those who work for it and you who buy it. The British people.

This is why the Mirror today carries our new slogan: "Forward with Britain."

That slogan is my policy.

● THREE moments in history as seen by the Daily Mirror. Today the Mirror itself makes history with a new owner and the start of a new era.

In July 1984 Maxwell finally bought a national newspaper. For the first year he would not leave it alone and the *Mirror* devoted columns to his own concerns. Five years later, through his early decision to buy colour presses, Mirror newspapers were making progress.

the promise of making some *Mirror* reader into a millionaire, fondly believing that the *Mirror* sale would leap by ten to fifteen per cent. But he was outsmarted when other newspaper groups heard of his plans and blanketed his announcement. Bruce Matthews, managing director of Murdoch's News International, proved faster on the draw and on his own initiative was able to produce a millionaire before Maxwell's game had been properly launched. Then for a time Maxwell cut the price of the *Mirror*, only to put it up again seven weeks later; that was highly unpopular with the newsagents. And his newspapers gave ceaseless exposure to Maxwell himself; he was thrusting himself forward at every opportunity, vainly trying to solve the miners' strike, and flying with relief supplies to famine-stricken Ethiopia. After six months the gap between the *Mirror* and the *Sun* had grown by nearly 100,000. For some time Maxwell's enjoyment of his new possession continued to blanket the good things in the *Mirror*. Much space was given to his meetings with leaders in various countries – Bulgaria, Poland, China, Russia. By the end of his first year the sale of the *Mirror* had dropped by 500,000 and the paper was still barely profitable.

At the beginning of 1985 he showed that if he wasn't a Beaverbrook in journalism, he was learning fast as a newspaper publisher. He launched a major cost-cutting exercise; and, while Murdoch was still publicly scorning newspaper colour, he ordered twenty-one MAN-Roland colour presses at a total cost of £68 million. His efforts to trim costs went slowly at first despite a warning that the papers would close if massive cost reductions could not be secured. In August he stepped up the pace and demanded that *Sporting Life*, the racing paper which was losing £3 million a year, should be printed outside Fleet Street. That was a fundamental threat to the Central London print workers and of course they resisted savagely. The battle followed traditional lines: disruption to London print, closure of the papers, resumption of publication, disruption, an offer of more pay in return for guaranteed production and the elimination of practices that padded the pay packets, more disruption, threats of dismissal and closure unless 2,000 redundancies were agreed. But then the unions and the chapels cracked; Maxwell had what other publishers failed to achieve – credibility. Further, the atmosphere in Fleet Street was changing; the unions could not fight Murdoch and Maxwell at the same time. By December, assisted by the release of £35 million from the Mirror Group Pension Fund to beef up redundancy money, he had shaved 1,600 jobs out of some

6,500, a cut of a quarter; and the *Sporting Life* was printed out of Fleet Street. Frank Barlow, managing director of the *Financial Times*, described it as 'the greatest single achievement in Fleet Street for twenty-five years'. Later Maxwell purred at the fact that his break-through at Holborn Circus preceded Murdoch's take-off to Wapping by at least a month and claimed his success had influenced the timing of that decision. The facts are given in the next chapter.

Maxwell's next move was to revive his plan for a second London evening newspaper; he asked me to act as editorial consultant. 'I would want it to be like the *Standard* in the great days of your editorship', he said flatteringly. This is not the place for a full account of what went wrong, and what went right, with the *London Daily News*. Magnus Linklater, the editor I recommended and whom Maxwell accepted without question (getting Linklater to accept was another matter), assembled a magnificent team of journalists with full support from Maxwell (who only quibbled once). Management was another matter. On arrival I had enquired about the managing director and was told by Maxwell he had just the man in mind. The following week I asked again. This time Maxwell said he had three possible candidates and needed to interview them. Then I asked a senior group executive what was planned. 'Funny you should say that,' said the executive, 'R.M. asked me only this morning if I had any ideas.' I initiated an executive search, only for Maxwell to produce Bill Gillespie, a senior executive from News International, whom he first over-loaded with work, and then found lacking. Gille-spie, for his part, was baffled by Maxwell's methods and eventually resigned. Although an MD was eventually found, much time had been lost.

The most serious mistake was to launch with the twenty-four-hour concept. When Maxwell told a small executive group that this was what he wanted I said it would increase costs by at least sixty per cent. Maxwell simply shrugged his shoulders. I believe he thought he could get two newspapers for the price of one and a half. In fact – a failure for which I must take my share of the blame – we did not realise until launch day that it weakened the evening paper without producing an effective regional morning paper. Senior editorial executives never quite knew whether they were fighting the *Mail* or the *Standard*. There were other major weaknesses, particularly in production and distribution, and to a lesser extent editorial. There had been too much instant decision-making, too much over-opti-mism, too much waste. In the end the losses were too heavy and

Maxwell shut it down after five months. Rothermere could not resist a public chortle. 'What gave me the greatest pleasure recently,' he told the *Financial Times*, 'was the squashing of Bob Maxwell's *Daily News* – that gave one enormous pleasure.'[7] Maxwell's immediate instinct was for revenge. 'I have a very long memory,' he told the author, and it was clear that he did not intend Rothermere to have the last word.

He is not called the Bouncing Czech for nothing. Soon there were major new take-over successes, more plans for new free newspapers in London and Manchester and detailed preparations for the launch of his *European* daily newspaper some time in 1989 (this was later changed to a weekly, and the launch delayed until 1990). The Mirror papers began to improve; they all had new editors – two of them women – since the day Maxwell took over. Maxwell himself was less in evidence on their pages. Above all, the use of colour was increasingly well handled. With the colour presses coming on stream month by month it looked like money well spent. Maxwell took comfort from the fact that the *Mirror* and the Scottish *Daily Record* were selling about 4 million, within sight of Murdoch's *Sun*. And it would still be months before Murdoch's colour presses were running.

Renewed talk of laying down some of his 'peripheral' burdens began to sound more convincing. His target of securing $3–5 billion turnover by 1990 was abandoned but the prospect of securing at least a partial success in the circulation battle with Murdoch seemed more promising. Like his great rival he had now firmly established himself as an international publisher and media magnate. With the successful take-over of Macmillan behind him he was even becoming more benign. 'I think Rupert recognises now there is room enough in the world for both of us,' he told the author. The two tycoons even did a deal together; Murdoch bought the right to put Sky, his slow-moving satellite television service, through Maxwell's cable network. But what would Maxwell do next? 'Walking in the mountains, looking at the flowers, cruising on the sea . . .'[8] The dream sounded a little unreal, but he added, 'I would devote myself mainly to the Maxwell Foundation. So many of the big charitable foundations are run by bureaucrats. We would have a more human face.' The primary purpose of the Foundation, whose investments are now worth in excess of £25 million, is to promote scientific research, but a secondary purpose is to provide financial assistance to both Jews and Arabs with the objective of promoting lasting peace between them. So the one-time lean and hungry Jewish boy from the pits of Ruthenia, whose success story is one of the most bizarre and remarkable in the post-war era, will make what could be seen as final restitution to his massacred family before he dies.

Notes:

1. There are two recent biographies: *Maxwell* by Joe Haines, Macdonald, 1988; and *Maxwell, the Outsider*, by Tom Bower, Aurum Press, 1988. Haines, a senior *Mirror* executive, had the full co-operation of Maxwell and his family which included access to the record of clippings and photographs compiled by Mrs Elisabeth (Betty) Maxwell – an invaluable source. Breezily and affectionately written, it is essential for an understanding of the man but some events are covered more briefly than their importance may warrant, and the story is always told, of course, from Maxwell's viewpoint. Bower interviewed 350 people for his book which, for some reason, Maxwell has tried to suppress. In fact, although Bower gives proportionately more space to the original problems of Pergamon and to Simpkin Marshall, the wholesale bookseller, Maxwell emerges in some ways as a more sympathetic, vulnerable and human figure than in the Haines biography. I have also read *Maxwell, a Portrait of Power*, by Peter Thompson, former editor of the *Sunday Mirror*, and Tony Delano, a former *Mirror* reporter and later executive, published by Bantam Press in 1988 and now pulped, following legal action by Maxwell.

2. See report by Robert Ballantyne, *The Times*, 15th August 1988. Other details in report by Andrew Hill, *Financial Times*, same day.

3. In an interview on 17th November 1988. (It illustrates the pace of Maxwell's life that this half-hour talk was postponed six times and eventually took place late one evening over the telephone.)

4. *Robert Maxwell & Pergamon Press, 40 years' service to Science, Technology and Education*, Pergamon, 1988.

5. From *Rupert Murdoch, a Business Biography*, by Simon Regan, Angus & Robertson, 1976. Quoted by Haines, op cit.

6. In conversation with the author.

7. Interview with Raymond Snoddy, 6th June 1988.

8. In conversation with the author.

11

Rupert Murdoch, the Invader from Adelaide

Opportunity Knocks

Title of popular TV talent show

'Rupert Murdoch[1] is one of the greatest risk-takers in the business. With him whatever is dangerous is possible.' It was Bruce Matthews's reading of Murdoch's character which fortified him to pick up the phone early in 1985 and suggest there might at last be the glimmering of a solution to the endless and sterile negotiations designed to relieve the ruinous production record of News International.

Matthews was one of those Australians whom Murdoch likes to have in senior positions; he has a rather bowed figure with a face that looks lined and lugubrious until he breaks into one of his frequent puckish smiles. As managing director of News International he had felt angry and frustrated at the failure of his efforts to open the company's new plant at Kinning Park, Glasgow, for the printing of the *Sun* in Scotland. By cutting out nightly air freight charges and faxing the pages to Scotland, he could save at least £3 million a year and the *Sun*'s robust circulation would increase still further. But despite the fact that he was proposing at least one hundred new jobs in Glasgow he had run up against the entrenched hostility of the Scottish journalists and print unions to a development which initially offered no Scottish input. Journalists on the Mirror Group's Scottish *Daily Record* seemed worried that the *Sun*, which had defeated the *Mirror* in the South might repeat the process in the North, and the SOGAT compositors, equally concerned, saw nothing in it for them. Matthews had been ready to allow some pages to be originated in Scotland, but Harry Conroy, then the Father of the Chapel for the *Daily Record* and *Sunday Mail* and now general secretary of the National Union of Journalists, wanted twelve

pages and seventy jobs for journalists. (News International were
convinced that he had been encouraged to make impossible demands
by his own employers.) And the print unions were worried that the
News of the World's Manchester print might be phased out altogether
and the work transferred to Glasgow on a lower cost basis. Bill
Keys, general secretary of SOGAT, promised Murdoch that he
would put pressure on the Scottish printers and that the plant would
be running by Christmas; but it was an empty pledge and nothing
happened. Shortly before Christmas 1984 Matthews saw no benefit
in prolonging the acrimonious negotiations any further; the two sides
were nowhere near agreement.

Apart from Kinning Park, News International had also built a
new £80 million print hall at Wapping so that the print of the *Sun*
and the *News of the World* could be transferred there from the
clapped-out presses in Bouverie Street, together with some sections
of the *Sunday Times* from Gray's Inn Road. It was known in the
firm as 'Hardy's Folly' after Matthews's predecessor, Bert Hardy,
who had built it – 'It just swallowed money and nothing ever came
out,' said Murdoch. The two developments had cost News International nearly £100 million and the interest on the money was
running at £10 million. Further, printing of *The Times* and *Sunday
Times* was constantly being disrupted at Gray's Inn Road and the
profitability of the company was being sapped by endless petty disputes. Attempts to use the new presses on an economical basis came
to nothing.

Over his Christmas break, which he took in his native country of
Australia, Matthews had been pondering over what had happened
when a Finnish firm had transformed an old steel mill at Shotton
Park, North Wales, into a paper mill. The Finns had wanted a
single-union deal with SOGAT's Manchester branch. Keys,
SOGAT's general secretary, agreed this could be done; the Manchester branch had been led by the moderate Brenda Dean, soon to
become first president and then general secretary of the union in
succession to Keys. But the national executive of the union, while
endorsing the principle, insisted that because of the location of the
plant the branch should be Merseyside, known to be among the
most militant. So the Finns decided to look elsewhere for their deal.
They talked to Eric Hammond, leader of the Electrical, Electronic,
Telecommunications and Plumbing Union (EETPU) and secured a
single-union deal with him. There were threats of trouble from
SOGAT if the Finns went ahead. The Finns had consulted

Matthews and he had told them to go ahead with the EEPTU. He was proved right: the single-union deal had worked and SOGAT's protests fizzled out.

Matthews began to think that if a single-union deal could work at a new plant in North Wales it would be worth looking at Wapping from the same angle. Why not regard it as a greenfield site, with a new title? That could get round TUC rules forbidding 'poaching' at existing plants. And might not the electricians be ready to help again since it was notorious that a SOGAT London machine branch had tried to recruit the EEPTU's Fleet Street branch after the Park Royal dispute?* SOGAT's action was still bitterly resented by the EEPTU. Would this be the longed-for chance to break the union stranglehold on the newspaper industry? (Whether Matthews had had any tentative conversation at this early stage with Hammond is far from clear, but it seems quite likely.)

There were other factors. The new industrial legislation outlawed secondary action, that is sympathy action against an employer to support a case or a cause even where there was no dispute directly affecting that employer and that union. Other Fleet Street employers had already used the law to good effect. Further, the miners' strike was failing to break the resistance of the Coal Board, and behind them, the government. Maybe they could work the plants after all. Maybe this was the time to break out. Matthews said as much to Murdoch in his telephone call from Australia to the States and was told he had better fly over.

They met in up-state New York. Matthews expounded his thinking and Murdoch 'quickly warmed to the idea'.[2] It is clear that when Murdoch warms to an idea, all systems go. He has a slight figure which sometimes gives the impression of positively quivering with suppressed energy. His Australian birth is evident in his voice which has a bit of a rasp to it. His deeply furrowed face is watchful; he listens, sometimes doodles, and reacts. This time he reacted very fast indeed. Early in February he appears to have given a warning to John Keating, his technical director in the United States, that he might want a large computer system for Britain. But the crunch meeting took place in his New York apartment on Sunday, 15th February 1985. Matthews had flown there by Concorde with a small group of key executives from London. They included Ken Taylor, the technical director of News Group (publishers of *The Sun* and

---

* Previously mentioned on p. 208.

News of the World); Christopher Pole-Carew, whom Murdoch had hired as a consultant on computer technology after he had fallen out with the owners of the *Nottingham Evening Post* (where as managing director he had forced through direct input after an abrasive confrontation with the unions); Geoffrey Richards, a lawyer from Farrer and Co, the company's solicitors in London; and Charles Wilson, deputy editor of *The Times*, who had recently been in Chicago as acting editor of Murdoch's latest purchase, the *Sun-Times*. Inured to the British way of negotiating change, Wilson had asked for one or two make-up modifications, thinking it would take months, and found the alterations implemented in the next edition. He could scarcely believe it.

Murdoch was realistic from the start. He saw that if they moved into Wapping with a single-union deal that excluded SOGAT and the NGA, there was every possibility of a strike both at Bouverie Street and at Gray's Inn Road. So it was not enough just to have the presses at Wapping. There had to be setting capacity as well. 'That was the first time we began to lay out a plan to have typesetting facilities there, and it was the first time we saw that we'd have to move the journalists there too.'

He also realised that the plan must allow for all four papers to be there from the beginning. But was there enough space in the buildings? Was there enough room for all the equipment, and for the staffs as well? At first the task seemed impossible; after all the place was built only as a print hall. Then someone remembered the old warehouses across the road inside the site. It was the breakthrough. 'I got excited about it and threw everything into it. It became *imperative* that we do it,' said Murdoch, looking back nearly four years later on the genesis of the plan.

He had not quite abandoned all hope of doing a deal with the print unions. He called back his industrial trouble-shooter Bill O'Neill from Australia to try to push the unions into Wapping. The terms were now very tough: a legally binding no-strike agreement with one union; complete flexibility of working practices; no closed shops; and with the management having the right to manage, including the right to determine manning levels. To get into Wapping the unions would have to swallow their pride completely and lose a lot of jobs as well. O'Neill was Murdoch's best union negotiator and had tried to get the unions into the plant in the earlier negotiations which had broken down at the end of 1984. ('We were presented with claims for manning levels and work practices which would have meant an actual financial penalty for moving into this great new plant,' said Murdoch.) But this time round the rest of the management would be working on the fall-back position, the alternative plan. Some of them felt they were 'living in two worlds' and did not find it too easy.

Key to the implementation of the plan was the computer typesetting system. Some people urged the most advanced system available. Murdoch would not have it; he said, 'We want something off the shelf. We want simple processes because we are going to have half-trained manpower.' The simplicity of the system became a blessing. 'It wasn't high tech; it was low tech,' he said later. There was no electronic page make-up; pages would be pasted up. The system selected was Atex, the most widely used electronic typesetting system already with some 500 customers. A few days after the crisis meeting with the British executives Murdoch called in the Atex people and asked if they could provide a system big enough for all the News International papers, in complete secrecy, and aim to instal it by the beginning of June. The order was worth around $10 million. Atex said they could do it.

Officially the whole plan centred on the launch of a new evening paper, the *London Post*, with Wilson as editorial director, but it is doubtful if Murdoch ever wanted it. He did not believe there was room for a second evening paper in London; his experience of Sydney and New York had convinced him that a second evening paper could be a nightmare. Later Bruce Matthews would press him to make the commitment, if only to keep the EEPTU happy, and Murdoch would go along with the idea on a 'maybe' basis. If the print unions had finally accepted his terms then he would have started a paper – but it would have been a middle-market morning paper and he would have had some doubts about its prospects. It seems certain that Murdoch had little expectation that the unions would bend. In retrospect, the *London Post* was a cover plan, although Matthews and Wilson believed in it and kept working at it seriously. There is no question that the management's past experience of union bloody-mindedness was a major factor in their stark determination to defeat the unions. When Murdoch met the union executives at the end of September, at their request, he finally felt able to tell them exactly what he thought. 'I have strained myself and my senior colleagues physically, emotionally and financially to build this business and we have met with nothing but cynicism, broken promises and total opposition,' he said in his opening statement. 'All national newspaper production departments are overmanned by from fifty to 300 per cent, with working practices that are a continuing disgrace to us all . . . It is difficult to see any point in going through another series of long, unpleasant and emotionally draining negotiations with so little prospect of success.'

Reflecting on the move to Wapping a few years after the event, it is easy to assume that Murdoch was always going to win. In fact the margin between success and failure was wafer thin. The big gamble could so easily have failed hopelessly. There were perhaps five critical points. The first was the recruitment of the production staff. Without question this was facilitated by Tom Rice, a former Communist who was then a national officer of the EEPTU, and by the union's area office in Southampton. By the summer scores of workers, not only technicians, were being bussed to Wapping from Southampton every day. The EEPTU area was not the only recruiting agent – some of the key people came from Australia – but it was crucial. There were mounting objections from the print workers as the facts of this recruitment became known, but an element of executive drag seemed to intervene at the EEPTU before recruitment stopped. (It is ironic that in the end the EEPTU failed to secure a single-union deal with News International at Wapping, but at the end of 1988 some thirty-five to forty per cent of the staff there still had some affinity with the EEPTU and when their current three-year contract runs out there might be talks about union recognition.)

Then it was essential that the existence, the extent and the capability of the computer system should be concealed so that the unions would misjudge the real strength of the management's position until it was too late. Although chapels had been allowed to see the presses at Wapping they never saw the computer equipment. By the autumn it seems certain that some London print union leaders had a pretty good idea of what was going on at Wapping, but most of their members had become arrogant after years of running Fleet Street their way. They believed they could defeat Murdoch in their own good time just as they had defeated the management of the Thomson *Times*. In September the SOGAT London Machine Branch Committee at the *Sun* actually recommended a strike after seeing dummy copies of the *London Post* smuggled out of the plant. To the amazement of the committee the strike call was turned down three to two. Yet if the strike had started that autumn, before Wapping was ready to produce, the cost to News International would have been enormous, and it might have proved even more difficult to persuade the journalists to move. To strike at the last moment, when preparations were complete was the worst course. In mid-December Matthews had a chat with Tony Dubbins, general secretary of the NGA.

'Tony,' he said, 'you must realise you could lose this one.'

'My members would expect me to take them out on strike,' replied Dubbins, showing that he was now trapped in a situation he could no longer control.

The third critical point was in fact the decision of the journalists. Without any previous warning or consultation they were suddenly told by their editors, in separate meetings, that they should move to Wapping tomorrow. As Kelvin Mackenzie, editor of the *Sun*, told his staff, 'The only people who matter any more are the journalists'[3] and it was crucial that enough journalists should go to bring the papers out. The management had sensibly arranged for the *Sun* journalists, who had vivid memories of the NGA walking through NUJ pickets eighteen months earlier, to be given their marching orders first. Mackenzie addressed the chapel around six on Friday, 24th January. After an ineffectual effort by Conroy to stem the tide with a call to support the TUC line of collective action, those journalists voted to go to Wapping by 100 to eight. Shortly after the *Sun*'s vote Charles Wilson, now editor of *The Times* after the death of Charles Douglas-Home, told his staff that they had lost that night's paper but would be producing at Wapping on Sunday night. 'I am inviting you to come along and help us do it.' After long and anguished discussions *The Times* staff voted decisively to go to Wapping. So did the *News of the World*. The meeting of the *Sunday Times* staff did not take place until the Monday morning and was the most tortured of the four. Andrew Neil, the gritty Scot from *The Economist* whom Murdoch appointed editor in succession to Frank Giles, had found the paper complacent, self-satisfied and living in the past; some of the staff had resented his unyielding determination to make it an altogether tougher, more news-oriented paper. Further he had publicly and deliberately identified himself with management policy over Wapping and as a result he was not popular. The meeting was remarkable for a dignified but bitter speech by Don Berry, the talented and much respected executive features editor. He attacked the manner in which the moral authority of the *Sunday Times*, as he saw it, had been undermined by the management and by what he described as the contemptuous treatment of his staff by the editor.

After a long and agonised debate the chapel voted sixty-eight to sixty in favour of going to Wapping. It was a narrow victory, but it was enough. Some journalists still refused to go, but the bulk of all four editorial staffs went over.

The fourth and most critical point concerned the ability of the police to keep the highway clear. Distribution of the papers was entirely dependent on the lorries which were delivering the papers to wholesalers and retailers throughout the country. At the start of the dispute, although the numbers outside the gates were large, picketing was relatively peaceful and the lorries had little difficulty getting through. But tension rose and so did the numbers, many of them from outside Fleet Street. Sir Kenneth Newman, the Metropolitan Police Commissioner, had learnt from the failure of outnumbered police to protect the coke depot at Saltley Gate, Birmingham, during the 1972 coal dispute and also from the handling of the miners' strike; so he ensured there was no shortage of manpower. There also seems to have been some local sanction for the police to get tougher. One night they charged a large crowd of pickets across the highway; there were 250 injuries and eighty arrests. Murdoch was fortunate that the government was friendly; the lorries continued to get through.

Finally the London print branches had made themselves so unpopular with their excessive rates of pay and airs of superiority that they found little support for their action among their fellow members in the provinces. SOGAT members continued to distribute the papers when they arrived at wholesalers. SOGAT and NGA members continued to print and handle the colour supplements, and Transport and General Workers' members drove the newspaper lorries through the pickets.

So what had seemed like an amazing gamble a year earlier paid Murdoch off in gold. No other publisher *could* have done it, for no one else had an alternative printing plant, but, Bruce Matthews adds with conviction, 'No other publisher *would* have done it.'

It was not only members of the print unions who lost their jobs as a result of Wapping. There was a clear-out of production management, virtually from top to bottom. All but two or three of the young executives who went to Wapping 'had to go', said Murdoch later. 'They could not get it into their heads that there was no departmental chapel to talk to. They were used to having a long lunch with the FOC to negotiate something. Now we have a production manager who came from Australia and a deputy production manager who came from *The Times* – almost the only one who made the transition. All the other production executives have been promoted from within the plant.'

Wapping was Murdoch's most spectacular success but it had taken many years of hard work before he was in a position to pull it off. He had already caught the newspaper bug when he succeeded to his inheritance at the early age of twenty-one. His father, Sir Keith Murdoch, had made his name by exposing the incompetence of the military command in the Gallipoli campaign during the First World War. Northcliffe had taken him up and helped him in his early struggles and Keith Murdoch had been so influenced by the great man that he was known in some circles as Lord Southcliffe. While he owned control of two papers in Adelaide he had only a small shareholding in the powerful Melbourne *Herald*, of which he was chief executive.

His son still vividly remembers the excitement of it all. He saw his father sitting up in bed in the morning marking up all the papers with shorthand notes all over the pages; he heard of the intense competition for circulation; he saw the travel involved – for his father was far more of a journalist than he was a businessman; and he realised too that there was a degree of political influence, for his father would meet prime ministers and other important political leaders and discuss the state of the world with them. 'It was very intoxicating stuff for a kid to see all this,' said Murdoch recently.

It is also possible that his drive to succeed was intensified by a desire to prove that his father's early anxieties about his abilities were ill-founded. At Oxford he was a fairly casual student and a member of the Labour Club; his father was uncertain for a time whether he would prove a worthy successor. Rupert was still at Oxford when his father died at the relatively early age of sixty-six; his absence at that time may have accentuated a feeling that there was something unfinished about their relationship; that he still had something to prove. (But his mother, the formidable Dame Elisabeth, remembers with pleasure that her husband read a long letter from his son only a few days before his death, and that he said, 'Thank God, the boy's got it.')

Rupert flew back to Australia and then returned to England and spent six rewarding months with the *Daily Express*. After a fortnight sitting around at the editor's conferences and observing what happened on the backbench and going over to the old Press Club for a drink he went to Edward Pickering (then the managing editor),* and told him that while everyone had been terribly kind he would never learn anything more just sitting around. 'Do you think I could have a job, down at the bottom of the subs' table?' There he came under the benign tutelage of Eric Raybould, a sausage-and-mash man who was the brilliant production editor at the heart of the *Express* engine room. 'My biggest moment came when I was given the Korean story for page one; I had to condense about 500 pages of cable into three paragraphs,' he recalled. 'I loved it; it was just fabulous.'

At the age of twenty-two he returned to Adelaide and became publisher of the *News*. After his spell in London it seemed a pretty small place and the *News*, which made about £10,000 a year, seemed a pretty small paper; it could not even afford its own cartoonist. So, for every reason, Murdoch looked for opportunities to expand. A few years later he bought a small Sunday paper in Perth; and then in 1958 he obtained the licence to run the Channel 9 television station in Adelaide; he followed that up two years later by moving out of Adelaide for an important acquisition and buying the Sydney *Daily Mirror* from the Fairfax group in 1960. It was losing money at the rate of nearly A$500,000 a year and for a time Murdoch was really worried he had so over-reached himself that his company would go broke. Just at that moment the television station in Adelaide came good and began to make A$1 million a year. Soon he was able to expand still further, with weeklies published in Brisbane and Melbourne, other magazines, more television interests and finally he founded Australia's first national daily, *The Australian*.

Murdoch, still under forty, survived the bruising wars of Sydney and was now a growing force in Australian publishing, said to be worth as much as A$50 million. But after his college days at Oxford and his early training on the *Express*, Fleet Street looked tempting. He had always admired the London *Daily Mirror* and he could see that Cecil King's obsession with politics was causing problems for IPC, the paper's owners. So he began buying shares in IPC with a view to 'getting inside and playing it from there';[4] eventually his shareholding rose as high as ten per cent. Then Maxwell launched his bid for the *News of the World*. Ever since the day when he had received a call out of the blue, 'Captain Maxwell here. I've got to see you,' leading to their abortive negotiations about Pergamon,

---

* Pickering later became editor (p. 96) and also played a part at IPC (p. 129).

Australia, he had been watching Maxwell's moves. Now he was informed at once. 'I could *smell* that the establishment wouldn't let Maxwell have it. So I put my hand up.' He did not have enough money to top Maxwell's bid, but he was much more welcome to Sir William Carr (see previous chapter) than a Czech-born socialist. Eventually his proposal to inject some of his smaller Australian properties into the News of the World company in exchange for shares won the day against the bigger bid from Maxwell and the combined chorus of City scribes. 'All over town people were saying, "What this country needs is more Robert Maxwells. This is the white hot revolution coming." ' Not for the first time did the City pages fail to affect the result of a take-over battle.

What the scribblers did not know was that the *News of the World* was in terrible shape. 'It could have made us broke. It was very hard work. I remember the first day. Carr was in hospital. I walked into the office at eight am and found the SOGAT cleaning ladies having tea on the chairman's desk ... Formative experiences those first few years,' said Murdoch later.

Perhaps it was because of a need to have some clear-headed advice from a man who had clearly mastered one aspect of the English publishing scene that Murdoch invited his friend Paul Hamlyn, the wealthy Hungarian-born publisher, to join his company as joint managing director. Although that position didn't last long, Hamlyn remained a director of the company for sixteen years – an unusual alliance which emphasises Murdoch's relish in the unorthodox.

His real steal was the *Sun*. Again Maxwell was in first, and it was the unions which rejected his proposal, allowing Murdoch to buy a paper for an astonishingly low price (see previous chapter). What seemed inexplicable at the time was the decision of the IPC board, with Cudlipp in the chair, to sell at all. In retrospect it is clear that the key factor was its fear that closure, with the loss of 2,000 jobs, might cause SOGAT to damage the rest of the business, the profitable *Mirror* and the mass-selling women's magazines – another example of the way in which the print unions terrorised weak managements. Now, with the help of his editor Larry Lamb (later Sir Larry) in dragging the paper into the topless trade and producing a light-hearted larky entertainment sheet, Murdoch transformed the title into the most popular daily in the country and one of the biggest money-earners in the business. (In three years the sale of the *Sun* increased from 800,000 at the time of the take-over to more than

3,000,000; in six years it had overtaken the *Mirror*.) Contemplating
the two deals which made his fortune in Britain, Murdoch says of
Maxwell, 'A very fascinating man, of enormous capacity. In a sense
I've got a lot to thank him for.'

He could say the same of Donald Trelford, editor of *The Observer*.
For in August 1976 David Astor, the owner of the paper and previously its editor, had decided that he could no longer afford to fund
the losses from his own pocket and that a buyer must be sought.
Murdoch, encouraged by Bert Hardy his managing director at the
time, who believed the *Sunday Times* was over the hill, said in answer
to an enquiry that he was interested but would not keep Donald
Trelford, the new editor, in that position. Lord Goodman, chairman
of the trustees, was worried about this disturbance to *The Observer's*
way of doing things and asked Trelford to see Murdoch in New
York, no doubt in the hope that the problem would resolve itself.
The reverse occurred. Murdoch wanted Bruce Rothwell as editor-
in-chief and Anthony Shrimsley as editor. Trelford could stay on as
editorial director, whatever that meant. After agonised consultations
back in London the news leaked, and the reaction of *The Observer's*
journalists was one of horror. Murdoch was furious and issued a
statement saying that News International was no longer interested.
But before long it was clear that no other publisher was prepared
to fund the losses and invest further money to put the paper into
the black. The board of the paper met again and were on the verge
of inviting Murdoch to take over; what is more, the journalists,
fearing the breadline, were becoming less hostile. For his part Murdoch still said he was not interested, but he was ready to be invited
back to negotiate. At the last moment, through a chance dinner
invitation to Kenneth Harris, a senior *Observer* journalist, from
Douglas Cater of the Aspen Institute which was funded by Atlantic
Richfield, the American oil company emerged as the saviour. When
Murdoch heard the news from Goodman he said his first reaction
was of tremendous relief, then one of personal grievance and annoyance. 'Lastly, I've got to admit that it's all for the best.' Just how
much it was for the best he wouldn't know for four years, when
Times Newspapers came on the market. If he had then owned *The
Observer*, not even a Conservative government could have cleared
the way for him to take over the *Sunday Times* as well.

By this time Murdoch's main expansionary drive was in the United
States. A number of factors combined to move him out of England.
On the suggestion of Somerfield, the *News of the World* editor he

inherited from Carr, he agreed to buy another instalment of Christine Keeler's memoirs, inevitably dragging up again the sins of John Profumo, the disgraced ex-Minister who was rehabilitating himself in the East End. There was an outcry from the establishment, ranging from the Press Council, spurred on by Denis Hamilton, to Cardinal Heenan. Murdoch appeared on the Frost Programme to defend himself but Frost was in one of his prosecuting moods and savaged Murdoch, who had been lulled into a state of unpreparedness. For a time Murdoch and his very attractive wife Anna were not particularly welcome guests in some circles. (Paul Hamlyn recalls that at one dinner party he attended, a guest stormed out saying, 'I won't sit at the same table as anyone involved with Rupert Murdoch.') Then there was the horrible murder of Muriel McKay, wife of a News International executive who had been lent the Murdochs' car. It seemed certain she had been kidnapped for a ransom in the belief that she was Anna Murdoch and killed when it emerged she was not; it was enough to put anyone off the country where such a terrible event could happen. The exposé of Lord Lambton's sexual activities in the *News of the World* caused a further frisson in some circles. Finally the media scene in the United States far surpassed that of Britain. The film and television markets were vast in comparison. The publishing world was much more open to attack. The profits to be made were glittering. And American society was much freer and less closed than the British. It is not surprising that Murdoch moved there in 1973 and soon started acquiring publishing properties, first in Texas and then in New York, Chicago and Boston, following them up with television stations, film studios and major interests in satellite and cable. Since this book is concerned with British newspaper publishing these deals are outside its scope. But it is true to say that Murdoch's habit of firing editors who didn't fit the job and of spicing up most of the papers he acquired led to much the same reaction in the United States as he first met in Britain. But his expansion has never been halted.

Undoubtedly the onward march has been helped by the profits from his British newspapers and Times Newspapers are now playing their full part. When Sir Gordon Brunton announced that the International Thomson Organisation was putting the *Sunday Times, The Times* and the various supplements up for sale, and would close the papers by March 1981 if a suitable buyer was not found, Maxwell was once again first in the field. Brunton did not even put him on the shortlist which he narrowed to Rothermere and Murdoch, with a strong preference for Murdoch. (See Chapters 9 and 10.) Once again the unions also preferred Murdoch since they liked what he had done for the *Sun*. The journalists of the *Sunday Times* in a poll conducted by their editor, Harry Evans, also preferred Murdoch over the other contenders.

Murdoch submitted to scrutiny by a vetting committee set up by Hamilton and gave various guarantees relating to the independence of the editors. Their appointment and dismissal had to be approved by the national directors; Murdoch would issue instructions only through the editors; the editors would retain control over the appointment, disposition and dismissal of journalists; the editors had control of the selection and balance of news and opinion; the consent of the independent national directors would be needed for the sale or disposal of an interest in the *Times* and the *Sunday Times*.

Murdoch's acquisition of Times Newspapers proved a financial triumph. When he took them over they were losing money at the rate of £14 million a year. In 1988 *The Times* was breaking even and the *Sunday Times* was said to be making more than £80 million a year. In addition the Reuters shares brought in a fortune. Editorially the record is more mixed. After a sticky start, with staff discontent enlarged by the hurried move to Wapping, Andrew Neil grew in confidence and the more relaxed atmosphere, together with the recruitment of his own men, led to the production of an impressive and serious newspaper wide in range, strong in cultural coverage, and, while clearly of the Right, increasingly independent of Thatcherism. The sheer bulk of the paper, which increasingly looks like an outcrop of the *New York Times* has led to a profusion of columns, some of them all too boringly predictable. Though harder, rather less entertaining and surprising and crusading than the paper produced by Harry Evans, the *Sunday Times* can now rank again among the world's great newspapers.

Murdoch's experience on *The Times* has been less fortunate. He persuaded Evans to move from the *Sunday Times* and take over the editorship from the academically inclined Rees-Mogg. Then, with difficulty, he persuaded the national directors to accept Evans. Unfortunately he also persuaded Gerry Long to become managing director of Times Newspapers. Long, a brilliant but irascible man with an obsession about how food and drink should be served, had transformed the fortunes of Reuters through the development of electronic data transmission, but he was neither well-fitted to put the brake on Harry, nor to use the resources of diplomacy and

THE NEW STANDARD

Incorporating the *Evening News*

Thursday, January 22, 1981. Price 12p.

THE TIMES — Sun owner to take over Times papers

MURDOCH BUYS THE THUNDERER

AUSTRALIAN PRESS magnate Rupert Murdoch has won the race to buy The Times.

A formal statement with details of the sale by Lord Thomson was to be made in London at 3 p.m. today.

It follows a period of intense negotiation. Lawyers worked throughout today to work out and finalise stages in the purchase package for *The Times, Sunday Times* and the supplements.

Mr Murdoch still has three main hurdles to clear before he can finalise the deal. He has to obtain the approval of the Times union, satisfy the national vetting committee which was set up to guarantee the newspapers' editorial integrity and

by Norman Leith and John McLeod

Independence—and faces a possible reference to the Monopolies Commission.

Mr Murdoch, proprietor of the Sun and News of the World newspapers—Britain's biggest selling dailies and Sunday papers—was in London for the announcement.

The final deal is still subject to agreement being reached between Mr Murdoch and members of the print trade unions. Unofficial talks have already taken place.

Mr Murdoch said he was still hopeful of satisfying vetting committees that he will honour the conditions on the troubled group.

Print union talks

The committee which consists of Sir David Nicolson, editor-in-chief, Mr William Rees-Mogg, editor of The Times, and Sir Harold Evans, editor of the Sunday Times, and four other members, each was told today discussing the takeover.

Mr approval of the commercial aspects of the deal formal general postponements in the official announcement throughout the day. A press confirmation, initially scheduled for 11 a.m., was delayed until 3 p.m.—and then later.

Both newspaper editors were standing by to address members of the staff before the formal statement is made. There are more than 4000 employees on the two papers.

The deal ends weeks of speculation about the future of The Thunderer, its about Sunday paper

and the little educational and literary supplements.

It makes Mr Murdoch, who has a newspaper, magazine and television empire in Australia, America and Britain, one of the most powerful press proprietors in the world.

The concentration of press interests in his hands has already aroused intense criticism.

MPs from both parties have agreed a Commons motion condemning the sale of Times Newspapers to anyone with major press interests in Britain or abroad.

Financial trouble

Mr Jonathan Aitken, Tory MP for Thanet, has described Mr Murdoch as "The unacceptable face of journalism."

The group came on the market last October. Lord Thomson, son of the man who brought The Times and Sunday Times together a decade ago, said he wanted to sell the papers at once then (buyers them March 6).

The group has been in desperate financial trouble since the eleven-month closedown from November 30, 1978 to November 13, 1979.

It cost the group a reported £40 million, and a further £20 million has been claimed for the current financial year.

Other factors were the future of management and trade unions to agree over the introduction of new technology at the Gray's Inn Road plant.

Mr Murdoch has been a favourite front-runner to take over the group since they went on sale.

Other press bidders included Lord Rothermere, Sir Maxwell family, Sir James Goldsmith, as well as two separate production groups.

The new owner—up and from *Down Under*: Page Two

KILLER CHASE • THE BULL FROM • MICHAEL CRAWFORD, HOW THE LEFT PUT
GUN BATTLE • THE BRONX • TIGHTROPE WALKER AGREED IN MARSH

THE Sun

Members of all The Sun production chapels refused to handle the Arthur Scargill picture and major headline on our lead story. The Sun has decided, reluctantly, to print the paper without either.

Sam's assets insured for £1m

£40,000 BINGO! Today's lucky numbers on Page 16!

ON THE EVE OF THE MEDIA TYCOON'S GREATEST TRIUMPH . . .

IT WAS 7 a.m. on a cold damp New York morning when Wall Street first digested the news

Rupert Murdoch in Geneva announced that the battle for control of the giant Warner Communications Industry had started.

It was sensational news. A two-billion-dollar empire was at stake, and the man who wanted it had a personal fortune of only £150 million. Brokers were woken up in Los Angeles and investors were roused from their beds in Sydney.

By then 52-year-old Rupert Murdoch was in London. He had dispensed with the editor of the News of the World, replaced him with the editor of the People and ordered the machinery necessary to turn the paper from a broadsheet into a tabloid.

Hunger

While Fleet Street was still discussing the ramifications of the Warner takeover bid, Murdoch was getting an assessment report by telephone from Chicago where he has just bought the Sun Times for £90 million and set the scene for a newspaper war in the windy city.

He ordered one of his top executives on the London Times — a Glaswegian with little respect for sensitivities — to fly to Chicago. His 'leaving present' was a plastic 'Tommy gun' . . . to 'pep' up the staff of the Sun Times.

Murdoch wants it in fighting shape to compete with the arrival of an afternoon newspaper in the city which looks certain to have as its Editor Mr Harold Evans, whom Murdoch sacked nearly two years ago from the editorship of The Times.

As the clock ticked on he ordered the reprinting of a sell-out book in Australia on the America's Cup and placed two reports on the possibility of buying two Hearst newspapers in the United States.

As millions of Londoners streamed home in the rush hour he took calls from two editors, altered the front page of a weekly magazine and heard a first-hand report from an undercover team exploring the backgrounds and life styles of the top executives in Warner Communications.

Murdoch is a one-man whirlwind, with a hunger for power and ownership that seems to simply feed on acquisition. In many ways he is the most

astonishing businessman in the world today, bounding from one country to another like a demented kangaroo.

And he's got plenty of people running scared. Yesterday's news in Hollywood was that Clint Eastwood and ET director Steven Spielberg wouldn't make any pictures with Warners if he gets control. Murdoch would just smile at that. Harsh words never worry him. He just gets on with business.

In the middle of all the activity Murdoch, who controls a publishing empire of 90 newspapers, 11 magazines, seven broadcasting stations and a TV network, in addition to a lottery, an airline and gas and oil interests, took time to approve an editorial project that involved just a few thousand pounds—the launch of

satellite TV in this country, in swindon of all the unlikely places.

Such attention to detail holds the key to the astonishing success of Rupert Murdoch, who started out 31 years ago with a failing afternoon newspaper in Australia and turned it into a $1·37 billion empire.

No aspect of his empire is overlooked. He knows the name of almost every key employee, their failings and their potential. Each satellite has to make its contribution and when they falter he personally intervenes to tighten the bootstraps or fire the failure.

His quest for Warner with its movie interests, extensive film library and cable TV is a gigantic step forward into a new dimension. There are those that doubt his ability to raise the money.

But his track record shows he has never failed to raise the cash in a takeover deal. What puzzles Wall Street, and in particular the American journalistic community which deeply resents his takeovers on their home ground, is where the Australian is going.

Asked about it recently, he said : 'People think I work to some ten-year plan. I don't. We look at opportunities as they come along.'

It is partly true. If the immediate acquisition is not always clear the ultimate goal is. Rupert Murdoch is on the road to becoming the world's biggest and most important media mogul.

What Murdoch has understood ahead of rivals in both the publishing and communications world is that in the new world of electronic media, entertainment and news are merging.

Money is his driving force. Once asked why he went on, he simply explained that more assets allowed him to acquire more assets. He dresses conservatively, he drinks modestly and prefers plain food.

Once invited to lunch with him, I was picked up in a Cadillac and delivered to a modest restaurant in New York's fish market. We had fish and chips on an oil-cloth table.

He sent the waiter to get a pack of beer from a nearby supermarket. After lunch he pocketed one of the cans left over for the chauffeur and handed me the other.

Formula

He resents spending what little spare time he has at social functions. 'This sort of stuff,' he observed at an exclusive New York party 'can wreck your working day.' And his working day is 'never routine.'

When his supermarket magazine was struggling, he dragged the executives through lines of shoppers, rearranged magazines on the racks and because enraged when one woman picked up his magazine, glanced through it and then replaced it before she reached the cash counter.

'That's fraud, plain fraud!' he repeated. In dealing with brokers, bankers and lawyers his style is no different. The formula is simple.

He is the boss . . . and he makes all the decisions.

Lust for power that drives Murdoch on

from George Gordon IN NEW YORK

Snore the merrier

IT'S the latest weekend holiday g i m m i c k — the SNORE-away break.

People normally embarrassed by their anti-social habit are being positively encouraged in it during weekends in a new wing, well away from other guests, at the Hotel Norwich in Norwich.

A porter carrying a decibel meter will take readings outside the doors of the 15 bedrooms. The loudest snorer of the week-end will receive a 'golden clothes peg' and a duvet. And any guests whose snoring can be heard from the hotel car park will get their bill cut in half.

The weekend costs £44 per person and ear plugs for partiners are thrown in free.

Peter Rudd, the hotel's manager, says : 'I'm a snorer myself and I know how awkward it can be. So when our new wing was built I decided to organise weekends where snorers will be encouraged to give off their beds without any worries.'

And during the days he is laying on special car trips . . . to the nearby villages of Great Snoring and Little Snoring.

IAN BROWN

Murdoch's rise to worldwide media power excited envy, hatred and scorn both among his rivals and the print workers, but it has never stopped him expanding whenever opportunity offered. Despite his interests in film, television and satellites, newspapers remain the foundation of his fortune, and his first love.

experience to smooth the relations between two highly-strung individuals with completely differing outlooks.

Although Evans speedily introduced a number of improvements to *The Times*, the benefit of which can still be seen, he also made a number of unnecessary blunders, possibly due to an understandable wish to drive through change in a hurry. Within a week of his appointment he had hired at least a dozen journalists, many of them to take senior positions on the paper. It soon became apparent that these were his favourites; further, the new men did not conceal their contempt for the old *Times* hands whom they referred to as 'dead wood'. So the staff was split from the very outset. It was also a mistake that he was ready to discard Louis Heren, an outstanding *Times* foreign correspondent and later deputy editor to Rees-Mogg, even if Heren was disappointed not to get the editorship himself.[5] Nor did Evans realise that with all the pressures of daily production there was simply no time for him to fiddle with as much detail as he enjoyed tackling on the Sunday paper. As it was, he both delayed production and cut down time for reflection. On the *Sunday Times* he was known as a fairly profligate spender, just kept in check by 'Duke' Hussey. On *The Times* he complained bitterly that he was never given the editorial budget which had been promised, but staff numbers instead of falling actually rose. By the end of 1981 fifty-three people had left under the expensive redundancy scheme, but fifty-six had been hired, and some of the new men were being paid more than the people they replaced. When Evans told John Grant, the managing editor, that Murdoch had promised to find the money for two months of feature serials during the summer months, Grant looked at Evans for a long time before saying, accurately enough. 'It'll all end in tears. Mark my words.'

For his part Murdoch was remarkably casual about implementing the guarantees he had given. According to Evans, Murdoch told Fred Emery, then the home editor of *The Times*, 'I give instructions to my editors all round the world. Why shouldn't I in London?' On another occasion he stated his attitude very clearly (although he was not talking about *The Times*).

'Of course I intervene. I intervene because I am the one who is responsible – not only for the paper that is produced, not only to the law, not only to the shareholders and to the banks who have staked us, or the mortgagers or whatever, but also to the people working for the newspaper – and that means everyone depending on it for a living. A publisher cannot abdicate his responsibility to an editor. All successful companies are personalised.[6]

No doubt it was in this spirit that he attempted to slide through a transfer of *The Times* titles to News International without obtaining the consent of the independent directors; the manoeuvre went badly wrong and Evans ensured the problem was fully ventilated in the columns of *The Times*. Then, while initially enthusiastic for the Evans reforms, he became increasingly hostile to his editor's middle-of-the-road political views. Soon he also found the level of editorial spending 'intolerable' and attempted to institute various checks, implemented by Long, to restrain some of the excesses.

The end came when both the deputy editor, Charles Douglas-Home (who later succeeded Evans as editor) and Grant decided to resign; Murdoch asked them to stay and asked Evans to resign instead. Initially Evans refused and challenged Murdoch to explain why. 'The place is in chaos,' said Murdoch. 'You can't see the wood for the trees ... your senior staff is up in arms.' He told Evans that it was really tough to take decisions like this. (Later he told the author, 'I am pretty weak, but sometimes you have to be tough. You have to wind yourself up.') That Evans recognised the real weakness of his position is shown by the fact that he never asked the national directors to support him. As Rees-Mogg later commented, 'You can't fight the staff and the proprietor simultaneously.'[7]

For *The Times*, Murdoch's inability to channel Evans's tremendous talents into constructive channels was a tragedy. A more emollient go-between such as Pickering might have succeeded in preventing the upheaval which deprived British journalism of its brightest star. The new editor, Douglas-Home, although crippled by a fatal disease, was able to draw the staff together and settle the paper on a more orthodox route. His successor, Charles Wilson, much improved some sections of the paper without as yet quite making it sing.

There was yet another score over Maxwell in 1987. Lonrho had bought Eddy Shah's loss-making *Today* for £10 million plus a £14 million investment; then they had bought most of his fifty-one per cent shareholding. But they found the losses too heavy and the drain on management time too severe; they wished to get out. At first it seemed that Murdoch would get it, but Tiny Rowland, chairman of Lonrho, was upset by some story in the *Sunday Times* about his endless and obsessive feud with the Al Fayeds over Harrods and cancelled the deal. Maxwell was alerted to the fact that *Today* was for sale and soon appeared to make a deal to buy the paper for £10 million cash plus taking over £30 million in loan stock. Then he made the fatal mistake of ringing Murdoch, who was in California, to tell him that *Today* would continue to honour the contract to print copies of the *News of the World*. From their conversation Murdoch gleaned the fact that the contract had not yet been signed; he telephoned London where David Montgomery, then editor of the *News of the World*, had long been pressing Murdoch to take over the paper. Montgomery was able to discover that £40 million cash would secure the paper. Murdoch, now in Colorado, flew on to London and sealed a provisional deal. On hearing the news Maxwell dropped out, saying that he would not engage in an auction. Rowland, after some show of reluctance, now had only Murdoch left to deal with and soon sold the paper to him for £38 million. The investment had not paid off at the time of writing but circulation had risen by more than 250,000 since Montgomery took over as managing director and editor. A well focused newspaper seemed to have the *Daily Mail* in its sights. So Murdoch had wound up with a quality, middle-market and mass-market daily – the original flight to grab the *News of the World* had certainly paid off.

Murdoch watches over all his papers with loving attention, casting his eye at them every day.[8] Believing that the head of a company should concentrate on the strategic decisions he delegates 'enormously' once the annual budgets have been set. For instance 'the management in Australia has total autonomy', although if they want to spend $50 million on a new printing press then 'obviously' that's referred. He displayed his financial monitoring system to the author with pride. Every Friday wherever he may be in the world he received a foolscap book in sections for each country where he's active; the book showed the figures right up to the previous Sunday, all processed by 'a computer in Holland or somewhere'. A book about half an inch thick covered London. 'Here it is for all the papers – how much money they budget to make, how much they did make, what they made last year, or lost, and how much for the year to date. And here at the front, just one paragraph on what went right or wrong. Then you get into the breakdown; this is for the administration costs of Wapping – I have it here in case things are starting to go wrong.'

He flipped some pages. 'This is last week's *News of the World*. Sales – circulation revenue, advertising revenue, sale of waste. And costs – editorial costs all broken down and . . .' he grinned, 'they're outrageous. Production costs – newsprint, administration, distribution, promotions. And profit. Then on another page you get the number of pages, actual and budgeted, the number of copies printed, gross circulation, net circulation, and the actual price per copy right down to a thousandth of a penny. Advertising – the rate for display and the rate for classified with the overall rate per column against last year – and what we thought we would get.

'The management gets that here and works through it. But I have it too, so if I get worried or have nothing else to do on a Saturday or a Sunday I can pick up the phone and make a nuisance of myself.' His old friend Paul Hamlyn commented, 'He can deal with and digest an enormous amount of detail. Most people in the company are convinced he can do their job better than they can – and they like it!'

Murdoch continued, 'And then I go around. What I enjoy most is spending time with the editors. For instance Andrew Neil came to supper last night for two or three hours. We had dinner on our own, just the two of us. I went to the reporters' room at the *Sun* twice yesterday, once with Kelvin [Mackenzie, the editor], just chatting. You get a feel for it; a bit washes on to them, and a bit washes on to you. You add a bit of excitement to it.' Says Hamlyn, 'His staff are obsessed by him. I have had to threaten to leave a dinner party unless people stopped talking about him.'

Murdoch added, 'I try to spend a month in Australia every year, fitting in with the school holidays so that I can take the family. Then I can see the people. I can do an awful lot by telephone, but you have to keep renewing. You have to physically go round once a year. Here in London it's very easy. I've been on the board of Reuters for six or seven years and I've used that almost as a discipline to make me come. I spent a very large proportion of both the years of 1985 and 1986 in this country, and I should have spent more.'

It is said that he has dynastic ambitions, perhaps reinforced by his mother, Dame Elisabeth, an immensely powerful figure in her own right. How had he kept family control over the whole vast business? It was simple. 'I don't give people shares. I just borrow the money. At one time it was very difficult, but you grow in stages.' The previous day he had been asked by another newspaper executive how his company could expand. 'I said, "Go and buy a big company." He said, "But we're only just starting." Well, I said, "Go and buy a medium-sized one." You build a record, based on two factors; first, a record of success, and that has to be on average; then you have to build a reputation as a straight dealer, and that's more important than anything else. So when we agreed to pay $3 billion for Triangle [publishers of the American *TV Guide*], and that's an enormous sum, we had no difficulty at all. We will sell some things, and we will pay back $1 billion, perhaps more, in a year. Our balance sheet at the end of nine months will look very strong.'

Of course a big media group operating in a highly competitive industry experiences some hiccups along the way. Not so long ago Murdoch's papers were in a dangerous position in Australia. 'We really had to face being pushed out of Australia. It was a very rough passage.' Now that position has been consolidated. Then there is the question of colour. At the time of the move into Wapping Murdoch took the view that there was no evidence that readers preferred colour in their newspapers, and that advertisers preferred the quality provided by pre-printed gravure colour. But Murdoch had now ordered MAN-Roland colour presses at a total cost of DM 1 billion, the biggest-ever contract in the world printing industry. Had he changed his mind? 'No, I got frightened,' he told the author. 'We have this huge and very successful investment in this country depending on technology that is almost two generations old. I concluded I was taking a risk that I should not take. If I was right, the opposition could go broke. If I was wrong, we could have no business. So we moved.

'We are getting the next generation of colour presses, better than Maxwell's, they *tell* us. There's a five-year roll-out programme in London, Liverpool and Australia. And there's another fifty per cent on the budget at the end for the Swiss Ferag equipment that goes with it. Then, if advertising gets very buoyant or if big business becomes fashionable, you can print during the afternoon and insert during the night, even four or five million copies a night, without stopping the presses.'

On the editorial use of colour it was clear that Murdoch and the *Sun*'s executives were watching the *Mirror* very closely. They admitted that the *Mirror* was learning to use it better and the colour was printing well. However Murdoch did not seem unduly worried, 'I am sure good words, better black and white, will always outsell colour just used for its own sake. But if you can have both, why not?' Perhaps he was about to change his mind after all.

What Murdoch means by 'good words' in this context, are, of course, words that grip the attention of a mass audience. Many condemn him for that. An American editor derided his New York

Post as 'a force for evil'. Lord Cudlipp, chairman of IPC when it sold Murdoch the *Sun* at a knock-down price, has said that in the current tabloid press, 'significant national and international events [were] nudged aside by a panting seven-day seven-night news service for voyeurs, the massage-parlour relaxations of polo players, and the exclusive definitive autobiographies of kiss-and-tell nymphets aged eighteen and a half.' Murdoch's reply to these attacks has been, 'A press that fails to interest the whole community is one that will ultimately become a house organ of the elite engaged in an increasingly private conversation with a dwindling club.' It is a remark which could well have been applied to *The Times* or IPC's *Sun* before he took them over. The people who attack the mass tabloids most strongly are usually those who feel most distaste for the masses and their interests. Of course there have been gross excesses and if the Press Council did its job properly they might be curbed. A more effective method may well be the imposition of enormous libel damages, far in excess of any actual damage caused to the plaintiff. Perhaps British juries are moving towards such a solution. Not even the *Sun* can contemplate the payment of £1 million – the payment the paper made to Elton John in December 1988 – with total equanimity.* A particularly unhealthy development has been the crude propaganda for Murdoch's Sky Television being pumped into all his papers. Yet critics of Murdoch's tabloids rarely commend the other side of the coin – brilliantly sub-edited papers† which bring a sense of fun and enjoyment into millions of homes. *The Times* was in an unhealthy state, financially and editorially, when Murdoch took over; he appointed the man everyone believed was an outstanding editor and it was not altogether his fault that the appointment failed. But at least, seven years later, the paper was breaking even and the pressure for improvement continued.

The critics are also inclined to forget the positive side of Murdoch's move into Britain. He has made modern electronic technology acceptable. The print unions have been compelled to change their attitudes. Some credit is due to Eddy Shah's pioneering efforts; he had the vision, but he possessed neither the resources nor the

* The appointment of a tough ombudsman at the *Sun*, which published his trenchant criticisms, provided an alternative approach to containing the paper's worst errors of judgment.

† The late Judge Morris Finer, chairman of a report on One-Parent Families, told me that in his view the *Evening Standard* (which used a Press Association report) and the *Sun* carried by far the best account of his work.

patience to see his dream through to fruition. Some credit is due to Maxwell's indefatigable struggles to secure rational deals with the print unions. And Brenda Dean, the general secretary of SOGAT, deserves credit too for attempting to educate her union in the realities of the modern publishing scene. But in my view it was only through the outright defeat of the unions at Wapping that the great liberation of the British newspaper industry was finally secured. It is no longer a rarity for new national newspapers to be launched and at least one of them, *The Independent*, deserves to be ranked among the best. So if Murdoch is to be rubbished for the rather grubby aspects of his tabloids, the salutary aspect of his Wapping gamble should be placed to his credit.

Television did not exist when Rupert Murdoch was born; films and sound radio were still at an early stage of development. The exploration of space was still a dream. So his life has coincided with a revolution in history: the revolution in communications. Now there is satellite television, and the use of satellites to pass information and messages round the globe. Murdoch seems to own a stake in every important development. Impelled by memories of his father; ready to 'put my hand up' whenever good prospects came along; never, as Matthews said, afraid of the impossible; eager to ride the whirlwind of change; Murdoch has built the second biggest media conglomerate[9] in the world. Until 1988 the bids may have been wholly opportunistic in origin but the pace may finally be more deliberate. He told the author, 'No doubt cleverer people will come along and do the same thing or do it better, but now we've arrived where we have, I am beginning to form a plan,' He thought about satellites for a moment and smiled happily. 'It's the most enormous gamble,' he said.

Notes:
  1. The most readable biography of Rupert Murdoch is *Barefaced Cheek* by Michael Leapman, Hodder & Stoughton, 1983, later updated in a Coronet paperback. *Rupert Murdoch, a Business Biography* by Simon Regan, Angus & Robertson, 1976, has some interesting material on Murdoch's business approach. *Rupert Murdoch, a Paper Prince*, by George Munster, Viking, 1985, has excellent material on the early days of the *Sun*. Linda Melvern, working at great speed, produced a highly informative book on the Wapping move called *The End of the Street*, Methuen, 1986, with some well-documented disclosures on which I have drawn. It is particularly strong on the union side.

2. From an interview with the author on 11th October 1988.
3. Quoted from a tape of his speech by Melvern, op cit.
4. Quoted in Regan, op cit.
5. Louis Heren writes a moving and convincing account of his days at *The Times* – he began as a messenger – in *Memories of Times Past*, Hamish Hamilton, 1988.
6. Quoted in Regan, op cit.
7. Quoted by Heren, op cit.
8. This section is based on an interview with the author.
9. Bertelsmann, the German media group, is the biggest at the time of writing. If the Time Inc – Warner Communications merge is consummated, it will be larger than Bertelsmann.

12
The Abuse of Power

There are the trade unionists, once the oppressed, now the tyrants,
whose selfish and sectional pretensions need to be bravely opposed.

J. M. Keynes

Cecil King was seldom complimentary about the management of
rival newspapers, but in relation to the print unions he was as
spineless as everybody else.[1] When Ted Blackmore, labour relations
director at the *Mirror*, refused a demand from men in the warehouse
for a payment, copies were lost until he paid up. Next day a meeting
of directors gave him a tremendous rocket and told him, 'Young
man, we are in the business of producing newspapers. Don't ever
do that again.' Blackmore appealed to Cecil King and complained
both that his treatment was unfair and that his brief was not clear.
King replied that the brief was perfectly clear, 'Always get the paper
out, but do it at the cheapest cost.'

It was this attitude to production, which the chapel officials understood all too well, that led to many of the excesses in money and
manpower which scarred Fleet Street so horribly in the post-war
years. King may have believed that the *Mirror* could always afford
to pay. He was wrong, of course, but in the short run his attitude,
which was very similar to that of Lord Beaverbrook whom he disliked
so much, did cause serious difficulties for less successful newspapers. Weak newspapers simply could not afford to lose production.
Without a newspaper they still had to pay most wages and salaries,
pay for the maintenance and upkeep of the building and plant, pay
the interest on any loans they had outstanding and pay the rates.
But there was no money being earned; there was no circulation
revenue, no advertising revenue. Every day a stoppage continued
meant that the company's financial position got worse. So the pressure to settle was immense. The only hope for the industry was to
put up an united front against excessive demands but time and again
the efforts to hold that front broke down. And it was always someone

238

else's fault. At one time or another I heard blame for failure to hold the line put on the Mirror Group, the News Group, Associated Newspapers, the *Telegraph*, the *Financial Times* and Express Newspapers. There wasn't really anyone else to accuse.

It is to be hoped that before long some economic historian will write a full and balanced account of industrial relations in Fleet Street during the forty-year period 1945 to 1986. Future readers would find it an almost incredible story. Here I intend only to sketch the barest outline of the labour situation that ultimately led to the Wapping revolution, for it explains what a fantastic upheaval that caused. The origins of print union power certainly owed much to failings of management, both individually and collectively. But the transient nature of newspapers – yesterday's newspaper looks even staler than yesterday's loaf of bread – gave the print unions unparalleled power to inflict damage on their industry.

None the less the national leadership of the principal print unions attempted to steer their London members into a more moderate attitude of mind on several occasions. After lengthy negotiations a Joint Standing Committee for the Industry was established in 1975, strongly supported by Bill Keys, the chairman of the TUC Printing Industries Committee. This produced a Programme for Action which was designed to trim back manpower through improved redundancy payments and better pension arrangements, and also to eliminate unnecessary 'casual' working. In its final form the Programme proposed to smooth the introduction of electronic technology through an obligation on the employers to submit their manpower and technology proposals to the Joint Standing Committee every year. And in every plant a Joint House Committee would have been set up to improve the industrial climate. Despite the fact that the national print union leaders endorsed these ideas the London branches were sceptical. The issue went to the vote. The NGA's London and Manchester members voted against by 3,778 to 889. the NATSOPA members (later incorporated into SOGAT) were against by the narrowest of margins – 4,598 to 4,296. That effort at reform was dead. Much later Brenda Dean took a small delegation of SOGAT officials to the United States and produced an excellent well-illustrated brochure on what the group had seen and what the lessons were for their members. But too few of the London members were listening, so their subsequent plight cannot be blamed on the general secretaries who were indeed sometimes driven to anger and despair at the activities of the London chapels.

These chapels had been exploiting their power quite ruthlessly and with no thought of tomorrow. As one NGA official has said, 'Once you have learnt a trick or two and learnt that it pays off, it is only human nature to carry on.' Sometimes the unskilled unions seemed to be more interested in expanding jobs than in money. Frank Rogers, at the time when he was production editor of the *Mirror*, pointed to the period when paper rationing was lifted and newspapers sought an ever larger quota of advertisements and hence bigger papers.

> The chapel negotiators wanted more men, mainly casuals, rather than more pay. At one stage we had negotiated for 800 people each in the machine and publishing rooms. If they had all turned up on one night they would have suffocated. It had become so bad that the larger the pagination, the higher the manning and the greater the loss.[2]

None the less more money for shorter and shorter hours was the normal objective. Graham Cleverley's excellent little paperback *The Fleet Street Disaster* set out four principal methods by which the print unions pushed up their earnings in the post-war period. These were 'ghost' working, 'blow' systems, double-working and 'fiddles'. When as an innocent young journalist I was first told that the *Evening Standard* was negotiating on the number of 'ghosts' in the machine room I thought that the services of some suitable exorcist would solve the problem; but more brutal methods than divine intervention were necessary to eliminate these shadowy penalties on production. Cleverley records that when Thomson had to move the print of the *Sunday Times* from the *Telegraph* presses in Fleet Street to Gray's Inn Road, the union pointed out that owing to the rising sale of the paper an extra press beyond the normal eight would have been needed in Fleet Street *if* the paper had stayed there. However it was conceded that the newer presses in Gray's Inn Road could cope with the print. The union therefore demanded that the payment for the unneeded extra crew should be shared out among the men who were actually going to work the eight presses at Gray's Inn Road. And they got it, although the mangement pretended it was due to the conditions of work while installation was in progress. (It will be remembered that Thomson was really working against the clock to transfer the print in time, so the unions had additional bargaining strength.) The *Telegraph* wire room staff were also manned up on

Saturdays to allow for transmission of material to Manchester (as needed by the *Sunday Times*), even though the *Sunday Telegraph* never printed in Manchester.

The 'blow' undoubtedly began as a sensible method for workers to take a breather during a long night's work. But it developed into a ritualistic method of extracting more money and men from weak managements. In some publishing houses one hour's 'blow' was taken in every three worked; these 'blows' were not taken at times convenient to the management when there was little work to be done, but on a strict rota basis. If more workers were required than were actually available for work, then the men having their 'blow' would graciously return to work but at overtime rates. The Economist Intelligence Unit produced a report for the National Newspaper Industry Board in 1966 which showed that forty-five man-hours were worked during a five-hour machine run, including all men who worked at all during that period. But the number of man-hours that were being paid for came to 115 hours, so that 'blow' time was in excess of fifty per cent.

Double-working was another device which in origin was a perfectly respectable method of increasing one's earnings by doing two jobs. It is certainly still being done on a large scale in the building trade. The system was fortified in Fleet Street by the fact that it was the unions rather than the managements who controlled the supply of labour and the unions exercised a rigorous closed-shop policy; only members of the appropriate union could be employed either as regular members of the staff, as 'regular casuals' or as 'casuals'. Since demand for labour fluctuated considerably between one day and another, the most obvious example being the Sunday newspapers which had high demands on Saturday nights and very little on other days of the week, casual working was endemic in Fleet Street. Some casuals were able to take advantage of a 'blow' in one office to work as a casual in another. And it seems clear that over-manning was tolerated to such an extent that some workers were able to draw pay packets made out in fictitious names for a totally fictitious night's work. An old Fleet Street joke has an MP asking a Minister how many people work producing national newspapers. The Minister replies, 'Oh, about one in four.' There was more than a grain of truth in that story.

There were also a whole variety of fiddles, varying from stealing and racketeering to legitimate but indefensible 'deals'. In one plant where I worked a keen manager was able to detect that certain men were 'hammering the docket'; they were charging for work they had not done – in other words they were stealing from the firm. There was no doubt they were guilty, but despite many meetings no one was ever sacked. I have also little doubt that in some areas there was considerable traffic in stolen goods. A legend at the *Evening Standard* held that one December day the Flying Squad swooped on our vanway in pursuit of a load of stolen whisky. They found nothing, but that afternoon every seller of the *Evening Standard* in central London found a bottle of whisky had been wrapped in his bundle of papers. Mistakenly they gratefully toasted the management for presenting them with such a generous Christmas box. I also recall that shortly before Christmas men from 'below' would appear on the editorial floor of the *Daily Express* bearing trays of shirts, watches, toys and other seasonable gifts at remarkably competitive prices. Of course many print workers had other businesses and the goods may have been legitimately acquired. But I was once given, as a parting present, a Swiss watch from one of those trays; a customs officer looked at it long and hard when I returned from an overseas holiday wearing it on my wrist and questioned me in detail about how and where I had come by it. He certainly gave me the impression it had escaped duty. A milder and entirely legitimate racket would occur in charging for advertisements which were delivered from outside. It was agreed in 1894 that the composing room should be paid on the basis that it had set the advertisement in the smallest type actually used in that advertisement. This payment was graphically known as 'fat'. Similarly classified advertisements, once set, could be used again in a repeat series, but setting had to be paid for each time the advertisement was used.

A frightening passage in Tom Bower's biography of Maxwell[3] reads as follows:

The machine room in the *Mirror* building had by 1970 become an unendearing model of anarchy and villainy. During the nights, especially Saturdays, large numbers of highly-paid but unneeded printers sat in the basement . . . watching blue movies or playing high-stake poker . . . Many had even clocked in under two names and were receiving double wages for no work. Others had registered but were working or sleeping elsewhere. It was not unknown at the end of a shift for wage packets to remain unclaimed because the printers were too drunk to recall which phony names they had registered under on arrival . . .

Bower quotes no authority for these statements but claims to have interviewed 350 people about Maxwell and his companies. In my opinion the state of affairs he describes was exceptional in Fleet Street but may have reflected the lax management style that prevailed at the Mirror Group on every floor.

The principal method used to extract excessive manning (outside the composing room where lower numbers meant higher rewards) and excessive payments was of course the threat to interrupt, or the actual interruption of, production. This was normally achieved through the holding of a chapel meeting at a time that was particularly inconvenient for the management, leading to the missing of the vital newspaper trains that carried papers to the various regions of the country. If no other method seemed appropriate, a slit cut in the paper during the production run was certain to cause delay while the paper was rewound.

Owing to the prolonged dispute at Times Newspapers much detail has been published about the virtual state of anarchy that used to prevail there. In 1978 there were eight unions at Gray's Inn Road; they were divided into sixty-five chapels, each one determined to preserve its individual negotiating rights.[4] In the first three months of the year *The Times* had failed to complete its run on twenty-one occasions, and the *Sunday Times* on nine. The company lost £2 million in that period. The agreed disputes procedure had been ignored in each case.

Production difficulties at Gray's Inn Road were particularly acute because the board had decided to adhere to the government's pay policy. Other companies had found ways of making under-the-counter deals, but the Thomson Organisation was worried that its immensely profitable North Sea oil licences might be endangered if it was known to be paying too much to the print workers. It was also claimed that the layout of the presses (which had, of course, been installed in a hurry) was cramped and inconvenient. Further difficulties had been caused when *The Times* moved from Printing House Square near Blackfriars Bridge. Every chapel compared what its opposite number was getting, and the higher figure, usually paid for weekend working, became the basis of endless claims and dissatisfaction.

None the less the arrogance of the unions enlarged every problem. When Roy Thomson took over the paper he met one of the FOCs and introduced himself by saying, 'I'm Roy Thomson, the new owner of this paper.' The FOC replied, 'You may own it, but I run it.' My wife worked at the *Sunday Times* as an assistant editor and clearly needed a secretary; after a long delay the union, who were of course in charge of recruitment, produced a Chinese girl who could barely speak English and was quite unable to understand the simplest telephone message, let alone use a typewriter. Somehow she had gained a SOGAT card and was therefore deemed by the chapel to be suitable. The cessation of publication had failed to alter the balance of power in the slightest. As Denis Hamilton said, 'Production sabotage resumed with the same irresponsibility, even anarchic fervour as before.' In 1978 *The Times* had lost 4,277,000 copies and the *Sunday Times* 8,729,000. On the resumption of production there was a small improvement. *The Times* lost 2,999,000 copies in 1980 and the *Sunday Times* 5,262,000. But by 1984 the two papers lost more than 11 million copies between them. Brian MacArthur, at that time an executive on *The Times*, has written[5] that 'the strain of dealing with the unions killed some managers, who suffered early deaths from heart attacks'. I am not surprised at his statement; it took a very tough character indeed to ignore the stream of insults, vilification and threats which accompanied so many union negotiations. It was all the worse when the labour managers so often found their efforts frustrated by weakness at the top. When work resumed at *The Times*, for instance, the general level of pay in the industry had risen and, according to one SOGAT official, in some instances Thomson 'had to pay double the previous wages to get his workers back'.

There were plenty of warnings about the consequences of union demands and management weakness. The second Royal Commission on the Press reported bleakly, 'The average earnings of manual workers in the newspaper production industry are the highest of any paid to manual workers in this country.' A study for the Commission found there was heavy over-manning in the machine room and the publishing room with excess staffing of some thirty-four per cent. When the pickings in Fleet Street were so lavish any suggestion of change met virtually automatic resistance. Nowhere was the unions' attitude to change exemplified more clearly than in their stand over the move of some News International production to Wapping. News Corporation, Murdoch's parent company, operated three-unit printing presses, manned by union members, in the United States and Australia as well as London. In Texas, four men and a 'rover' when needed operated the press; in Chicago up to a maximum of three; in New York (the most militant union city in the US) six; and in

Sydney six men were running up to four-unit presses. But in London the union demanded eighteen. And there was every indication that demarcation problems would have continued unabated. SOGAT wanted a fifty-fifty presence as machine minders in the press room. The NGA insisted that all minder positions should be filled by them. The NGA also sought to encroach on SOGAT's position in classified advertising with a fifty-fifty involvement in input.

When Murdoch finally let fly at the union leaders in September 1985 he told them, 'Today the *Sun* and the *News of the World* employ 4,700 people at an average weekly wage of more than £300. Put another way, about £75 million per year in wages, excluding other benefits.

'The vast majority of those people belong to your unions, enjoy a closed shop and all the privileges that go with that. Some of them are dedicated and skilled at their work, whilst, depending on their jobs, many others have little or no skills, and almost in inverse proportion to their skills they work fewer hours. Let us be honest about this! The great majority of night shift workers are at their jobs no more than twenty hours per week, at more than double the national average wage. Furthermore they get from six, eight and in some cases even twelve weeks' holiday, pensions, sickness and other benefits. We are allowed neither to hire nor fire them. All Fleet Street publishers are permitted to take only that labour which is sent to them by your branches.'

There was really no answer to those charges. When Murdoch moved to Wapping 5,500 men and women lost their jobs, but many of these were one-day-a-week casuals. The work they had been doing in Bouverie Street and Gray's Inn Road was accomplished at the new plant, using the electronic technology and other mechanical developments the unions had resisted for so long, initially by less than 600, most of them only half-trained. By the end of 1988 production staff employed at the various News International plants throughout the country totalled 1,129 and that covered five newspapers (including *Today*) some of them much fatter than before and others with bigger sales. Amazingly enough there were almost as many journalists – 1,049 for the four newspapers excluding *Today*. Direct comparison with the pre- and post-Wapping figures for four newspapers is fairly meaningless but dramatic growth in productivity is undeniable. Later, when the *Telegraph* moved to the Isle of Dogs, the composing room staff which in Fleet Street had numbered 540 including the 'readers' (who spotted the literals) and their assistants, reduced to fifty-four, with the journalists setting and 'reading' their own copy. It is estimated that the average numbers employed in London by the *Telegraph* on the actual printing of the two papers (as opposed to pre-press work) was reduced from 1,559 in the year ended March 1985 to only 400 in 1989. (The actual number of printers at the West Ferry Road plant was higher because Express Newspapers were also using the plant.) Casual labour was eliminated, and the number of printers employed on behalf of the *Telegraph* at Withy Grove in Manchester was cut from 450 to about 100 in the same period.

It would be quite wrong to suggest that the print workers as a whole were a shiftless bunch of layabouts. The compositors in particular had immense pride in their craft and the tempo at which they would work if excited by a big story was absolutely electrifying. Similarly the circulation staff at all levels took real pride in their paper's successes. Their morale was volatile, depending on scoops and beats and 'skinners' – the editions that sold out so quickly that the sellers were skinned of copies – but they wanted their paper to succeed and identified closely with it. It was not really their fault if some of them were trapped with skills they knew were obsolescent or locked into working practices which may have had some reason fifty years before but were just a drag on efficiency in a later age.

The process of union electioneering tended to throw up experts at confrontational tactics. There were 600 casual workers employed in the *News of the World* publishing room, but with modern equipment this could be cut by 500. The union negotiators simply would not give ground. Joe Wade, making his swan song speech as general secretary of the NGA in 1982 had warned, 'If we are not prepared to embrace new technology . . . then competition from alternative sources in this country, or from abroad, will spell the death knell of the newspaper industry as we have known it.' He might just as well have been speaking to a conference of the deaf. There was some movement in the more progressive provincial newspapers but the London branches were virtually Luddite in their opposition to change, and the London branch leaders could not visualise the possibility of defeat. On the night that Bouverie Street shut down Bruce Matthews tried to commiserate with a chapel official he knew. The official was unrepentant. 'Don't worry,' he said, 'we'll be back in a fortnight.' He still expected the dispute to end like every other he had ever known, with capitulation by the management. It is not only military men who are trained to fight the last war.

Notes:

1. Almost every book written about Fleet Street contains some horror story of production problems in the post-war era up to Wapping. Only one book, to the best of my knowledge, deals exclusively with management and production problems. That is *The Fleet Street Disaster: British national newspapers as a case study in mismanagement* by Graham Cleverley, Constable, 1976. Cleverley was for a time director of man-power development at IPC and thus in an excellent position to record some of the practices he saw on both sides of the negotiating table. There is also an excellent brief account of the background in *Eddy Shah and the Newspaper Revolution* by David Goodhart and Patrick Wintour, Coronet, 1986. The authors had both worked as labour correspondents, for the *Financial Times* and *The Guardian* respectively, and had thus witnessed at first hand the events which culminated in the Wapping revolution.

2. Quoted in Goodhard and Wintour, op cit.

3. *Maxwell, the Outsider*, Arun Press, 1988, op cit.

4. Full details are given in the admirably clear account of the stoppage at Gray's Inn Road from 25th November 1978 to 17th November 1979 in *Stop Press* by Eric Jacobs, a senior member of the *Sunday Times* staff and himself a union negotiator, André Deutsch, 1980.

5. *Eddy Shah*, Today *and the Newspaper Revolution* by Brian MacArthur, David and Charles, 1988.

13
New Beginnings

The golden years return,
The earth doth like a snake renew
Her winter weeds outworn

Shelley, *Hellas*

The crunch years for the British newspaper industry in the second half of the twentieth century were 1985 and 1986 when Robert Maxwell secured an agreed twenty-five per cent reduction in manning at the *Mirror* plant in Holborn Circus and Rupert Murdoch made an entirely new beginning at Wapping. These events totally changed the industrial climate and newspapers suddenly began to make very sizeable profits. The move away from Fleet Street, first highlighted by Eddy Shah's News UK, accelerated fast. He had his editorial offices in Vauxhall Bridge Road and his southern printing plant at Poyle near Heathrow. Associated Newspapers speeded their plans to move printing to the Surrey Docks, south of the river, and put their offices in Kensington on top of the old Barkers building. Telegraph Newspapers moved both their editorial offices and their printing plant to highly inconvenient sites on the Isle of Dogs. Express Newspapers were the last to announce their plans; they moved to the other side of Blackfriars Bridge. *The Observer* and the *Financial Times* moved as well. It was the death of Fleet Street as a newspaper publishing centre; it would rise again as an extension of the City. Journalists felt some relief at getting away from the hot-metal factories and all the restrictions that were embedded in traditional work practices, but they sadly missed the shop talk arising from the easy mingling with staffs of other newspapers. An interesting side effect was that talent-spotters found it difficult to know who were the coming men and women on opposition papers.

During this period a number of new press barons emerged as others stepped down; but so far the new men seem relatively unassertive compared with the larger than life characters who used to

248

inhabit the Street. Yet they deserve attention for among them may be figures who in future years will rank with Northcliffe and Beaverbrook as journalistic innovators of the first order. Their task will be much tougher. During my childhood there was no radio, no television. Newspapers really had to live up to their name. But my grandchildren are growing up in an age when satellite television is inaugurating an entirely new era of truly global communication. It is hardly surprising that Britain's two major media magnates are heavily involved in these fields as well as with newspapers and terrestial television. In such circumstances the progress of anyone just arriving on the newspaper scene is likely to be slow. Newspapers, while still very lucrative and likely to remain so, are now diminished in their primary role as information providers, even if their importance as reporters, analysts, entertainers and above all as instruments of free democratic debate is as great as ever. The doctrine of 'balance' may well be necessary for television and radio, but in a free society arguments must be forcefully stated if the public are to learn about the issues of the day. And that is a role for the newspapers that no other medium can match.

Of the new men the most interesting and important is the Canadian Conrad Black, now undisputed controller of Telegraph Newspapers. There was an element of luck about his arrival on the scene and more than an element of family tragedy in the departure of Lord Hartwell from personal control of the *Telegraph* which his father, Lord Camrose, had bought in 1928 when its sale was as low as 84,000. Hartwell, formerly Michael Berry and Camrose's second son, had accepted a peerage from Harold Wilson in 1968; he was a gentleman proprietor who took immense pains, in his role as chief proprietor and editor-in-chief, over every aspect of his papers. According to Bill Deedes (now Lord Deedes), editor of the *Daily Telegraph* for twelve years, one of his favourite and most characteristic phrases, used of a politician or journalist who had overstated a case, was to say drily, 'Rather over the top, I thought'.[1] His natural reserve made such a rebuke all the more telling. The reputation of his newspapers for the range of their reporting, accuracy and sober Conservative comment stood very high. But in the 1980s circulation, which had grown to more than 1,400,000 after the war, was slipping while the circulation of both *The Times* and *The Guardian* was growing; the profile of the readership was ageing; and the volume of classified advertising was showing signs of weakness. Hartwell had been bold enough to start the *Sunday Telegraph* to compete with the

Sunday Times which he felt his uncle Lord Kemsley had treacherously sold out of the family, but for years that was such a drain on his resources and his time that now and again he regretted launching it. He was always more interested in the content of his newspapers than in their profitability and totally failed to realise the dangers to family control until it was much too late. In four of the six years to March 1985 the two papers made a combined loss. The ageing management team, many in their seventies, had contracted to implement a £105 million modernisation programme with new plants in the Isle of Dogs and in Manchester, the second being of doubtful necessity, together with a major redundancy programme due to cost £38 million. Although Telegraph Newspapers benefited from owning Reuters shares worth £40 million and owned other assets such as the Telegraph building in Fleet Street, they had to set up a complex financing package to provide a total of £110 million. The banks refused to offer more than £80 million because they were not too happy with the quality of the *Telegraph* management as revealed in the profit figures. In consequence they would release the money only in tranches dependent on budget figures being achieved at set periods. Further, to reduce their exposure, the banks insisted that some new risk-bearing share capital should be raised to provide the £30 million that was still needed. Since Hartwell wished family control to remain intact, he refused to sell more than forty per cent of the company. That reduced the attractiveness of the shares to outside investors; many City institutions refused to subscribe. Meanwhile, one observer commented, 'From the beginning of 1985 week by week, fortnight by fortnight . . . someone else's bill fell due. It was like a Greek tragedy.'² The company was threatened with bankruptcy. Still short of £7.5 million needed to trigger the complete deal Hartwell, who was taking all the key decisions himself ('it was a family business'), desperately needed to find another large investor. Andrew Knight, the well-travelled editor of *The Economist*, suggested to Conrad Black, a Canadian entrepreneur of right-wing views who already owned some twenty newspapers, that he might be able to buy a substantial stake in the firm with longer term prospects of playing a major role. Black was interested and his name was then floated to Hartwell. After a brief telephone conversation Hartwell with two merchant bankers and his managing director flew to meet Black at Kennedy Airport outside New York. The deal was virtually clinched at an airport hotel. Black came up with £7.5 million for fourteen per cent of the equity, but realising the strength of his position, he agreed only on two conditions: first he had an option on any stock that became available and second he had the right to match any outside bid for the company. He had a lock on the company from that moment. Nicholas Berry, Hartwell's second son, was appalled but the decision had been taken.

After an internal audit committee had discovered there were no proper management accounts, a firm of accountants was hired and claimed that there were 300 more staff on the production payroll than the management had realised. Worse was to follow; the budget figures proved to be grossly over-optimistic and for the six months ending in September 1985 a loss of £16 million was reported on a turnover of £74 million. Advertising volumes were down but, more seriously, redundancy payments were far higher than had been anticipated. Only four months after the completion of the rescue package the final crisis had arrived – just how grave became evident later. In the nine months to December 1986 the group made a net loss of £21 million and had an accumulated deficit of £41 million.

Hartwell, who had taken much pride in forming a trust to keep the *Telegraph* in the family after his death, had to yield authority to Hollinger Inc, the Canadian company controlled by Black which, for another £23 million, obtained a total of more than fifty per cent of the votes in the company's shares. At once Black appointed a much younger management team with Andrew Knight as chief executive and later editor-in-chief. Knight chose new, more vigorous editors. He formed a sales and marketing team. The redundancy programme, greatly expedited by Murdoch's success at Wapping, was completed, and in a shrewd move Sir Frank Rogers, the veteran chairman of EMAP, was appointed deputy chairman. Hollinger bought another group of shares from the Telegraph Newspaper Trust for £10.25 million in November 1987. The results of the new approach were rewarding: circulation and advertising picked up and in the half-year to June 1988 pre-tax profits of £15.5 million were recorded. Black then increased his total shareholding to eighty-two per cent paying £31 million for a further twelve per cent. The company was then valued at £260 million. Hollinger's share was worth about £213 million, for which it had paid in total about £95 million. It was an impressive investment. The full year figures gave Black further grounds for confidence, showing pre-tax profits of £29 million, a record in the history of the company. Hartwell and his family had the consolation of having sold shares from their Trust for about £15.5 million and also retaining eleven per cent of the company, worth about £28 million, considerably more than the value of 100 per cent of a debt-ridden loss-making company that had lost its way. His bitterness was reserved for the banks. Three years later in a letter to *Campaign*, the advertising magazine,[3] he wrote, 'I do not for one moment deny . . . that at one moment the *Telegraph* was nearly bankrupted. For this latter I blame the banks who, in spite of their long association, always took a short-term view. At seven pm one day I was threatened with foreclosure by three pm the next day unless my family put up more than £3 million.'

Probably of greater importance to Hartwell than the money was the increased vigour of the *Daily Telegraph* under its new editor, Max Hastings, a distinguished alumnus of the *Evening Standard* school of journalism. He recruited a much younger and abler editorial team, aided by defections from Wapping and, despite the arrival of *The Independent* (of which a brief account will be given later), checked the decline in sale and introduced a livelier more independent spirit in its pages. He initiated gradual changes in layout while the Sunday magazine was switched to Saturday allowing a vast increase in its advertising rates. The *Sunday Telegraph* was less successful despite the introduction of *Seven Days*, yet another colour magazine, and circulation continued to decline. Knight decided on a bold experiment; he decided to move towards a seven-day newspaper on American lines. Hastings was placed in overall editorial command while Peregrine Worsthorne, previously editor of the *Sunday Telegraph*, continued his own idiosyncratic political commentary and took responsibility for political features. Meanwhile the content of the Sunday colour magazine was changed again. On the production front United Newspapers took a half-share in the Isle of Dogs plant as it was expanded to meet the requirements of its subsidiary, Express Newspapers.

The partnership between Conrad Black, a rather rumbustious tycoon, and Andrew Knight, a cool and enigmatic figure who enjoyed patrolling the corridors of power, thus restored the profitability of the company just as Hastings restored the authority of the *Daily Telegraph*, sometimes voicing sharp criticisms of government policies in a manner which might have been alien to the Hartwell regime. If Knight's reforms had failed, no doubt Black would have made his presence felt much more heavily and the independence of the editors might have been considerably circumscribed. Black had said on one occasion, 'My experience of the working press is that they are a very degenerate group'. He also wrote a letter to *The Spectator* criticising most British newspapers as 'habitually snobbish, envious and simplistic'. After taking over control, however, he kept such thoughts, if he still had them, to himself and seemed to relish occasional editorial brushes with the British Prime Minister. He also engaged in a brisk exchange with Robert Maxwell over Quebec calling Maxwell's views 'buffoonish and demagogic.' By the end of 1988 Black and Knight were talking of entering a period of expansion, and it looked as if Black was emerging as a major force in British newspaper publishing – an impression which was strengthened when he emerged with a 'friendly' stake in United Newspapers which he quietly enlarged.

No greater contrast could be imagined than that between the patrician Lord Hartwell and Eddy Shah who made a fairly brief but significant appearance on the newspaper scene.[4] Eddy was more than thirty years younger; he was an outsider in British society despite being educated at Gordonstoun. Of Anglo-Persian stock, a direct descendant of the first Aga Khan, he was bubbly, innovative, outgoing, fascinated by technology, temperamental and fiercely hostile to the old Fleet Street way of doing things. He was burly and effervescent; Hartwell was thin and impassive. His principal activities were firmly based in the North of England; Hartwell was a Southerner. Eddy was a teetotaller; Hartwell mixed an exceptionally dry martini. They were however alike in two respects: they were both workaholics, and, alas, their wives both suffered from cancer. Lady Hartwell, better known as the famous hostess Lady Pamela Berry, sadly died in 1982; Jennifer Shah, formerly the actress Jennifer White, was given only five months to live that same year, just as her husband's battle with the NGA was reaching a climax, but she survived and has now been cleared. She remains a powerful influence on her husband, just as Lady Hartwell had lightened her husband's days with laughter and fierce support for all he did.

Hartwell was always destined for the newspaper business. Shah drifted into it after a variety of jobs; he was a stage hand, a television floor manager, a salesman for double-glazing and eventually an advertising salesman for a Manchester free sheet. When that job folded he mortgaged his house and with the help of two friends started the Sale and Altrincham *Messenger* from an office over a curry shop. After a rocky start he got going and by 1980 owned four newspapers in the Manchester area. They were making good money, about £600,000 a year. In 1980 he decided to transfer the typesetting of his papers from Carlisle to his new headquarters in Stockport. He agreed to an NGA closed shop there and also agreed to pay good money. But he soon fell out with the strict rules of the NGA. Eddy ran a family business where everything was done Eddy's way. The NGA men did not join in. So Eddy began to prepare a way out by buying a small printing plant at Winwick Quay, an industrial estate just outside Warrington. He told some of his staff but warned them that the NGA was not to be told. The plant was housed in what amounted to a large shed. The forecourt there was to witness the battle that decided the future of the newspaper industry.

Shah was also arranging for some computerised type-setting to be transferred from Stockport, which was unionised, to Bury, which was not. Meanwhile Warrington was handling some of the printing. The NGA's national officers were becoming increasingly worried about Shah but they still under-estimated him. They demanded an NGA closed shop in both Bury and Warrington. When that was refused, the eight members of the NGA employed at Stockport were told to strike. After a short interval two of the eight went back to work for Shah. The so-called 'Stockport Six' then began a picket of their office. Negotiations between Shah and the NGA continued surprisingly amicably at first; perhaps Shah was preparing the ground for his real breakthrough. But he would not re-employ the six strikers. Then the NGA started mass picketing at the Warrington works and that was illegal for the dispute was at Stockport, not Warrington. Shah began taking legal action which led to ever-increasing fines on the NGA and the eventual seizure of all their assets. The crunch of the whole dispute came when on Tuesday 29th November, some 4,000 pickets attempted to stop the *Messenger* vans from leaving the works. At one moment it looked as if the steel doors of the plant were buckling under pressure. Shah rang up Andrew Neil, editor of the *Sunday Times* and his chief supporter in the national press, and told him he might not be able to hold out. (Inside the plant there were only ten workers, six security guards and two dogs.) Neil had a terse conversation with the Home Secretary, Leon Brittan, who said he could not interfere in operational matters. Neil threatened to report their conversation in the *Sunday Times* if Shah was defeated owing to lack of police support. But the police had already made their preparations and around midnight went on the offensive. There was a rough fight – the NGA had been reinforced with the rent-a-mob gang that flourishes in these situations – and the struggle was violent. Eventually the Tactical Aid Group in full riot gear cleared the road with batons lunging. Shortly before five am Shah's vans emerged and the papers were distributed. The battle of Winwick Quay had ended in the utter defeat of the NGA, and Eddy Shah had emerged in frequent press and television interviews as an appealing symbol of the little man fighting the big bad unions; he was a national figure.

It was Andrew Neil, meeting Shah for the first time, who pointed him towards a national newspaper suggesting he should take a look at *USA Today*, printed in colour at seven different plants with the pages distributed by satellite. Shah became increasingly excited by the idea and went firm on the plan in March 1984. Then he had to raise the money. It took nearly a year and soured Shah's view of the City for ever. Eventually he raised £8.5 million, with three major investors – one was Trust House Forte – putting in £2 million each; the smaller investors included Sir Richard Storey's Portsmouth and Sunderland Newspapers (£500,000) and Messenger Newspapers (£250,000). The Hungarian Bank agreed to loan £6.5 million for four MAN-Roland colour presses. Other loans would pay for the rest of the equipment. In the end Shah raised £18 million for his new baby. It was 19th February 1985 when the investors finally gave the project their blessing – just four days after Murdoch had held his critical meeting in New York and decided secretly to equip Wapping with computerised type-setting so that he could go it alone without Sogat or the NGA.

Everything that Shah planned, on the other hand, was done in the full light of publicity. While Murdoch was going for 'low-tech', Shah wanted nothing less than state of the art equipment. So, apart from the Hastech word processors and sub-editing terminals, he demanded page layout terminals. Colour pictures were held in computer data bases, later called into colour page assembly terminals. All the pages were then transmitted electronically to the three satellite printing plants at Poyle near Heathrow, Birmingham and Manchester. No newspaper in Britain had ever used such a system before.

Journalists don't come in state of the art models, and Eddy made the task of recruiting his editorial team unnecessarily difficult by his deep suspicion of Fleet Street, which he regarded as inherently evil. After taking advice about potential editors from such sages as Rees-Mogg, former editor of *The Times*, Brian Nicolson, formerly a senior executive at the *Express* and *Observer*, and myself, he saw various people, including Harry Evans. He finally plumped for Brian Mac-Arthur who had held senior positions at *The Times* and *Sunday Times* but had earned Brownie points in Shah's eyes by abandoning Fleet Street for the salubrious air of South Devon as editor of the *Western*

Morning News, which he had considerably improved. While Shah's ideas about technology were all too clear, his thoughts on the paper were woolly and fluctuated wildly. MacArthur translated his ideas into an appeal to a clean-living 'Middle England' with a 'qualipop' paper. Senior executives were recruited mainly from the *Mail* and *Express*, but down the line – under Shah's influence – there was a strong preference for the provinces. Early research on some dummies seemed very favourable. Then the powerful influence of Wight Collins Rutherford and Scott was brought to bear; this was a relatively new advertising agency with a strong creative streak, and they entranced Shah with suggestions that he could, and should, sell a million. Originally he had been saying he could break even on a sale of only 300,000;[5] now as he tapped bigger sales figures and higher advertising rates into his portable computer, his ambitions grew until reality went out of the window and he saw potential profits of £27 million a year. Shortly before the launch I told MacArthur that his sale was very unlikely to be any higher than 700,000. Shah telephoned within the hour, betting me £50 that it would be over a million.

In fact the launch was a disaster. A serious blunder in the electrical wiring of the offices in Vauxhall Bridge Road – the wiring had not been earthed and walls were getting red hot – led to a shut down of the whole building while it was rewired. Consequently there had been no full rehearsals using all the equipment. The system easily became over-loaded; there were not enough terminals; page make-up took two or three hours instead of ten minutes and colour was not registering properly. Postponement was discussed, and rejected. There would have been heavy costs involved in delaying the £4 million promotional campaign – the words shouted by the staff, 'We're ready, Eddy' in the final commercial were typically over-optimistic – and MacArthur felt editorial morale would suffer. The paper had been sold on its colour, and unfortunately that was the worst feature of all. There was a provincial feel about too many of the pages, and as the staff were totally exhausted from their daily battles with a recalcitrant system it is hardly surprising that the paper lacked any feeling of zest and surprise. In the end everything would work satisfactorily, but inexperienced operators and undermanning in some crucial areas – initially only seventeen sub-editors were allowed for a seven-day week operation while the *Express* had sixty-eight for six days – caused further delays.

Whatever the problems Eddy was still euphoric. He told me three

days after the launch, 'I've done it. I've pulled off the impossible
again. We have taken a company with untrained people, untrained
printers, people who have never even seen a newspaper office,
journalists who have never been used to working this sort of equipment. We've started from absolute scratch. We said we'd go on 4th
March two years ago and we were an hour and a half late. I think
it's bloody magic.'

Shah had every right to feel he had pulled off a minor miracle in
production terms. But as the sale sagged as low as 400,000 in June,
despite marked improvements in the paper, and advertising rates
were cut, his backers became increasingly restive. Storey, leader of
the critics, said, 'The first rule of Venture Capitalism should be:
Shoot the inventor.' Eventually the board sensibly demanded the
appointment of a general manager. (In Warrington Shah had the
redoubtable Helen Graham looking after his money-earners but she
had nothing to do with *Today*.) Shah's home-made road distribution
service was working badly *and* costing him money. The cash-flow
position was chronically critical and there were no proper management accounts. Shah was getting desperate; he even instructed
MacArthur to offer Nigel Dempster, gossip columnist of the *Daily
Mail*, the ridiculous sum of £200,000 a year, if he would transfer to
Today. And he began looking for a saviour. Various names were
canvassed, among them Richard Branson of Virgin, Kerry Packer,
the Australian entrepreneur, Robert Maxwell, anxious to buy the
presses for his forthcoming London evening, Lord Rothermere,
anxious to stymie Maxwell, and the Al Fayeds, presumably anxious
to have a weapon with which to match the boring vendetta run
against them on *The Observer*'s City pages. As it happened *Sunday
Today* had been investigating the long-running feud between Rowland and the Al Fayeds and carried a carefully vetted story at the
crucial weekend. The Al Fayeds were offended and pulled out;
suddenly Rowland stepped in. (The Al Fayeds' lawyer hurriedly
asked for the return of some documentation about Lonrho which
they had supplied for *Sunday Today*'s investigation.)

Lonrho agreed to inject £10 million of new money into the company, and to buy out the original shareholders for another £10
million. More importantly they persuaded Terry Cassidy, managing
director of their Scottish newspapers, to take over the same job at
Today. Formally Shah remained chairman and chief executive but
the real power lay with Cassidy as was quickly demonstrated by their
first showdown over the editorship. Shah wanted to fire MacArthur;

Cassidy refused on the grounds that he needed time to make up his own mind. At a crucial board meeting Shah lost, but had already appointed Sir Larry Lamb, first editor of Murdoch's *Sun*, as a consultant. Cassidy's hand was strengthened when he established that *Today*, instead of losing £1 million plus a month, the management figure, was really losing £3 million a month. While MacArthur was taking a brief holiday Shah offered the editorship to David Montgomery, editor of the *News of the World*, at a salary of £100,000 a year, with a bonus of £100,000 if the circulation hit 800,000. Cassidy who was now openly contemptuous of Shah told MacArthur that the decision was up to him. Despite a call from Rupert Murdoch saying that Neil would like him back at the *Sunday Times*, MacArthur decided to stay on. Shah sold more than half of his fifty-one per cent shareholding to Lonrho and was seen less and less in Vauxhall Bridge Road. Despite a reasonably successful relaunch Shah continued to press Rowland to fire MacArthur. Then Cassidy, who had become a strong supporter of MacArthur and his editorial team, decided to go back to Scotland. This time MacArthur accepted a renewed offer from Murdoch and resigned. Shah sent him a three page handwritten letter couched in the warmest terms saying 'I hope we can become friends again.' They did, and arrived arm-in-arm at *Today*'s first anniversary party.

Lonrho was however finding that *Today* was an expensive luxury. The paper was still losing money at the rate of around £28 million a year and would need further investment to make it pay. As previously related, both Maxwell and Murdoch made offers. In the event Murdoch won and bought it for £38 million. Shah sold out his final ten per cent shareholding for £350,000 and retreated to Warrington where he regrouped for another assault on the national newspaper market.

Shah's *Today* was a failure. When Murdoch's men moved in the sale was hovering between 300,000 and 350,000; Lonrho would have shut it down if there had been no bidders. But Shah's innovative free-thinking approach to newspaper production helped to unchain the fetters of custom and practice which had crabbed and confined Fleet Street for so long. It was Rupert Murdoch who defeated the unions, but Shah in effect by-passed them. He was the first to show that printing in inner London was no longer a necessity for a national paper. He made every management in Fleet Street re-think their attitude to colour. He demonstrated, as if it needed any further illustration, that the industry was grossly over-manned. And although

he botched his road distribution scheme, partly because the volume
was too small, he was a pathfinder in this area too. He was in fact
a catalyst for change. Far from destroying the Fleet Street he hated
so much he became an important agent of reform and helped to
ensure its continued and profitable survival.

His failure lay in the initial weaknesses of his production system
combined with uncertain direction of the editorial target. Next time
round, when he launched the *Post* from a base in Warrington, he
showed he had learnt some lessons but not all. Once again he
displayed his technical imagination by using desktop publishing
based on the Apple Mackintosh computer. It cost around £5 million
less than the system used at *Today* so that his launch costs were
considerably lower. And this time round there was no premature
announcement of the launch date and there was ample time to
produce full dummies. Yet Shah again failed to assess whether there
really was a market for a 'clean' down-market tabloid and the launch
attracted half the readers expected. As MacArthur wrote, 'The
lesson we were to learn [at *Today*] was that readers simply do not
want their papers to be "too nice"; it is gossip and malice that makes
the world go round.' Shah folded the paper (which had lost nearly
£7 million), sold his Messenger group for £25 million and concentrated on television production and other enterprises. As he frequently said of himself, 'I am much better at starting things than at
running them. I get bored too easily.' Bored he might be, boring he
never was.

One of the many ways in which Shah helped to change Fleet
Street was to provide the initial inspiration for the launch of *The
Independent*. When Shah made the announcement about his new
daily in February 1985 the American publication *Business Week* asked
Andreas Whittam-Smith, then City editor of the *Daily Telegraph*, for
his comments. He rubbished the whole idea and said it could not
possibly succeed. No sooner had he put the phone down, he told
me later, than he realised he was wrong. He telephoned Shah who,
typically, was extremely helpful, then and later. He found there were
two like-minded colleagues on his paper: Matthew Symonds, the
senior economics leader-writer, and Stephen Glover, a feature
writer. The group of three decided that there was an ideal opening
for a new quality paper. But they were loyal members of the *Telegraph*
staff and before they set up their company Whittam-Smith, who
admired Lord Hartwell very much, secured an appointment and
suggested how the *Telegraph* finances might be secured with a public

flotation. He gained the impression that Hartwell was somewhat offended at his presumption in delving into a family matter, and the proposal was not discussed again.

Being City-minded Whittam-Smith realised how he could best obtain the financial backing he needed. So he set about getting the best advice available on the basis of 'no foal, no fee'. Advertising agents (Saatchis), solicitors (Herbert Smith), accountants (Arthur Andersen), merchant bankers (Charterhouse Japhet), stockbrokers (de Zoetes) and headhunters (Korn Ferry) all pitched in and with their help he was able to raise a first tranche of £2 million. Eventually he raised a total of £18 million with a facililty for a further £3 million bank loan. Tall, florid-faced and amiable, Whittam-Smith does not look like a gambler, but before the money came in he mortgaged his house to the hilt so that he could secure suitable offices in the City Road, far from either the traditional haunts or the new Docklands environment.

Staff recruitment was assisted by the disillusionment of some journalists with Murdoch's ruthless move to Wapping. A third of the original staff came from *The Times* and *Sunday Times*. But there was no understanding about the need for classified *selling* and there were only four people in that department for the launch. After several weeks of producing full scale dummies the paper actually appeared in October 1986. It was a quality product with exceptionally comprehensive foreign coverage, well written sport, fine use of non-newsy photographs, exceptional City coverage and careful arts coverage backed by full listings. Its independence was emphasised when in the 1987 general election Whittam-Smith refused to back any political party.

By January Whittam-Smith was getting anxious; staff costs were higher than budget, newsprint was costing more than expected, advertising revenues were below budget, and sale had been dropping steadily, down to 257,000 in January. Then a steady improvement set in, and after a year circulation at 360,000 was higher than for the first month of publication and was still climbing. The price was raised, a Saturday magazine added, and the newspaper was firmly established. By the end of 1988 it moved into profit and was clearly heading in the right direction; sale now averaged in excess of 410,000 and was within striking distance of its competitors. It was a triumph for the journalists who had conceived the paper and brought their ideas to fruition. They had hurt *The Times* and above all *The Guardian* whose sale slumped by nearly 90,000 between

September 1986 and October 1988, weakened not only by the incursion of *The Independent* but also by an ill-advised facelift. The only danger for *The Independent* might be a mood of self-satisfaction which could occasionally be sensed in its columns. But Whittam-Smith had much to be pleased about; at least on paper he was now a self-made millionaire.

Other launches were less successful. *News on Sunday*,[6] a left-wing Sunday paper partly financed by trade unions, soon ran out of money. It had been founded on a mixture of idealism and an undue faith in some rather shaky market research. There was a vacuum of authority in the company, much muddled thinking, a total lack of financial discipline and confused objectives. A local property magnate took it over, but it did not last long. *North-West Times*, an attempt to produce a quality regional paper, totally failed to hit its modest circulation target and folded after a few weeks with debts of £850,000. *Plus*, an attempt to supply a national weekly colour supplement for provincial newspapers, ran into initial problems caused by the excess of colour capacity and consequent rate-cutting but gradually expanded its readership and improved its content. *The Independent* sensibly decided not to enter the Sunday field for the time being at least, but a new group, with significant backing from the *Chicago Tribune*, hoped to find a market gap with their *Sunday Correspondent*. The best result of the Fleet Street revolution was that the cost of entering the market had been drastically reduced. Hence the eagerness with which widely differing groups of people sought to enter the field and offer readers a wider and wider choice.

Of course the existing band of newspaper publishers sought to defend their titles. The most ill-advised of the new men was Lord Stevens, quickly promoted to the peerage after his victory over Lord Matthews on the ownership of Express Newspapers. Stevens, a small myopic looking man, was a financier whose successful expansion of United Newspapers owed almost as much to the sensible editorial guidance of Sir Gordon Linacre, deputy chairman and chief executive until December 1988, as to his own aggressive takeover tactics. Stevens went into partnership with a soft-porn merchant called David Sullivan in an effort to revamp his troublesome tabloid, the *Daily Star*. Sullivan was publishing a fairly successful Sunday newspaper called *Sunday Sport* and was threatening to start a daily which might have hurt the *Star*. United took a quarter share of Sullivan's company for £1.5 million and the editorial director of *Sunday Sport*, Michael Gabbert, became editor of the *Star*. Esoteric discussions on 'nipple count' took place in Stevens's office and the *Star* was transformed into the most vulgar and unpleasant daily tabloid in the country. 'Raunchy' – defined by my dictionary as 'lewd' or 'smutty' – was the word much used by Gabbert to describe its contents. According to Gabbert[7] Stevens was delighted at first, ringing from the South of France to say, 'It's a laugh a minute.' Readers and advertisers were less enthusiastic and some of the staff were so appalled that they left. Within a fortnight the management were saying the paper would be more 'restrained' in future. Within eight weeks Stevens had sacked Gabbert; the sale had fallen by 100,000 to barely more than one million. It was a devastating example of proprietorial bungling, as Stevens accepting 'full responsibility' was apparently ready to admit.

On the other hand new editors were appointed to both the *Daily Express* and *Sunday Express;* the slide in the sale of the daily was checked and the downward trend at the Sunday was slowed; major staff cuts were implemented from 6,800 in 1985 to 1,700 four years later; the famous black glass building was sold for £80 million; and the move out of Fleet Street took place. United Newspapers were highly profitable, even if Express Newspapers profits fell slightly from £33.1 million to £31.6 million a year later. The City was not entirely convinced when Stevens told an interviewer, 'People say I am a financial man. I consider myself to be a newspaper man'.[8] It still seemed possible that the parts of United Newspapers might be worth more than the whole, and could attract a predator. Yet, Stevens denied any such idea. 'There is nothing in this group which is for sale,' he said. 'I haven't spent eight years building this group up to flog bits off.'[9] Media magnetism had claimed another scalp.

Journalists were, of course, the principal beneficiaries of the Fleet Street printing revolution. They were at last in charge of their own words. They type-set their text and they 'read' it. And now that excessive manning and 'obscene' rates of pay, as Lord Matthews saw it, were being eliminated, more money was available for editorial budgets. There was much much less general aggravation; it was now a rarity for newspapers to lose editions, or even copies, except in the case of technical breakdown. And managements had to recognise that the *quality* of the editorial product within its chosen market was crucial in determining commercial success. Equally publishers and editors needed to share a clear idea of their target – what Vere Rothermere called the 'concept'. For a time that worked brilliantly for Cecil King and Hugh Cudlipp. Equally, towards the end of

1988, for instance, it was not completely evident to an outside observer that the editor and management of *The Guardian* were exactly of the same mind.

One important point remained the same: every newspaper needed a Chief who gave the lead. As Murdoch put it, 'Every successful company is personalised.' He, or she, could be the editor – and there are only a limited number of people who can do that job. But it was more often that the real spark came from the publisher. They might not always possess the most benevolent and altruistic of characters. They were not humble or reticent men. Northcliffe, with his 'ferrets', tried to dominate the Prime Minister. Beaverbrook, with his occasional vendettas, propagandised for his lost causes. Murdoch had few scruples in his search for mass readership. But somewhere, somehow, publishers like these were fired by a divine spark that shot their newspapers into a dazzling arc of success. Like any other rocket the starshell would burst sooner or later, but, be sure, there would be another one in the sky before too long.

Notes:
1. See 'A chapter of excellence' by W. F. Deedes, *Daily Telegraph*, 1st September 1987. I regret that Lord Hartwell declined to be interviewed.
2. Quoted by Raymond Snoddy, *Financial Times*, 14 December 1985.
3. 7th May 1988.
4. There are two good books about Eddy Shah: *Eddie Shah and the Newspaper Revolution* by David Goodhart and Patrick Wintour, Coronet, 1986; and *Eddy Shah, Today and the Newspaper Revolution* by Brian MacArthur. (Eddy does not really care whether his name is spelt 'Eddie' or 'Eddy' but the latter is correct.) The first book was completed before the actual launch of *Today* but is good on the industrial background. The second, by the first editor of *Today*, gives a harrowing picture of all the difficulties that beset the heroic editorial staff but includes an affectionate and attractive picture of Eddy himself.
5. See 'Who's Afraid of Eddie Shah?', *Sunday Times*, 12th May 1985.
6. A graphic account of the launch and the dive to doom is given in *Disaster! The Rise and Fall of* News on Sunday, *Anatomy of a business failure*, by Peter Chippindale and Chris Norrie, Sphere Books, 1988.
7. 'Why They Gave Me the Boot' by Michael Gabbert, *UK Press Gazette*, 16th November 1987.
8. Maggie Brown, *The Independent*, 8th March 1989.
9. Raymond Snoddy, *Financial Times*, 8 April 1989.

Appendix
The Value of the Pound

It may be useful to have a rough idea of the value of the pound sterling in the period covered by this book. The Central Statistical Office has compiled 'a continuous index of the purchasing power of the pound since 1750' but it warns that 'since this index is the result of linking several indices on different bases and measuring price changes of different groups of commodities, the index can only be taken as showing very approximate price movements over the whole period' (CSO press release dated November, 1988).

The CSO index is presented in percentage terms, based on January 1974 as 100. Thus 1890 is shown as 9.9; 1932 as 16; 1964 as 55.8 and 1984 as 351.8.

Here is a simpler table based on the index which shows what £1 would be worth in current (November 1988) purchasing power for each decade from 1850.

This is the result:

Year	Value of the £1 today	Year	Value of the £1 today
1850	£40	1920	£15
1860	£36	1930	£24
1870	£35	1938[1]	£25
1880	£37	1950	£12
1890	£44	1960	£9
1900	£44	1970	£6
1910	£40	1980	£1.65

These figures must be regarded as very approximate.

Note:
[1] There are no figures for the war years, 1939 to 1945.

Index

Ackerman, Jack, 70, 71
Agate, James, 90
Ainsworth, Harry, 52–3, 58, 62
Aitken, Jonathan, 168
Aitken, Peter, 99, 100
Aitken, Sir Max, 78, 96, 99–100,
   103–4, 154, 155, 156, 157, 175,
   181
Aitken, Timothy, 168
Amalgamated Press, 143, 144
Anderson, Sir John, 140
Angell, Norman, 11
Asquith, Margot, 41
Astor, David, 226
Astor, Gavin, 117
Astor, Lord, 117
Attlee, Clement, 93, 140

Baldwin, Stanley, 59, 94
Balfour, Lady Betty, 15
Balfour of Inchrye, Lord, 113
Bareau, Paul, 72
Barlow, Frank, 212
Barry, Gerald, 72–5
Bartholomew, Harry Guy ('Bart'),
   132, 135, 139, 140, 141, 142
Bartlett, Vernon, 72, 73
Bathhurst, Lady, 26, 40
Baxter, Beverley, 89–90, 95
Beavan, John (later Lord Ardwick),
   144
Beaverbrook, Lord, 11, 16, 26–7, 35,
   40–41, 56–8, 65, 68, 80–1,
   82–104, 107, 116, 134, 139, 141,
   142, 151, 156, 173, 175, 176,
   178, 187, 238, 249, 263

Benn, Tony, 146, 206
Bennett, Arnold, 52, 88, 90, 97
Berry, Don, 221
Berry, Gomer *see* Kemsley, Viscount
Berry, Michael *see* Hartwell, Lord
Berry, Nicholas, 251
Berry, Sir William Ewert *see*
   Camrose, Lord
Bevin, Ernest, 55, 95, 141
Binder, Bernhard, 70, 71
Birch, Reg, 159
Birk, Ellis, 128–133, 149
Birkenhead, Lord, 88
Black, Conrad, 249–53
Black, Sheila, 182
Blackburn, Sir Tom, 66, 96, 100
Blackmore, Ted, 238
Blumenfeld, R. D., 13, 85, 86, 87,
   88, 89
Bolam, Sylvester, 142
Bonham-Carter, Lady Violet, 64
Bottomley, Horatio, 50–52
Bower, Tom, 242–3
Boxer, Mark, 116
Bracken, Brendan, 45, 66, 74
Branson, Richard, 257
Brex, Twells, 15
Brittan, Leon, 254
Brown, Douglas, 77
Brown, George, 120
Brunton, Sir Gordon, 106–7, 118,
   186, 207, 227
Bulmer-Thomas, Ivor, 73
Burnham, Lord, 32–3
Burton, Pomeroy, 14
Bystander, 35

Cadbury, George, 68–9
Cadbury, Henry, 67, 70
Cadbury, Julian, 80
Cadbury, Laurence, 65–8, 70, 73–4, 75–6, 77–9, 80, 151
Cadbury, Richard, 68
Cadbury, Sir Adrian, 80
Caird, Sir Andrew, 3, 14, 20, 21–3, 27, 134
Cameron, James, 75, 77, 79, 83, 90
Campaign, 206, 252
Campbell, Sam, 52
Camrose, Lord (William Ewert Berry), 33–41, 43, 44–46, 52, 58, 87, 151, 249
Carpenter, Leslie, 209
Carr, Sir William, 201–3, 225, 226
Carthew-Yourston, Brigadier, 195
Cassandra, 141
Cassidy, Terry, 257–8
Castle, Mrs Barbara, 148
Cater, Douglas, 226
Chamberlain, Neville, 41, 43, 60, 73, 140
Chancellor, Sir Christopher, 143–4
Chat, 186
Cheadle, Sir Eric, 107
Christiansen, Arthur, 95–6, 176
Churchill, Winston, 13, 44–45, 73, 92, 94–5, 139–41
Clarke, Tom, 13–14, 23, 49, 71, 91
Cleverley, Graham, 240
Coltart, James, 112, 115
Connor, Sir William, 140, 141, 142
Conroy, Harry, 215–6, 221
Cooke, Jack Kent, 110
Coope, John, 77, 78, 142
Coote, John, 179
Corbett, Howard, 22
Cousins, Frank, 67
Cowdray, Lord, 26, 70, 71
Cowley, John, 134, 136, 139, 142
Crossman, Dick, 136, 199
Cruikshank, Robin, 74, 75–6, 80

Cudlipp, Lord (Hugh Cudlipp), 128–31, 132, 135–36, 139–40, 142, 144, 146–8, 205, 225, 234–5, 262
Cudlipp, Percy, 59–60
Cummings, A. J., 72, 73, 77
Cursley, Norman, 77
Curtis, Michael, 76–7, 78

Daily Chronicle, 35, 54, 64, 70
Daily Dispatch, 35, 44, 76, 88, 176
Daily Express, 13, 27, 56, 57, 58, 83, 85–8, 92, 94, 95, 99–100, 101–103, 141, 151, 155, 156–7, 159–61, 162, 165–6, 169, 173, 175, 176, 178, 179, 181, 182, 208, 223–46, 242, 255, 256, 262
Daily Graphic, 26, 35, 44, 88
Daily Herald (later the *Sun*), 54–60, 67, 117, 132, 144, 199, 205
Daily Mail, 11, 12, 15, 16, 20, 23, 25, 26, 27, 32, 39, 56, 64, 79, 89, 92, 117, 134, 172–3, 176–85, 212, 232, 256, 257
Daily Mirror, 11, 15, 17, 95, 128, 132, 134, 135, 139, 141, 142, 144, 145, 148, 157, 159, 161, 178, 191, 208, 209–11, 213, 215, 224–5, 235, 238, 240, 248
Daily News, 26, 64, 68, 69–70, 81
Daily News Trust Ltd, 68, 71, 73, 74, 79
Daily Record, 213, 215
Daily Sketch, 36, 172, 174–9
Daily Star, 161–2, 165, 169, 261–2
Daily Telegraph, 26, 30–31, 33, 37–41, 44–5, 58, 117, 122, 240, 245–6, 249, 250, 252, 259
Daily Worker, 141
Dane, Surrey, 55
Dean, Brenda, 216, 236, 239
Deedes, Lord (William Deedes), 249
Delmer, Sefton, 90
Dempster, Nigel, 257

Denning, Lord, 160, 205
Dent, Alan, 79
Dietrich, Dr Otto, 43
Douglas-Home, Charles, 221, 231
Douglas-Home, Sir Alec, 117, 119
Driberg, Tom, 83
Dubbins, Tony, 221
Duncan, A. C., 62
Dunnet, Alistair, 112, 114

Ecclestone, Jacob, 123
Economist, The, 57, 65, 70, 221, 250
Eden, Anthony, 43, 142
Edinburgh Evening Dispatch, 111–2,
 119, 116
Elias, Julius Salter *see* Southwood,
 Lord
Ellerman, Sir John, 26
Emery, Fred, 230
Empire News, 44, 64
English, Sir David, 172, 174–7, 181,
 182, 184, 185, 187, 188
Esquire, 187
Evans, Harry, 108, 119, 120, 157,
 186, 205, 228–30, 255
Evening News, 10, 11, 64, 134, 154,
 162–3, 182, 183, 184, 186–7
Evening Standard, 46, 78, 88, 89, 96,
 100, 121, 154, 155, 162–3, 177,
 179, 182, 183, 184, 186, 205, 212,
 240, 242, 252
Exchange and Mart, 167

Family Living, 118
Fawcett, Mrs, 15
Felker, Clay, 187
Fenton, West de Wend, 34
Ferris, Paul, 3
Financial Times, 35, 40, 45, 47, 132,
 157, 168, 212, 248
Fish, Walter, 3
Flower, Sir Newman, 4
Foot, Michael, 91
Forrest, William, 73

Freeman, John, 117, 119
French, Howard, 177
Frost, David, 227
Fyfe, Hamilton, 15

Gabbert, Michael, 261–2
Gaitskell, Hugh, 136, 144, 146
Garvin, J. L., 3, 4, 87
Getty, Paul, 181
Giles, Frank, 114–15, 221
Gillespie, Bill, 212
Glaser, Milton, 187
Globe, The, 86
Glover, Stephen, 259
Gold, John, 180, 182
Goldsmith, Sir James, 102, 154, 155,
 207
Goodman, Lord, 179, 182, 226
Gordon, John, 88, 142
Graham, Helen, 257
Grant, John, 230, 231
Guardian, The, 157, 249, 260, 263
Guardian Weekly, 50
Gwynne, H. A., 41

Haines, Joe, 192, 194, 196, 202, 203,
 204, 209
Haley, Sir William, 117
Half-penny Marvel, 9
Ham and High, 6
Hamilton, Sir Denis, 44, 47, 117,
 118, 119, 120, 122, 123, 126,
 227, 228, 244
Hamlyn, Paul, 129, 130, 132,
 136–7, 225, 227, 233
Hammond, Eric, 216, 217
Hardy, Bert, 185, 226
Harmsworth, Alfred *see* Northcliffe,
 Lord
Harmsworth, Geraldine (later King),
 8, 132
Harmsworth, Harold *see*
 Rothermere, Lord
Harmsworth, Hildebrand, 86

Harmsworth, Vere *see* Rothermere, Lord
Harriman, Averell, 95
Harris, Kenneth, 226
Hart, Charles, 12
Hartwell, Lord (Michael Berry), 37, 45, 46, 115–16, 143, 249–52, 253, 259–60
Hastings, Max, 37, 252
Healey, Denis, 146
Hearst, 12
Heren, Louis, 230
Hetherington, Peter, 154, 155
Hibbert, Christopher, 18
Hobson, Oscar, 72
Hodson, H. V., 119
Holland, Noel, 78
Holmes à Court, Robert, 166, 161, 208
Hooley, Ernest Terah, 49
Hopkins, Harry, 95
Hopkinson, Tom, 74
Horder, Lord, 5
Howard, Peter, 83
Hudson, Sir Robert, 1–2, 5, 18
Hulton, Sir Edward, 35, 88–9
Hunt, Thornton Leigh, 31
Hussey, Marmaduke, 122, 123, 126, 179, 230

Ideal Home, 51
Iliffe, Sir Edward, 35, 38
Iliffe, William, 7, 35
Independent, The, 236, 252, 259, 261
Inge, Dean, 90
Investor's Chronicle, 178
Investor's Guardian, 33
Irvine, Bert, 172–3
Irvine, Ian, 167, 168
Isaacs, George, 27

Jackson, Professor Derek, 201
Jacobson, Lord (Sydney Jacobson), 142, 148

Jameson, Derek, 157–8, 161
Jarratt, Sir Alex, 208
Jay, Peter, 190
Jealous, George, 6
Jenkins, Simon, 155, 157, 182–3
John Bull, 50–52, 61
Johnston, George Lawson, 87
Jones, Kennedy, 10, 11
Junor, Sir John, 164

Kearton, Lord, 207
Keating, John, 217
Kemsley, Viscount (Gomer Berry), 33–6, 39, 40, 41–4, 45, 76, 106, 115, 250
Keys, Bill, 159, 160, 216, 239
King, Cecil, 8, 12, 17, 25, 28, 38, 44, 66, 67, 68, 75, 78–9, 80, 99, 101, 103, 117, 118, 128–49, 178, 204, 224, 238, 262
King, Francis, 131
Kirby, Louis, 163, 182
Kisch, John, 196
Kitchener, Lord, 12, 18
Knight, Andrew, 251, 252–3

Lamb, Sir Larry, 166, 225, 258
Lancaster, Osbert, 91
Lange, Dr Tonjes, 196–7
Lansbury, George, 54
Law, Bonar, 84–5, 87, 88, 94
Lawson, Fred, 38
Lawson-Levy, Edward, *see* Lord Burnham
Lawson-Levy, Lionel, 30
Layton, Lord, 64, 65–77
Leasco, 204–5
Leese, John, 185
Le Sage, John, 32
Leigh, Sir John, 26
Levin, Bernard, 178
Levy, Joseph Moses, 30–31
Linacre, Sir Gordon, 261
Linklater, Magnus, 186, 212

Lloyd George, 2, 15, 24, 35, 68, 70–1, 73, 92
Lloyds Weekly, 19
Logan, Jimmie, 113
London Daily News, 163, 185, 212–3
London Post, 219, 220
Long, Gerry, 228

McCarthy, Ralph, 74
MacArthur, Brian, 244, 255–8, 259
Macdonald, Ramsay, 55–6, 59
Mackay, Ian, 72, 75
Mackenzie, Kelvin, 221, 233
Mackenzie, Sir James, 4
Macmillan, Harold, 65, 92, 101, 117, 119
Mail on Sunday, 163, 174, 183, 185
Manchester Guardian (later *The Guardian*), 94
Marks, Derek, 175
Marlowe, 16
Martin, Kingsley, 72
Marwan, Dr Ashraf, 168
Matthews, Bruce, 211, 215–17, 219, 222, 236, 246
Matthews, Lord, 102, 151–70, 183, 262
Maxwell, Robert, 166, 167, 185, 188, 190–214, 224–25, 227, 231–2, 242–3, 248, 253, 257
Miles, Lori, 186
Milne, J. V., 6
Minney, R. J., 41
Money, 168
Montgomery, David, 232, 258
Moorehead, Alan, 90
Morden, Grant, 52
Morison, Stanley, 14
Morning Leader, 68–9, 76
Morning Post, 26, 40–41, 54
Morrison, Herbert, 141
Mosley, Leonard, 90, 130
Mountbatten, Lord Louis, 101, 146–7

Mudford, William, 12
Muggeridge, Malcolm, 101
Murdoch, Sir Keith, 16, 223
Murdoch, Rupert, 16, 102, 156, 161, 166, 186, 187, 190, 199–205, 207, 209, 211, 215–236, 245, 248, 251, 255, 258, 263

Neil, Andrew, 221, 228, 233, 254, 255, 258
New Statesman, 72
Newnes, George, 7
News Chronicle, 56, 59, 63, 64–8, 70–71, 73–80, 92, 117, 176
News of the World, 184, 199–203, 208, 216, 221, 224–5, 226, 227, 232, 245, 246, 258
News on Sunday, 261
Nicholson, Brian, 182, 255
Northcliffe, Lord, 1–28, 54, 71, 88, 142, 151, 173, 249, 263
Nottingham Evening Post, 218

Observer, The, 11, 87, 186, 208, 226, 248, 255, 257
Odhams, 51–2, 59, 60–62, 67, 117, 143–4
O'Neill, Bill, 218
Owen-Browne, Colin, 121

Packer, Frank, 67
Packer, Kerry, 257
Pall Mall Gazette, 26
Pappas, George, 121
Parker, Eric, 161, 163, 165
Pearson, Arthur, 85
Pearson, Clive, 71
People, The, 52–4, 60–1, 117
Pergamon, 193, 197–98, 200, 202, 203, 204, 205, 207, 224
Pickering, Sir Edward, 96, 129, 224, 231
Pole-Carew, C., 218
Post, 259

Prior, Jim, 160
Profumo, John, 227

Radio Times, 53, 208
Railton, Dame Ruth, 142–3
Railway Times, 50
Randall, Mike, 174, 176
Raybould, Eric, 224
Raymond, Detlev, 196
Redhead, R. A., 78, 80
Rees-Mogg, 228, 230, 231, 255
Reith, Lord, 53, 101
Reve, Emery, 45
Reynold's News, 199
Rice, Tom, 220
Richards, Geoffrey, 218
Richardson, Michael, 200
Ritzema, Thomas, 68–9
Robens, Lord, 146
Robertson, E. J., 100–2, 176
Rogers, Sir Frank, 129–31, 137, 240, 251
Rothermere, Lord (Esmond Harmsworth, second Lord Rothermere), 139, 173–4, 179, 181
Rothermere, Lord (Harold Harmsworth, first Lord Rothermere), 8–10, 27–8, 33, 39–40, 89, 134, 135–6, 154, 173, 181
Rothermere, Lord (Vere Harmsworth, third Lord Rothermere), 102, 154, 163, 172–189, 262
Rothschild, Evelyn de, 155
Rothschild, Jacob, 201
Rothwell, Bruce, 226
Rowbottom, Brian, 167
Rowland, Tiny, 155, 168, 208, 231–2, 257
Russell, Leonard, 36, 43
Russell, Sir Charles, 4
Ryder, Lord, 129, 130, 131, 144

Sala, George Augustus, 31–2
Sandilands, Sir Francis, 161
Saturday Review, 30–31
Scargill, Arthur, 166
Schofield, Guy, 174
Scotsman, The, 46, 111–2, 114
Scottish Daily Express, 206
Seven Days, 252
Shah, Eddy, 188, 231, 235, 248, 253–9
Shawcross Commission, 78–9, 80, 142
Shawcross, Lord (Sir Hartley Shawcross), 65, 204
Sherren, Graham, 164
Shields, Mick, 163, 177, 180–1, 186
Shrimsley, Anthony, 226
Shrimsley, Bernard, 184
Sleigh, Colonel Arthur Burroughes, 30
Smith, Lints, 20, 22–3
Somerfield, Stafford, 201, 226
Southwood, Lord (Julius Salter Elias), 49–62, 65
Spectator, The, 252
Sporting Chronicle, 52
Sporting Life, 52, 211–2
Stairs, John F., 84, 94
Standard, 31
Star, The, 59, 64–7, 69, 78–9
Stead, W. T., 19
Steed, Wickham, 3–5
Steinberg, Saul, 204
Steven, Stewart, 174, 185
Stevens, Jocelyn, 154, 155, 156, 157–8, 160, 161, 162, 163–6, 179, 181, 182, 183
Stevens, Lord (David Stevens), 168, 261–2
Stevenson, Frances, 71
Stevenson, Sir Edward, 112
Stuart, Sir Campbell, 14
Sullivan, David, 261
Sun (formerly *Daily Herald*), 10, 128,

132, 139, 148, 160, 161, 166, 187, 205, 207, 209–11, 213, 215–16, 220, 221, 225, 228, 233, 235, 245, 258
Sun-Times, 218
Sunday Chronicle, 36, 41, 44, 88, 135
Sunday Citizen, 199
Sunday Dispatch, 175
Sunday Express, 27, 88, 90, 102, 116, 142, 158, 164, 169, 175, 179, 183, 187, 262
Sunday Mail, 215
Sunday Pictorial, 136, 139, 142
Sunday Sport, 261
Sunday Telegraph, 241, 249, 252
Sunday Times, 30, 32, 34–6, 40, 43–4, 46–7, 98, 106, 108, 114–17, 118, 119, 120, 122–24, 157, 160, 162, 186, 190, 205, 207, 216, 221, 226, 227, 228, 230, 231, 240, 241, 243, 244, 250, 254, 255, 257, 258, 260
Sutton, Sir George, 14, 36, 39
Swaffer, Hannen, 55
Symonds, Matthew, 259

Tatler, 26
Taylor, A. J. P., 56, 86, 98
Taylor, Ken, 217
Thomas, Cecil, 135
Thomson, Kenneth, 118, 123, 126, 207
Thomson, Lord (Roy Thomson), 46–7, 64, 67, 68, 98, 106–26, 143–4, 162, 240, 243
Thornton, Clive, 209
Tillett, Ben, 54
Times Newspapers, 118, 121–24, 186, 228, 243
Times, The, 11, 14, 15, 18, 19, 20, 26, 27, 31, 32, 37, 117–18, 122–24, 155, 178, 182, 186, 216, 221, 223, 227, 228–30, 235, 243, 244, 249, 255, 260
Tit-Bits, 7
Today, 188, 231–2, 245, 257, 258, 259
Tracy, Louis, 10
Trelford, Donald, 226
Treves, Sir Frederick, 2
Turner, Lloyd, 162

Vallance, Aylmer, 71–2
Vicky, 72, 75, 91

Wade, Joe, 246
Walker, Patric, 174
Walter, John, 4
Ward, Christopher, 166
Waters, Frank, 66, 75, 80
Watson, Arthur, 38
Wells, H. G., 1, 28
Westminster Gazette, 19, 26, 69–70
Whittam-Smith, Andreas, 259–61
Williams, Francis (later Lord Francis-Williams), 57–8, 59
Wilson, Charles, 218, 219, 221, 231
Wilson, Harold, 128, 139, 145, 146, 199, 249
Winn, Godfrey, 135
Winnick, Maurice, 46
Winnington, Richard, 73
Winnington-Ingram, John, 172, 177
Wolfson, Isaac, 46
Woman, 128
Woman and Home, 143
Woman's Weekly, 143
Women's Own, 128
Woolton, Lord, 44
Worsthorne, Peregrine, 252
Wright, Roy, 157

Zec, Philip, 141
Zuckerman, Lord Solly, 148